D1291564

The
Underside
of History

Revised Edition   Volume 1

To all the women,
of every time and space,
who are this book

The Underside of History

Revised Edition   Volume 1

A View of Women Through Time

Elise Boulding

Original line drawings by *Helen Redman*

SAGE Publications
International Educational and Professional Publisher
Newbury Park   London   New Delhi

Copyright © 1992 by Sage Publications, Inc.

All rights reserved. No part of this book may be reproduced or utilized in any form or by any means, electronic or mechanical, including photocopying, recording, or by any information storage and retrieval system, without permission in writing from the publisher.

For information address:

 SAGE Publications, Inc.
2455 Teller Road
Newbury Park, California 91320

SAGE Publications Ltd.
6 Bonhill Street
London EC2A 4PU
United Kingdom

SAGE Publications India Pvt. Ltd.
M-32 Market
Greater Kailash I
New Delhi 110 048 India

HQ 1121
. B64
1992
vol. 1

Printed in the United States of America

Library of Congress Cataloging-in-Publication Data

Boulding, Elise.
   The underside of history: a view of women through time / Elise
Boulding.—Rev. ed.
     v. cm.
   Vols. 1-2 include bibliographical references and indexes.
     ISBN 0-8039-4768-2 (v. 1).—ISBN 0-8039-4816-6 (v. 2).—ISBN
   0-8039-4769-0 (v. 1: pbk.).—ISBN 0-8039-4817-4 (v. 2: pbk.)
     1. Women-History. I. Title.
   HQ1121.B64 1992
   305.4′09—dc20   92-28926

92 93 94 95 10 9 8 7 6 5 4 3 2 1

Sage Production Editor: Diane S. Foster

Contents

Gift 08/05/01

AUG 2 8 2001

Part II. Women as Civilizers

List of Tables

List of Figures

Foreword

T*he Underside of History* was originally conceived to correct a massive injustice—the wholesale omission of recognition for the contributions to the histories of civilizations by one half of the human beings ever to have populated the earth.

It has been nearly two decades since *The Underside* first appeared and, while there have been excellent special-focus histories of women's roles through time, such as Gerda Lerner's *The Creation of Patriarchy* (1986), Rosalind Miles's *Women's History of the World* (1989), and edited books on the underside theme such as *Becoming Visible* by Renate Bridenthal and Claudia Koonz (1977), the more complete story has yet to appear. In the meantime, fine studies of every period covered in *The Underside* have appeared, and women scholars of every continent are producing documentation on the lives of women, past and current, on the continents that colonialism rendered invisible.[1] Yet mainstream histories continue to ignore women.

The division of the book into two volumes, the first on prehistory and the early civilizing roles of women, and the second moving from the first millennium to the current time, makes the volumes usable separately or together for a greater variety of readers. Readers familiar with the first edition will note that I have shifted from the Christian-based dating systems of B.C. (Before Christ) and A.D. (Anno Domino) to the more universalistic terminology of B.C.E. (Before the Common Era) and C.E. (the Common Era).

In rereading *The Underside* to prepare this edition, I realized what a regrettably strong male orientation undergirds the conceptual structure of all the social science disciplines, particularly sociology and demography. I did not realize just how much this orientation affected the leading women social scientists of this century who were my mentors, and how much it affected me. (Cavin 1985, has a label for this: "patriscience.")

As I have been updating my own knowledge of research on women in preparation for this second edition, I have become aware of the increasing differentiation among women scholars in terms of the range of theories under development, types of data and methodologies used, number of subcultures from which women scholars emerge, and differences in worldviews and preferred social and political strategies for changing society found among them.

Some very exciting new types of writing on women are becoming available that were in very early stages and not yet known to me when I was writing *The Underside*. They have to do with exploring the nature of women's identity and culture beyond the existing critique of patriarchy and with how women think, how they do art and science, and how they make ethical and moral valuations. Lesbian feminists have asked radical and searching questions about the organization of human society, questions that cut the ground right out from under more familiar liberal equity-feminist approaches to making society better for women (for example, Cavin 1985; Duberman et al. 1989). Lesbian deconstructionist analysis of culture takes us well beyond the general social science recognition that all cultures are social constructs (Kitzinger 1987).

No less radical in their implications are recent studies of women's ways of knowing—how women process information and arrive at judgments about empirical reality—with a fuller involvement of experiential and intuitive dimensions (Belenky et al. 1986). Studies of how women perform scientific investigations have uncovered a pattern of differences in how women observe, relate to, and work with scientific phenomena as compared with many of their male colleagues (Keller 1983; Goodfield 1981; Bleier 1986). Because science has played such a central role in the development of the modern world, particularly in creating a sense of alienation from nature, the feminist organic approach to science offers new hope for an increasingly gaia-conscious world.

Another discovery has abruptly brought into question long-accepted theories of stages in the moral development of human beings (Kohlberg 1966) and the meaning/definition of *minority*. I refer to Gilligan's (1982) findings that women's moral judgments tend to be arrived at by a different route than men's, being less abstract and rule based and relying more on contextual and relationship elements in the situation requiring judgment.

With the increasing role human rights and social justice concepts are assuming locally and internationally, feminine ways of evaluating justice, violence, and oppression will assume increasing importance. This is an arena in which feminist peace researchers are making important contributions (Brock-Utne 1989). I also welcome continuing research on goddesses in human history.[2]

Another older research tradition, one that is being renewed with the development of new computer technologies, is the tradition of studying the changing role of women through the prism of the household-in-society, using a life-course methodology. Having been personally involved in developing this new approach to an old problem through my association with the United Nations University, I would like to celebrate the recent publication of the first cross-national study using the new technologies, *Women, Households and Change,* ably organized by my long-time colleague Eleanora Masini (Masini and Stratigos 1991). The household has not lost its relevance as a unit of analysis of women's lives!

To consider sex and gender roles throughout history, as if all women were heterosexually partnered, widowed, or single, and to ignore the reality that a significant lesbian culture has most probably existed in every society from tribal to industrial, in every era, seems ridiculous to me now. Yet this is what I did. For the record, I find Cavin's (1985) estimates of the omnipresence of gay and lesbian life ways throughout history, although differing widely in cultural forms and frequency of occurrence, very plausible. This carefully avoided segment of human experience requires the same kind of in-depth research called for in every aspect of women's history and the history of humankind.

Wherever possible, I have inserted modifications in passages that cry out for recognition that *female* does not necessarily signify *heterosexual*, and I have also added references throughout both volumes to more recent research on women's roles in each historical period.

I was very moved by the report of the major effort launched at the 1988 National Women Studies Association meeting at the University of Minnesota to deal with those differences, creating bridges of understanding and workable multicultural alliances in the face of apparently irreconcilable conflicts (Albrecht and Brewer 1990).

My own thinking has undergone many changes in the past 18 years. Some readers will find me too conservative, others too radical. Many of my generation of scholar-activists, while recognizing the importance of conflict and confrontation, have our own style of dealing with conflict, based on how we have experienced the past seven decades. I do, however, see the need, like many of my younger sisters, for drastic change in social structures. This is essential if the ways of thinking, perceiving, and responding of women and men are to change to release the gentler, more nurturant qualities in everyone. And the gentling of society must, under no circumstances, diminish the love of adventure and discovery that makes humans such a special breed among all living things! While I do not agree with Riane Eisler's (1987) oversimplified view of human history (where did that sudden eruption of fierceness in men come from?), I warmly welcome the interest her book has aroused and share her view that the future lies in a genuine partnership between women and men. I also agree that much of the teaching required for the development of that new society will have to come from women.

Notes

1. Note especially the excellent annotated bibliographies of both recent and earlier research on women's roles in each historical era now available in the three-volume collection of teaching packets, *Restoring Women to History*, prepared for the Organization of American Historians (1988). While the packets are primarily directed to teachers and researchers, any women's history buff will enjoy browsing through them.

2. I am less convinced, however, of the significance of today's "goddess fad," complete with catalogues and marketing strategies. There is, however, an associated movement that represents a genuine search for a buried feminine spirituality—overdue and badly needed in these times. A body of research on goddesses in history was already available in 1974 and was therefore included in the original edition of *The Underside*.

References

Albrecht, Lisa and Rose M. Brewer. 1990. *Bridges of Power: Women's Multicultural Alliances.* Philadelphia: New Society.

Belenky, Mary Field, Blythe McVicker Clinchy, Nancy Rule Goldberger, and Jill Mattock Tarule. 1986. *Women's Ways of Knowing: The Development of Self, Voice and Mind.* New York: Basic Books.

Bleier, Ruth, ed. 1986. *Feminist Approaches to Science.* New York: Pergamon, Athena Series.

Bridenthal, Renate and Claudia Koonz, eds. 1977. *Becoming Visible: Women in European History.* Boston: Houghton Mifflin.

Brock-Utne, Birgit. 1989. *Feminist Perspectives on Peace and Peace Education.* New York: Pergamon, Athena Series.

Cavin, Susan. 1985. *Lesbian Origins.* San Francisco: Ism Press.

Duberman, Martin, Martha Vicinus, and George Chauncey, Jr. 1989. *Hidden from History: Reclaiming the Gay and Lesbian Past.* New York: Penguin.

Eisler, Riane. 1987. *The Chalice and the Blade.* San Francisco: Harper & Row.

Gilligan, Carol. 1982. *In a Different Voice: Psychological Theory and Women's Development.* Cambridge, MA: Harvard University Press.

Goodfield, June. 1981. *An Imagined World: A Story of Scientific Discovery.* San Francisco: Harper & Row.

Keller, Evelyn Fox. 1983. *A Feeling for the Organism: The Life and Work of Barbara McClintock.* San Francisco: Freeman.

Kitzinger, Celia. 1987. *The Social Construction of Lesbianism.* Newbury Park, CA: Sage.

Kohlberg, Lawrence. 1966. "Moral Education in the Schools: A Developmental View," 74:1-29.

Lerner, Gerda. 1986. *The Creation of Patriarchy.* New York: Oxford University Press.

Masini, Eleanora and Susan Stratigos. 1991. *Women, Households and Change.* Tokyo: United Nations University Press.

Miles, Rosalind. 1989. *Women's History of the World.* Topsfield, MA: Salem House.

Organization of American Historians. 1988. *Restoring Women to History.* 3 vols. Bloomington, IN: Organization of American Historians.

Preface

This book was started during a year of retreat spent in my hermitage in the mountains near Boulder. It was a year of reading, reflection, withdrawal, a year needed to develop a deeper sense of connectedness after a very crowded life. This is the kind of book that can only be written in solitude. Like all macro history, it is autobiographical—the story of the author's search for meaning in human existence. The underside theme came naturally. A woman activist in the twentieth century cannot avoid identity struggles because society gives her little ground on which to stand. Because I am a sociologist as well as an activist, I saw that struggle in historical terms. Women have for millennia had to work for the public good from privatized spaces. Why?

The tension between the activist, the sociologist, and the inwardly inclined Quaker, in the process of trying to answer that question in this book, has been almost unbearable. On the one hand, there was the problem of establishing an adequate knowledge base to write a macro history. The awareness of my lack of training as a historian, and of the hit-and-miss quality of my scholarship, has been so acute that I have repeatedly decided to give up the project because of my lack of competence to do it—only to be driven back to it by some more powerful counterforce. It is necessary for women to be willing to stick out their necks when an unprecedented task presents itself. Perhaps the hardest problem of all was to justify to myself attempting to write a scholarly book at a time when I felt called to an inward, spiritual journey. Bending the mind to a major analytic task when the spirit is attuned to prayer is a very special discipline. I held to the discipline for the two years required to finish the book.

The entire book was written at the hermitage, a little one-room cabin in the woods above our family cabin. I carried every one of the hundreds of books used for the work up the steep hill on my back, so I have a physical as well as mental sense of the weight of history. After my university leave was over and I returned to teaching, I came out each weekend to continue work on the book. The hermitage was the only place where there was mental space enough to lay out all the chronologies and all the maps of civilizations I needed to unroll in my head to write the history. It was the only place where there was room enough to unreel before the inward eye all the dramas of the past that the books evoked. For two years, the hermitage was bursting with images. Images of the overside of history, images of the underside, and always images of women; so many women— half the human race—and so magnificent. How could I capture and portray what I saw?

The book itself is a failure—a travesty of the history I wanted to record. But it is a necessary failure, because there has to be a first attempt. In reading it, others will see what needs to be done to recover the underside of the human experience and particularly to recover women as part of history.

If I were to begin this book now, with what I know after two years of work, I would write it differently and, I think, better. I would be able to give a better balance to the presentations of the life situations of women in different social classes, especially the situation of laboring women, slaves, prostitutes, and laboring children. I have not been able to convey adequately the human suffering of the underside. There have been times when it has almost overwhelmed me. The elites have invariably had more than their share of attention in the book. They too have suffered, however, and again I have failed to portray the heavy burdens of their lives—it seemed so important to point to their accomplishments.

If suffering has been underrecorded, so has joy. In a book such as this, a macro history, how do you capture the laughter of young working girls on holiday, the joy of sunrise for a solitary old woman glad to be alive? How do you capture the sound of children playing in the street, the rhythm of kitchen work by busy mothers to the music of clicking pots and pans on feast days, the contentment of the grandmother by the fireside with her granddaughter on her knee? The frontispiece picture of the sculpture of St. Louis and Marguerite of Provence captures something of the complexity of the underside. The expression on Marguerite's face as she looks up at her husband is not wholly attributable to the trappings of authority of church and state that he bears, dressed in Crusaders' garb, holding a model of the

Holy Sepulchre in his right hand and the shield of France in his left. Does it convey a contented dependency, or is there a private, affectionate autonomy in her stance?

I never wanted to write a "big-name" history, but it is relatively easy to dig out the names of the great women achievers, names that are often missing from the standard histories. Thus I found myself continually slipping into big-name history, in spite of myself. Those names had to be put back in the record!

There are wild imbalances in the book in terms of macro-historical perspective. The major one is the excessive attention to Western history. I could not master the necessary scholarship, in the time I had, to write the world history I originally intended. Also, the nineteenth century gets far more attention than it should. Yet, it seemed right to present the nineteenth century as I did, because the twentieth-century activities of women make little sense without a knowledge of their nineteenth-century roots. As a sociologist, I could not resist a somewhat lengthy discussion of nineteenth-century women social scientists, because my profession has no image of its own underside.

The breathless summary of 1,000 years of "Two-Thirds World" history in Chapter 4, Volume 2 ("A Historical Note on the Underside of the 'Two-Thirds World' ") should perhaps not have been attempted, but I could not be content to enter the last chapter without it.

I have become increasingly aware in recent months of the number of historians who are now doing in-depth studies of particular historical periods, the kind of studies that I so keenly felt the lack of while writing this book. Where their work has come to my attention, I have mentioned them, but there is much more work going on than I have been able to uncover. Every specialist will find that the period she or he knows best has been badly treated here and will find much to criticize. I regret this, but had I been a period specialist I would never have dared to write this book. The justification for macro history is supposed to be that it has a validity of its own, independent of individual historical facts. I rejoice that there will be not only one but many successors to this work, each with new facts and new insights about the underside.

As with every historian, my own commitments and beliefs have shaped the emphases I have given to history. I have given more weight to religious currents as a crucial force in the development of the human potential than others might give. Militarism has been treated as pathology, and the development of the sequence "urbanism/societal differentiation/hierarchy/centralization" has been treated as one among several possible patterns of human development. I have presented no "grand theory" of history. I have not even fully "explained" the role of women in history. Rather, I have tried to develop a perspective, a way of thinking about these roles, that can help us all to connect better with the new developments that are unfolding as we move into the twenty-first century.

The fact that the book has been completed during International Women's Year gives me particular satisfaction. It is a rare experience for a nonconformist to have one's inner agenda coincide with an agenda set by the world. During the 1975 activities, I have become increasingly aware of the quality of leadership that U.N. Assistant Secretary General Helvi Sipila has given to the women's year. Her leadership gives me hope that the United Nations itself will help to open up for women the futures that I have seen glimpses of while writing this book.

Acknowledgments

As I noted in the original edition, *The Underside of History* would not have been imaginable to me were it not for the support, encouragement, and life-enriching stimuli of my husband, Kenneth, who learned homemaking skills while in his sixties to free my time for writing. He cheered me on when I was discouraged, served as an invaluable sounding board, and even stimulated my own thinking during our disagreements about the interpretation of history!

Also, there were several outstanding husband and wife partnerships, among them:

Alva and Gunnar Myrdal (Alva was my first scholar-activist role model as a young bride when she and Gunnar were working on *The American Dilemma*)

Clara and Robert Park

Marie and Charles Johnsen (among my splendid teachers at Fisk in 1942-43, who helped me discover the black underside of U.S. society)

Helen and Everett Hughes

Evey and David Riesman

Marion and Reuben Hill

Esther and Robert Angell

Fred Polak and Louisa Polak Moor

(teachers, friends, partners whose lives taught me insights about the relative invisibility of faculty wives whose creativity has flourished in private spaces)

Three organizations exerted, in different ways, powerful influences on both the events in my life and the formation of my views during the 1950s and 1960s:

the Women's International League for Peace and Freedom

the Center for Research on Conflict Resolution (University of Michigan)

the International Peace Research Association (which grew out of a newsletter I edited during this period)

A book that celebrates women's lives throughout time must certainly celebrate my own family, who have brought such richness into my life. Here I say thank you from the heart to

my children, whose companionship has been as important in my personal and intellectual development as any other influence in my life,

Russell, Mark, Christine, Phillip, and William

five daughters-in-law—Bonnie, Susan (whose untimely death has left an unhealed wound), Pamela, Elizabeth, and Patricia—and one son-in-law—Gregory

my grandchildren: Bjorn, Carew, Frances, Abram, Kit, Peter, Krista, Geoffrey, Brenin, Marshall, Morgan, Brittany, Meredith, Emily, and Luke

my parents: Birgit-Marianna Johnsen, my ever-eager, ever-exploring mother, and Josef Biorn-Hansen, my gentle father

my sisters: Sylvia (whose loss I still mourn) and Vera, who as younger siblings brought fun and joy to their staid older sister

In my late-launched career, I found supportive colleagues and inspiration from many sources, among them

Charles Moskos, who always heard what I was saying

my fellow members on the American Sociological Association's Committee on the Status of Women in the Profession

the women who worked with me on the International Sociological Association's Research Committee on Sex Roles in Society

the women I have known in the women's movement—sisters in the Women's International League for Peace and Freedom and women in Japan, Jamaica, Canada, Latin America, North Africa, and in all the countries of Eastern and Western Europe (but most especially the women of my own native land, Norway)

the women I have known as neighbors in the many communities where we have lived; the women I have worked with in local political and community action programs; the many Quaker women I have known—each in their way helped prepare me to write this book

During this book's early stages of preparation, I discussed historical perspectives on women's roles with a number of people; their encouragement helped me to go on with the project. I particularly want to thank

Margaret Mead,
Jessie Bernard,
Berenice Carroll,
Saul Mendlovitz, and
Johan Galtung

for listening and being supportive at that early stage. Of course, none of them bears any responsibility for the way the book later developed.

For their insight into the ways of women religious and the role of women in the Christian church, I thank Brother Victor Antonio of the Benedictine Monastery of Our Lady of the Resurrection in La Grangeville, New York. I also thank the sisters in various contemplative and apostolic orders who have greatly deepened my understanding of the importance of monastic life in releasing women's creativity.

Many thanks for her facilitating skills are due to Gloria Scott of the United Nations' Social Development and Humanitarian Affairs division.

My colleagues Shirley Nuss, Dorothy Carson, Robert Passmore, and Michael Greenstein have made an important contribution to our understanding of the global situation of women based on the data they gathered for the *International Women's Data Handbook* (Boulding, Nuss, Carson, and Greenstein 1976), which was used in the tabular material of the 1976 edition of *The Underside*. Although these tables were omitted from the current edition, the data inform much of the discussion in the current Chapter 5 in Volume 2.

My colleague Anna Spradlin, at the University of Colorado's Department of Communication, helped in locating literature on lesbianism for this new edition, which has helped me in turn to understand the diversity of lesbian cultures.

I am grateful for research support to the University of Colorado Committee on Creative Research and the United Nations.

The contribution of the readers of the manuscript proved invaluable. They set me straight when I had the history wrong. They helped me get a better perspective on the whole book. They, however, bear no responsibility for errors of commission and omission, which are my own. For their assistance in reviewing the entire original manuscript, I thank

Sheila Johansson, demographic historian
Susan Armitage, historian

Anita Cochran, librarian
Suzanne Tessler, sociologist
Brian Giffen, craftsman and inventor

I am also grateful to the period specialists who provided invaluable comments on specific chapters: Professors William Proctor and E. H. Hallgren, medievalists, and Joy King, classicist. My thanks also go to anthropologically trained editor Sharon Bryan, who read the first five chapters, and to my sister Vera Larson, who read Chapter 2 in Volume 1 (one of the hardest and most rewritten chapters in the book), whose perspectives as a family therapist helped me with an especially difficult part.

The 80 students in the Social History of Women class I taught in the fall of 1975 played a special part in the preparation of the original edition. I am grateful for the insights we generated together as well as the willingness of several individuals in that class to share their work with me, as noted in the notes and references.

For their help in the long and arduous task of preparing *The Underside* for publication, I wish to thank:

Dorothy Carson—my friend and administrative assistant (during the preparation of the original edition);

Anita Cochran, the type of creative librarian who reduces the pain and enhances the joy of scholarly work;

Kathy Hamilton of Boulder Graphics, who produced many beautifully readable graphics as needed;

Bonnie Boulding, who, with great care, rendered the drawings for the village layouts in Chapter 4 of Volume 1;

Judy Fukuhara, who typed multiple versions of each chapter in the original edition with speed, accuracy, and loving care;

Alanna Preussner, who did a mammoth reference checking and editorial job;

Mario Holgu, Maureen Mee, and Holly Hollingworth, who also greatly assisted in the final stages of manuscript preparation;

Marty Gonzales, my gifted current administrative assistant, who kept me organized to undertake this revision at a busy time in both our lives; and

Ellen Wild, who assisted in turning an untidy jumble into a beautifully readable manuscript copy for the publisher of this new edition.

I was fortunate to have Lynne Rienner's careful and discerning copyediting skills for the original edition.

Helen Barchilon Redman brought a whole new dimension to both editions of the book by becoming both art consultant and illustrator. Indeed, one of the pleasures of this new edition has been to reconnect with

Helen. Her drawings of women through the centuries, based on a pains-taking search through archives for authentic historical representations of women engaged in precisely those activities that male historians failed to record, are an essential part of this book.

Thank you also to the wonderful team of women at Sage Publications: Janet Brown, for fine copy-editing and heroic tracing of lost permissions; Diane Foster, clear-headed orchestrator of production; and Judy Rothman, with her energy, imagination, and instinct about the audience for whom this book was written, who directed the whole publishing process.

And a very special thank you to Sara Miller McCune, founder, Chair, and Publisher at Sage Publications: I am deeply grateful for her willingness to work patiently with me on figuring out the revised format for the current edition out of her conviction that *The Underside* was worth republishing. Thank you, Sara, for your friendship, your keen awareness of the many dimensions of women's search for identity, and for your vision of what publishing is all about.

The last word (in addition to the first word) of gratitude goes to my husband of 50 years, Kenneth Boulding, who enjoys insisting that the trouble with women is that, like men, they are human beings!

PART I

Setting
the
Stage

1

Sampling the Invisible

H istory is a problem in sampling. Depending on the point in time at which one considers that one's ancestors became fully human, there have been somewhere between 60 and 77 billion of us around, women and men, weaving an infinite variety of gossamer social webs to girdle the planet. We are an interesting lot, we humans. Yet the most informed of the 4 billion of us alive today know precious little about our story. We know little enough about our contemporary family and, when we start probing back through history, we find huge blank spaces relieved here and there by fragmentary images of kings, pyramids, temples, and battlefields. If we try to go back much beyond 5,000 years, our imaginations give out entirely. Yet we and the immediate ancestors to the human race, *Homo* and *Mulier erectus*, have been around for about 2 million years.[1] Anyone wandering in the bookstores of Stockholm, Brussels, Frankfurt, or Chicago looking for history books will find hundreds on the history of Western civilization and only dozens on the history of the rest of the world. Yet most of the human beings who have walked through history have lived elsewhere. They have lived all over the planet, of course, but most have lived in Asia. The sampling of human experience in our history books is, in short, very poor.

It would not matter so much that those of us who live in the West focus on our own recent corner of history if we kept it in the proper perspective. But, of course, we do not. We have created a myth called the "Evolution of Mankind" from our fragments. One of the many strange things about this myth is that it does not include woman. The history of humankind has been written as if it were the history of Western man. An otherwise excellent world history widely used in college courses, McNeill's *The Rise of the West* (1963), contains two mentions of women in 1,000 pages.

The elimination of most of the human race from the historical record shrinks our human identity. We don't know fully who we are. We know even less what we might become. Obviously, this book cannot answer these broad questions, but it will deal with some specific questions of the role of women in history. In failing to see what was happening to women, we have misunderstood the story of the rise of cities and empires, the thrust of "social progress." I propose an attempt to recover some of the wholeness of the human identity by going back to sample the underside, the invisible side, of history and bring its women to life.

This is not intended to be an exercise in polemics, although polemical elements will inevitably appear. The history of polemics about the role of women is a long one, and this book is written in the context of the twentieth-century version of an old battle. The last round of polemics previous to our own time began about 100 years ago, when Bachofen wrote *Das Mutterrecht* to show that society had once been a matriarchy and that humankind had once lived under the rule of women. The flurry this book and others caused died down when it was demonstrated that the evidence had been misinterpreted. Women, briefly regarded with suspicious awe, could safely be allowed to lapse into invisibility again. Now we have more complete anthropological data on contemporary tribal societies, including "Stone Age-type" hunting and gathering bands. We have archaeological reconstructions of ancient Paleolithic camp sites, of the first agrovillages of the Near East, of the first cities of the Mediterranean.

We also have new studies of the literature of antiquity, of ancient laws, and of the political structures of city-states, kingdoms, and empires. A whole new light has been thrown on the European Middle Ages through studies of parish records. Medieval writings in praise of women, as well as denunciations, have been uncovered. The history of the industrial revolution has been rewritten. Out of all this, a very different picture of the role of women emerges than the one reflected in the polemics of the nineteenth century or the new polemics of the twentieth. Yet, when we turn to standard contemporary histories, women disappear from sight. Queens and courtesans are the most likely female characters to survive the historians' sorting process.

When Cora Castle in 1910 undertook a statistical study of eminent women in history, on the basis of names that appeared in any three out of six major European encyclopedias, she was only able to come up with 868 women, given all of history on which to draw. The categories of women treated as most eminent by the encyclopedias, in terms of numbers of lines of biography, were, in rank order: (a) queens, (b) politicians (mostly French salon women of the 1600s), (c) mothers, (d) mistresses, (e) beauties, (f) religious women, (g) women of tragic fate, and (h) women important only through marriage. Substantive achievements of women as the basis for mention trailed in the last seven categories (Castle 1913).

This kind of treatment of women in history is now outmoded and yet strangely persistent. The view of Western history as an evolutionary unfolding from the time of the first post-Roman "barbarian" kingdoms led to compelling conceptions of individualism in the nineteenth century, but they were applied to men of the middle and upper classes only. In the twentieth century, these conceptions reappear as leftover agenda items for populations excluded from nineteenth-century developments, particularly women, the working classes, the poor, and colonized peoples. The excluded folk are now applying these conceptions to themselves. The nineteenth century was the century of the celebration of individualism, but the twentieth century is the century of the celebration of the individuality of all human beings, including women.

The celebration of the individuality of women has taken diverse forms. There have been social science analyses of the occupational segregation and the status inequalities that characterize women's roles everywhere, throwing light on the dynamics of inequality.[2] There has been reconsideration of the theories of the golden age of matriarchy, some more ideological than scholarly, as in Diner's *Mothers and Amazons* ([1932] 1965) and Davis's *The First Sex* (1971). Reed's *Woman's Evolution from Matriarchal Clan to Patriarchal Family* (1975), also ideological, attempts to synthesize earlier materials into a new statement about matriarchy. Other books in a more polemical style and focusing on the "woman as victim" theme are as varied as Millet's *Sexual Politics* (1970) and Firestone's *Dialectic of Sex* (1970).

In between are a variety of efforts to understand the meanings for women of equality, of participation, and of liberation in the context of the human condition in the twentieth century. It has been the accumulated work of my contemporaries in the decades between the close of World War I and the onset of the women's liberation era, providing a fresh unclouded look at women, that has made this book possible. Margaret Mead, Alva Myrdal, Viola Klein, Mary Beard, Jessie Bernard, Athena Theodore, Mirra Komarovsky, Barbara E. Ward, Harriet Holter, Evelyn Sullerot, and Ester Boserup are among the leading social scientists of Euro-North America who contributed to the ways of thinking that this book represents. The book has been written out of a Western tradition of thought but looks to a future when all the major cultural traditions of the planet will be drawn on to delineate the shapes of women's roles in human society.

Margaret Mead was a pioneer in drawing attention to the processes that shaped male and female roles, through cross-cultural analysis. Mead was also among the first to spell out the character of role transition in the modernization process, both for women and for men (Mead 1955, 1968, 1970).

Alva Myrdal did a pioneering analysis of the structural constraints that shaped women's roles, first in a policy-oriented study of Sweden (1945) and then, jointly with Viola Klein (Myrdal and Klein 1968), in a cross-cultural analysis of women's double role as homemaker and producer. Myrdal and Klein were the first to see the large-scale entry of women into the labor force in this century as a return to a former economic productivity, as the "recovering of women's lost territory" (1968: 1-2).

Mary Beard (1946) was the first of the mid-twentieth-century historians to use the best of modern techniques of documentation and analysis to portray women as significant actors in the public arena throughout history. Documenting the role women played in public affairs in Egyptian, Greco-Roman, and successive European eras from the early Middle Ages to the current time, she also drew a picture of the successive opening and closing of roles to women.

Jessie Bernard (1975) uncovered and described the underlife—the socially hidden activity and movement—of academic women and has gone on to uncover the underlife of women in their twentieth-century roles. Athena Theodore did the same for professional women (1971), and Mirra Komarovsky provided an early sociological analysis of sex roles in terms of cultural contradictions (1946). Barbara E. Ward (1963) forcefully drew the attention of Westerners to what modernization was doing to women in those civilizations of Asia that had traditionally given a more egalitarian status to women than Western values permitted. The essays she assembled from Asian women scholars showed, among other things, how women were being forced out of independent economic roles and relegated to wife-hostess roles by Westerners accustomed only to dealing with men in public decision-making spheres.

Sullerot (1968), initially examining contemporary occupational data on women in France, was led to an examination of earlier occupational roles of women in Europe and opened up the old, long-forgotten subject of times when women held more equal participatory and decision-making roles than they do now.

Holter (1970) was the first to do a systematic analysis of how practices of stratification lead to power discrepancies between men and women; Boserup (1970) was the first to document in detail, from a precise analysis of agricultural practices, the "how" of early sex-based division of labor leading to that stratification and loss of power. The 1958 International

Institute of Differing Civilization Conference on Women's Role in the Development of Tropical and Subtropical Countries (Carr-Sanders 1959) laid the foundation for a general understanding of the effect of modernization on women's roles, and a series of U.N. conferences and associated research on the status of women over the last two decades demonstrate that the problems continue.

The women scholars so briefly mentioned in this roster represent only the most visible top rank of a large body of women who have during this century laid the basis for a reconceptualization of the roles of women and men in society. The reader will note that most of the scholars I have cited are women. While their perspectives are very different, one from the other, their work collectively does represent a special stream of thought in mid-twentieth-century sociology. One name that I would add here because of the importance of the global perspective he introduced is William Goode. In looking at the sweep of changes on the entire planet from the perspective of the family, he has made a significant contribution to the understanding of the underside (Goode 1963). While his analysis has been confined to the past half-century, the depth of his historical insight gives his work a macro-historical dimension. It took courage for Goode to write his book, and his achievement helped give me courage to write this one.

Uncertainty about the whole phenomenon of role differentiation based on sex, compounded by uncertainties engendered by continuing economic and environmental crises, makes the women's liberation era a time of considerable tension in male-female relationships. As we move toward the twenty-first century, we need new perspectives on society, on history, on the human identity. It is a good time to view the historical process as experienced by women and men. The problems of sampling will continue to dog us: The very invisibility of women in the historical record makes the effort to include them in a resurvey of the past problematic. The fact of that invisibility tends to pull us toward the women-as-victim position on women in history. The meager reporting on women in the documents we turn to compounds the conviction that they have been excluded from decision making, recognition, and reward and left to do the dirty work of society. The middle position, however, between the victim theory and the decline-from-golden-age-of-matriarchy theory, is the one that best fits the materials assembled in this book.[3] It is the position eloquently put forward by Beard (1946). In antiquity and in the Middle Ages, there were women who took leadership roles and were involved in public affairs. Events associated with the developments of the industrial revolution and postmedieval political and legal institutions reduced the leadership roles of elite women.

The thrust of this book is different than that of Beard in several important respects, however. In examining leadership roles of elite women, there is more emphasis on the structural constraints that shaped their roles. There is also a continuing emphasis on the contrast between the predominantly human welfare orientation of women's activities, in all social classes, and the predominantly conquest-and-dominance orientation of men's activities. That contrast remains essentially unchanged once city life becomes a focal point of human existence. In the twentieth century, as in the Mediterranean civilizations of 2000 B.C.E., there are no women in the national security councils of any country, no women in top-level military commands, and no women among the top ecclesiastical authorities (who have historically also had armies at their disposal) of any major religion. Women heads of state, then as now, can be counted on the fingers of one hand, with several fingers left over. Even at local levels, few women will be found in any historical period in positions of responsibility in any of these centralized hierarchies. The visible world continues to be male. There is a continuing effort throughout this book to look at what women *have* been doing in all classes of society, not just among the elite, and to document the range and variety of their occupations in the hidden underlife. Finally, there is a commitment to viewing women's roles in the context of the total time span of human experience, going back before the appearance of our own species to the 2 or 3 million years when *Mulier* and *Homo erectus* explored the earth and bringing the exploration up to the threshold of the twenty-first century.

Some of the perspectives that went into the making of this book are not directly rooted in any of the recognized traditions of the study of women, stemming rather from the other major involvements of my own life. The concern with victimization, oppression, and violence as human problems, and the concern with the extension of the concept of human community from the tribe to the world as a whole, with all the social and political ramifications of that extension, come out of my work as a peace researcher and social activist. The concern for the spiritual dimension in human development comes out of my struggles to integrate the intellectual, spiritual, and activist dimensions in my own life as a homemaker, mother, scholar, teacher, and activist. Finally, the concern to understand the sweep of history comes out of my own profound conviction that the current time is intolerable unless understood in the context of the long slow processes of human development on the planet.

It seems appropriate to bring all these concerns together in a book about women because the status of women, as many scholars have now noted, is indeed a useful indicator of how society is doing in its historical enterprise of making humans more humane. When we look at the imbalances regarding women both in the social record and in society itself, we are getting clues about general social imbalances, not just about the status of women. Women's biological attributes do not affect the generalizability of the discoveries we make. With what we know now, it can be said that the social invisibility of women is a cultural artifact rather than a biological necessity. It is also in part a conceptual artifact, due to an underestimation of the role of the household in society dating perhaps from the first empires of antiquity. The faulty conceptualization has made understandings of and policies about sex-based roles peculiarly resistant to those processes of social change that reshape other social roles.

The household unit in society through the first millennium C.E. was responsible for about 90% of the total production of the city-states and empires.[4] If we define as *household production* all that is produced inside and adjacent to the home, including courtyard and kitchen garden, family workshop, and farm fields (workshop and fields are psychologically adjacent to the household but may be geographically distant and require long walks for women to their "household" work sites), then we may say that women have at the very least been equal partners in production through most of history. Not infrequently, and particularly in wartime, they have been the major contributors to that production. As long as the household was also the major work base for men, the equal partnership concept would hold. Long before the industrial revolution, however, a substantial amount of craft production was being carried on by both women and men in village and city workshops owned by others. In work outside the household site, women were always disadvantaged.

It happens that many studies of the industrial revolution have focused on the textile industry, which happened in its preindustrial phase to be a family industry carried out in the home as workshop. This has led scholars mistakenly to conclude that the majority of men and all women were carrying out their productive activities within their own households up to the time of the industrial revolution. See, for example, Smelser's (1959) analysis of the impact on families of the shift from home to factory work sites in the British cotton industry. Even Myrdal and Klein make the same mistake (1968). This issue will be further explored in Chapter 2 in Volume 2.

In household-based production, then, women have historically probably been an equal and sometimes dominant partner in terms of productivity and decisions about resource allocation. It was the 10% of production carried on outside the household, increasing in proportion from C.E. 1000 to the time of the industrial revolution, that placed women at a disadvantage and in menial roles. As we shall see, women of the elite were much less disadvantaged beyond the household.

Women's economic partnership roles throughout history deserve more attention. Recent research indicates that the capital available to women in their domestic partner role, through dowry, inheritance, and management of production activities, was considerably larger than hitherto realized

(Goitein 1967-71; Jennings 1975; Herlihy 1962). Their use of this capital in civic projects also has not been recognized. With the industrial revolution and the shrinking of domestic productivity down to one-fourth to one-fifth or less of the total productivity of a society, capital available to women also shrank and nondomestic work sites became more important. That shrinkage was accompanied by political changes that abolished the public roles of elite women, compounding economic deprivation with political deprivation at the very time when new ideals of political participation were developing. The old household partnership model could no longer serve, and industrialization seemed to spell disaster for women.

An Alternative "Development Story"

The old nineteenth-century theme of inevitable progress through industrialization has worn thin. Though enthusiasm can still be found for the view that there is one basic upward path for human societies, with clearly marked stages on the way, prophecies of the decline of the West have moderated this enthusiasm.[5] We are also more knowledgeable about alternative ways of entering modernity stemming from different cultural traditions, with China and Japan as notable examples. This has brought into favor the more modest concept of the multilinearity of social evolution. Other ways of conceptualizing the historical process that sidestep the "onward and upward" issue have been developed by the demographer and the ecologist.

According to the ecological view of history,[6] *Homo erectus* lived for 2 or 3 million years in a state of equilibrium in relation to available environmental resources, in a condition of zero population growth. Two factors contributed to population limitation: (a) babies in hunting and gathering bands must be carried when moving from camp site to camp site and in the daily search for food, and (b) bands seem to operate on a principle of limiting the population to a number that can be comfortably cared for and supported by gathering the most desirable and readily available plant and animal foods. This means that there is always more food in the environment than a given band uses, and in times of drought there are ample resources available. (Farmers are more apt to starve during droughts than food gatherers.) Population control mechanisms among humans (techniques for abortion and contraception are known in most if not all tribal societies) are apparently suspended, or at least practiced more selectively, once nomadic existence has been replaced by a settled agricultural way of life.[7] Children become an asset rather than a handicap. The change in attitudes regarding childbearing that took place about 10,000 B.C.E. seems to be very difficult to reverse now that environmental constraints once more require limitation of population.

Significant population expansion began about 10,000 B.C.E. But, because there was plenty of room in which to spread out, and the initial number of settled agriculturalists engaged in this new enterprise of actively breeding children was small, it took a long time to create the kind of population densities that laid the basis for urban civilizations, census taking, and a decline in the status of women.

Ever since this great transition from the Paleolithic to the Neolithic, we have been dealing with increasing problems of scale. From nomadic camp site to agricultural village, from village to trading town, trading town to city, city to city-state, city-state to empire, and empire to nation-state, from raw nationalism to the modified nationalism of a U.N. system, each step represents an increase in population concentration and in the complexity of the sex- and class-segregated patterns of organizing that concentration.

Resource shortages continually developed as societies outgrew their ecological niches. These shortages might come from population growth, but they might also come from the development of structural inequalities in a society that created a nonproductive, overconsuming sector that could not continue to be supported by the existing resource base. Either way, there was pressure for the development of new production technologies.

Shifts in production technology have usually squeezed women out of formerly central roles. Thus women were the cultivators under the old slash-and-burn agricultural system, but, when higher yields required the invention of the plow, men took over[8] and assigned auxiliary tasks to women. Women are the builders when housing involves twig shelters, skin tents, and woven grass huts; they may hang on through the making of adobe houses; but, when it comes to fired bricks and processed materials, men take over.[9]

The shift in roles comes about each time because more hands are needed. In the process of inventing productivity-enhancing technologies, auxiliary tasks requiring less skill than the former production role are generated, and, if the new technology displaces women, it is women who perform these auxiliary tasks.

Problems of Scale and Dominance Traps for Women

Repeatedly in history, humans were pushed to the threshold of necessary innovations—pushed by socially and biologically created wants in the face of environmental constraints. From the time of the earliest agricultural settlements, women carried a heavy double load of providing a continuing supply of babies throughout their reproductive years—as contrasted with careful spacing in the nomadic state—while participating in the full productive work of society on the farm, in the cottage industry of the home, or in workshops outside the home. As long as the household was the main work site, technological change did not disadvantage women too seriously; they still retained control of some capital. But, as we will see in Chapter 4 in this volume, I am suggesting that they never had sufficient leisure in the early agrovillages to grasp adequately the new problems of scale that were created in village settings. Hence inventions to deal with problems of scale became a male task, and women were simply left with new work residues.

In the egalitarian band society, and in what Fried (1967) calls the ranked societies—tribal societies with special prestige roles that involve responsibility for redistribution of goods but not personal access to more goods—no individuals, women or men, are removed from the primary producer roles. Kinship structures form the infrastructure of society, and most political roles are embedded in kinship roles. It is in the shift from the ranked to the stratified society that some individuals are removed from primary producer roles, with the consequences that differential access to resources develops. In the stratified society, the individuals who cease to be primary producers control the labor, and the products, of their fellows. A class society has come into existence. Neither the ecological model, in which population concentration forces that shift, nor the Engels-Marx model, in which domination by men over women in the monogamous household patterns all later stratification and differentiation of access to resources, really accounts for the dynamics of dominance, nor for the fact that one of the forms dominance takes is male control over the female's access to some of her means of production.

In the next chapter, we will be exploring the determinants of male dominance as seen by the sociobiologist. For the purposes of this discussion, it is enough to point out that hunting-gathering bands are generally monogamous and sex egalitarian. The domination of female by male stems from other sources than physique and monogamy, and its later forms are linked in complex ways to accumulation and the reward system. No doubt, domination of the female has been a powerful reinforcer of all other dominance systems.

In this chapter, we are looking at the historical situation of women primarily in terms of social structure. Social historians have pointed out the special role that urbanism has played in the development of stratification systems. Sullerot (1968) sees urbanism as providing the opportunity for "thinker males" to free themselves from producer roles by lumping breeder and producer functions together for cattle, slaves, and females. This in turn gave the major impetus to stratification processes in general and to the domination of the woman by the man in particular.

I suggest that the accumulation of the power to dominate may be a push-pull process involving pressure both from above and from below. The stratification system that emerges from this push-pull process is one in which women are found to be marginal in terms of command roles. A loose stratification of tribes into have and have-more groups could have set in motion a dynamic that led to work loads within households that are heavier for women than for men. As we will see in Chapters 3 and 4 in this volume, the male hunting role played a special part in the tilting of work loads toward women. Hunting was arduous work while in process but much more sporadic than women's work. This dynamic resulted in women becoming a special category that has persisted as a social phenomenon through 10,000 years of history. The biological breeder-feeder role of women very likely reinforced other tendencies to place extra work loads on women.

Ceremonials, ranking, and stratification all in their way helped the societies that evolved them in dealing with problems of scale. In stratified societies, only elite women participated publicly in policy planning and decision making. They used their male-derived status for a parallel, if secondary, exercise of power. Ceremonies and rituals are interesting because they have the unique property of being relevant techniques of social organization at every level of community. Women play an important role in the ceremonial life of every society, and much Paleolithic and early Neolithic ceremonial was probably created by women in their priestess roles.

Each increment of size and complexity of social organization has its implications for women's roles, including the twentieth-century rediscovery of the Paleolithic dictum that population must be held in balance with environmental resources. I sometimes wonder if our motto today does not need to be: "Forward to the Paleolithic!" The folk of the Neolithic, with their cozy farm communities, working like dogs and breeding like rabbits, have little that is useful to say to us. And, while I am not prepared to join Richard Lee and Irven De Vore's (1968) bushmen, or Colin Turnbull's (1968) forest people, bands like these have sometimes been called the only leisure societies left on the planet. They have had population control and (relative) abundance, leisure time, a rich ceremonial life, and relative peace throughout the entire period that Eurasia has fought to ever higher levels of struggle.

On the other hand, we cannot simply write off the experience of the last 12,000 years. However we evaluate the achievements of these millennia, they are in fact the products of the human experience. Empire and military glory have no doubt been valued too highly, but they do belong somewhere in the story. Revaluing our own creativity as we look at a fuller record of human history, to gain an understanding of how to nurture the best of the human potentials in the future, is a task not to be ignored. As we understand better what women were actually doing century by century through recorded time, we will have a better comprehension of our own behavioral repertoire and of the social inventions at our disposal.

The Approach of This Book

The Long Look

The reconstruction and revaluing of women's roles undertaken in this book necessitate a long walk through history, from the time of our earliest primate ancestors onward. We will move through the 100,000-year wanderings of the Paleolithic, on into the great transition from hunting and gathering to herding and planting, on to life inside city walls and life outside it for the nomads and the forest dwellers, to the great primary civilizations of the Middle East and Asia, and the feudal civilizations on its fringes, on to the more recent sweep of culture from the Greco-Romanic-Islamic empires to "European Enlightenment," and finally to the last two centuries of gradual industrialization-urbanization of large parts of the planet. I originally intended to keep this a world history right up to the twentieth century. The impossibility of covering developments in Asia, Africa, and Latin America with the limited research time available has led me, reluctantly, to focus on "the West" after the fall of Rome. A sweeping historical survey of the *Two-Thirds World* (a term I use rather than the pejorative *Third World*) is included as Chapter 4 in Volume 2, before the final chapter, to bring that whole sector of underlife experience of Two-Thirds-World women into focus before launching into a discussion of the future.

The immediate stimulus for this work came from a study in the middle 1960s of the current participation of women in the economic, educational, and civic sectors on four continents (Boulding 1969). It was finding an enormous variation in traditional participation patterns in Africa and Asia, compared with a narrow range of participation in modernized societies, that led me to the questions I am asking here and to the historical survey that this book represents.

I found that women's traditional roles were the most autonomous and participatory in countries that entered modernization from the essentially preurban kingdoms of Africa and the outpost empires of Asia and from tribal societies. Women in the central empire countries from the anciently urbanized Syriac-Palestinian area had the least individuated roles.

While for Western countries the "floor" of participation is higher than for preindustrial societies—that is, there is a participatory level below which women do not fall in the West—the ceiling is also lower; women do not rise to the heights of participation that they do in some traditional African and Asian countries. This means that the theories that equate societal differentiation with increased autonomy and participation are inadequate. Nevertheless, because social structures pattern individual participation, attention must be paid to the differentiation process.[10]

An important feature of structural differentiation is the relative independence of the various systems within the society. In the simplest societies, economic, political, legal, religious, and educational systems are all embedded in the kinship structure. The idea of the completely differentiated society assumes that each sector operates to a degree independently in terms of definition of tasks and responsibilities and that each individual operates on the basis of universalistic principles rather than from special interest. In fact, of course, such terms as *military-industrial complex* and *power elite* indicate that both embeddedness and particularism continue into the current time.

On the one hand, the old view of "primitive societies" as ones in which all human activities, all value judgments, and all loyalties refer back to family groups, and of "modern societies" as ones in which every individual regardless of sex, race, or class carries out specialized functions with an objective and sophisticated commitment to the universal good, is gradually breaking down. On the other hand, we continue to define—and experience—differentiation and centralization as leading to a higher, more all-encompassing social good and to progress. We certainly conceptualize these phenomena as progress in our social theories. Have differentiation and centralization meant progress for women?

Sampling by Means of the Random Walk

Initially, I had developed a societal-complexity profile and a women's participation profile to measure the extent of differentiation of societal and of women's roles in each society through history. This plan had to be abandoned for two reasons. First, it would require a social historian knowledgeable enough to make proper judgments about societal complexity in different historical eras. Second, I found that information on women in the easily available history books in every period of history was so spotty, so like chance eruptions of hot springs in areas where thermal waters run close to the earth's surface, that it was impossible to do the systematic codification I had hoped to do. A number of women historians are now working with primary sources to correct this situation, and in coming decades we will have much more adequate data on women through time than were available to me. It is not my purpose to try to do badly what the trained historian can do well but to develop a new way of thinking about women in the historical process. I hope this rough preliminary survey of the terrain has some usefulness as an interim statement while the research of trained historians is being undertaken. An adequate macro history of women's roles lies in the future.[11]

Instead of a sophisticated historical study of societal differentiation and women's roles, then, I offer my personal "sociological" walk through history and accounts of the activities of the women I have seen there. Whatever their social class, they have invariably been more productive and more overworked than would be suspected from an examination of the male diatribes against them that can be found in every historical era from Sumerian times forward. Each one described should be taken as illustrative of countless of her sisters who remain invisible.

Although I do not present a systematic macro-historical analysis of societal differentiation, I have given some attention to the structural features and cultural uniqueness of each society studied through time. Because both women's and men's roles are shaped by social structures and cultural patterning, it may be useful to list the kinds of societies we will be studying as we move through history. These do not necessarily represent an evolutionary sequence, and in fact some variant of each major type of society still exists in some form somewhere today. Hunting-gathering societies are found on all continents. Remnants of "forest civilizations" are found in Africa. Singapore is a city-state. Southeast Asia still contains remnants of centralized empires, as in Thailand. Table 1.1 lists the societal types considered here, and Table 1.2 indicates the chronology of the appearance of each new type. Each of these new types develops a characteristic social technology. Each set of new social inventions represents adaptations to increasing size and the need for a new scale of activities. These inventions will be referred to as appropriate in each chapter as we discuss women's adaptations to new levels of complexity.

Women and "Underlife" Structures

In this section, I will share some of my thinking about the meaning of underlife structures for women and how these structures have shaped women's lives and behaviors.[12] The underlife concept implies an overlife as well, which consists of overtly articulated role structures—the visible terrain of society. Woman's sex-designated position, resistant to social

TABLE 1.1 Societal Types

1. Band or tribal
   a. hunting and gathering, egalitarian
   b. hunting and gathering, horticulture base, ranked
2. Preurban
   a. agriculture base, "forest civilizations," ranked transitional
   b. nomadic, herding, no agriculture, ranked
3. City-based state
   a. city-state, agriculture, craft industries, urban administration, stratified
   b. feudal kingdom, same as city-state but with weaker urban administration
4. Centralized bureaucratic empire

   Agriculture, large-scale industries, trade, strong central administration, diplomatic relations with other societies, stratified
5. Modern industrialized or transitional

   Mass production, communication infrastructure permitting some local autonomy coordinated to varying degrees of strong, central planning; stratified, agricultural activity involves as little as 5% of the labor force

changes that alter other parts of the social structure, tends to keep her in the underlife sector. From time to time, there is a further contraction of roles formally designated for women, and then the feminine half of society reorganizes and readapts to carry out its functions under new cultural constraints. The role of women in societies where these constraints have

TABLE 1.2 Chronology of the Emergence of Societal Types, 50,000 B.C.E. to Current Time

Time Period	Type of Society
50,000 B.C.E. - 10,000 B.C.E.	Hunting and gathering
10,000 B.C.E. - 6000 B.C.E.	Settled agricultural
6000 B.C.E.-	Trading town
3500 B.C.E.-	City
2500 B.C.E. - 1500 C.E.	City-state: most city-states come to an end by the time of the Roman Empire; another series of city-states in Europe in Middle Ages
2000 B.C.E. - 500 B.C.E.	Empire: Type A. Archaic empires (Hittite, Assyrian)
500 B.C.E. - 400 C.E.	Empire: Type B. Early empires (Persian, Hellenic, Roman)
400 C.E. - 1000 C.E.	Empire: Type C. Late Roman, Christian, Byzantine, Moslem, and Chinese
1000 C.E. - 1500 C.E.	Empire: Type D. Medieval feudal
1500 C.E. - 1800 C.E.	Empire: Type E. Mercantilist colonialism
1800 C.E. - Current time	Nation-states and the new imperialism

NOTE: Because every type that has ever existed in history still exists somewhere today, this table is only meant to indicate approximately when each new type first emerged. The dates for the city-state and the empires overlap because of different stages of development in different societies.

been particularly harsh can be likened to that of the inmates in what Erving Goffman (1961) calls the "total institutions"—such as prisons, mental hospitals, or army barracks. The temptation to treat the household, wherever one meets it in history, as a total institution imprisoning women and children is, however, one that must be resisted. There will be wide variations in the amount of capital and resources for production available to women in the household, depending both on the socioeconomic status of the family and on the time and place in history. Except among the very poor and the slaves, women householders are never resourceless. Normally, they are both producers and traders. Yet, it is also true that women in most societies are *to a degree* stripped of identity, autonomy, and privacy as Goffman describes that stripping for inmates of total institutions. With some variation, women in every part of the world are treated in part as prisoners, mental patients, and dependent children. Their names come from their fathers or their husbands. Their obligations to provide 24-hour domestic service to their fathers, husbands, and children leave them perpetually on call at any time of day or night. There are substantial limitations on their rights to transact business and get credit in their own names, and they have limited rights in courts of law. They will not be found in large numbers among the bureaucrats and administrators of any society or in many of its public spaces.

Yet there is an interface between the private, household-centered life of women and the public life of every society, and that interface is in the law court. While law codes place restrictions on women, they also establish rights. We shall see women of substance entering the law courts to fight for their rights of property and freedom of person and freedom to do business even in societies that apparently have secluded women completely. They could do this in ancient Greece, in the Moslem world, in Byzantium, and in Europe. This interface between the women's underlife and the overlife of society, available chiefly to the wealthy, acts in every age to mitigate the severity of victimization or restraint of women.

The underlife itself, which exists in societies as different as urban Turkey and suburban America, is enormously varied and often harbors a rich unrecorded culture. That underlife has been recognized in various ways but takes its conceptual origin from what Sullerot calls the *dedans* and the *debors*—the within and the without. She cites Xenophon's classic justification for the servitude of women:

> The gods created the woman for the indoors functions, the man for all others. The gods put woman inside because she has less endurance for cold, heat, and war. For woman, it is honest to remain indoors and dishonest to gad about. For the man it is shameful to remain shut up at home and not to occupy himself with affairs outside. (1968: 31-32)[13]

The *dedans* concept is simply descriptive to the extent that women's major workplace is in the household. What turns the *dedans* into a victimization concept is the notion of confining women to the home at all times and denying her other work sites. This application of the *dedans* concept is indeed suggested by Xenophon in the passage quoted, although it was never practiced by more than a small group of urban middle-class women, even in Xenophon's time.

Another way to think of the underlife/overlife, within/without dichotomy is in terms of private versus public spaces. The kitchen and the courtyard, society's service areas, are for women. The *agora*, where the public interest is defined and acted on, is for men. Whether we call it the "underlife," the "within," or the "private space," the basic concept tends to carry connotations of the clandestine. To the extent that the males of a society consider women's activities and thought trivial and inconsequential, there is a clandestine quality about the accompanying women's culture. The implication is that this underlife is not serious and consequential for the overlife of the society.

The presentation in literature of the women's world as inconsequential alternates with depictions of women as the source of evil. Various compilations listing all the nasty things men have said about women strongly reinforce the image of women as "outlaws" and the underlife as clandestine. Much energy has been expended on psychological analyses of the tendency of men to fear women and ascribe evil to them. H. R. Hay's *The Dangerous Sex* (1964) summarizes much of this analytical material. What really has to be explained, however, is not why there is an antiwomen literature but why the majority of writers who deal with these matters focus exclusively on the negative references to women. As Sheila Johansson points out, from any cultural or religious tradition or set of laws, it would be equally easy to compile "praise books" consisting of all the admiring and appreciative things that men have said about women. From the "praise books," including Ashley-Montagu's *Natural Superiority of Women* (1953), one could construct a very different image of the underlife, showing it as the source of human strength and capability.

There is in fact nothing inherently clandestine or superior about underlife as a concept; it has to do with spatial differentiations. To the extent that women are forcibly confined to these spaces, however, connotations of the clandestine are appropriate. Because differentiation between men's and women's spaces are found in all societies, the underlife concept becomes crucial to an analysis of women's roles. Ignorance of it has been a major factor in failures in development planning and aid schemes. Some examples follow.

Occasionally, the underlife erupts into public view with large-scale actions by women, which are invariably treated as utterly mysterious phenomena. In Nigeria in December 1929, apparently peaceable, home-loving Ibo village women changed overnight into a frenzied mob of thousands who attacked administration authorities while their men stood passively by. This uprising, precipitated by an unfounded [sic] rumour that Ibo women were to be taxed by the government, arose from uneasiness on the part of the women concerning their economic position, which had already suffered from the world depression, and which they envisioned as being further threatened, as well as from other non-economic grievances. (Ottenberg 1959: 205)

In 1948, when the first mass-education teams were starting work in Ghana, they wanted to begin by organizing courses in the rural areas for the educated few, who could then teach their illiterate compatriots. Although publicity about this program was carefully aimed at educated women, 300 illiterate women turned up at the first course, held at Peki-Blenko, and demanded instruction. Wherever the education teams went in Ghana, they were confronted with the same situation: Appealing for educated women to train, they were overwhelmed by hundreds of illiterate women who demanded education (Prosser 1963). Stories of other types of public gatherings of women for a variety of purposes abound. For example,

in January of 1964, the Tanganyikan army mutinied. On the morning of February 3, women assembled by the thousands outside the United Women of Tanganyika headquarters, bearing banners from Morogoro, Kisaraw, Bagamoyo, and a hundred other towns.

The capital had never seen anything like it. For three and a half hours a procession of more than a mile of women marched from their headquarters in the south part of town, along Independence Avenue, through the business district, and around the water front to the government office area. The drums beat. The song of TANU (Nyerere's political party) was sung in powerful chorus. Placards flashed in the sun: Down with Violence, Mutiny and Treason! . . . the great procession halted outside the State House and waited for the President. When Nyerere appeared at the door a mighty shout arose, mingled with the weird half-whistle with which tribal women acclaimed their warriors. (McDonald 1966: 187-88)

How did the "submissive and downtrodden women of Africa" come to engage in such actions? The answer in each case lies in the existence of traditional women's councils that were organized into communication networks covering great geographic distances. These organizations existed long before colonial powers appeared on the scene and have made all kinds of interesting adaptations to modernization. West Africa is covered with these networks. Very occasionally, a Western woman has had the opportunity of seeing one of the meeting places traditionally used by African women—nothing but a clearing in an otherwise dense bush—to which they come when summoned by drums. Messages by drumbeat, addressed to the women only, carried the word from village to village among the Ibo women in 1929; among the Akan, Transvoltan, and Ashanti women of Ghana in 1948; and among the Tanganyikan women (who included the rugged women of the Masai warrior tribe) in 1964.

One particularly invisible counterpart to these all-women's councils is the woman-headed household. A persisting feature of underlife structures that we will be encountering from time to time is the phenomenon of households without men. Because the traces history leaves us concerning women almost always involve their identification as the daughter of X, the wife of Y, or the mother of Z, it is easy to overlook the fact that a certain number of these women were, and are, heading their own households and carrying out the work of both economic production and family nurturance either unpartnered or with a woman partner. While there were wealthy widows among them, most of them belonged to the working class. Their capacity to maintain households and rear children is another reminder of the extent of resource management by women and of the importance of their producer roles. In Chapter 6 in Volume 2, the figures on the percentage of women around the world who were unmarried (including those with a woman partner) widowed, separated, or divorced as of 1968 are given. Comparable figures are, of course, not available for other historical periods, but the following estimates on widowhood for women in nonindustrialized countries today give some clues to the number of women who have headed households as widows in the past (Ridley 1968: 21). These estimates are based on the simplified assumptions that life expectancy at birth is 43, that all women take male partners at 20, that all husbands are five years older than their wives, and that conditions are "normal"—that is, famine or war conditions do not obtain.

Age of Married Women	Percentage Becoming Widowed
20-29	8.4
30-39	10.7
40-49	16.6
50-59	27.1
60-69	43.6
70-79	57.8

Because, in both famine and war, more women survive than men (Mayer 1975: 572), rates of widowhood may have been higher in times past than are estimated in this table. On the other hand, life expectancies of women have been shorter than those of men at some periods of history, depending both on the mortality rates for women in childbirth as compared with the mortality rates for men in battle and on the character of other societal risks for males and females (J. Lawrence Angel, as discussed in Pomeroy 1975: 45). In any case, the widow appears often in history. While widows sometimes remarried, the evidence from the historical record is that they frequently chose to remain without men in the face of great pressure to remarry, and they were often protected by law in their right to do so. A systematic historical study of this phenomenon must await the skills of the demographic historian, but readers of this book are alerted to look for evidence of nontraditional women householders as they appear from time to time, peeking out from the underside of their times.

To account for the roles that women play in a society, we must identify the overlife and underlife structures in terms of the social spaces women can move in and the kinds of social learning that take place in them. *Social space* in this book is used in the full ecological sense of niche space available to a species. The term *social learning* is used rather than *socialization* because it emphasizes the active role of the individual rather than treating the individual as an object of the social process. The term *cultural conditioning* will be used in the next chapter to refer to the more mechanical aspects of the actions of a culture on its members.

As we move through different periods of history, we will see the ways in which structural differentiation enlarges or constricts the social learning spaces for women, and how and when constraints have been transcended.

Related to a structural differentiation is the extent of dominance relations in a society. While a great deal has been written about authoritarian versus democratic political structures, very little of it touches on the issue of the role of women in society. The Marxist critique of capitalism addresses itself directly to the situation of women but still misses some key aspects of the woman problem by relying too much on what the public sector can do for families.[14] Neither the United States nor the United Kingdom, often pointed to as models of the democratic society in the capitalist camp, nor the former Soviet Union, long considered a model in the socialist camp, avoided sex stereotyping and serious inequalities of opportunity for women. Neither has Sweden, another model country, avoided the sex dominance trap. Women are in a special way the "victims" of dominance structures in most societies.

Because of the special importance of conceptions of dominance in the analysis of women's roles, Chapter 2 in this volume will be devoted to an analysis of dominance systems in the animal world and an examination of biological, environmental, and cultural determinants of human dominance systems. After a concluding examination of the potentials of alternatives to dominance and hierarchy in social organizations and human relationships, we can begin our walk through history.

Appendix

How and Where Women Learn

The factors associated with social learning for young women growing up in any society can be divided into (a) the genetic substrate; (b) developmental sequences of physiological, emotional, intuitive, and cognitive maturation and the associated accumulation of the social knowledge stock; (c) specific learning processes, that is, cognitive construction, trial and error (social reinforcement), modeling, and intuition; and (d) the social spaces within which learning takes place, that is, home, community, specialized settings such as schools, church, place of work, and others.[15]

There is some genetic and developmental variation between the two sexes, but the variation is also wide within each sex. The overlap between the sexes is great. It is reasonable to conclude that, given adequate social-learning opportunities, women can learn to fill any social roles available in a society. Historical accounts of great women hunters, warriors, queens, poets, artists, and scientists support this view of the potential performance capacities of women.

To know how a woman will actually perform in a given society, we must know something of her opportunities for training, what kinds of social reinforcement she is getting for specific kinds of behavior, and who her role models are. We must also know in what social spaces the learning takes place. Is she confined to the private space of the home? If not, what public spaces are accessible to her? For large parts of human history, the church has been the primary public space accessible to women, which accounts for the important role women have played in the great religions even when they have not had positions of political power in them. If women and men share the same public spaces, women will have a broader kind of training, more varied social reinforcements, and a wider range of role models than if the spaces of women are restricted.

If marriage acts to limit social space for women, then age at marriage will be of crucial importance in determining their opportunities for social learning. Societies with child marriage usually—though not always—limit drastically women's opportunities for learning. Marriage is not necessarily a limiter of social space, however, and in some cultures it is marriage itself that frees a woman into the larger

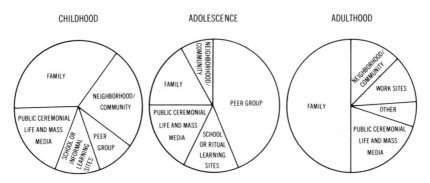

Figure 1A.1. The Context of Social Learning for Women. Drawn by KH.

society (or, in some Moslem societies, the second marriage, which the woman may arrange for herself). In a stratified society, the social spaces for the wealthy elite, for the group with the middle range of skill and material resources, and for the poor are very different for both sexes but vary more for women than for men. As we shall see, social space and learning opportunities are relatively more restricted for women of the middle group than for either the rich or the poor, though poverty places its own kinds of restrictions on learning opportunities.

The emphasis in the above discussion on access to social spaces and kinds of learning opportunities should not obscure a very important point: All human beings have more or less active minds. Everyone engages in cognitive construction, in the "creative imitation" we call modeling, and in intuitive, nonverbal formulations of reality. The interior mental work of mapping social reality and creating new social roles out of raw materials of observed behaviors of others and one's own values and preferences is unique to every woman and man. Settings and training sequences can trigger this interior creative work but can never determine the product. In one sense, then, all social roles are created by the individuals who perform them, as social psychologists have long asserted. This means that there are always significant degrees of freedom for women (and men), over and beyond their training and opportunities, in every society. The rags-to-riches, and slave-to-king, and prostitute-to-queen stories found in every stratified society testify to this omnipresent possibility.

Having said this, we must nevertheless return to a recognition of the constraining effect of limited social space on the learning of women. Figure 1A.1 presents diagrammatically the shifting social spaces in which development takes place over time in the life of a maturing female. While the relative size and appropriate labels for various spaces will vary from society to society, one constraint is the relative importance of the family space in the life of a woman. Also, she has some kind of "ceremonial space" in every society, no matter how limited she is in respect to other spaces. If we were to do a comparable diagram for men, the family slice would be smaller, and neighborhood/community, work sites, and "other" would be larger. "Other" represents everything beyond the local community.

Notes

1. The Leakeys report that new *erectus* finds have been uncovered dating back 3.5 million years! ("The Oldest Man," *Time* (November 10, 1975: 93).

2. We have, for example, from the economists, the papers from the "Workshop Conference on Occupational Segregation: Past, Present, and Future" (Wellesley College, May 1975, in *Signs: Journal of Women in Culture and Society, 1,* no. 1, 1976); also Hilda Kahne's "Economic Perspectives on the Role of Women in the American Economy" (1975); from the anthropologists, *Woman, Culture and Society* (Rosaldo and Lamphere 1974) and *Women and Men: An Anthropologist's View* (Friedl 1975); from the historians, *Liberating Women's History: Theoretical and Critical Essays* (Carroll 1976) and *Clio's Consciousness Raised: New Perspectives on the History of Women* (Hartman and Banner 1974); from the sociologists, *Academic Women on the Move* (Rossi and Calderwood 1973) and *Changing Women in a Changing Society* (Huber 1973); and from the field of comparative and cross-cultural studies, *Our Many Sisters: Women in Cross-Cultural Perspective* (Matthiasson 1974), *Cross-Cultural Perspectives on the Women's Movement and Women's Status* (Leavitt 1976), *Women and Work: An International Comparison* (Galenson 1973), *Women and Work in Developing Societies* (Youssef 1973), and *Women in Perspective: A Guide for Cross-Cultural Studies* (Jacobs 1974, a bibliography for region and by topic).

3. I am indebted to Sheila Johansson (historian, Seattle, Washington, personal communication, 1975) for pointing out to me the underlying contradiction that is never fully resolved in this book: The victim theory is indeed stated and invoked from time to time, yet most of the data describe women as creative actors. Given that the social reality concerning women's roles is also full of contradictions, the best I can do now is to acknowledge the inconsistencies and let them stand.

4. The only alternative production sites were palace and temple workshops and state-owned mines and public construction enterprises.

5. The progress optimism of Comte ([1855] 1974) was countered by Spengler, who cried doom in 1922 in his *Decline of the West* (English edition, 1926-28). Nevertheless, Weber's great works in the sociology of history, and particularly *The Protestant Ethic and the Spirit of Capitalism* ([1904-5] 1930), remain classical sociological statements of development theory. Parsons's "Evolutionary Universals in Society" (1964) is a further development of Weberian theory. Eisenstadt, who has also worked in this tradition, has provided in his edited book of essays by Two-Thirds-World scholars (1972) a searching examination of classical development theory from the perspective of change agents using traditional institutions on behalf of change. Polak, in *The Image of the Future* (1961), questions the development potential in the Western self-image of the twentieth century. Nisbet (1969) provides a searching examination of what he calls the metaphor of growth in his study of Western theories of development.

6. The exposition of the ecological view draws in part on Wilkinson (1973).

7. The shift from zero population growth with the end of the nomadic way of life continues today as formerly nomadic bands go sedentary. A very dramatic description of the change in fertility behavior among the Kung people as they shifted from nomadism to agriculture as recently as in the decade of the 1960s appeared in *Science* (Kolata 1974).

8. Boserup, in *Women's Role in Economic Development* (1970), discusses in detail the exclusion of women from the productive process at the point of technological innovation in agriculture.

9. Cole, in *From Tipi to Skyscraper* (1973), documents women's gradual loss of construction roles concurrent with technological development.

10. It is by no means easy to get a picture of the progressive structural differentiation of societies as they deal with their ever-changing, ever-the-same problems of subsistence.

The work of Eisenstadt (1963) in political sociology and Fried (1967) in political anthropology has been very helpful in developing a framework for observation of the historical process. Fried's work helped make clear the early transitions from egalitarian bands to ranked tribal groups to stratified societies. Eisenstadt's study of 32 societies that could be categorized as developed political systems has clarified the subsequent development process.

Etzioni's concept of epigenesis (1965), an alternative approach to the analysis of progressive social complexification, has not been used in this book although it offers a very useful additional model for historical development. I would agree with Etzioni that some structural changes are preformist, and some epigenetic, and regret that my own need to keep the analysis as simple as possible kept me from introducing these distinctions.

11. Sheila Johansson (personal communication, 1975) has developed a women's role analysis instrument suitable for the macro historian. It contains many of the features of my own discarded instrument but is a more sophisticated tool. As of this writing, the future of "herstory," as Johansson calls it, looks promising.

12. While in this book I am looking particularly at the underlife of women, there are other groups who also live on the underside of history: peasants, the urban poor, slaves, and oppressed minorities. They too are finding their chroniclers in current decades.

13. This is my translation of Xenophon from the French.

14. The following correction to the above statement is offered by a reader: "A Marxist critique does not deal with isolated elements of a structure. It does not 'address itself directly to the situation of women' because women are not seen as an analytical category of oppression. Rather they are members of a class which in part comprises the entire structure of a capitalist system" (from Suzanne Tessler, a student, 1975).

15. For a fuller discussion of learning models, see E. Boulding (1978).

References

Ashley-Montagu, M. F. 1953. *Natural Superiority of Women*. Rev. ed. New York: Macmillan.

Beard, Mary R. 1946. *Woman as Force in History: A Study in Traditions and Realities*. New York: Macmillan.

Bernard, Jessie. 1964. *Academic Women*. University Park: Pennsylvania State University Press.

———. 1975. *Women, Wives, Mothers: Values and Options*. Chicago: Aldine.

Boserup, Ester. 1970. *Women's Role in Economic Development*. New York: St. Martin's.

Boulding, Elise. 1969. "The Effects of Industrialization on the Participation of Woman in Society." Ph.D. dissertation, University of Michigan, Ann Arbor.

———. 1978. "The Child and Non-violent Social Change." Pp. 68-100 in *Strategies Against Violence: Design for Nonviolent Personal Relationships, Communities and International Relations*, edited by Israel Charmy. Boulder, CO: Westview.

Carr-Sanders, Sir Alexander. 1959. "Economic Aspects of Woman's Role in the Development of Tropical and Subtropical Countries." In *Women's Role in the Development of Tropical and Subtropical Countries*. Report of the 31st Meeting of the International Institute of Differing Civilizations, Brussels.

Carroll, Berenice A., ed. 1976. *Liberating Women's History: Theoretical and Critical Essays*. Urbana: University of Illinois Press.

Castle, Cora. 1913. "A Statistical Study of Eminent Women." *Archives of Psychology* 7(August).

Cole, Doris. 1973. *From Tipi to Skyscraper: A History of Women in Architecture*. Boston: I Press.

Comte, Auguste. [1855] 1974. *Positive Philosophy*, translated by Harriet Martineau. New York: AMS Press.

Davis, Elizabeth G. 1971. *The First Sex.* New York: Putnam.

Diner, Helen. [1932] 1965. *Mothers and Amazons,* translated by John Philip Lundin. New York: Julian.

Eisenstadt, S. N. 1963. *The Political Systems of Empires.* New York: Free Press.

———. 1972. *Post-traditional Societies.* New York: Norton.

Etzioni, Amitai. 1965. *Political Unification: A Comparative Study of Leaders and Forces.* New York: Holt, Rinehart & Winston.

Firestone, Shulamith. 1970. *Dialectic of Sex: The Case for Feminist Revolution.* New York: Morrow.

Fried, Morton H. 1967. *The Evolution of Political Society: An Essay in Political Anthropology.* New York: Random House.

Friedl, Ernestine. 1975. *Women and Men: An Anthropologist's View.* New York: Holt, Rinehart & Winston.

Galenson, Marjorie. 1973. *Women and Work: An International Comparison.* New York: Cornell University Press.

Goffman, Erving. 1961. *Asylums: Essays on the Social Situation of Mental Patients and Other Inmates.* Chicago: Aldine.

Goitein, Solomon D. 1967-71. *A Mediterranean Society: The Jewish Communities of the Arab World as Portrayed in the Documents of the Cairo Geniza.* 2 vols. Berkeley: University of California Press.

Goode, William J. 1963. *World Revolution and Family Patterns.* New York: Free Press.

Hartman, Mary and Lois Banner, eds. 1974. *Clio's Consciousness Raised: New Perspectives on the History of Women.* New York: Harper & Row.

Hays, H. R. 1964. *The Dangerous Sex.* New York: Putnam.

Herlihy, David. 1962. "Land, Family and Women in Continental Europe, 701-1200." *Traditio* 18:89-120.

Holter, Harriet. 1970. *Sex Roles and Social Structure.* Oslo: Universitetsforlaget.

Huber, Joan, ed. 1973. *Changing Women in a Changing Society.* Chicago: University of Chicago Press.

Jacobs, Sue E. 1974. *Women in Perspective: A Guide for Cross-Cultural Studies.* Chicago: University of Illinois Press.

Jennings, Ronald C. 1975. "Women in Early 17th Century Ottoman Judicial Records: The Sharia Court of Anatolian Kayseri." *Journal of Economic and Social History of the Orient* 8 (part 1):53-114.

Kahne, Hilda. 1975. "Economic Perspectives on the Role of Women in the American Economy." *Journal of Economic Literature* 13(December):1249-92.

Kolata, Gina Bari. 1974. "Kung Hunter-Gatherers: Feminism, Diet, and Birth Control." *Science* 185:932-34.

Komarovsky, Mirra. 1946. *Blue-Collar Marriage.* New York: Random House.

Leavitt, Ruby R., ed. 1976. *Cross-Cultural Perspectives on the Women's Movement and Women's Status.* The Hague: Mouton.

Lee, Richard B. and Irven De Vore, eds. 1968. *Man the Hunter.* Chicago: Aldine.

Matthiasson, C., ed. 1974. *Our Many Sisters: Women in Cross-Cultural Perspective.* New York: Free Press.

Mayer, J. 1975. "Management of Famine Relief." *Science* 188(May):571-77.

McDonald, Alexander. 1966. *Tanzania: Young Nation in a Hurry.* New York: Hawthorne.

McNeill, William H. 1963. *The Rise of the West: A History of the Human Community.* Chicago: University of Chicago Press.

Mead, Margaret. 1955. *Cultural Patterns and Technical Change.* A manual prepared by the World Federation for Mental Health, UNESCO. New York: Mentor.

———. 1968. *Sex and Temperament in Three Primitive Societies.* New York: Dell.

———. 1970. *Culture and Commitment.* Garden City, NY: Natural History Press.

Millet, Kate. 1970. *Sexual Politics.* Garden City, NY: Doubleday.

Myrdal, Alva. 1945. *Nation and Family: The Swedish Experiment in Democratic Family and Population Policy.* Cambridge: MIT Press.

Myrdal, Alva and Viola Klein. 1968. *Women's Two Roles: Home and Work.* 2nd ed. London: Routledge & Kegan Paul.

Nisbet, Robert A. 1969. *Social Change and History: Aspects of the Western Theory of Development.* Oxford: Oxford University Press.

Ottenberg, Phoebe V. 1959. "The Changing Economic Position of Women Among the African Ibo." Pp. 205-33 in *Continuity and Change in African Cultures*, edited by W. R. Bascom and M. J. Herskovits. Chicago: Phoenix.

Parsons, Talcott. 1964. "Evolutionary Universals in Society." *American Sociological Review* 29(June):339-57.

Polak, Fred L. 1961. *The Image of the Future.* 2 vols., translated by Elise Boulding. New York: Oceana. (1973 ed., abridged by Elise Boulding, San Francisco: Jossey Bass/Elsevier)

Pomeroy, Sarah B. 1975. *Goddesses, Whores, Wives, and Slaves: Women in Classical Antiquity.* New York: Schocken.

Prosser, U. R. 1963. "The Role in Community Development, with Particular Response to West and East Africa." *International Social Service Review* 9(April):46-53.

Reed, Evelyn. 1975. *Woman's Evolution from Matriarchal Clan to Patriarchal Family.* New York: Pathfinder.

Ridley, Jeanne Clare. 1968. "Demographic Change and the Roles and Status of Women." *Annals of the American Academy of Political and Social Science* 371(January):15-25.

Rosaldo, Michel Z. and Louise Lamphere, eds. 1974. *Woman, Culture and Society.* Stanford, CA: Stanford University Press.

Rossi, Alice and Ann Calderwood, eds. 1973. *Academic Women on the Move.* Menlo Park, CA: Russell Sage.

Smelser, Neil J. 1959. *Social Change in the Industrial Revolution: An Application of Theory to the British Cotton Industry.* Chicago: University of Chicago Press.

Spengler, Oswald. 1926-28. *Decline of the West*, translated by Charles Atkinson. New York: Knopf.

Sullerot, Evelyne. 1968. *Histoire et Sociologie du Travail Féminin.* Paris: Societé Nouvelle des Editions Gonthier.

Theodore, Athena. 1971. *The Professional Woman.* Cambridge, MA: Schenkman.

Turnbull, Colin. 1968. *The Forest People.* New York: Simon & Schuster.

Ward, Barbara E., ed. 1963. *Women in the New Asia: The Changing Social Roles of Men and Women in South and South-East Asia.* Paris: UNESCO.

Weber, Max. [1904-5] 1930. *The Protestant Ethic and the Spirit of Capitalism*, translated by Talcott Parsons. London: Allen Unwin.

Wilkinson, Richard B. 1973. *Poverty and Progress: An Ecological Model of Economic Development.* London: Methuen.

Youssef, Nadia. 1973. *Women and Work in Developing Societies.* Population Monograph Series no. 15. Berkeley: University of California, Institute of International Studies.

2

Dominance, Dimorphism, and Sex Roles

The question of why women are everywhere the "subordinate sex" has never failed to interest both women and men, and many interpretations have been advanced to explain the phenomenon, including the interpretation that women are not really subordinate at all. It will be useful to review the evidence for the subordination of the female from the points of view of sociobiology, archaeology, and anthropology before beginning the journey through human history. Evidence about the status of the female from the mammalian world in general, from our near "relations" among the primates, and from current hunting and gathering societies, added to archaeological evidence about the kinds of tools the protohominids used, by no means leads to one simple, clear picture of the situation of the earliest human female. The facts of dominance and subordination in the human experience can still be interpreted differently. Because sexual dominance and dominance systems in general are so closely intertwined, this chapter deals with both.

The construct of social dominance represents an ideology as well as a set of behaviors and social structures, an ideology reflecting basic value judgments about the nature of the social order and of sex differentiation. In this chapter, we will therefore also explore briefly the alternative construct of egalitarianism as an ideology and as a set of behaviors and social structures having implications for sex differentiation.

Because there are significant social roles in every society that stand outside dominance structures and yet relate to them, these are explored also, under the label of "interstitial" (in-the-cracks) roles. Both family and community roles are examined for their interstitial qualities. Finally, the symbol systems that support ascription of weakness and submissiveness to women are examined, along with the physiological bases for the pervasive symbolism of the dominance-submission dichotomy. This chapter is an attempt, in short, to examine some of the contributions from the social sciences, from sociobiology, and from folklore to conceptions about the subjugation of women.

The Politics of Subordination

In discussing sex role dominance, people easily tend to extremes. From one side, embattled champions of the downtrodden sex put forward the enslavement concept, which evokes the image of the helpless food-gathering child-breeding-feeding female in the hunting and gathering society who is both protected and victimized by the brute strength of the male, who gains a brief respite as mother-goddess and matriarch after her invention of agriculture in a world of dwindling animal prey, who then loses all claims to power and status as man invents the plow and takes over farming, the gods, and the descent-reckoning system, letting his woman work for him as slave-helper-breeder.

From the other side, champions of serene womanhood put forward the concept of the gentle queen who in an unobtrusive way rules the mighty world of men through the power of love. Reality cuts across all theories. To the extent that women do indeed help shape human destinies, enslavement theories are absurd. To the extent that women do find themselves in both de facto and de jure situations of subordination in most societies known to us, the queen theory is equally absurd. Detached perceptions of the geography of power as it relates to the status of women are rare. The drive to plead the cause of feminism has increasingly overwhelmed analysis.

In the fourteenth century, "feminist" Christine de Pisan asked simply to be accepted as a human being, free to do the things that humans do. The nineteenth-century suffragette said we are political animals, like men, and must participate in decision making; give us the vote. In the twentieth century, some feminists are saying we have been subjugated by men and must learn to exercise power; we don't want it as a gift—we will take it as a right.

Power is taken here simply to mean the ability to achieve desires in the face of opposition or obstacles: the power to "get what one wants." We will be concerned with that aspect of power known as *dominance*, a concept that has both structural and behavioral components. Both components are relevant to discussions of the subjugation of women but must be kept conceptually distinct. The widespread practice in many cultures, including the Western European, of beating women to discipline them—best symbolized by the whip said to hang over the Russian peasant's bed in the days of the czars—is an example of the behavioral aspect of dominance. Behavioral dominance may be as crude as "beating someone up" or as refined as "staring someone down." It does not necessarily involve physical aggression, but it implies it as a potential in the situation. An example of the structural aspects of dominance is the limited personhood of women in the courts, which limits their rights to transact business and administer property in their own names.[1] No individual actor can be identified as the source of this type of domination. The former is personal and immediate in its effect; the latter impersonal and indirect but all-pervasive. *Conscienticization* is a term used to refer to the process of awakening, on the part of a subjugated group, to a consciousness of the facts of structural dominance.

When women have been conscienticized and talk about taking power as a right, questions inevitably arise about their intended relationship to existing dominance structures. History asks the same question of all revolutionaries: Will you destroy the old structures and behaviors of dominance and replace them with new models for human relationships, or will you introduce new personnel into old dominance systems?

The conscienticization of women is a particularly complex process, however, given that women have never been simply a subjugated people. They have always participated in a secondary way in the prevailing dominance structures of society, from the times of the earliest incipient social stratification. The tribal chief had a queen-wife and their daughters were princesses.

In a stratified society, members have control over their own lives and control of resources generated by others according to the status assigned to them by birth or skill and achievement. There are other criteria used to assign control of resources, however. Therefore, at each level of social rank, power is differentially distributed to men, women, old people, children, and racial, ethnic, and religious minorities. The fact that some women have traditionally had high social status as the wives of their husbands and daughters of their fathers and lower status in terms of their own achievements has usually been discussed under the heading of status incongruities. While status incongruities are both painful and unjust, they tend to mask the underlying phenomenon that women too have slots in the dominance structures of society (as do the various minority groups). An upper-class woman may not have as much power as her husband, but she has a lot more power, in the sense of control of her own life and of social and economic resources, than the middle-class woman. Whether she uses it or not is another matter. There is always an element of achievement in the use of power, whether acquired by birth or not, because the effective exercise of power requires skill.

What we see throughout history is a series of class or status alliances between women and men to dominate and exploit lower-status social groups. This is not necessarily conscious exploitation. How could the lady bountiful of the medieval manor or the Victorian household, hurrying on her errands of mercy, be said to exploit the poor she worked so hard to help? Her exploitation lay in supporting the dependency structures that created the helplessness of "her poor," dependency structures that provided her life with meaning. We will see many examples in the chapters to follow of women who have contributed in important ways to the shaping of society through their use of the structures of dominance available to them. They have frequently created service-oriented social institutions.

Structures of dominance are ordinarily hierarchical. When the work of a number of people needs to be coordinated, hierarchical organization with successive levels of overview of the social science eliminates a lot of explaining and teaching. If people do completely what they are told, "aboveness-belowness" works well. We have had 10,000 years of experience with progressive centralization of social organization. Few social scientists, let alone laypersons, could imagine doing without it. Centralization generates the power that "is the resource that makes it possible to direct and coordinate the activities of men" (Blau 1964: 99).

In addition to being efficient and pervasive throughout recorded history, is hierarchical dominance also a biologically determined feature of human relationships? The question can be divided into two parts: (a) Are humans genetically programmed to enter into dominance-subordination relations— regardless of sex? and (b) Are males programmed to dominate females?

Dimorphism and Dominance

Possibly such questions arise only with the genetic diversity that accompanies the development of dimorphic life forms. It is hard to visualize amoeba-like creatures dominating each other. A study of dimorphics, the new discipline recently proposed by Kenneth Boulding (1976), may throw some light on the relationship between two-formedness and dominance behaviors. Do the extent of sexual dimorphism and the intrasex variability dimorphism has produced affect subjugation efforts? Is there a linear relationship between differentiation and dominance?

Sociobiologists say yes, finding that anatomical and behavioral dimorphism covary among nonhuman primates. What we find among these primates is a striking range of variation in dimorphism and the accompanying extent of dominance behavior. Gibbons, hardly distinguishable as to sex and with no easily detectable ranking systems, are at one end of the scale. At the other end are the highly sex-differentiated baboons with a highly visible dominance structure both among males and females (Martin and Voorhies 1975: 123-33). The picture is more complicated than that, however. The extent of sexual dimorphism is also related to the extent of danger in the environment. The look-alike gibbons live in a friendly arboreal environment with few predators. The baboons, with males almost twice the size and weight of females, live in the dangerous savanna, full of enemies to their kind. Chimpanzees, halfway between gibbons and baboons in extent of sexual dimorphism, are half arboreal, half terrestrial in their habits. They have a dominance system but are fairly casual about it. Following Wilson's (1975: 13) arguments that behavior is the pacemaker for evolution, it appears that the need to be able to defend their kind operated as a powerful selector for increased size and weight among the baboons.

There is considerable difficulty, however, in going from these primate cousins to humans. Compared with baboons, we are minimally differentiated in size and weight. Without observation of secondary sex characteristics, it is sometimes hard to tell male and female humans apart. We are more like gibbons than we are like baboons. Yet the primate behavioral model put before us by writers like Tiger (1969) is based on the baboon, not the gibbon. Our choice of a primate role model is clearly culturally determined. Who wants to be like the unaggressive, vegetarian, food-sharing gibbons, where father is as much involved in child rearing as mother is, and where everyone lives in small family groups, with little aggregation beyond that? Much better to match the baboons, who live in large, tightly knit groups carefully closed against outsider baboons, where everyone knows who is in charge and where mother looks after the babies while father is out hunting and fighting.[2]

The chimpanzees, our closest cousins anatomically, will not do as primate role models in spite of their brains and skill with tools, because they are too casual about their sex lives. They can take it or leave it. Humans are not that casual about sex.

The issue is, of course, not one of the appropriateness of role models but of the facts of environmental challenges and protohominids' response to them. Martin and Voorhies (1975: 175) quote Jolly's findings about Lower Pleistocene tools being primarily hand axes and simple flakes, associated with scouring and processing vegetable matter rather than with processing meat. "We" may have been vegetarians for hundreds of thousands of years before hunting was adopted. Food gathering is not a dominance-oriented activity and points us right back to the gibbon. Even when the shift to hunting took place, probably as a result of environmental challenges, there is no proof, as Wilson points out, that women were not also hunters side by side with men. Among the lions, "the females are the providers, often working in groups and with cubs in tow, while the males usually hold back" (Wilson 1975: 567). Among the African wild dogs, males and females hunt side by side.

However hunting began, at some long-ago point in human history, it became a male specialization. The effect of that specialization on hunting and gathering societies, as we will see shortly, was distinct but possibly minimal. Hunting and gathering societies do not have generalized dominance structures but give recognition to special skill as it appears in various occupations (Martin and Voorhies 1975: 190).

We must draw on Wilson's principles of the "multiplier effect" and "social drift" for an explanation of why the hunting specialization developed such complex and divergent ramifications in most societies over time. The multiplier effect is a process by which "a small evolutionary change in the behavior pattern of individuals can be amplified into a major social effect by the expanding upward distribution of the effect into multiple facets of social life" (Wilson 1975: 11).

Social drift is the "random divergence in the behavior and mode of organization of societies or groups of societies" (Wilson 1975: 13). An example of social drift is found in the phenomenon, described by Wilson, of vastly differing social structures, owing to differing sexual habits, arising among two closely related and interbreeding subspecies of baboons. This type of divergence is paralleled in the ethnographic literature by Douglas's study (1965: 183-213) of the Lele and the Bushong in Africa, who live in very similar habitats. One is a poverty-stricken society that heavily overworks its women and the other is more affluent and gives a higher status to its women. When such divergences occur in basically similar settings, it is easy to understand how the shift in activity patterns from food gathering to a combination of hunting and gathering could trigger great role variations between women and men.

The simplest determinant of dominance orders in those animal societies where they exist are size, age, androgen-determined levels of aggression, and luck (Wilson 1975: 251-54). With animals of greater intelligence and more durable group formations, other factors quickly come into play. Notable among these are childhood history, mother's rank, peer group alliances, and special ability (Wilson 1975: 291). Luck triggers the multiplier effect, as one animal's "bad day" sends its status spiraling downward; another's "good day" sends its status spiraling upward (Chase, quoted in Wilson 1975: 295). It is clear that females are not simply passive supporters of male-defined dominance systems, as Maclay and Knipe (1972) would have us believe, but develop their own complementary systems, which are in varying degrees independent of the male systems. Top females are usually coupled with top males, but their status may have been independently derived, going back to their childhood and the status of their mothers as well as their own ability (Wilson 1975: 291-94). Dominant females breed leaders, both among their daughters and among their sons. Low-status females do badly all around. They seem to be less well nourished, and they do a poor job of mothering (based on Fraser's observations of sheep and reindeer, in Wilson 1975: 288).

Rowell's dissenting reports on baboon troops without dominance hierarchies must be mentioned here, because they call some of the above observations into question; her work may trigger a whole new set of field studies. Much of the dominance behavior reported to date, particularly in the case of baboons, where the male is twice the size of the female, may be a report of what observers expected to see, or it may represent observations on stressed troops. Rowell suggests that "hierarchy may be a 'pathological response' to stressful conditions" (1973: 602). This is an extreme but interesting position and deserves further exploration, both in primate and in human societies.

This discussion began with the question of whether there was a relationship between dimorphism and dominance. We have found that dominance patterns exist within each of the sexes as well as between sexes. For all that luck, mother's status, and ability contribute to an individual's dominance status, the simple fact of greater size seems to play a continuing role. Height is an advantage to both females and males in human dominance systems (Maclay and Knipe 1972: 42-45). As far back as 1915, it was found that bishops were taller than clergymen, university presidents taller than college presidents. The intangible of self-confidence, pointed out by Maslow (1968; he equates self-confidence with dominance; see Maclay and Knipe 1972: 30), is bolstered by being able to look down on the world. Women have grown taller in the twentieth century (in the United States they have gained two inches since 1900; Bois 1969: 9), but so have men, so the physiological supports for social equality continue to elude the female sex.[3]

Reproductive Behavior and Dominance

We have seen that determinants of the extent of dominance systems are partly genetic and partly environmental and that the extent of sexual dimorphism determines the range of potential dominance behavior both within and between sexes.

The basic fact that females give birth to and feed infants seems to establish the initial social patterning for animal societies. Among many mammals, there is no male involvement with offspring or family groups. Wilson points out that the

> key to the sociobiology of mammals is milk. Because young animals depend on their mothers during a substantial part of their early development, the mother-offspring group is the universal nuclear unit of mammalian societies. Even the so-called solitary species, which display no social behavior beyond courtship and maternal care, are characterized by elaborate and relatively prolonged interactions between the mother and offspring. From this single conservative feature flow the main general features of the more advanced societies, including such otherwise diverse assemblages as the prides of lions and the troops of chimpanzees. . . . [W]hen bonding occurs across generations beyond the time of weaning, it is usually matrilineal. (1975: 456)

The first helpers and defenders of the mother are thus adolescent and young-adult sons and daughters.

Among primates, the pattern varies considerably, but it is fairly common to find both adolescent offspring and adult male partners as helpers and defenders of breeding females. A number of sociobiologists, including Crook and Gartlan and Eisenberg (Wilson 1975: 523-25), have argued that there is an evolutionary development among primates toward increased involvement of the male in the society. For our purposes, this and other formulations are inadequate because they do not bother to spell out the changing role of the female in the evolutionary sequence; it is considered enough to spell out the role of the males. It is clear, however, that the larger the social aggregate, the more the adult male offspring are integrated into the group in the double role of offspring and mates to adult females. Unpredictability of food supply and an increasing number of predators in the environment appear to be among the factors that encourage larger aggregations and the more complex integration of males into the aggregates. The extent of dominance by males of the females is not, however, related in any obvious way to the extent of male involvement in the society. Among the chimpanzees, where there is a clear dominance system among the males, this has no influence whatsoever on access to females (Wilson 1975: 546). When chimpanzee bands meet, both single females and females with offspring may move from one band to another. The males have nothing to do with this movement at all (Wilson 1975: 539).

That the special responsibility of females for the young is associated with gender-specific behavior is not surprising. Sex-linked behaviors have been identified in vervet monkeys that give clear evidence of sex role differentiation in group bonding behavior. Nurturance comes from females, defense from males, vigilance from both (Wilson 1975: 300).

There is considerable debate about the extent to which the attempt should be made to trace human behavior from primate behavior. Similar debate exists about the relevance of information about contemporary hunting and gathering bands to the behavior of early human groups. Wilson has tabulated behaviors associated with such contemporary human bands, indicating the extent of variability of comparable behavior traits among nonhuman primates. On the basis of these tabulations, he has made cautious estimates about the possibility of the presence of each set of behavior traits in early humans. His table is reproduced here as Table 2.1. It will be noted that the only traits he concludes can be very reliably assigned to early humans are play behavior, prolonged maternal care, and extended relationships between mothers and children.

All the evidence seems to point to the development of different behavioral repertoires for males and females at some point in hominid development, along the lines of female specialization in the care of the young and male specialization in defense. Whether the male defender role and the male as dominator of the female developed together, in response to environmental threats, or whether the male as dominator of the female was more dependent on accidents of time and place, it is hard to say.

Wilson presents some very interesting material on dominance behavior of the female, but he does not develop it in terms of dominance theory in general. He describes the conflict between mother and offspring at the point where the mother is trying to force the offspring to independence while the offspring is trying to stay with the mother. Although infant urges to explore are a well-known component of the development of autonomy, Wilson quotes observations that all point to the fact that, for monkeys, the "release from maternal bondage was achieved in considerable part by responses of punishment and rejection" (1975: 341). Weaning conflict and territorial expulsion exist among many mammals. Because males are generally the ones expelled, while female offspring are kept as helpers for the next brood of offspring, it is males who get the experience of fighting for resources, and it is their mothers they fight. Later, the young males are accepted back into the home territory as helpers, but only after they have learned to forage for themselves. Female offspring have to learn to forage too, but their experience may be less traumatic than that of the young male.

This expulsion-from-the-nest behavior of mothers, while obviously adaptive, needs to be more fully analyzed in terms of female dominance behavior. It is related to, but separate from, the fathers' expulsion-from-the-nest behavior. The latter occurs when male offspring are near or at maturity. It is sometimes associated with the barring of young males from access to

TABLE 2.1 Social Traits of Living Hunter-Gatherer Groups and the Likelihood That They Were Also Possessed by Early [Man] (Sic)

Traits That Occur Generally in Living Hunter-Gatherer Societies	Variability of Trait Category Among Nonhuman Primates	Reliability of Concluding Early Man Had the Same Trait Through Homology
Local group size:		
mostly 100 or less	Highly variable but within range of 3-100	Very probably 100 or less but otherwise not reliable
family as the nuclear unit	Highly variable	Not reliable
Sexual division of labor:		
women gather, men hunt	Limited to man among living primates	Not reliable
males dominant over females	Widespread although not universal	Reliable
Long-term sexual bonding (marriage) nearly universal; polygyny general	Highly variable	Not reliable
Exogamy universal, abetted by marriage rules	Limited to man among living primates	Not reliable
Subgroup composition changes often (fission-fusion principle)	Highly variable	Not reliable
Territoriality general, especially marked in rich gathering areas	Occurs widely but variable in pattern	Probably occurred; pattern unknown
Game playing, especially games that entail physical skill but not strategy	Occurs generally, at least in elementary form	Very reliable
Prolonged maternal care; pronounced socialization of young; extended relationships between mother and children, especially mothers and daughters	Occurs generally in higher cercopithecoids	Very reliable

SOURCE: Wilson (1975: 568, Table 27-5); © 1975 by the President and Fellows of Harvard College; used by permission.

mature females by the dominant males in a troop. It may also be related to a limited food supply. Not enough attention has been given to the fact that male offspring usually have to "fight" their mothers before they have to fight their fathers. It may well be that mother-son conflicts over the right to nurturance are equally as important in the development of dominance behaviors on the part of the male as environmental threat and adult sexuality. From this perspective, increasing male involvement in social groupings would represent a gradual diminution of in-group aggression between mothers and offspring. With the introduction of the male, there is the new phenomenon of father-offspring aggression, which presumably also diminishes with time. The evolutionary development, then, would point in the direction of increasing peaceable involvement of both females and males in the continuing life of their offspring.[4]

The three evolutionary models of dominance behavior we have been examining are suggestive in both their congruences and their differences. They all indicate increasing male participation in society but differ in interpretations of the role of dominance and aggression in social development. The Martin and Voorhies and the Wilson models imply that the only evolutionary development that takes place is in the male. The role of the female does not evolve but remains static. If there is a theoretical possibility that the female as well as the male roles have evolved toward increasing peaceable involvement in the continuing life of their offspring, then this component would need to be added to both the Martin and Voorhies and the Wilson conceptions of increasing involvement of males with their offspring. The remaining issue—as to whether evolutionary development has been in the direction of dedifferentiation and lowered levels of aggression (the Martin and Voorhies position) or in the direction of continuing differentiation and continuing genetic selection of male ability to aggress and fight the enemy—cannot be settled by the evidence presented here.

A fourth approach, based on psychoanalytic theory, suggests that the structure of dominance evolves from the relationship of mother and infant into adult eroticism. The conflict between dependence and independence experienced by the infant plays out in opposite ways for males and females in adulthood, as fathering and mothering and the associated social role patterning provide different role models for boys and girls. This dependence/independence conflict thus translates into power and dominance for men, and surrender for women, in adult sex life and accompanying social roles. Both Dinnerstein (1977) and Benjamin (1988) demonstrate in different ways how this locks masculinity and femininity into master-slave relationships, and both suggest the possibility of breaking this sequence—Dinnerstein in particular—by changing conceptions and practices of parenting.

It would appear that the data suggest a wide range of behavioral alternatives available to humans and that behavioral dominance is not a genetically specified feature either of male-female relations or of same-sex relations. Behavioral dominance may have been produced via social drift and the multiplier effect, by any one of a series of environmental constraints or by interaction sequences involving temporary periods of female helplessness due to childbearing. The female role as provider of milk for both male and female young can act both to modify and to enhance male dominance tendencies. Similar basic sequences were bound to recur in a

wide variety of settings, giving rise to the cultural variations we recognize
in male-female relationships.

Dominance as a Cultural Requirement

Although we have seen that many animal societies have far more complex social patterns than they have generally been given credit for, they
are very simple in comparison with human society. Given the human talent
for cultural elaboration, is there something in the elaboration process itself
that might inevitably lead to generalized male dominance among humans?
It is by no means clear that there is such a generalized dominance of the
male over the female in hunting and gathering bands. There is, in fact,
cultural variability in the presence and extent of male dominance among
such bands. Partly this variability may have to do with the predispositions
of the ethnographer. Martin and Voorhies (1975) would argue that shifting
dominance is the more common pattern and that dominance in any particular instance tends to be situational, related not to sex but to activity and
skill.

Can more complex societies exist without well-defined dominance
structures? The popular conception of history as the story of successions of
conquest states would suggest the answer is no. Evolutionary views of
historical development offer contradictory insights on this subject, and
simple evolutionary theories of development, as suggested in the last
chapter, are inadequate to explain twentieth-century realities.[5]

Dominance systems organize most of our political and economic lives.
Furthermore, because they are also primarily male dominance systems,
they cast an extra shadow over the lives of women, both in the public and
in the domestic spheres. Men and women alike, but men more than women,
are used to being rewarded for doing what society values by being given a
"dominance" bank account. The growth of exchange relationships does not
necessarily change this, although exchange has strong egalitarian elements
because exchanges can also take place within dominance systems.[6] People
of very unequal status can exchange goods or services that lead both to
feeling richer than they were before without changing the inequality. Nor
is cooperation incompatible with dominance. In fact, one of the notable
historical features of oppression is that the downtrodden comply in their
own oppression. The discovery by the oppressed that they have power is
the discovery that they can gain a kind of dominance through the withdrawal of compliance. This is the power of the women's liberation movement and of all other liberation movements. Noncompliance is by no

means an insignificant technique in human history. A recent compilation of the historical uses of noncompliance gives numerous examples of an important tool in lessening social violence while still working to remove injustice (Sharp 1973).

The use of noncompliance merely to gain social power, however, leaves us where we were before: facing a society that operates by the manipulation of dominance systems. The fact that there are sets of social interactions that operate outside dominance systems lets us know that hierarchical relations are not an across-the-board requirement for social organization. Let us look at the alternative modes of relating and how they affect the generalized submissive stance considered culturally appropriate to women.

Alternatives to Dominance Systems

Egalitarianism

The most obvious alternative to the dominance-submission relationship is the relationship of equality. For any two people—any dyad—to remain in a relationship of complete equality for even a short stretch of time is extraordinarily difficult, as Simmel has vividly described (Wolff 1950). Through the entire gamut of relationships that any married couple faces, for example, an exact tit-for-tat in mutual services would require an extraordinary degree of calculation and rationality. Marriages can become mutual nonaggression pacts having many of the characteristics of a cold war. What makes interpersonal relationships bearable, especially intimate ones, is that each partner from time to time throws a little bit "extra" into the relationship, and neither keeps an account book. This is what Gouldner (1960) calls the reciprocity multiplier, what Blau (1964) calls accumulating a capital of willing compliance, and what Fried (1967) calls generalized reciprocity. Kenneth Boulding (1973) adds to this the concept of serial reciprocity—passing on the extra to a third party.[7]

No dominance system could operate without at least small amounts of generalized reciprocity. Egalitarian systems need very large reciprocity multipliers in order to work. Stable egalitarian systems are in fact very fluid systems of alternating dominance, with each partner "taking command" when the available resources lie more fully within her or his domain, without prejudicing the participation pattern for the next situation. When we move from the dyad to the triad, we move from the interpersonal to the social, but Simmel points out that an egalitarian system of three partners has the same difficulties that inhere in the two-partner system. Most triads resolve themselves into dyads, with the third party either teaming up with one of the others or exploiting them both (Wolff 1950: 118-74).

The principle of social drift discussed earlier explains why equality is such an unstable relationship. Small situation-specific changes in behavior between partners in an egalitarian relationship may be amplified into substantial shifts in participation patterns, resulting in the development of unanticipated dominance roles.

Some recent research, such as Winch's work (1972) on complementarity in the marital relationship, has pointed to the possibility of sustaining shifting patterns of dominance. At the societal level, Robert Bales's research technique of interaction analysis, which identified "task leaders" and "emotional support" leaders in problem-solving groups, pinpoints such complementarities (Bales et al. 1965). Some techniques of group dynamics involve teaching participants to avoid dominance behavior, although "overthrowing the leader" is also a standard group dynamics routine. The very scarcity of examples demonstrates clearly enough that dominance-submission relations are the easiest pattern for any dyad, triad, or group to fall into when faced with tasks or problems.

Altruism

There is a third mode of relating, distinct from both dominance-submission and equality: the mode of altruism. In fact, although it is not usually described in that way, altruism and egalitarianism may be thought of as lying at opposite ends of the dominance-behavioral spectrum, with submission merely a midpoint on the continuum. Like dominance, altruism is an active mode of relating and is evoked by environmental challenge. It is the obverse of dominance in that it involves using one's own resources to better the condition of another rather than doing something at the expense of another to better one's own condition. In the language of the sociobiologist, it is increasing "the fitness of another at the expense of one's own fitness" (Wilson 1975: 117). Wilson discusses the genesis of altruism among animals, where it has been clearly identified, in terms of the phenomenon of kin selection. He imagines a network of blood relatives who

> cooperate or bestow altruistic favors on one another in a way that increases the average genetic fitness of the members of the network as a whole, even when this behavior reduces the individual fitnesses of certain members of the group. The members may live together or be scattered throughout the population. The essential condition is that they jointly behave in a way that benefits the group as a whole, while remaining in relatively close contact with the remainder of the population. This

enhancement of kin-network welfare in the midst of a population is called kin selection. (1975: 117)

While the mathematics of altruism is too complex to discuss here, this line of reasoning is attractive in offering an explanation of apparently antisurvival behavior on the part of individuals. Natural selection operates to reinforce predispositions to behavior in the phylogenetic substrate that optimize group rather than individual survival. It is not sex linked. Both females and males have capacities for altruism. In Wilson's presentation, emphasis is put on altruism as displayed by the male. It is also clear from his discussions, however, that food sharing, alloparenting (caring for offspring not one's own), and a variety of helping behaviors between parents and offspring, and among adults, are included as altruistic behavior. Helping behavior can apparently be triggered by a variety of circumstances, according to cultural conditioning.

In the stressful environments created by complex high-density human societies, altruism is presumably a response option just as dominance is. We already know that altruistic behavior—of which the reciprocity multiplier is a mild form—acts as a modifier in an otherwise unbearable world. Altruists range all the way from the totally life-spending St. Francis, or the kidney donor who faces the rest of her life at risk, to the helpful person in the office downstairs. Altruism in women and other disadvantaged groups is sometimes hard to distinguish from oppression-coerced behavior, as in the pseudoaltruism of the downtrodden, submissive wife, but the distinction can be made. Altruism arises from some inner surplus of resources. The behavior can be described physiologically, but among humans it may have other, nonphysiological components that are not well understood. While the goal of altruism is often equal status in the future for the one being helped, it does not necessarily lead to equality, any more than dominance behavior on behalf of social justice necessarily leads to equality.

Egalitarianism, Altruism, and Natural Selection

The relationship of equality of give and take, finely tuned to the respective capacities and resources of individuals or groups, is the hardest kind of social relationship to establish. It is much harder than dominating, and it is also harder than simply helping. Yet, as Tocqueville pointed out in 1848,

the gradual development of the principle of equality is . . . a providential fact . . . it is universal, it is lasting, it constantly eludes all human interference. . . . all men have aided it by their exertions, both those who have intentionally labored in its cause, and those who have served it unwittingly. (Tocqueville [1848] 1944)

Could natural selection operate on behalf of a "passion for equality that incites [men] to wish all to be powerful and honored"? Or is natural selection operating on behalf of a depraved taste "which impels the weak to attempt to lower the powerful to their own level" (Tocqueville 1944: 56)? Both are ways of conceptualizing equality. The first has an altruistic cast, the second is an inverted approach to domination. Is the social force we know as egalitarianism something that is emerging from these two preexisting dispositions?

The need to understand what it is like to be inside the skin of another, to make appropriate responses in social interactions, was identified as sympathy by Adam Smith in *The Theory of Moral Sentiments* ([1759] 1966). Smith considered that sympathy is the basis for all society; it certainly lays the basis for the possibility of egalitarianism. Darwin saw in the need for animals to "understand each other's expressions, sounds, and signed movements" (Gruber 1974: 97) the basis for that same sympathy. He puzzled over the process, for it could be as often painful as pleasurable to recognize another's condition. It was also clear to him, however, that communities having "the greatest number of the most sympathetic members, would flourish best, and rear the greatest number of offspring" (Gruber 1974: 318).

If the passion for equality is the significant evolutionary force Tocqueville believed it to be, it nevertheless had to contend with equally significant drives for domination. As an emergent capacity among humans, its future will depend on the social values and enabling structures that come to prevail in the next few centuries.

To summarize what has been said about the alternatives to dominance relationships in the social order, they point at most to *possibilities*. Altruism appears to be as much genetically determined as aggression, which means that it is part of a possible behavior range subject to cultural modification. Neither trait is sex linked, though behavioral emphases for the two sexes may be different. The capacity for egalitarianism is at best emergent. To the extent that various types of cooperative movements and community experiments in different parts of the world develop viable egalitarian patterns, future developments in that direction will be enhanced.

Women have, for the most part, adapted themselves to existing dominance structures. When possible, they have used their own positions in the dominance structure—linked to that of the males in their family though with fewer resources—as a power base. Women are highly skilled at converting the power they do have—deriving from the important personal services they render to men—into influence, a special and privatized "underside" power that gives women more leverage than a formal analysis of their authority roles would suggest. The theme of the power base from which women operate will be explored in each historical period in the chapters that follow, and alternative modes of operation—when they can be identified—will also be described.

Family Roles and Roles "in the Cracks"

Marriage Bonding

In some ways the family stands outside the dominance structures of the larger society, and in other ways it mirrors these structures. There are few dominance patterns within hunting and gathering type families and in the matrilocal villages of simple subsistence farming communities. But, once women began to leave the villages of their mothers to marry, and had to enter the villages of their husbands' fathers (patrilocality), the fluidity of earlier relationships disappeared and the practice of male dominance began. (Male dominance of the female in the household was, of course, never complete, because both altruistic and egalitarian modes were always present in the behavior potentials. What kinds of environmental constraints and interband relationships made patrilocality a more adaptive solution than matrilocality to the problem of household formation will be discussed in Chapter 4.) The development of patriarchal dominance was accompanied by the maintenance of a maternal "subdominance" over children. There would be the occasional situational dominance of the wife over the husband, when circumstances permitted (all societies have some stories of wives beating husbands). This entire dominance system was modified by the range of helping behaviors required of both males and females in the family unit. "Bachelor" males and females (also found in animal societies) sometimes roved as loners, sometimes attached themselves to family units as helpers/defenders.[8] Multigenerational dominance along patriarchal lines with appropriate subdominant roles for women framed the household dominance system.

With the establishment of patrilocality and male dominance, women developed a special set of interstitial or in-between roles that lie outside dominance structures and are not hierarchically ordered. These in-between roles play a special part in social bonding, conflict resolution, and crisis management within and between social groups. Women have played a historically unique role in the creation of alliance structures at all levels, from interfamilial to international. Many examples will be given of this in the chapters to follow.

Women's bonding roles operate at two levels. The first level is local and represents the type of bonding that occurs through ordinary marriage procedures, when two kin groups become allied through the marriage agreement. The woman plays a dual role here. First, she bonds the two groups as daughter of one and wife of the other. Later, as a mother herself, she extends the bonding process as parental agent on behalf of her offspring in search of mates. The second level is international and takes place when a woman is sent as "wife-diplomat" to the court of a chief, king, or emperor who poses a threat to the sending group. This too has the same double aspect: woman bonding as daughter and wife, and woman bonding as parental agent on behalf of offspring.

The absurdity of the treatment of bonding as a male specialty, as in Lionel Tiger and Maclay and Knipe, has been widely exposed in recent feminist writing, but even so there is a tendency to underestimate the significance of women's bonding roles in contemporary society. This is partly because there are many other institutional mechanisms for bonding in the twentieth century in addition to marriage.

Historically, however, marriage has been the major alliance mechanism of every society, and little girls are trained for roles as intervillage family diplomats. Except in cases of matrilocal residence (husband coming to live in wife's village), the married woman straddles two kin networks, two villages, sometimes two cultures. In traditional societies, in a social world framed by patrilocality, women experience an uprooting in the teen years that men do not generally undergo. During this time, their capacities to engage in new learning and adaptive behavior may well be at the maximum. Having been thoroughly trained by the women (and men) of their home village in necessary productive skills and required social behavior, they are then very frequently removed from the environment they were trained to function in and taught new social behaviors. They also often shift social roles overnight from that of loved and protected daughter to "on-trial," sternly disciplined daughter-in-law. Men in patrilocal societies do not undergo such a drastic family-role shift, nor do they have to adapt to the mores of a new village after marriage. Sterling describes the woman's situation in his *Turkish Village:*

> Thus any set of women who meet daily and share their tasks, their child-minding and their gossip will include some who are neither kin nor childhood neighbors to each other. Such a set will change its composition fairly steadily over time, by marriages in and out, and divorces, as well as deaths and the growing up of daughters.
>
> The women explicitly recognize this situation. One group told my wife that *akrabalike*, kinship, did not count for women as it did for men. What mattered to women was neighborliness, *komsaluk*. They did not mean that kinship does not count at all. Ties with kin are kept up by occasional visits, by gossip and news, by children going back and forth. (1965: 173-74)

The visiting back and forth between childhood home and nuptial home means that women are in a position to engage in an intellectual synthesis of two sets of mores and two sets of life-styles, which gives them a perspective that their one-village husbands may lack. While one may assume that men also get acquainted with more than one village in a lifetime, they do not do so with the degree of intensity, and under the conditions of divided loyalties, that women necessarily experience. When this results in the valuing of a capacity for neighborliness independent of the kin relationship (as Sterling described above), one has the ingredients for a wider range of expectations and tolerance for social behavior. The social skill a woman develops in learning first to *receive* neighborliness in a new setting and then in turn to give it to later comers than herself, and the skills of cross-cultural analysis she develops as she compares ways of doing things in her natal with those in her nuptial village—both are vital to the development of expertise in social networks.

This network expertise becomes particularly important in negotiating marriages for the next generation. It is the women who have the most relevant knowledge about problems between villages and how best to place marriageable offspring in relation to those problems. Whether their role is publicly acknowledged or not, women play an important part in decisions about marriage alliances in every society from tribal to imperial.

Marriages that are essentially diplomatic alliances are a much more complex affair. When a young bride is shipped from the refined and elegant court of twelfth-century China to be the wife of the nomadic chieftain who has been pillaging one of the provinces of her father's kingdom, her role is a delicate one indeed. This will be explored in detail as we build up documentation of "negotiation by marriage" in the period of the primary civilizations and later among the kingdoms of Europe.

To say that women shipped off to villages or palaces are being treated as objects is nonsense. In diplomatic marriages, women have been highly educated as an investment in diplomacy. The whole image of the "woman as pawn" in marriage is misleading and uninformed. As a potential partner, she is indeed manipulated, but so is her young spouse. When she in turn becomes the mother of marriageable offspring, she is herself among the manipulators. While it can be argued that the whole marriage process takes place on behalf of male-dominated systems, interesting insights emerge when marriage systems are looked at from the point of view of female interests. Martin and Voorhies have "rewritten" the ethnographic account of marriage among the Tiwi from the female perspective, paralleling the traditional male perspective (1975: 203-10), and it is clear that the same overt behaviors can be interpreted in ways that give a much higher status to women in relation to men—with much more emphasis on shifting dominance and actual egalitarianism—than ethnographers sometimes depict.

In general, marriage alliances are systems of redistribution of resources and represent institutionalized sharing behavior (Service 1962) as well as techniques for conflict reduction, within and between communities. The role of women in relation to all these functions is an active, not simply a passive, one. Variations in the scope of activity open to women after marriage stem from cultural patterns in localities; they are not necessarily inherent in the marriage negotiation process.

The conflict specialization role for women as a consideration in marriage alliances is particularly important. Mair (1972) describes situations where tribes deliberately marry their daughters into the tribes (or villages) with whom they fight. Tyler makes the same point more dramatically in explaining the origin of the incest taboo: "Again and again in the world's history, savage tribes must have had plainly before their minds the simple practical alternative between marrying-out and being killed out" (as quoted in Farb 1968: 26). Farb points out that the *levirate* (the rule that a man must marry his brother's widow) and the *sororate* (the rule that a woman must marry her deceased sister's husband) are institutions that function to preserve marriage alliances after the death of one of the partners (1968: 27).

Women in traditional societies often have other highly specific conflict-related responsibilities. The formal function of deciding when war is justified, and of adjudicating a conflict if it can be adjudicated, was a woman's role among the Germanic tribes of Europe in Roman times and continues in some contemporary African and native American tribes. As a woman's role, adjudication does not usually survive urbanization for long.

Paid and Unpaid Work Roles

Another important in-between role for women is as unspecialized labor able to fill a variety of slots in times of crisis. We have seen this most recently during the twentieth-century wars as well as in the social aftermath of a high male death rate in war. When conferences on women's role in development refer to women's historical role as "an extra pair of hands" (Carr-Sanders 1959), the emphasis is usually on the demeaning aspects for women of belonging to a reserve labor force, perpetually subject to call on short notice. This, however, sidesteps the difficult problem of how a society is to generate needed labor in times of shortage and stress, and it also minimizes the opportunities for structural change in labor force composition that times of crisis afford.[9]

Interstitial roles do not generally confer status in themselves, though they may at times be highly valued for their contribution to the maintenance of dominance systems. Since the time of the Renaissance, feminists have been coming around gradually to the position that they should not undertake work that does not confer status—that does not, in other words, give them clear access to some kind of valued social power. When income from paid jobs became the generally accepted status indicator, feminists focused on the position of women in the job market.

This was an important development. It provided for the first time an objective measure of how women were doing in their drive to participate as equals with men. Women who worked as volunteers in the community always suffered from the equivocal and ambiguous character of their status and never knew when they would be taken seriously or have the door shut in their faces. The use of wages as the criterion in determining whether work should be done at all—the local consequence of focusing on wage-sector status—has presented some problems, however. By abolishing the voluntary sector, we abolish most household and child-rearing tasks, many community services, many religious and cultural activities, and much of the process of social and technological invention.

The question then becomes this: Should interstitial roles be abolished in the reconstruction of society or should all paid jobs be stripped of conventional measures of worth? To place all work in the public sector, or at the least to see to it that all productive labor is remunerated by wages, would require a vast reconstruction of society. Of course, such a reconstruction would not necessarily ensure the equality of wages, as the experience in some socialist countries with large wage inequalities has demonstrated. Essentially, it would abolish all interstitial roles and give society the job of officially allocating status and monetary worth to everyone. The opposite approach would be to abolish the wage sector and give all work an interstitial character. In modified form, this is what Scott Burns (1975) suggests. He proposes an alternative approach to the economic system, an approach that focuses on the household[10] and the volunteer sector as the most significant productive sectors and replaces monetary measures of worth with "units of time spent." This would produce something like the world that Martin and Voorhies foresee, because it would lead to decreased differentiation of sex roles and more time spent on nurture by both males and females.

Women and the Left Hand: Further Thoughts on Dimorphism and Dominance

We have examined the sociobiology of sexual dimorphism and concluded that the extent of behavioral differentiation found in most human societies has to be environmentally and culturally explained, because both

sexes have wide behavioral ranges available to them in relation to dominance and aggression. Small differences in ability to cope with rapidly
changing and hostile environments on the part of female hominids with
offspring could set in motion the multiplier effect that would create substantial behavioral amplifications of apparently insignificant adaptations.
Social drift could carry these amplifications in the direction of the various
patriarchal dominance patterns we find in the later stages of agriculture
and with the development of trade.

Every society patterns all creation anew and develops symbol systems
that support the order they impute to the cosmos. We would therefore
expect a strong tendency for societies to rationalize the de facto subordination of the female by building into their symbol systems images of women
as weak, helpless, and passive. We do indeed find this and find it built into
a system of dimorphic thinking that calls for a review of the significance of
dimorphism in the evolutionary process. Dimorphic sexual selection, it will
be remembered, expands the gene pools and increases fitness for survival.
Dual classification systems confront the diversity resulting from the expanded gene pool and find ways to weave that diversity into the pattern of
the social order. Hertz (1973) suggests that these dual systems arose out of
the primitive pattern of social organization based on dividing a tribe into
two moieties (or halves).

Originally, this would be a reversible dualism. The Chinese concepts of
yin and yang reflect this reversible dualism. There is no imputation of good
or evil, superiority or inferiority, per se, to either half of the duality. The
reversibility is, however, evidently unstable:

> The evolution of society replaces this reversible dualism with a rigid hierar-
> chical structure: instead of separate and equivalent clans there appear
> classes or castes, of which one, at the summit, is essentially sacred, noble,
> and devoted to superior works, while another at the bottom, is profane or
> unclean and engaged in base tasks. The principle by which men are assigned
> rank and function remains the same: social polarity is still a reflection and
> a consequence of religious polarity. (Hertz 1973: 8)

The point at which reversible dualism shifted to irreversible dualism is
the point at which women became symbolically pegged as weak and bad.
In his study of dual classification systems, Hertz notes the great frequency
with which they are based on the right and left hand, across a variety of
societies.[11] The basic system goes as follows:

right	left
strong	weak

day	night
male	female
life	death
good	bad
high	low
sacred	profane

At some point during the Paleolithic, our previously ambidextrous forebears shifted to right-handedness, a posture that evidently had survival value for hunters. As a result, the capacities of the right hemisphere, governing the left hand, began to be underexercised, and consequently undervalued, a long time ago. These capacities include the capacity for spatial and temporal orientation and for the kind of instantaneous comprehension of complex wholes involved in analogic and intuitive thinking. It is possible that the slower, verbal-analytic (left-hemisphere) approach to problem solving was necessary to build up the neural circuitry that could later be used for analogic purposes. In any case, the possible role played by the experience of right-hand dominance in shaping our interpretation of the dominance-submission relationship as part of the cosmic order should not be overlooked (Ornstein 1972; Walters 1953).

It would appear that the symbolic classification system—right-left, male-female, strong-weak—has in effect powerfully reinforced small adaptive behavioral differences that probably go back to the beginning of hunting and has acted to amplify these differences in ways that affect almost every type of activity in which women engage. How long it took for the new behavior pattern of right-handedness to predominate among the protohominids is anyone's guess. Presumably, in one millennium, it didn't matter which hand was used. By the next millennium, it did. There must have been, as indicated earlier, some evolutionary advantage (at least in the short run) in this dominance, and it may well have aided the development of speech. Learning to talk with both hemispheres of the brain actively involved may be a much more complicated process—it would perhaps be like conducting two simultaneous conversations at all times. As it is, our second conversation is relatively nonverbal and easier to handle. We turn over our spatial judgments and analogic intuitive thinking to our "spare brain."

In the West, the dominance of the right hand—that is, of verbal-analytic thinking—is for the first time being seriously examined instead of assumed. It is presumably this dominance that has led both to the success of the industrial revolution and to the ecological disasters that have followed. Educators are increasingly giving attention to training the intuitive faculties along with the cognitive.[12] A journal[13] has been devoted entirely to the integration of the two spheres. The human potential movement in a sense represents a "declaration of independence" for the right hemisphere of the brain and therefore for the left hand. Are we witnessing a revolution against the right hand?

To the extent that this movement simply results in inverted dominance patterns, valuing the left *over* the right, it is self-defeating. In terms of the women's movement, neither elevation of femininity nor a women-can-do-everything-men-can-do approach really carries us out of the current impasse. The subordination of women historically has not done society much good. The deification of women and courtly love in the Middle Ages fit easily into an overall pattern that included the bloody Crusades. Robert Graves's poetical pursuit of the *White Goddess* (1966) through the ages pretty much leaves women and men right where they are now—to the satisfaction of neither. And, while some readers may glory in thoughts of a matriarchal age as they read Briffault's *Mothers,* or thrill to the smell of women hot with battle as they read Diner's *Mothers and Amazons,* these attempts at the reconstruction of human experience leave the concept of dominance untouched.

Meanwhile, another concept—that of social ambidexterity—gets short shrift. A certain amount of philosophical deference is paid to the idea of a society in which women and men both have their analytic and intuitive sides equally developed—what Margaret Mead (1967) called the androgynous society—but people are generally unenthusiastic about this. Someone always calls out *"vive la différence!"* And we do tend to think of sex role equality as a lessening of differentiation. This is not at all, however, an inevitable outcome.

In our examination of dominance and dimorphism as it affects human sex roles, many related concepts have been introduced. Some will recur later in this book; some will not. Readers are invited to make use of these concepts in whatever ways seem useful, in pondering the chapters that follow. All of the concepts will contribute something to our understanding of why women are found both in subordinate and in dominant roles throughout history. They will also help us to understand why it is necessary to look on the underside of history to find out what most women are doing.

Appendix

New Concepts in Dominance Theory

Sociobiologists are increasingly replacing old concepts of dominance with more sophisticated conceptualizations, as earlier terminology fails to describe what observers see. One group of scholars (K. R. L. Hall, I. S. Bernstein, Thelma Rowell, J. S. Gartlan, and others, in Wilson 1975: 282) has begun working with the concept of *control animal:* one who intervenes and manages conflict but does not exercise personal dominance. Control animals have been identified among monkeys having no clear-cut dominance order. Dominance potential is used much more to keep order, to keep others from fighting, than was earlier realized.

Another nonaggressive set of behaviors earlier associated with dominance fall into related categories of *greeting behavior*—signaling the gang when one has found something good, showing off, and play. Chimpanzees engage in a good deal of noisy chest beating and arm waving, particularly when two bands meet, but these behaviors seem to be a form of greeting ritual; while they may also establish relative dominance positions of males, no aggression is involved. There is a whole range of showy behavior among chimpanzees, and it is not always clear when it is simply play or when it is performing other functions. Play, itself—a special characteristic of higher species who do much of their exploration and invention as well as anticipatory socialization, through play—is distinct from aggression and efforts to dominate and yet has some of the characteristics of dominance behavior. We have all watched what began as rough and tumble play, both between animals and between humans, turn into a real fight. No doubt, excess androgen is discharged through play, and a comparative study of male and female play behavior in animals might throw light on the distinction between play as manipulation[14] for fun and play as an exploration of dominance possibilities.

If Martin and Voorhies (1975: 168) are right, females have less time to play than males. Apparently, even among the primates, the female has the typically longer working hours we find widely prevailing in the human experience. The female is busy feeding and caring for the young, and she must also find time for grooming the males; the males have time on their hands, and they play. Adolescent males play more than adult males, and they often play roughly, although it usually stays at "play." Is this anticipatory socialization of the young male for dominance?

The fact that the same species in different environments exhibit different degrees of aggressiveness has led sociobiologists to introduce another concept into their treatment of behavioral dominance. When baboons move out of the savanna and into the forest, they become more peaceable. Not as peaceable as the gibbon, but more peaceable than they were in the savanna. *Behavioral scaling* is the explanatory concept used to deal with this phenomenon: "Behavioral scaling is variation in the magnitude or in the qualitative state of a behavior which is correlated with stages of the life cycle, population density, or certain parameters of the environment" (Wilson 1975: 20). The potential for aggressive behavior is adaptive to the range of needs of the individual. The entire behavioral scale, not isolated points on it, is what is genetically fixed.

Humans too have their genetically fixed behavioral scales and can perform at one end or the other, depending on the circumstances. What they cannot do is "go over the top" or "under the floor" of their particular behavioral scale (Maslow, summarized in Maclay and Knipe 1972: 30-31). Human males, with generally higher androgen levels than females, have higher ceilings on the average. Cultural conditioning and social learning, however, can shift the behavior of individuals of either sex toward the top or the bottom of their scales. Mead's *Sex and Temperament* (1968) is a classic illustration of the consequences of this conditioning for individuals in societies with different values about acceptable levels of aggression. Individuals who are forced by their society to move too near the top or bottom of their particular behavioral scales become misfits.

Territoriality is another concept that goes beyond simple dominance. It is an interesting discovery of sociobiologists that crowding elicits increased aggression and a stronger dominance order in any animal species. When species have more space, they organize their relationships around territoriality, and aggressive behavior is seen only infrequently—and then chiefly at "public" sites such as water holes. Among humans, the sequence—nomadic-agrarian-urban—has on the whole been accompanied by rapidly accelerating elaborations of dominance structures and aggressive behavior.

Still another concept that can be used to explain dominance behavior is the sex ratio. Guttentag and Secord (1983) suggest that, when the sex ratio (the number of men per 100 women) deviates appreciably from 100 in the cohort of marrying age, this affects the status of women and the structure of the family. An undersupply of women would be associated with high status for women, and an oversupply, with the reverse. Because, as the authors admit, many other factors come into play in determining the status of women (scarce women might be kept as valuable chattels), this phenomenon has limited, but nevertheless significant, explanatory value. The opposite approach to the significance of the sex ratio is taken by Cavin (1985, chap. 4). For a bit of intellectual fun, read these two analyses one after the other.

Finally, there is the interesting thesis of Karen Sachs (1979), which differentiates between the position of women as sisters and women as wives. She suggests that societies in which women relate to the means of production as sisters generate a different status for females than societies in which men mediate the relationship between women and production. "Sisterhood" in the kin sense could thus literally cut away the ground from under male dominance.

Notes

1. While the courts provide the arena in which some women can defend what rights they have, the courts also set the limits to their rights.

2. New information on baboons from Rowell's field studies in Uganda call into question generalizations about baboons based on other studies. Rowell finds that "adult females serve as a focus of the group's social activity, and that they 'lead' the group in the sense of selecting the direction for the day's march; adult males change groups frequently, and the stable core of a group is the subset of adult females; the adult males of the Ishasha troops were not arranged in dominance hierarchies; and adult males failed to defend the troop against external threat, choosing rather to lead the retreat" (1973: 602).

3. For a discussion of some new concepts in dominance theory that go beyond what is discussed in this section, see the Appendix to this chapter.

4. This means, among other things, the development of a capacity to teach self-help skills and foster autonomy in the young without engaging in rejection behavior. It can be argued that human parenting is still in a fairly primitive stage in this regard.

5. The utopian anarcho-socialist version of development theory, foreseeing the withering away of hierarchical organization and the development of local self-organized modes of production and sharing, has had little confirmation in the experience of the last 100 years. Nevertheless, the cooperative movement that developed out of utopian social-ism embodies a continuing nonhierarchical tradition. The writings of Melman (1969) and McGregor (1960) on nonhierarchical systems in contemporary enterprises, including kibbutzim, provide continuing evidence of the workability of the egalitarian ideal under certain conditions; so do accounts of anarchist socialism during the civil war in Spain (Dolgoff 1974).

6. Blau's *Exchange and Power in Social Life* (1964) deals with some of these same issues in a somewhat different context. Blau would argue that all social interaction creates power imbalances. See especially his Chapter 5, "Differentiation of Power," and Chapter 12, "Dialectical Forces."

7. These are all specialized meanings for reciprocity. In one sense, all human inter-actions are reciprocal, in "that each partner has a part in permitting a transaction to take place," as in victimization (Vera Larsen, family therapist, La Grange, Illinois, personal communication, 1975).

8. See Wilson's very interesting discussion on alloparenting, referring to assistance given by other members of a society in the care of offspring. This phenomenon is chiefly found among the more advanced animal societies (1975: 349-52).

9. Arthur Marwick (1965), in his history of Britain during World War I, builds a strong case for the *permanent* changes in participation levels of women in the labor force made possible by wartime upheavals.

10. Burns estimates that the household economy is one-third the size of the total market economy. This figure is probably much too high for a highly industrialized country like the United States, though it might apply in some European countries. His main point is, however, substantially correct: While the forms of household craft have changed over the centuries, it is surprising how persistent skilled and semiskilled labor in the household is as a feature of the human economy.

11. The dual classification system has nothing to do with left-handedness in women but operates only at the symbolic level.

12. Jerome Bruner (1965) was one of the first to make this academically respectable, with the publication of his *On Knowing*.

13. The journal is *Synthesis: The Realization of the Self* (104 Dogerty Way, Redwood City, California).

14. Wilson (1975: 165) emphasizes the manipulative character of play, defining it as movement of the body and manipulation of known objects and environments in novel ways.

References

Bales, Robert, et al., eds. 1965. *Small Groups: Studies in Social Interaction*. New York: Knopf.

Benjamin, Jessica. 1988. *The Bonds of Love, Psychoanalysis, Feminism and the Problem of Domination*. New York: Pantheon.

Blau, Peter M. 1964. *Exchange and Power in Social Life*. New York: John Wiley.

Bois, J. Samuel. 1969. *Breeds of Men: Toward the Adulthood of Humankind*. New York: Harper & Row.

Boulding, Kenneth. 1973. *Economy of Love and Fear*. Belmont, CA: Wadsworth.

———. 1976. "Comment on 'The Social Institutions of Occupational Segregation'. " *Signs: Journal of Women in Culture and Society* 1(supplement, Spring):75-77.

Briffault, Robert. [1927] 1959. *Mothers: A Study of the Origins of Sentiments and Institutions*. New York: Humanities Press.

Bruner, Jerome. 1965. *On Knowing: Essays for the Left Hand*. New York: Atheneum.

Burns, Scott. 1975. *Home, Inc.: The Hidden Wealth and Power of the American Household*. Garden City, NY: Doubleday.

Carr-Sanders, Sir Alexander. 1959. "Economic Aspects of Woman's Role in the Development of Tropical and Subtropical Countries." In *Women's Role in the Development of Tropical and Subtropical Countries*. Report of the 31st Meeting of the International Institute of Differing Civilizations, Brussels.

Cavin, Susan. 1985. *Lesbian Origins*. San Francisco: Ism Press.

Diner, Helen. [1932] 1965. *Mothers and Amazons,* translated by John Philip Lundin. New York: Julian.

Dinnerstein, Dorothy. 1977. *The Mermaid and the Minotaur: Sexual Arrangements and Human Malaise*. New York: Harper & Row.

Dolgoff, Sam, ed. 1974. *The Anarchist Collectives: Workers' Self-Management in the Spanish Revolution 1936-1939*. New York: Free Life Editions.

Douglas, Mary. 1965. "The Lele-Resistance to Change." Pp. 183-213 in *Markets in Africa: Eight Subsistence Economies in Transition*, edited by Paul Bohannan and George Dalton. Garden City, NY: Doubleday.

Farb, Peter. 1968. *Man's Rise to Civilization: As Shown by the Indians of North America from Primeval Times to the Coming of the Industrial State*. New York: Dutton.

Fried, Morton H. 1967. *The Evolution of Political Society: An Essay in Political Anthropology*. New York: Random House.

Gouldner, Alvin. 1960. "The Norm of Reciprocity: A Preliminary Statement." *American Sociological Review* 25(April):161-78.

Graves, Robert. 1966. *White Goddess: A Historical Grammar of Poetic Myth*. New York: Farrar, Straus & Giroux.

Gruber, Howard E. 1974. *Darwin on Man: A Psychological Study of Scientific Creativity; Together with Darwin's Early and Unpublished Notebooks*, edited by Paul H. Barrett. New York: Dutton.

Guttentag, Marcia and Paul Secord. 1983. *Too Many Women? The Sex Ratio Question*. Beverly Hills, CA: Sage.

Hertz, Robert. 1973. "The Pre-Eminence of the Right Hand: A Study in Religious Polarity." Pp. 3-31 in *Right and Left: Essays on Dual Symbolic Classification*, edited by Rodney Needham. Chicago: University of Chicago Press.

Maclay, George and Humphry Knipe. 1972. *The Dominant Man: The Pecking Order in Human Society.* New York: Delacorte.

Mair, Lucy Phillip. 1972. *An Introduction to Social Anthropology.* 2nd ed. Oxford: Clarendon.

Martin, M. Kay and Barbara Voorhies. 1975. *Female of the Species.* New York: Columbia University Press.

Marwick, Arthur. 1965. *The Deluge: British Society and the First World War.* Boston: Little, Brown.

Maslow, Abraham. 1968. *Toward a Psychology of Being.* New York: Van Nostrand Reinhold.

McGregor, Douglas. 1960. *The Human Side of Enterprise.* New York: McGraw-Hill.

Mead, Margaret. 1967. "The Life Cycle and Its Variation: The Division of Roles." *Daedalus* 96(Summer):871-75.

———. 1968. *Sex and Temperament in Three Primitive Societies.* New York: Dell.

Melman, Seymour. 1969. "Industrial Efficiency Under Managerial vs. Cooperative Decision Making: A Comparative Study of Manufacturing Enterprises in Israel." In *Studies in Comparative Economic Development.* Beverly Hills, CA: Russell Sage.

Ornstein, Jack. 1972. *The Mind and the Brain: A Multi-Aspect Interpretation.* New York: Humanities Press.

Rowell, Thelma. 1973. *The Social Behavior of Monkeys.* Baltimore: Penguin (as reviewed in *Science* 180, May 11: 602-3, by James Loy).

Sachs, Karen. 1979. *Sisters and Wives: The Past and Future of Sexual Equality.* Westport, CT: Greenwood.

Service, Elman R. 1962. *Primitive Social Organization.* New York: Random House.

Sharp, Gene. 1973. *Politics of Non-violent Action.* Boston: Porter Sargent.

Smith, Adam. [1759] 1966. *The Theory of Moral Sentiments.* New York: Augustus M. Kelley.

Sterling, Paul. 1965. *Turkish Village.* New York: John Wiley.

Tiger, Lionel. 1969. *Men in Groups.* New York: Random House.

Tocqueville, Alexis de. [1848] 1944. *Democracy in America*, translated by Phillipps Bradley. New York: Knopf.

Walters, W. Grey. 1953. *The Living Brain.* New York: Norton.

Wilson, Edward O. 1975. *Sociobiology: The New Synthesis.* Cambridge: Belknap Press of Harvard University Press.

Winch, Robert F. 1972. *Mate Selection: A Study of Complementary Needs*, edited by Ann Greer. Dubuque, IA: William C Brown.

Wolff, Kurt H. 1950. *The Sociology of Georg Simmel.* London: Free Press.

3

The Paleolithic:
The Evolution of Home Base
and Sex Role Differentiation

Hominids Make Themselves at Home

We are in the Great Rift Valley of East Africa, 350 miles from Kiliman-jaro. Runoff streams from the mountains have made a brackish lake; the grasslands of the savanna creep up to the edge of the rift, and if we were standing up above we would see herds of wildebeests, small baboon troops, and other savanna animals moving about. We are in the valley, and the sun has just set. The year is 2,000,000 B.C.E. An 18-year-old *Australopithecus* male is hauling a freshly killed animal toward an area blocked off by a semicircular stone wall, where two females are sitting on the ground feeding babies and several small children are running about. The females shake their heads as the boy approaches and point over to an area where three males and some youngsters are busy smashing bones with rocks.

AUTHOR'S NOTE: Because this chapter covers nearly 2 million years, the reader is urged to study the chronology in the Appendix to the chapter. The Leakey data, which pushes hominid existence back another million and a half years, became available after the original publication of *The Underside*. Readers are urged to study Richard Leakey's *The Making of Mankind* (1981) for updated information.

"Into the kitchen, not here!" is the message. The males growl with pleasure as they see more meat arriving. They were getting the last bits of marrow out of yesterday's bones, because today had not been a good hunting day. The females, as soon as they have finished feeding the infants, bring the small children and join the males to get their share of meat—it has been saved for them. The bulbs and tubers gathered earlier during the day have long since been eaten, in the foraging places where they were gathered. Only the meat is carried back to camp, because the best chopping tools are here. One of the females puts a hand on the boy's shoulder. She remembers how sickly and weak he was during the bad droughts when he was little, and how he nearly died. Now he is able to bring home meat.

We can't call this little band—about 12 individuals in all—human. But they look like our second cousins, at least. They are hominids, early representatives of the human species. The particular band we have been watching really did camp on the shores of the lake in what is now Olduvai Gorge. The remains of its members, including the 18-year-old who had several times nearly died of malnutrition as a small child, have been dug up and examined by the Leakey family, a remarkable two-generation archaeological team (Pfeiffer 1969: 72-92). Three hundred feet of volcanic ash had been covering that site for millennia. It was a mere 50,000 years ago that the Rift Valley, part of the great geological fault that winds in almost continuous fissures around the planet and back on itself again, heaved and cracked once more and exposed part of the ancient site where this hominid band had camped.

The total site is a 3,400-square-foot living floor. One area contains a rough semicircle of rocks, perhaps a windbreak (and protected place for little ones to be left?); an area about 15 feet in diameter, "thick with shattered pieces of rock and bone and choppers" (the kitchen) and, a few feet away, a place containing larger bone fragments and unshattered bones (the "dining room"). Eleven different kinds of stone implements have been found among the 4,000 artifacts and fossils at this one living area. Fifty known sites remain to be excavated in the valley.

Tools, Diet, and Development

These tools are a million years older than prehistorians expected.[1] "It is almost as if one opened up a musty vault in the Great Pyramid of Egypt and found vacuum cleaners and television sets," writes Pfeiffer (1969: 79). For our purposes, this site throws unexpected light on the way of life of protohuman familistic groupings. Like some of their primate cousins, the hominids moved about in small bands. The Olduvai site was not a permanent settlement but a camping site returned to over and over again in the course of millennia; perhaps it was a favored "home base."

Because hominid infants did not have the ability of other primates to cling to their mothers, they tended to be carried. This means that mothers, just as their hands were freed by walking upright, found those hands fully occupied with babies. This was not too much of a problem in early hominid days, when males may well have carried the babies too, as some other primate males did. Moving around through the grasslands by day, there were many opportunities to set infants down while gathering roots and tubers. In these early millennia, the hominids were primarily vegetarians. Once in a while a hominid—male or female—would either come upon a newly dead small animal and try eating it out of curiosity or, almost accidentally, actually kill a rabbit or other small creature. An account of baboons killing and eating meat in Royal Nairobi National Park is suggestive about the development of this new behavior pattern:

> Suddenly we saw directly ahead a large male baboon with a freshly killed hare in its mouth, a noteworthy event in itself since meat eating is rarely observed. But there was more to come. A whole troop was crossing the stream, and a few seconds later another large male passed with another hare, and not long after that a third male carrying the remains of a small antelope.
> . . . The whole troop seemed excited, jittery. Since baboons eat small animals in a matter of minutes, these animals must all have been killed recently and almost simultaneously. Perhaps one baboon came upon a hare lying in the grass and picked it up casually, and the sight of the act aroused other baboons to go after hares and other small game in the vicinity. In other words, it might have been a spontaneous flurry of activity. (Pfeiffer 1969: 108)

De Vore, who was on this expedition, suggests that meat eating can be established by several recurring incidents like this as a new cultural tradition in a baboon troop.

More was involved in the development of hunting than an accidentally acquired culture trait, however. Droughts that drastically reduced usual food supplies helped turn hominids to hunting. Their first easy pickings would be the crippled and weak animals around them who could cope with the drought even less well than they. Studies of hunting and gathering societies in Africa and Australia today indicate that many miles are run per pound of meat caught. Richard Lee (1968) reports four days of hunting for each animal caught. Phyllis Kaberry (1939) writes of the kind of physical endurance required for hunting. She tried twice to accompany men on hunting trips, and each time had to give up because she could not maintain their speed. We do not know whether the women members of the bands she studied could have kept up if they tried. We do know, however, that they rarely participate in these trips; they confine their hunting activities to hares and other small animals found near the camp site. It is interesting to note that, when women do hunt, they usually do so without weapons, relying on their knowledge of animals' habits to catch an animal with their bare hands. Or, like the Tiwi women, they may hunt with dogs (Goodale, in Martin and Voorhies 1975: 197-98).

In the Pleistocene, female hominids were being slowed down as the pelvis, enlarging to accommodate their brainier, larger-headed hominid offspring, was widening their hips and reducing their running speed.

The combination of drought-induced shortages of vegetable foods, biological accommodations of the female to hominid evolution, and the need for babies to be carried as they lost their grasping facility limited the females' freedom of movement at the same time that it expanded the males'. The female continued to hunt for tubers but also depended on what the male could bring back. Herein lies the importance of the invention of the home base: a place to put babies down and a place to share the meat. The home base introduced another revolutionary possibility: a place for the sick and injured to recover. In a troop constantly on the move, minor illnesses could be fatal because a sick member must either keep up or be left behind to become some predator's dinner: "It is the home base that changes sprained ankles and fevers from fatal diseases to minor ailments" (Washburn and De Vore 1961: 101). It also gave the female a new role: that of nurse.

The shift to hunting also encouraged food sharing. Meat was hard to tear into with the vegetarian-type teeth with which hominids were equipped. Tools were needed for cutting and for crushing. Females and males both became adept at making tools from pebbles, bones, and shells[2] and developed increasingly cooperative habits of food and equipment sharing in the small bands in which they lived and moved.

The emergence of camp sites would not necessarily have to relate to hunting. In fact, there is evidence that much of the activity that went on at the camp site related to the preparation of vegetable foods. Hominids were very inventive about converting the environment into food and were accomplished seed eaters before they were meat eaters. Foraging bands in North America, at a much later time, are estimated to have used 2,000 different plant foods (Farb 1968: 10). Many of the plants could not be easily chewed or digested without pounding and scraping, and many of the hominid's stone tools were used for this purpose (Jolly, in Martin and Voorhies 1975: 172).

Hominid bands, like hunting and gathering bands today, ranged from 12 to 25 individuals. Today, at times of severest drought, both baboons and Kalahari bushmen divide into small groupings to search for food. They recombine into larger bands when conditions are better. Similarly, food pressure probably caused the hominid bands from time to time to divide into small groups of female plus male plus children. Individualization of male-female relationships was happening at the same time. While the first bands may have consisted of females and adult offspring, at some time during these very early hominid wanderings, females began stable pairing with an adult male from another band. There is no way to know whether pairing was linked to an increased dependency on animal food, increased protection needs, or both.

With the disappearance of estrus ("heat") in the female, neither males nor females were any longer propelled by a totally automatic sex drive. A milder state of continuous receptivity on the part of the female made it possible for choice to enter into the sexual relationship—choice both for the female and for the male.[3] The nurturant activities possible in the home base also added more dimensions to the male-female relationship.

The sex-based division of labor in food getting, the institution of home bases, and a pattern of social organization based on familistic groupings of male-female-children (sometimes in bands, sometimes separately) must all have evolved early in the hominid experience and long before the arrival of *Mulier* and *Homo sapiens* on the scene.

Territorial Expansion and Takeoff

Australopithecus family bands slowly started moving out of Africa. Compared with their primitive relatives, they were already "cosmopolitans," moving over a hunting territory of about 500 miles, while baboons usually travel over a 15-square-mile territory. This tendency to cover vast areas in their foraging for food, instead of adapting to micro environments, was one of the factors that led to the very rapid evolution of those early hominids into the brainy human species that succeeded them. It appeared they were always out exploring, always looking for new problems to solve.

In the course of another million years, these cerebrating hominids had circled the Mediterranean and found their way to China, always taking the valley routes, avoiding mountains, and leaving sites to be discovered millennia later by twentieth-century archaeologists. Toralba in north central Spain and Terra Amata near present-day Nice in France are two 400,000-year-old sites that give us a glimpse of the continuing evolution of the hominids.

By this time, hunting has grown in importance as a human activity. Males have become very skilled at it and can now bring down the largest animals in the environment—elephants and rhinoceros—as sites in Spain show. They have developed all kinds of hunting strategies, including working in coordinated hunting parties, and have continued to improve their tools. Cleavers, axes, borers, scrapers, and a bewildering variety of implements of stone and bone appear. While they are not marked "his" and "hers," we can infer that many of the improvements in tools during this period were also made by women. For all the variety, they still bear the marks of the basic Olduvai pattern—variations on a 2-million-year-old tool kit. Significant tool complexes appear that are labeled *Acheulean* and *Abbevillian*. Home-base camps now have huts that may be up to 50 feet long, made of long branches bent to interlock at the top. Food gathering remains a major activity for women, but now they also scrape hides and perhaps build the new twig houses. House building becomes an increasingly frequent activity for them.[4]

What has been happening to *Homo* and *Mulier erectus* over the past 1 million years, apart from their spread through the temperate zone? The size of their brains is in the process of doubling. While the Bible tells us that we cannot add a cubit to our stature by thinking, apparently the evolutionary process has involved adding cubits to the brain size by thinking—or rather has rewarded thinking and "selected" for cranial capacity.

Somehow, a deviation-amplifying feedback system[5] became effective early for our particular primate ancestors, leading to their ever sharper judgmental capacities. Every new advantage the far-ranging hominids experienced expanded their survival capacities. They kept discovering new things to eat, new places to take shelter, new ways to make tools. Each discovery equipped them for the next one. If we go back to very early developments in the prehominid line, we may consider with Pfeiffer the special evolutionary possibilities that life in the trees offered (1969: 21-34). While early primates may have been forced into the trees because they could not compete successfully on the ground, once up there they had to deal with a new dimension: treetop living. This kind of life involved so many gaps, discontinuities, and uncertainties that a species, to survive, had to develop extraordinary flexibility and skill in lightning-quick spatial judgments:

> Regarded from a ground-dwellers point of view, it is roughly equivalent to moving too rapidly to stop through tall dense grasses without being able to see more than a few feet ahead. At any moment, one may suddenly come upon a deep hole directly in the path, too wide to step across. Such hazards may be numerous and scattered at random over the terrain. Frequent swift decisions are required about how far to jump and in what direction. To live in trees is to be confronted continually with analogous emergencies, analogous "holes" in the form of gaps between branches. (Pfeiffer 1969: 10)

Research on learning in human infants emphasizes the importance of optimum discontinuities in triggering learning. Using representations of a human face from very conventional to wildly distorted, it has been shown that an infant glances quickly away from both the very familiar and the unrecognizably distorted faces and is held longest by representations that are suggestive of a face that needs "mental work" to fill in the gaps (Kagan 1967, 1971). Our primate ancestors, then, lived from moment to moment by figuring out, literally, how to bridge gaps.

Not all who took to trees became *erectus*, however. When competition got heavy in the trees, grasping and swinging skills alone were not enough. With changing climatic and environmental conditions, the premium came first on size, then on ability to survive in two environments: both in the trees and on the ground. Some primates became hominids in the process, thriving on the double set of discontinuities of tree and ground living. At each point in this long development, new neural pathways were developing, "the cerebral expression of new possibilities":

> The possible routes along which nerve signals may pass from sense organs to muscles increased enormously. The cortex is in part an organ of analysis, a dense network of billions of nerve cells which lies between stimulus mechanisms and response mechanisms, between experience and action. Its complexity reflected the new complexity of the apes' world. (Pfeiffer 1969: 35)

The additional complexes neural pathways set up—once the hand was freed from the necessity of the grosser grasping movements of treetop swinging for the finer hand-wrist-finger movements of a slower-paced exploration of the ground—must in themselves have enormously expanded the cortex. Our hands literally helped develop our brains. So, while the female hominid paid a high price for the loss of the more general grasping reflex in her infants, in terms of her own increased responsibility for toting them around, she gained in the long run, right along with her mate. The hand that grasped the tree limb, and clutched its mother's fur,[6] could never have wielded the bone sewing needle.

Hunting Versus Gathering and a New Division of Labor

The deviation-amplifying feedback process of challenge-response-new challenge went on as hominids began to explore the planet. Male and female were in this together. The process of mapping new environments, identifying dangers and resources, was a shared one. Because the females were often carrying babies, they may have developed somewhat different scanning skills than the males, but the cortical enrichment would have been the same. As long as hunting was confined to the pursuit of small game, caught not far from home base, role differentiation would be minimal.

We can make some guesses about what daily life was like on the basis of observations made by anthropologists who have lived with any one of the dozens of small hunting-gathering tribes found today in Africa, Australia, and South America.[7] Women in the Australian desert will walk a maximum of 10 miles a day, water bowl balanced on head, nursing child on hip and small children following, in search of food: five miles out from camp, five miles back. They are quite clear about their physiological limits. They have such intimate knowledge of an area, of say 500 square miles, that they know where each special water-bearing plant, each nut-bearing tree, edible root, and bulb are growing in that area. Careful conservationists, they leave certain emergency-type rations like the water-bearing plants "for next time."

The difference between male and female knowledge stocks in these bands is probably not large. Because the women supply up to 80% of the diet by weight, they must know a good deal about environmental resources (Lee 1968: 33). Both women and men are skilled ecologists, but women may know the names and properties of more plants and bushes than men do. What the men know was taught them when they were little by the women, before they were old enough to join their fathers on hunting expeditions. It has been said that hunting is a high-risk, low-yield activity and that food gathering is a low-risk, high-yield activity (Lee 1968: 40). In times of drought in Africa, people who can attach themselves to desert nomad peoples do so, for desert food gatherers rarely die of starvation in droughts. The women have a wide reserve knowledge of edible plants that are not normally used (being tough to chew, less tasty, and so on) but that see them through prolonged shortages of other foods (Lee 1968: 40). The "low-risk activity" has high survival value. Further information on women as gatherers can be found in Dahlberg (1981).

Although hunting and gathering tribes of today have a million years' more evolution behind them than the early hominid bands, it is nevertheless probably true that, then as now, there were women's rituals and men's rituals, based on different ways of spending the day. The rituals are a source of mutual challenge as well as of mutual pleasure; neither set of rituals is "better." Old women as well as old men play the role of tribal elders. In short, the cognitive-analytic, symbolic-aesthetic, and social-bonding talents of both women and men are fully developed and fully exercised in this type of society.

At some point in the million-year spreading out over the planet, hominids moved from small-game to large-game hunting. The Toralba and Terra Amata sites, with their huge piles of animal bones signifying large-scale kills, represent the large-game era and provide the materials for societies' favorite myth about the brawny hunter who drags his women by the hair into his cave to do his will. A great deal of attention has been given to the analytic and coordination skills, both individual and social, that developed in the course of big-game hunting. There is no doubt that both the behavioral learning "in the field" and the considered program of training that the males in hunting societies develop to educate their young boys involve a major evolutionary advance in capacity to deal simultaneously with large numbers of items of information, to achieve high levels of mental synthesis, and to integrate behaviors and cognitions with subtlety and speed. To infer from this that hunting was the "master integrating pattern of our species" (Laughlin 1968), however, is to forget the same set of capacities—to deal simultaneously with large numbers of items of information, to achieve high levels of mental synthesis, and to integrate behaviors and cognitions with subtlety and speed—involved with the gathering activities of the females.

Deetz (1968: 281-82) points out the absurdity of considering hunting as the master pattern for human activity, given the wide range of activities in which early hominids engaged. Why not, says Deetz, consider "Man the Gatherer" and "Woman the Potter"? The problem of how to use *man* in the generic sense, while imaging both women and men in our heads as we use it, compounds the difficulty of identifying particular activity patterns as crucial in human development.

The major impact of large-scale hunting was that it helped establish an asymmetrical division of labor that replaced the essentially symmetrical sharing found in gathering societies. The biological givens of childbirth and nursing then reinforced this new separation of men's work from women's work.

By 400,000 B.C.E., there may have been about 40,000 bands of hunter-gatherers scattered across Africa, Asia, and Europe, each with its own home base. There were haves and have-nots then, as now, given that some bands found the richest grassland areas with the largest animal herds and others managed in less fertile regions with a relative scarcity of food. It was hardly a situation of perfect competition, in the economist's terms, because most bands had no idea that there were alternative environments available to them. Some were just lucky. Over time, however, more and more bands found out about the good hunting and gathering to be had in Spain and France near the Mediterranean, and that region became an early area of population concentration.

When we see the remains of the Toralba and Terra Amata sites with their extensive building and tool remains, complex yet still stamped with the sameness of the Olduvai, we are seeing hominids already launched in the "development" process. They are about to reap the rewards of the accumulated experience and rapidly expanding brain size that, coupled with higher population density and more opportunity for social interaction, have brought them to a new phase of social evolution. The Swanscombe site near present-day London presents us with almost modern-looking women and men, nearly *sapiens*.[8] Their tools, including the two new types, Clactonian and Tayacian, are still modifications of very old patterns. The double-edged hand ax and a more sophisticated type of flint (Levallois technique) indicate, however, that they are using their brains to improve their tools. Postholes and other evidence suggest that women were building both animal-hide and twig huts. While many shelters were built in the open, evidence of tents of skin erected inside caves, probably to keep out the cold, are also found as far back as the Middle Paleolithic. Digging sticks with fire-hardened points indicate women had figured out that putting pointed sticks into the fire to dry and harden provided them with more efficient tools for food gathering.[9] Men got the idea of using the sticks to spear animals.

Neanderthals and New Skills

Fully modern woman, *Mulier neanderthalensis,* and her mate took another 300,000 years to evolve. ("Fully modern" may be a slight exaggeration, but it is generally agreed that a well-groomed and tastefully dressed Neanderthaler would not stand out as unusual in a New York subway.) By this time, her brain size had fully evolved and, if she had an oversized jaw, this would be corrected by an improvement in her cooking techniques. Emerging during an interglacial period, she was to face during the next ice age—from 75,000 to 50,000 B.C.—the greatest challenges her evolving species had yet met. One reason that she and her mate survived the cold was because of the superior stone tools they developed, known as Mousterian and Levallois; 60 different kinds of these tools have been identified, all a substantial advance over the 2-million-year-old Olduvai tool models (Constable 1973: 54).

Adventurous, *Mulier neanderthalensis* moved with her mate into a whole new set of habitats across the plains of what is now the Soviet Union and across forbidding mountain chains toward southern Asia to open up the area that was to become the birthplace of civilization. Her ecological knowledge would have been crucial in these movements. Without her sharp eye for new environmental features and her ability to make good judgments about the unfamiliar on the basis of what earlier had been familiar, her bands would have starved to death. Meat was sometimes abundant, sometimes not. Roots and tubers and nuts and berries were always needed.

Judging from her tool kits, she became a highly skilled dressmaker, preparing a great variety of animal skins for garments as well as for shelters.[10] As heavier and heavier winters descended on the European

Neanderthalers, her skill in finding and storing plant food was pushed to its utmost. The most important development in this period, however, was woman's learning to tame fire. This extraordinary achievement set her off from all animals, who feared fire, and it gave her and her children both protection against wild animals while the men were away hunting and warmth in winter. It made cave dwelling possible, because with fire it was for the first time feasible to drive animals out of the caves (they liked shelter too), and keep them out, so that hominid families could move in. Who knows what complex threads of thought and imagery were spun on her mental loom to enable her not to fear that which had surely burnt and hurt some members of her band, if not herself?

> She watched it carefully, calculatingly; [s]he accepted the odds and sought to improve them in favor of escaping fresh hurt. [S]he was learning which end of the stick [s]he could grasp with impunity. . . . the taming and use of fire raised [wo]man indeed to Promethean heights, [mistress] not of a tool but of a force. (Walters 1953: 38)

The taming of fire is usually ascribed to men, but it seems far more likely that women, the keepers of home base and protectors of the young from wild animals, would be the ones whose need for it would overcome the fear of it. Men's controlled use of fire in hunting may, however, have developed simultaneously with women's use of it at the home base. The hearth fire was for a long time "collected" from found fires and carefully saved and moved from site to site, as it is done today among the Congo pygmies described by Turnbull (1968). Learning to kindle fire was a much later development (Oakley 1961).

With a fire burning on the hearth, and animals brought in by the men to supply food and warm skins, some Neanderthal bands survived a 30,000-year ice age. Death came often. A hunter injured and frozen to death in the snow could mean a whole band wiped out. Children died of malnutrition; women died in childbirth. Each new birth would be a stern time of silent weighing of possibilities. Should this child be allowed to live? Could they feed it? As with the Australian aborigines today (Pfeiffer 1969: 517), this decision might be primarily the mother's. She will know what the food prospects are, how much is left of last summer's plant-food store, what the weekly take-home pay in animal meat has been lately. And knowing that girl babies will be destined to be further producers of offspring, she is less likely to let girl babies live than boy babies, in the leanest times. She has learned to look ahead, to be practical.

The extent to which cannibalism was practiced to extend the food supply during hard times among the Neanderthals is not clear. Probably infants that were not to be reared were eaten, a practice that has continued to this century among some foraging people in times of drought and great hardship (Hogg 1966: 168). Bashed human skulls and charred human bones at various cave sites leave a double trail of evidence. Sometimes fellow hominids were used for food, sometimes brains alone were consumed in a special kind of communion ritual (Constable 1973: 104-5). We will see shortly that the ritual use of skulls, both animal and human, is one of the early cultural traits of the protohumans. On the whole, the Neanderthals appear to have been a peaceable folk. Evidence for raiding parties and interpersonal violence are infrequent; most of the archaeological records tell a pacific story.

The Flowering of Neanderthal Culture

By 100,000 B.C.E., then, the human species has had a long experience behind it of making increasingly sophisticated adaptations to an environment it is coming to know better and better. The capacity to symbolize and record experience is beginning to emerge. The startling and still controversial work of Alexander Marshack (*Roots of Civilization,* 1972a) points straight back to this Neanderthal culture as the time when the first systematic observations of lunar time periods were made and the basis for later calendrical developments established. On the strength of the fact that his work has had a surprising degree of acceptance among those scholars most involved with calendrical research, and because his line of analysis fits so well with the kind of picture I am trying to develop here, I am going to elaborate on the Marshack thesis. It should be understood that this is an imaginative reconstruction that will have to be modified when more research data are available.

Marshack's basic thesis is that *patterning events over time*—what he calls "time-factoring"—and *creating stories around repeated human experiences* that become the basis for complex ritual enactments—are capacities that developed in the Neanderthal culture and came to full flowering in Magdalenian systems of notation and of symbolic representation in painting and sculpture and in associated rituals that made use of the notations and representations. His demonstrations, based on painstaking microscopic analysis of apparently chance scratches or decorative markings on paintings and engravings, evoke calendrical overtones and suggest lunar cycles. A whole new interpretation of Neanderthal culture is emerging from his work. (See also Marshack, 1972b, 1975, and 1976.)

With the human brain now fully evolved, is it so strange to imagine the Neanderthals beginning to conceptualize lunar and solar cycles and to relate them to changing seasons? All human experience in nonurban settings is framed by the risings and settings of the sun by day and the moon by night, by the movement of the seasons and the associated ripening, harvesting, and "dead time" of plant foods. Animals as well as humans respond to these cycles, so Neanderthals had two sets of teachers—the cyclic events in nature itself and the animal responses to these events. Side by side with these environmentally determined cycles are the biosocially determined cycles of the human lifetime: birth, puberty, pairing, death. Many other cycles develop out of the interrelationship between humans and their environment and out of their relationships with each other in dyads, familistic groups, and bands. It is the conceptualization of all these cycles that Marshack refers to as "storying." The acting out of these conceptualizations gives an in-depth quality to the human experience, provides social support and nurture, a sense of identity, and courage to face the unknown.

Most of our knowledge of the Neanderthals comes from their burials, and quite a number of Neanderthal burials have been uncovered. They all give evidence of ceremonies having been performed at the time of the burial and of preparations for burial implying a set of beliefs about death. Flint, stone, and bone tools were buried with bodies, and in at least one case (Shanidar cave burial) the body was set on a mound of wild flowers and covered with more flowers (Constable 1973: 25). At another site, six pairs of goat horns, still attached to skulls, form a circular arrangement around a grave. A child's grave at La Ferrassie contains a piece of stone (see Figure 3.1) "intentionally engraved with linear sequences" comparable to calendrical notations found much later, in the cave-art era (Marshack 1972a: 349). Careful removal of the base of the skull, or *foramen magnum*, seen in some skeletons indicates the possibility of ritual cannibalism of the kind practiced in Bronze Age Germany and, until recently, by nomadic subsistence peoples in various places (Marshack 1972a: 121; Hogg 1966).

Figure 3.1. Line Rendition of an Intentionally Engraved Stone Found at La Ferrassie. Redrawn by HBR.

Cave sites also give evidence of ritual use of red and yellow ocher and of a fairly elaborate bear cult. A cave containing a stone chest with seven bear skulls, and niches with six more bear skulls carefully arranged, and a second cave with a larger chest and even more bear remains, point to large-scale ritual preparations. While bear-cult remains are relatively specific, some imagination is needed to figure out how the ocher was used. It has been suggested by Constable and others that men painted their skins with ritual patterns in ceremonial preparations for hunting. This would certainly fit with observations of present-day hunting and gathering cultures, where such ritual painting is found. In fact, painting the body with ritual symbols may be the earliest form of "written communication" as well as an early art form. Frobenius (1974), examining the elaborate tattooing of the Maori, sees this ritual adornment as having become record keeping as well as communication, because each tatoo mark on a woman or man indicates parentage, status, and so on.

The appearance of ornaments in burials (for example, animal-tooth and seashell necklaces) almost as early as that of tools indicates that the impulse to decorate is about as old as the impulse to create artifacts. Frobenius (1974) suggests that all human labor is a consequence of the desire to have materials for decoration. That seems too extreme a position, but we certainly cannot ignore the fact that humans from Neanderthal on have decorated surfaces (their own bodies, tools, cave walls) in ways that did not add "utility" in the sense of economic productivity.

Join all this speculation to the evidence that Neanderthals sometimes allowed crippled babies to live and sometimes cared for helpless old people,[11] at least during periods when there were no serious food shortages, and we must realize that we are dealing with a complex culture.

The fact that Neanderthals met at special times and places to perform burial rites associated with gathering food and hunting cannot be directly related to more sophisticated calendar consciousness except through the one marked stone buried with a child, but it does lead directly to the various lunar and lunar-solar markings that come in the Aurignacian-Magdalenian times that follow. Calendar consciousness may have developed in women first, because every woman has a "body calendar"—her monthly menstrual period. She would be the first to note the relationship between her own body cycle and the lunar cycle.[12] Urban women are much less likely to notice or be affected by the phases of the moon, so that particular calendrical potential is much less obvious in modern times. This calendaring by women will be further discussed below. The marking of seasons was equally important for women, the food gatherers, and men, the hunters, so the development of a combination lunar-solar calendar was probably a joint enterprise. (Death rituals, because they are often for infants in the first year of life—many infant burials have been found—would fall perhaps more in the women's sphere than in the men's.) The two sets of rituals that we have evidence for among the Neanderthals, then—those associated with food gathering and those associated with death—are likely to have had full participation by both women and men. Because they suggest elaborate advance preparations and patterned ceremonials repeated over and over, probably both women and men spent part of their work days in preparation for ceremonials.

The burden of all this discussion is that conceptualization and ritualization of social life happened very gradually, over a long period of time, and that females were fully involved in that process throughout "prehistory." The roots of ritual in the experience of death and bereavement may go back to the nonhuman primates. Mother baboons give evidence of considerable grief when their babies die, and male baboons also seem to be aware of the death of infants as a puzzling discontinuity (Altmann and Altmann 1970: 178). It is not so strange that, over a 20-million-year period, from our primate ancestors until the Neanderthal era, *Mulier* and *Homo sapiens* evolved from feeling a baboonlike grief over the death of an infant to perceiving a time-patterned quality in death and in birth. In addition to the three sets of teachers I mentioned earlier, the cyclic events in nature, the responses of animals to them, and the biosocial cycles evinced most clearly in the woman, they had something else of crucial importance—the "home-base" setting in which to organize their perceptions night after night.

The long, slow evolution of home base must have been very basic to the development of a sense of the relatedness of the seen and the unseen in the face of the discontinuities of everyday life. When fire-lit caves became home base, and the dangers of death by freezing were added to the dangers of death by starvation, injury from hostile animals, and other perils, a new quality must have entered into both the solitude and the togetherness of the small bands. In the hardest times, bands probably rarely exceeded 12 persons. Neither large bands nor "nuclear families" could have survived.

House hunting in the Paleolithic for caves to live in, especially at the height of the ice age, was not exactly easy. The range of choice was limited. Archaeologists have estimated that a cave for a Paleolithic hunting band would need to be about 250 square meters, allowing 10 square meters per person for an average band of 25. In fact, this seems to be the average cave size in sites in France. In South German and Yugoslavian sites, the same number of people (judged by concentration of tools) squeezed into 10 square meters as their total space. It would appear that the first housing shortages developed in the last ice age. The alternation of experiences of ranging over great spaces and being crowded into small caves was probably very important in developing the special social characteristics that were to produce *Homo* and *Mulier sapiens*.

For survival, at least two adult males and two adult females would be needed in each band. What kind of communing went on among them? Many anthropologists have given accounts of how small hunting and gathering bands sit in silence around a campfire in desert or forest. Some extraordinarily beautiful photographs of the tiny Tasaday band living in a cave on the slope of a jungle mountain on Mindanao in the Philippines (White 1973: 137 ff.) show pensive faces by firelight. The Neanderthals had limited voice box equipment and therefore a limited speech capacity. Their performance, however, shows that their intelligence was as keen as ours. Did they have better nonverbal communication modes than we? Very likely. Their culture, however, was not to last. (See Marshack 1976: 141-45, for a discussion of the origins of language.)

A New Development in the Near East: The Cro-Magnons

The Neanderthals reached their peak and then "disappeared" from history. Some of them remained in Europe and coped with the severities of the ice age, but by 50,000 B.C.E. many of them had moved to the Near East. Genetic isolation for the series of bands that stayed behind in Europe, as contrasted with the great intermingling in the Near East, inevitably made the Cro-Magnons of the Near East look like a different species. They did not have the oversized jaw, not having to eat so much undercooked meat in the warmer, more resource-filled environment. While a lot of their large-jawed cousins probably did die out because of environmental hardship, the ones who were left apparently intermarried with their relatives from the Near East when these trickled back to Europe, some thousands of years later. The older Neanderthals may sometimes have been hunted as "wild men" by returning Cro-Magnons, but, on the whole, with their superior intelligence, they probably found a way to adapt. It was only the oversized jaw that died out.

The Near East corridor became the focal point of the next evolutionary development. While the ice age was still on, hunting was at its very best here, because this was the retreat site of the herds. "Transitional type" humans are found here in places like the Mt. Carmel rock shelter, along with successive layers of tool kits from Neanderthal to "modern" (Cro-Magnon). The experience of higher population density and intensive big-game hunting had evolved a whole new set of tools and new patterns of social organization. When the Neanderthals' culture was at its peak of development in Europe, the species probably numbered about 1 million on the entire planet. In the favorable environment of the Near East, the population expanded rapidly, so that, by the time the new people were spreading back into Europe, humankind had tripled in size, to more than 3 million by 35,000 B.C.E.[13]

With open land and a few forests in the new terrain, bands met one another much more frequently. This is the time, Hawkes suggests (Hawkes and Woolley 1963), that alliances between bands became tribal-type associations. We can imagine that the already elaborate ceremonies the immigrant Neanderthals brought with them from Europe became much more elaborate in the friendlier climate. They would become the occasion of the coming together of a number of bands. The habit of females changing groups at the time of interband encounters, already noted in Chapter 2 as a practice among chimpanzees, would by now have been developed into interband alliances. While it is not possible to reconstruct Neanderthal "family life," the evidence from cave sites and camp sites is not inconsistent with the possibility that monogamous lifetime pairing had developed. At first, there would be spontaneous movement of young unpaired females from their birth band to another, and a similar movement of young males, resulting in a random pairing of "eligibles." Once speech had developed, it does not seem like such a great step to go from random pairing to interband discussion about that pairing. Once coupling became a matter for interband agreement, it would be another short step to the development of interband pairing rituals. (Note Auel's 1980 imaginative reconstruction of Neanderthal "family life" in *The Clan of the Cave Bear*.)

Setting the Stage

Contemporary hunting-gathering bands have had 50,000 years since Neanderthal times to elaborate marriage alliance patterns. Yet it is interesting to note that polygamy is rare, and where found it does not account for more than 5% of marriages in a band (Gardner 1968: 210). Polygamy is also commonly associated with serial marriages for both women and men, in what Gardner calls "gerontogamy"—older males marrying younger females or vice versa. The first marriage then becomes a kind of adoptive parent-child relationship, to be succeeded for the child by other marriages. In the Paleolithic, in small bands with short life expectancies, this might well have been adaptive behavior at times.

The fact remains that stable monogamous pairing is nearly universal among hunters and gatherers today, as the two major reviews of studies of hunting-gathering societies indicate (Lee and De Vore 1968; Bicchieri 1972). The fact that in some of these tribes the children call all the adults mother and father does not at all mean that there is a group marriage practice, as Lewis Henry Morgan ([1877] 1963) erroneously thought when he studied the Iroquois.[14]

Considerable affection between spouses is often described by observers of hunting and gathering bands. Spouse exchange between men takes place, if at all, under very well-defined conditions. Marriage rituals may in themselves be simple, but the process of two families within a band, or two bands, exchanging women (or men) to set up new household units is one that always receives a lot of attention. Each hunter needs a partner, just as each gatherer needs a partner, and bands are careful that a new marriage does not leave one family short of the necessary personnel to carry on their subsistence activities. We could say that the women exchange men, or that the men exchange women, although the latter is the usual statement of the process. However one phrases the personnel exchange, the underlying fact remains that marriage is indeed an affair of the entire band. Turnbull (1968) has described with humor and sympathy how that personnel exchange occurs. The wishes of the young people are probably taken more into account in these small bands than in more urban settings. The very fluidity of the hunting band, with groups splitting off at various times of the year for various specialized types of hunting, coming together at other times, and continually recombining in various ways, makes the fact that the married pair remains stable through these changes all the more noteworthy.

With the help of the clear skies of the Near East, the early sky calendars of the Neanderthals must have become elaborated beyond the simpler European forms. But, because of the nature of the camp sites, there is no archaeological evidence for this. All kinds of notations may have been made on unbaked clay tablets and on hides, none of which would survive the centuries. It is only when these peoples are back in Europe, circa 35,000 B.C.E., that we can interpolate back to what must have been happening in the Near East in the interim.

Back in Europe With the Cro-Magnons

It is hard to keep straight the rapid sequences and the clusters of simultaneous events that exploded on the European scene when the ebullient Cro-Magnons returned at the close of the ice age that originally drove them out. Two separate cultures, the Perigordians and the Aurignacians, apparently trickled in simultaneously about 35,000 B.C.E., coexisted peacefully for about 15,000 years, and then blended with a transitional European culture, the Chatelperronian. The Perigordians had roomy cave homes with public hearths out front, with stone wall dividers, and a longhouse built at the back for comfortable group living quarters. Their tools and living patterns are easily identified, but they turn out not to be "mainstream people." The Aurignacians were somewhat different. Their tools were more elaborate and specialized; their settlement patterns involved a large central living site and satellite quarters for specialized activities. It is in their caves that we find the first cave art. In caveless regions, such as Czechoslovakia, southern Russia, and Siberia (Gravettion culture), they erected substantial longhouses and left much evidence of a rich ceremonial life. Similar evidence is found in the rare cave sites of those who stayed behind in the Near East, such as the Shanidar cave. From 20,000 to 17,000 B.C.E., there was a brief resurgence of glacial cold, and during this period a people labeled the Solutreans emerged with tools that were beautiful elaborations of the earlier Neanderthal tools, including the breathtaking laurel-leaf blade that in its most elaborate form could never be used as an implement. Were these people hide-out Neanderthals? Finally, there was the Magdalenian culture, lasting from 17,000 to 12,000 B.C.E. and bringing cave art to its greatest heights at a time when many of the animals depicted were disappearing from Europe. The Magdalenians represented the peak of the population explosion that began after the last glaciation. As ice caps receded, there was more food, both on land and at sea, and more social technologies to exploit them than *erectus* or Neanderthal had had.

What part did women play in this explosion? I suggested earlier that women's ecological skill was crucial in making the trek eastward and in making the successful settlements in new environments possible. Once migrating bands connected with the great animal herds roaming the mideastern corridor, however, band life-styles must have changed considerably. There was no longer the same dependence on plant food and less reason to practice infanticide; there was enough food for any number of babies. *Erectus* bands had first begun to cluster in France and Spain 300,000 years before, but they saw each other relatively rarely. In the Mideast, they learned to live together, to develop interband relationships. While men were organizing communal hunts, women were exercising their building skills in developing new kinds of shelters with wood, stone, and skins and in making new kinds of tools to work the animal skins the men were bringing home. (See Figure 3.2 for an imaginative reconstruction of women's activities.)

During this period, it is likely that a further development of women's interband bonding skills took place. High-density living made increasingly important the question of how children of mating age should pair. In isolated bands, or bands that at most had contact with one or two other bands, there was little choice. With more bands in contact, there was more choice.

The habit of thinking of children in terms of interband alliances, which I have suggested might have begun as far back as 50,000 B.C.E., would now be reinforced by the expanded alliance opportunities. Because many of the work settings for women in food-gathering societies are communal settings (especially for food preparation and child care), women had if anything more time for discussion of alliance possibilities than did the men, who were away tracking down bears.

Figure 3.2. Reconstruction of Cave Dwelling Life, Neanderthal.

NOTE: The top left of the figure depicts a woman painting cave wall; the foreground: girl caring for baby, woman making stone utensils, woman scraping with antler tool, older woman tending fire and infant; the middle area: cleaning hide, assembling hide into garment; far ground: foraging for food, woman and boy catching fish, woman gathering plants. Drawn by HBR.

The women might discuss the relative hunting skills and strategies used by men in different bands, particularly in regard to their effectiveness in bringing back meat to the camp sites. Making alliances with the best hunting bands through exchange of children ready for pairing would be an obvious strategy to evolve. Another characteristic to look for in a band would be the skill of its women in food gathering and in the preparation of skins for clothing and shelter. Then, finally, there were the skills of the individual young people ready for pairing. There were many things to take into account, and what the women discussed during the day would be talked over with the men around the campfire at night.

The interaction of women became more complex as environmental pressures lessened. It has already been mentioned that, with ample food supplies, there was less pressure to practice infanticide and more babies who needed care. We can imagine a period of some thousands of years in which women worked in small groups up and down the valleys of Europe, sharing new knowledge about what was edible in the environment and how to prepare it, learning from each other how to make new kinds of scrapers and bone implements as they prepared meats and hides together. As they worked, they would discuss seasonal changes in plant and animal food supplies. They would also discuss babies. It is hardly possible that menstrual cycles and their relation to birth, lactation, and weaning were not thoroughly explored in these thousands of years by women working in communal groups; it was too obvious a part of their lives to be ignored. The more primitive awareness of Neanderthal women would now be replaced by a gradually dawning comprehension not only of the fact of cycles but of their function. The lore of sun and moon and stars developed during the millennia of living in the Near East was now woven together with the recognition of menstrual cycles into a complex whole that made it possible on the one hand to predict seasonal changes in food supplies and on the other to predict the time of birth of a new infant from the time of cessation of menstruation. It was obviously useful to be able to predict both sets of events. We know that men developed the habit of making notches and lines on bones (archaeologists call them *batons*) to count sequences of lunar changes that related to seasons and to significant ritual events.[15] (Also interesting is the deciphering of lunar-phase notations on one such bone by Marshack 1972a: 89.)

Why make marks on bones?

A bone slate is small and long-lasting, it can take exceedingly fine scratching better than woods. Being relatively small, a bone slate can be carried in pocket or pouch more easily than one carries a large wooden stick, and in a culture of high mobility, where a [person] could not carry too many belongings, the small slate would be the more practical. (Marshack 1972a: 90)

How would the bone slate be used? It was partly used for ceremonies,

> but in a culture that counted "moons" there may also have been other persons keeping a notation for other purposes: perhaps for a voyage, visit, or march, or for a menstrual or pregnancy record, or for a private period of initiation. (Marshack 1972a: 90)

If the baton tradition was primarily masculine, we must look elsewhere for the women's notations, and we find them on highly abstracted female images as old as the earliest batons and animal images scattered across Europe all the way from Spain to Siberia. Marshack has studied some of these figures under a microscope and reports that they give evidence of having been marked repeatedly by different tool points, presumably at different times. The periodic markings would appear to be "evidence of a female symbol system or a form of record keeping, very likely by adult women. The markings seem to indicate a knowledge and use of symbols to document human processes and activity" (Marshack 1975: 84). Some of the female images shown in Figure 3.4 very probably had record keeping as well as ritual functions, but I do not have the information to substantiate such a statement.

To what extent men taught boys a "masculine" system of record keeping and women taught girls a "feminine" one we cannot know. Because both sexes were working on the basis of the same lunar cycle, and had to cooperate closely in use of the environment for survival, there was probably a substantial common knowledge stock passed on by both women and men to the children of a band. It is not improbable that there were special teaching ceremonies connected with puberty rites for both girls and boys. It would be at puberty that girls would be taught to keep calendars, possibly in ways not very different than those used in tribal societies today. Marshack tells us that, among Siberian people of today,

> women calculate child-birth by the phases of the moon. . . . Pregnancy has a duration of ten lunar months, and the woman keeps a sort of lunar calendar (it was always the woman who was the custodian of the lunar calendar among these nationalities). (Boris Frolov, "Stone Age Astronomers," *Moscow News*, September 4, 1965 in Marshack, 1972a)

Also,

> women among the Yurok Indians had menstrual calendars and could predict birth within a day, and . . . the Yuroks also had other tally systems. The women apparently kept a menstrual count by dropping a stick each day into a basket and kept a pregnancy count by dropping a

"month" stick each lunar month into a second basket until they reached a count of ten. (Piltina in Marshack 1972a: 337)

Calendar keeping and the design of ever more elaborated rituals around life cycle and seasonal events seem logical activities for the women, who spent so much more time at the camp sites than the men did.

I am not suggesting, however, that women were the sole designers of ceremonies. Men, deeply involved in hunting, would be more familiar with the appearances of animals on the move. When the ceremonies included painting these animals on cave walls, men may have painted the animals and women the calendrical notations or the women may have instructed the men in how to make them.

Cave art was a part of ceremonial activities ritually repeated over and over again at the same site. Many caves have been discovered in France containing well-hidden ceremonial sites. The evidence that the animals on the nearly inaccessible walls have been painted and repainted, sketched and resketched, many times, and that children and adults have performed special walks or dances before the pictures, all makes it clear that these are ceremonial rather than living centers. Because of the size of handprints and heelprints, and the occasional presence in paintings of "animal-headed" women as well as men—that is, shamans dressed to perform their rituals— it seems clear that women, men, and children were all involved.

These cave painting ceremonies were not simple hunting magic, given that they appeared to involve so many different elements of symbolism and ritual as well as references to food gathering. There are plants, fish, and birds included in the paintings, all portrayed in relation to certain seasonal concurrences. For example, spawning salmon, foaling horses, and growing grain are placed side by side. The symbolism is complex and the notation itself sometimes approaches looking like hieroglyphics. Figure 3.3 shows the range of symbols. They are simpler in the Aurignacian period, more complex in the Magdalenian, but there are similarities that point to some common tradition being evolved over large areas over a long span of time. The symbols represent a higher order of abstract intellectual conceptions of cycles in relation to environmental resources as well as skillful observations and recordings of environmental detail. Because plant food and fish as well as animals are all involved in the record, I suggest that there were women recorders as well as men. Observation of plant life was women's specialty, and we may find the foundations of their later development of agriculture in these paintings, symbolic notations, and calendrical markings. Because many of these paintings and engravings are so beautiful, we have tended to think of them as individual artistic creations. Once we think of them as reflecting the emergence of art, science, philosophy, and religion in a

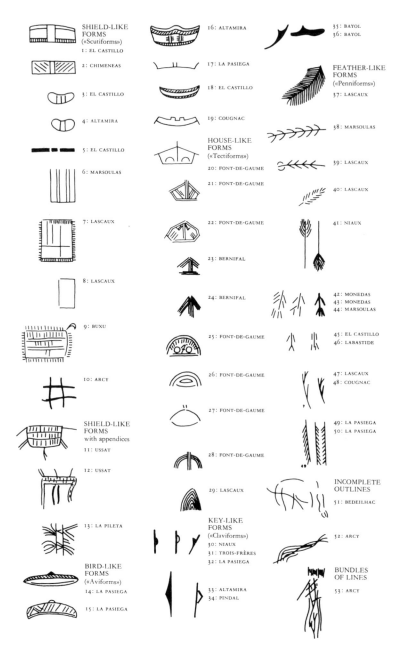

Figure 3.3. Cave Painting Symbols

SOURCE: André Leroi-Gourhan classification of Ice Age cave-painting symbols. In Marshack (1972a: 198); used by permission.

TABLE 3.1 Female Figurines From Periods Ranging From Aurignacian Through Magdalenian, Listed in Order of Completeness of Representation

Type	Use	Period
a. Faceless, otherwise realistic pregnancy figure	rock-shelter bas-relief	Upper Perigordian
b. Abstract full figure	for ritual placement	East Gravettian
c. Abstract full figure	"baton" for holding during ritual observation	Magdalenian
d. Geometric female figure	calendar bone	Upper Magdalenian
e. Abstract full figure	pendant	Upper Magdalenian
f. Abstract full figure	"disposable" for once-only use	Magdalenian
g. Double breast	pendant	East Gravettian
h. Forked image with vulva	pendant	East Gravettian
i. Forked image with vulva	pendant	Middle Magdalenian
j. Buttocks silhouette	cave wall painting, stone slab engravings	From Aurignacian to Magdalenian
k. Ritual vulval disc	"charm"	Aurignacian Through Magdalenian
l. Hand (praying female?)	on bone batons, cave walls	Aurignacian to Magdalenian

SOURCE: Data from Marshack (1972a).

delicate synchronization of recorded observation and ceremonial life that unfolded over many centuries, it gives us quite another sense of the quality and complexity of life of the Upper Paleolithic peoples.

Not only was there cave art and its associated ceremonial life, there was also "home art," or "camp-site art," and its associated ceremonial life.

Most of the calendar bones belong to home art, as do animal and fertility figurines and engraved stone slabs. If we keep in mind the users of these ritual objects, then it seems at least likely that the men might make the animal figurines and engravings and the women the fertility figurines.[16] Marshack has made a very interesting photographic collection of these figurines, which makes it possible for the first time for the layperson to see the range of styles and possible uses for them. Prior to the Marshack analysis, the sheer diversity in the figurines, as well as their ubiquity all over Europe, was puzzling. Now it is possible to suggest some themes and functions for the figurines.

Table 3.1 presents all the different kinds of figurines, grouping them thematically rather than chronologically and listing them in order of completeness of representation.[17] Some of the figurines are pendants, meant to be worn around the neck. Some are "disposables," made perhaps by a woman as a prayer for a successful pregnancy and then thrown away.[18] Others are clearly ritual objects to be held in the hand during ceremonies, and they bear evidence of much handling. Still others were evidently placed on some kind of stand for ritual display and/or veneration. Figure 3.4 consists of a series of sketches and line drawings of the figurines listed.

Some of the earliest and some of the latest figurines have similar styles, so no particular thematic evolution emerges here, although it well might if I had fuller information. In addition to the classification by type of use—pendant, statuary object of veneration, disposable prayer, charm—there is probably an implication of different ritual meanings in the different aspects of the female emphasized—breast, vulva, buttocks, hands, full figure. Currently, however, there is no way to interpret these. It is useful to be aware of a probable wide range of meanings so that we do not underestimate the extent of ceremonial observances associated with female figurines. At this time, the functional and impersonal quality of these figurines should be appreciated. There is no hint of the existence of an "adoration of women" in these faceless and variously styled figures. The whole mother-goddess phenomenon and the accompanying complex of male-female attitudes and relationships comes later. The one exception to this is the very first figurine (a) listed in Figure 3.4; it comes from early Perigordian times yet has many of the attributes of the much later agricultural mother-goddess; the half-moon (or horn) that she holds in her hand becomes part of the rich symbolism associated later with mother-goddesses. Because this figurine is so early, it would be a mistake to associate later symbolic meanings with it, but we see the early signs, perhaps, of the mother-goddess idea here.

We will probably never know how many of these figurines were made by males, how many by females, and to what extent females rather than males presided over the ceremonies associated with their use. It seems reasonable to infer, however, based on other evidence mentioned of women's participation in ritual, that some of them were made by women and some of the ceremonies presided over by women.

The cave art, the bone records, and the figurines all point to a highly developed capacity for both abstract thought and imagery in the late Paleolithic. A great deal has been written, particularly by Jungian "human potential" theorists, about the superior capacity for imagery of early humans. McCulley (1971) suggests that the development of verbal thinking overlaid the imaging capacity but that it is possible for persons to be in touch with the deep psychic structures that generate archetypal forms and patternings for contemporary experience. These forms are generic to the human observer-responder from ancient days. McCulley (1971) draws heavily on the work of André Leroi-Gourhan in interpreting cave paintings

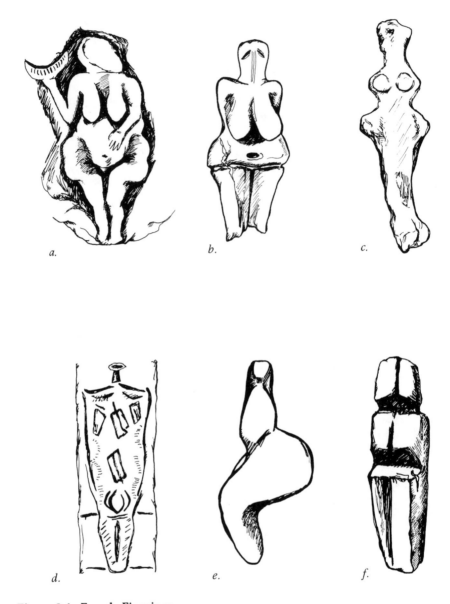

Figure 3.4. Female Figurines

NOTE: a. faceless female in bas-relief; b. buxom female image, fired clay; c. pregnant female, reindeer antler; d. female with tiny head on calendar bone; e. stylized female, polished coal pendant; f. crude female figurine, coal. Redrawn by HBR.

to suggest the omnipresence of archetypal forms in the paintings to the exclusion of any recognition of abstract, notational representations.

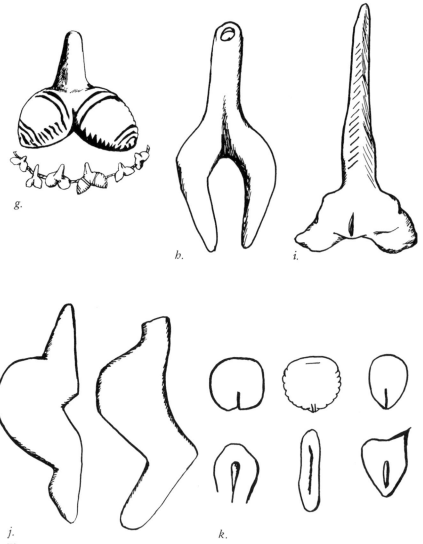

Figure 3.4. Continued

NOTE: g. ivory bead double breast pendant; h. forked image with vulva, ivory pendant; i. forked image with vulva, baton; j. sculpted female buttocks; k. ritual vulva disks. Redrawn by HBR.

Without in the least minimizing the importance of archetypal forms that may very well reflect basic psychic structures found in all humans in every culture and time period, I suggest that an exclusive focus on archetypal imagery in the analysis of cave art is a disservice both to Cro-Magnon and to modern woman and man. If the human race "dreamed before it thought," dreams soon taught thinking. The sheer growth in the area of the cortex of the ancestral brain assured the evolution of a new series of processes: observation, memory, comparison, evaluation, and selection (Walters 1953: 38). Humans, interacting with their environment in ways discussed earlier in this chapter, equipped with the remarkable scanning, storing, retrieving, and synthesizing mechanisms of these new brains, were thinking essentially as we think. Their powers of observation and recording were the product of capacity, social need, and training. If our contemporary educational techniques leave some of these capacities untouched, that is our problem, and a remediable one. In short, we should neither romanticize the imaging capacity of Paleolithic peoples nor downgrade their intellection capacities. We are recognizably the same family, in terms of mental functioning.

Along with the evidence of the development of an increasingly rich culture from Aurignacian to Magdalenian times, we also find that by the time of the Magdalenians weapons were being used not only against animals but also against humans. By 12,000 B.C.E., the Magdalenians were occupying three to four times more sites than their predecessors ever had, taking up land that had never had human settlements before.[19] It is extraordinary not that we begin to find evidence of interband hostilities but that we find it so late in human history. It is certainly true that bands did not meet each other often. Estimates of territorial ranges for contemporary hunting and gathering bands are from a low of one person per 300 square miles up to three persons per 1 square mile (Fried 1967: 55). Even though territories can be identified, there is seldom exclusive use of them (Fried 1967: 60, 67). There are always conditions under which other bands may hunt on one's territory. Our notions about the importance of territoriality have little basis in either primate or human history. Most primates have overlapping territories, sometimes even overlapping central cores, just as human bands do (Fried 1967: 45-49).

Evidence from existing hunting and gathering bands supports the archaeological finding of peaceableness in the Paleolithic. Hostilities would be confined to raiding parties with very limited objectives, probably a consequence of interband ceremonial observances as societies developed ranking and ceremonial specialists and came to notice each other's rudimentary surpluses. Larger aggregations of bands—tribal and prestate associations—were much more the consequence of interband ceremonial gatherings than of competitive interaction or conquest. Fried (1967) points out that the organizing potential of ceremonial occasions is far greater than the organizing potential of warfare. War is irregular, brief. Ceremonials are regular, frequently lasting for weeks, and require a lot of preparation. Berndt (1962) reports a pig festival in an Australian New Guinea tribe that requires six years of preparation. The war leader, a temporary figure, would have far less status than the ceremonial leader, who would always have a great deal to do in preparation for the next intercommunity ceremonial. Because the work of women is important in ceremonial preparations, this suggests active participation of women in Paleolithic "public life."

We can think of Magdalenian times, then, as an era in which there was a great increase in interband ceremonial occasions with increasing population density and interband contact. The larger caves became more and more important not only as a setting for ceremonies and the elaboration of ritual art but for all kinds of public uses. Pfeiffer suggests that

> the caves represent protoinstitutional sites before the coming of separate specialized institutions; from time to time they probably served as prehistoric archives, shrines, offices, schools, vigil places, theaters. Indeed, for limited periods at least some of them may have been as bustling for those times as downtown business and cultural centers are today. (1969: 236)

Some of these caves were very large indeed. Howell (1968: 288) mentions an occupation site in Spain, covering more than 4,000 square meters and opening into another, adjacent occupation site. It is not hard to imagine a complex social life in such a setting. Something happened to the Magdalenian culture, however, and it died out. Perhaps it was too specialized and failed to adapt when certain of the resources it had counted on too heavily were depleted. Whatever the cause, the "petered-out" Magdalenian was replaced by a less advanced culture, the Azilian.

The Magdalenian period, however, saw a very significant shift in the hunting-gathering way of life that was to pave the way for the agricultural revolution both in the Middle East and in Europe. Binford (1968) identifies the lever for change in the rapid development toward the end of the Paleolithic of *facilities* as contrasted with *tools*. The first breakthrough for hominids in the development process came with the mastery of tool making, which facilitates energy transfer (spears, digging sticks, and so on; Binford 1968: 272). The second breakthrough involved the construction of facilities that conserve energy: fish weirs, nets, pottery. Containers, and the storage principle they embody, developed *before* agriculture.

One important aspect of the container revolution was the discovery, presumably by the women foragers, of seeds as food. Seeds are nutritious, abundant, and store easily, but only if one has containers. Also, seeds are hard to digest without grinding and boiling. Grindstones and containers for storing and boiling food appear in Europe and the Middle East well before the discovery of agriculture. Washburn and Lancaster suggest that the grinding-boiling technologies spread along the Arctic route to the New

World, "setting the stage for nearly simultaneous discovery of agriculture in both the New and Old Worlds" (1968: 295).

In this view, it is the seed-using technology developed by women that paves the way for agriculture. The seed-using technology is not the whole story, of course, but is part of the great worldwide explosion in food technology that leads to the use of river and sea food and a whole range of nuts as well as seeds. Boats, which made water a resource instead of a barrier, were constructed for the first time during the late Paleolithic. This is also the time when dogs were first domesticated and used for hunting. The first bows appeared also. Everything points to a severe pressure of existing population on a dwindling supply of game. If game shortages led to these discoveries, the vast increase in food supplies that the new technology made possible immediately led to higher population densities in many areas. This cycle of increasing food supplies and increasing population densities was particularly dependent on the discoveries, skill, and ingenuity of women as food gatherers and processors. The old vegetarian diet could be eaten by foragers on the very spot where it was gathered. The new vegetarian diet needed preparation to be made digestible. Unlike meat, which could be simply roasted whole, grains had to be processed before they could be cooked.

It would be absurd to say that all these new developments stemmed from the increasing interaction of the women in the bands all up and down the valleys of Europe. Some part of the developments did happen there, however, and we have the records of the evolution of the new preagricultural knowledge stock on the walls of the caves of France, with their detailed notations of plants, animals, and fish and the seasons of seeding and harvest for each. Some part of the developments happened too in the hunting expeditions in those valleys, as many braved frightening waters to find food when game gave out.

What was the status of women toward the end of the Magdalenian? It may well have been a time of sex egalitarianism, given that both sexes were being noticeably inventive. Women may have had more time for the development of ceremonials than they did formerly, as their new seed technologies led to more time spent on food processing as compared with gathering, thus increasing the amount of time spent at the home base. With food supplies abundant, and with the possibility of storage against future scarcity, children would be valued more. Accordingly, female fertility would also be valued. The fertility figurines hint at the importance of fertility for both women and men and also at the continued elaboration of ceremonial status for women as well as men.

It must be confessed that the evidence for the patterning of women's roles in relation to men from early hominid times down through the

Paleolithic is scanty to the extreme. Readers will have noted this for themselves. Most of the evidence is about the band's way of life, not about the presence or absence of sex-based division of labor. This chapter has thus largely been a work of imaginative reconstruction, relating as far as possible to the available archaeological evidence. The full participation of the female in discovering environmental resources and inventing tools with which to use those resources has been emphasized at every turn, as has her participation in the creation and elaboration of social bonds and ceremonials. While an egalitarian society has been depicted, these millennia should hardly be thought of as a utopian era in human history. Droughts, ice ages, and danger from powerful animal predators framed a very uncomfortable and insecure existence. Bands sometimes turned on each other in violence, though not often. Infanticide was a necessary feature of responsible parenthood, and cannibalism a consequence of food shortage. The extraordinary message that comes through the evidence of camp and cave home sites, and from cave paintings and stone and bone carvings, is that hominids were continually finding new ways to respond to their changing environments. The early emergence of home sites shows the conserving, protecting side of hominid evolution, and the long treks over every continent show the adventurous side. Because male and female hominids maintained home sites together, and trekked together, one can hardly argue that the inclination either to conserve or to adventure is sex linked. Both are basic traits of the human species.

We have come now to the threshold of the Neolithic, and we are ready to examine the special roles that emerged for women with the development of the first settled societies.

Appendix

TABLE 3A.1 Simplified Chronology of Archaeological Ages and Cultures (Focus on Europe)

Geologic Age	Archaeological Age	Number of Years Ago	Species	
Lower Pleistocene	Lower Paleolithic	2,000,000	Erectus	Oldowan, Acheulian, Abbevillian,
Middle Pleistocene				Clactonian, Tayacian
Upper Pleistocene	Middle Paleolithic	1,000,000	Neanderthal	Levallois, Mousterian
Holocene		70,000		
LAST ICE AGE	Upper Paleolithic	35,000-18,000	Cro-Magnon to Sapiens	Chateperronian, Perogordian, Aurignacian, Gravettian
		20,000-17,000	Sapiens	Solutrean
		17,000-12,000	Sapiens	Magdalenian
	Mesolithic	12,000-9,000	Sapiens	Azilian

NOTE: This chronology only includes cultures mentioned in this chapter and is by no means complete. It is based on the discussion in *Prehistory and the Beginnings of Civilization* (Hawkes and Woolley 1963) and *The Neanderthals* (Constable 1973) and has not been altered to include the additional 1 million years prior to 2,000,000 B.C.E. that the Leakey findings have since ascribed to *erectus* existence.

Notes

1. Note that since this was written the prehistory of *erectus* has been pushed back another million and a half years.

2. There is a consistent tendency to underestimate the female as toolmaker, whether in archaeological or ethnographic investigation. Because she was a tool user from the start, this is rather absurd. Seashells as kitchen tools, found in the earliest sites, were certainly being used by both sexes and may as well have been "invented" by women as by men. O. T. Mason, writing in the 1890s, was very conscious of the woman as toolmaker: "[She] will be seen in the role of potter, butcher, cook, beast of burden, fire maker and tender, miller, stonecutter (stone griddle maker), most delicate and ingenious weaver, engineer (devising a mechanical press and sieve in one woven bag and using a lever, baker, and preserver of food. Add to this her function of brewer, and you have no mean collection of primitive industries performed by one little body" (1894: 40).

3. If Rowell (1973) is correct, estrus is not that clear-cut a phenomenon in monkey troops either, which means that the evolution of the female-male relationship has been even slower and more gradual than we thought.

4. Although we do not normally think of house building as a female activity today, there are many references to house building by women in the ethnographic literature: Aberle (1962), Sterling (1965), Sullerot (1968), Mason (1894), Briffault ([1927] 1959), Fraser (1968), and Turnbull (1968). Most of these references describe contemporary (nineteenth- and twentieth-century) house-building activities of women. Others refer to the Middle Ages and to ancient times. Cole (1973) has written the most comprehensive study to date on women as builders and architects, but most of her material is drawn from North America.

5. This is a concept developed by Magorah Maruyama (1963).

6. I am not prepared to deal with the question of how the hominids got rid of their fur. The aquatic-period theory of Sir Alistair Hardy, described in Elaine Morgan's *Descent of Woman* (1972), is interesting, but we need a good deal more evidence before putting our early ancestors into the ocean for a prolonged period.

7. The possibilities and limitations of use of ethnological data on contemporary hunting and gathering societies to make inferences about the life of early hominid bands were repeatedly discussed by both ethnologists and archaeologists at the 1966 Man the Hunter Symposium held at the University of Chicago (see especially Clark 1968: 276-80). Given that each existing society is the product of as long a period of evolution as any other contemporary society of the twentieth century, there are no simple generalizations about ancient foragers that can be made from modern ones. Yet knowledge about technologies, and the use of resources and space, among current foragers can be combined with archaeological findings on such sites as Olduvai and Terra Amata to make possible some imaginative reconstructions of daily life. These images may turn out to be wrong when further information is available, but they are the best we can do at this time.

8. Information on the Swanscombe site is from Pfeiffer (1969) and Constable (1973).

9. Because the digging stick is a primary tool for women in subsistence societies today, both for food gathering and for horticulture, it seems reasonable to suggest that they discovered the fire-hardening process on their own.

10. Sally Binford (1968: 108) has written in some detail about the tools made and used by women for the preparation of skins. Another interesting source for exploring the life of Neanderthals and Sapiens in a presumed transitional era, from an imagined female perspective, is in the well-researched novels of Jean Auel, beginning with *The Clan of the Cave Bear* (1980).

11. A 40-year-old skeleton at the Shanidar site indicated that a Neanderthal band had allowed a boy baby with a serious birth defect of right arm and shoulder to live and nurtured him to a relatively ripe old age.

12. Dr. Jock Cobb, of the University of Colorado Medical Center, Denver, Department of Preventive Medicine (personal communication, 1974), reports that women living near the equator apparently have a marked tendency to ovulate during the full moon. If a biological regularity occurred in identical cycles with a large number of women, this would soon create a sense of social cycle. Some of the rapidly accumulating body of research on the control of ovulation by light is summarized by Gay Luce. According to Luce (1971), the city woman with irregular menstrual periods can simulate the effect of the full moon on ovulation by keeping a light on all night for the period when ovulation should normally be taking place—and thus become perfectly regular.

13. Estimates by E. S. Deevey (1960).

14. It was Morgan's misinterpretation of Iroquois practices that gave rise to Engels's view of marriage as introducing the domination of females by males after an earlier group marriage situation. Ceremonial interband pairing antedates any kind of economic surplus or seizure of political power (see Engels [1884] 1942).

15. Marshack has expressed himself strongly on this point in a communication to the author, and there seems to be no reason to question the careful linking of evidence and intuition that stands behind his statement that the baton tradition must be regarded as a masculine one.

16. An alternative interpretation of the use of the fertility figurines is that they were not ritual objects at all but simply dolls for children's play. It seems not unlikely that some of the figurines served as dolls, but until there is more evidence about play activities I prefer to follow the domestic ritual-object line of reasoning. The figurines could have served double duty for mother and daughter as fertility charm and doll. See the work of M. I. Finley (1971) for a different interpretation of all female figures and of the role of women in prehistory.

17. This organization of the figurines is my own, and I take full responsibility for any possible misinterpretations.

18. These, it seems to me, are the ones most likely to have been used as dolls in children's play.

19. There were then nearly 5 million humans, according to E. S. Deevey's (1960) calculations.

References

Aberle, David F. 1962. "Matrilineal Descent in Crosscultural Perspectives." Pp. 655-730 in *Matrilineal Kinship*, edited by David M. Schneider and Kathleen Gough. Berkeley: University of California Press.

Altmann, Stuart A. and Jeanne Altmann. 1970. *Baboon Ecology: African Field Research*. Chicago: University of Chicago Press.

Auel, Jean. 1980. *The Clan of the Cave Bear*. New York: Crown.

Berndt, Ronald M. 1962. *Excess and Restraint: Social Control Among a New Guinea Mountain People*. Chicago: University of Chicago Press.

Bicchieri, M. 1972. *Hunters and Gatherers Today*. New York: Holt, Rinehart & Winston.

Binford, Sally R. 1968. "Early Upper Pleistocene Adaptations in Levant." *American Anthropologist* 70(August):708.

Briffault, Robert. [1927] 1959. *Mothers: A Study of the Origins of Sentiments and Institutions*. New York: Humanities Press.

Clark, J. Desmond. 1968. "Studies of Hunters and Gatherers as an Aid to the Interpretation of Prehistoric Societies." Pp. 276-80 in *Man the Hunter*, edited by Richard B. Lee and Irven De Vore. Chicago: Aldine.

Cole, Doris. 1973. *From Tipi to Skyscraper: A History of Women in Architecture*. Boston: I Press.

Constable, George. 1973. *The Neanderthals*. New York: Time-Life.

Dahlberg, Francis, ed. 1981. *Women, the Gatherer*. New Haven, CT: Yale University Press.

Deetz, James F. 1968. "Hunters in Archeological Perspective" (Discussions, part 6). Pp. 281-85 in *Man the Hunter*, edited by Richard B. Lee and Irven De Vore. Chicago: Aldine.

Deevey, E. S. 1960. "Human Population." *Scientific American* (September):195-96.

Engels, Frederich. [1884] 1942. *The Origin of the Family, Private Property, and the State*. New York: International.

Farb, Peter. 1968. *Man's Rise to Civilization: As Shown by the Indians of North America from Primeval Times to the Coming of the Industrial State*. New York: Dutton.

Finley, M. I. 1971. "Archeology and History." *Daedalus* 100:168-86.

Fraser, Douglas. 1968. *Village Planning in the Primitive World*. New York: George Braziller.

Fried, Morton H. 1967. *The Evolution of Political Society: An Essay in Political Anthropology.* New York: Random House.

Frobenius, Leo. 1974. *Childhood of Man.* Magnolia, MA: Peter Smith.

Gardner, Peter M. 1968. Discussant in *Man the Hunter*, edited by Richard B. Lee and Irven De Vore. Chicago: Aldine.

Hawkes, Jacquetta and Sir Leonard Woolley. 1963. *History of Mankind. Vol. 1. Prehistory and the Beginnings of Civilization.* New York: Harper & Row.

Hogg, Garry. 1966. *Cannibalism and Human Sacrifice.* New York: Citadel.

Howell, F. Clark. 1968. "The Use of Ethnography in Reconstructing the Past" (Discussions, part 6). Pp. 287-89 in *Man the Hunter*, edited by Richard B. Lee and Irven De Vore. Chicago: Aldine.

Kaberry, Phyllis. 1939. *Aboriginal Woman: Sacred and Profane.* London: Routledge.

Kagan, Jerome, ed. 1967. *Creativity and Learning.* Boston: Houghton Mifflin.

Kagan, Jerome. 1971. *Change and Continuity in Infancy.* New York: John Wiley.

Laughlin, William S. 1968. "Hunting: An Integrating Biobehavior System and Its Evolutionary Importance." Pp. 304-20 in *Man the Hunter*, edited by Richard B. Lee and Irven De Vore. Chicago: Aldine.

Leakey, Richard. 1981. *The Making of Mankind.* New York: Dutton.

Lee, Richard B. 1968. "What Hunters Do for a Living, or, How to Make out on Scarce Resources." Pp. 30-48 in *Man the Hunter*, edited by Richard B. Lee and Irven De Vore. Chicago: Aldine.

Lee, Richard B. and Irven De Vore, eds. 1968. *Man the Hunter.* Chicago: Aldine.

Luce, Gay. 1971. *Body Time: Psychological Rhythms and Social Stress.* New York: Pantheon.

Marshack, Alexander. 1972a. *The Roots of Civilization.* New York: McGraw-Hill.

———. 1972b. "Upper Paleolithic Notation and Symbol." *Science* 178:817-28.

———. 1975. "Exploring the Mind of Ice Age Man." *National Geographic* 147:62-89.

———. 1976. "Implications of the Paleolithic Symbolic Evidence for the Origin of Language." *American Scientist* 64:136-45.

Martin, M. Kay and Barbara Voorhies. 1975. *Female of the Species.* New York: Columbia University Press.

Maruyama, Magorah. 1963. "The Second Cybernetics—Deviatio—Amplifying Mutual Causal Processes." *American Scientist* 51:164-79, 250-56.

Mason, O. T. 1894. *Woman's Share in Primitive Culture.* Ann Arbor, MI: Finch.

McCulley, Robert S. 1971. *Rorschach Theory and Symbolism.* Baltimore: William and Wilkins.

Morgan, Elaine. 1972. *Descent of Woman.* New York: Stein and Day.

Morgan, Lewis Henry. [1877] 1963. *Ancient Society*, edited by Eleanor Burke Leacock. New York: World.

Oakley, Kenneth P. 1961. "On Man's Use of Fire, with Comments on Tool-Making and Hunting." Pp. 176-93 in *Social Life of Early Man*, edited by Sherwood Washburn. Chicago: Aldine.

Pfeiffer, John E. 1969. *The Emergence of Man.* New York: Harper & Row.

Rowell, Thelma. 1973. *The Social Behavior of Monkeys.* Baltimore: Penguin (as reviewed by James Loy in *Science* 180[May 11]:602-3).

Sterling, Paul. 1965. *Turkish Village.* New York: John Wiley.

Sullerot, Evelyne. 1968. *Histoire et Sociologie du Travail Féminin.* Paris: Société Nouvelle des Editions Gonthier.

Turnbull, Colin. 1968. *The Forest People.* New York: Simon & Schuster.

Walters, W. Grey. 1953. *The Living Brain.* New York: Norton.

Washburn, Sherwood L. and Irven De Vore. 1961. "Social Life of Baboon and Early Man." Pp. 91-105 in *Social Life of Early Man*, edited by Sherwood L. Washburn. Chicago: Aldine.

Washburn, Sherwood L. and C. S. Lancaster. 1968. "The Evolution of Hunting." Pp. 293-303 in *Man the Hunter*, edited by Richard B. Lee and Irven De Vore. Chicago: Aldine.

White, Edmund. 1973. *The First Men.* New York: Time-Life.

4

From Gatherers to Planters: Women's Moment in History

The transition described in this chapter, from the hunting and gathering way of life to the agricultural settled way of life, ostensibly began about 12,000 B.C.E. In fact, the process really began at least 10,000 years earlier, as described in the last chapter. On the one hand, Neanderthal's and Cro-Magnon's improved hunting techniques led to a vigorous onslaught on the dwindling herds of large animals that roamed the warmer lands fringing the glacier country. On the other hand, women were developing the new seed-processing technology. While behaviors changed very slowly, there certainly were some "aha!" experiences preceding the development of agriculture. How excited the first person must have been who realized that seed spilled by chance near a camp site the year before had now sprouted into wheat. And the first baby lamb that missed the usual fate of being eaten when its wild mother was roasted must certainly have caused a flash in someone's mind as it tottered uncertainly after its new "mother" as camp broke: We don't have to hunt meat, we can raise it.

Nevertheless, the change in ways of procuring food moved as slowly as the glaciers themselves. We usually do what we know how to do best, and earlier humans knew gathering and hunting best. We can watch their slowly changing diet through the changing character of the debris that archaeologists have unearthed from ancient sites. Flannery describes how, after 20,000 B.C.E. in the Taurus-Zagros region (parts of modern Turkey and Iraq), large animal remains were increasingly supplemented by "traces of smaller, humbler creatures: turtles, land snails, fish, fresh-water crabs and mollusks, partridges and migratory water birds" (in Leonard 1973: 21). An increasing variety of nuts and seeds would also be found in such layer-by-layer analysis. When the 10,000-year transition was over, women and men stood in a different relationship to one another. The earliest development of agriculture, and the settlements around which it was pursued, were women's special work. The challenge of dealing for the first time in human history with continuing residence in a small area, with clear rules of access to land and the development of food-storage techniques and facilities, led to what might be thought of as women's brief period of "dominance" in history: the matrilocal period[1] in which the women of a village exchanged men with other villages.

In the previous chapter, we saw the Cro-Magnons living in clusters of up to 100 people. But those who moved on to Europe and those who stayed behind in the Middle East continued this clustering process even while they remained nomads, and the cave settlements described in Europe were matched by the caves of Shanidar in Iraq and of Belt and Hotu on the Caspian. Hunting and gathering bands were spread out all around the famous fertile crescent, the arc that inscribes the Arabian desert, curving northward from the Syrian coastal hills, east across the low hills that border the great Anatolian plain, and back down the foothills of the Zagreb Mountains. There, streams from the higher mountains, and a light rainfall, provide just enough moisture for a good grass cover without irrigation but not enough for forests.

Life was good for these people. The composition of their diet was changing, but there were plenty of grains, nuts, roots, and fruits to supplement the meat and fish. Archaeological evidence continues to point to a relatively peaceable way of life. Human violence against other humans occasionally shows up in bashed skulls, but infrequently. Alland (1962: 2), writing about a much later period, describes occasions of peaceful interpenetration of tribes in the African forests: Newcomers may settle in the "empty spaces" of another tribe's territory, amicably working out with that tribe who has the right to what resources in the area. If this could be true in times of greater population density, it is not hard to visualize a similar process of peaceful accommodation among the nomadic bands of Europe and the Middle East.

Declining supplies of game meant that women had to provide increasing amounts of plant food. Women would be very aware that the men were staying away longer at a time, even while coming back with less meat.

Women and men had different kinds of teachers and therefore were learning different kinds of things. The plants taught the women; the animals taught the men. The men knew things about speed and strategy and also about persevering. A man can wear out any animal he hunts because he can persist longer than the animal being chased, even though the man is slower moving. So, when animals became harder to find, more perseverance was required. Also, men killed everything they found. Women found that, if they left some of the plants and roots in the soil when they were gathering, they would grow again in the same abundance as before for picking on a return visit. They were learning to practice conservation.

The fact that meat was getting more scarce put greater pressure on the supply of plant foods that grew near home base. What was needed was for more things to grow—more plants, more animals. The problem was *fertility*. The Cro-Magnons and their Neanderthal cousins had both been pondering fertility a long time, as we saw in the last chapter. Who knows how the first thoughts about fertility came? Perhaps they initially came through the impact of human experiences rather than through animal and plant observation: puzzling over the death of a woman, the death of a child, moving from the sorrow of bereavement to the thought of a woman's womb, source of new life. Certainly, burial rituals already showed very complex human ponderings about meanings beyond the immediate present. The fertility of women may have been inseparable from that of animals in the minds of the early hunters, because they depended so very much on both. We find such a possible linkage in a discovery from the Gravettian period. A site containing a kiln and the remains of a round earth-and-twig hut produced broken pieces of animal figures mingled with parts of figures of women. Might this have been the quarters of a Paleolithic medicine man (Hawkes and Woolley 1963: 135)? While animal and human figurines are sometimes found together, the female figurines are often found alone. These figurines were examined in Chapter 3, where we assumed that, in addition to shamans specializing in cave art and figures, there were women who made these figures for their own use. The practice of making clay figurines (usually unbaked) came with hunting bands to the Middle East, where the custom flourished. We find these figurines everywhere, still primarily as depersonalized special-purpose objects, although occasionally a beautiful "Venus"-type statuette appears.

All this pondering about fertility sooner or later led to thinking about the procreative powers of female animals in a new way. If hunters captured a female with a baby, they could bring both home and *raise* meat, instead of killing it on the spot. It does not matter whether the thought came first to the men or to the women. Although it meant more work, it also meant more food.

Large animals would not be very convenient to bring home, but there were wild sheep and goats and pigs in the fertile crescent. Caring for sheep is currently a woman's job in some parts of Asia, and in New Guinea women breast-feed piglets when necessary (Leonard 1973: 79). It is likely that the women of the late Paleolithic were in charge of the first domestic animals. Whatever the sequence of events, goats and sheep began to be kept near the home base, and from then on it became more complicated to leave and move everything to a new home base.

There is some disagreement about whether the domestication of animals or plants came first. In fact, both were probably happening at the same time. There is evidence from campfire remains as long ago as 20,000 B.C.E. that women had discovered the food value of einkorn, a kind of wild wheat that grows all through the fertile crescent. An enterprising Oklahoma agronomist, Professor Jack Harlan of the University of Oklahoma (Leonard 1973: 22-24), noticed several years ago, on an expedition to eastern Turkey, how thick these stands of wild einkorn grew. He tried harvesting some, and once he had resorted to a 9,000-year-old flint sickle blade set in a new wooden handle (he tried to use his bare hands first, with disastrous results), he was able to come away with an excellent harvest. After weighing what he had reaped, he estimated that a single good stand of einkorn would feed a family for a whole year. He also found that the grains had 50% more protein than the wheat we now use in North America for bread flour. Einkorn grains are found everywhere on the ancient home-base sites of the fertile crescent, either as roasted hulls in cooking hearths or as imprints in the mud-and-straw walls of the earliest preagriculture huts.

It would be inevitable that grains from sheaves of einkorn carried in from a distant field would drop in well-trodden soil just outside the home base or perhaps in a nearby pile of refuse. When the band returned the following year to this camp site—perhaps a favorite one, given that not all camp sites were revisited—there would be a fine stand of einkorn waiting for them right at their doorstep. We might say that the plants taught the women how to cultivate them. Planting, however, was quite a step beyond just leaving some stalks at the site where they were picked, to seed themselves for the next year. There was less reason for deliberate planting as long as bands were primarily nomadic and there was plenty of game to follow. But in time there was a premium on camp sites that would have abundant grain and fruit and nuts nearby, and then there was some purpose in scattering extra grain on the ground near the camp site for the next year. Because of the construction of the seed, einkorn easily plants itself, so it was a good plant for initiating humans into agriculture.[2]

Gradually, bands lengthened their stays at their more productive home bases, harvesting what had been "planted" more or less intentionally and letting the few sheep they had raised from infancy graze on nearby hills. One year, there would be such a fine stand of wheat at their favorite home base, and so many sheep ambling about, that a band would decide just to stay for a while and not move on that year.

If any one band of nomads could have anticipated what lay in store for humankind as a result of that fateful decision (made separately by thousands of little bands over the next 10,000 years), would they after all have moved on? While it may have been a relief not to be on the move, they in fact exchanged a life of relative ease, with enough to eat and few possessions, for a life of hard work, enough to eat, and economic surplus. As Childe says, "A mild acquisitiveness could now take its place among human desires" (Childe 1963: 265).

Successful nomads have a much easier life than do farmers. Among the Kung bushmen today, the men hunt about four days a week and the women only need to work two and a half days at gathering to feed their families amply for a week. (At that, meat is a luxury item, and most of the nourishment comes from nuts and roots.) The rest of their time is leisure, to be enjoyed in visiting, creating and carrying out rituals, and just "being" (Lee and De Vore 1968).[3]

The First Settlements

For better or worse, the women and the men settled down. They settled in the caves of Belt and Hotu to a prosperous life of farming and herding on the Caspian. They settled in Eynan, Jericho, Jarmo, Beidha, Catal Huyuk, Hacilar, Arpachiyah, and Kherokitia in Cyprus, and in uncounted villages that no archaeologist's shovel has touched. These places were home-base sites first, some going back thousands of years. By 10,000 B.C.E., Eynan had 50 houses, small stone domes, seven meters in diameter, around a central area with storage pits. This was probably preagricultural, still a hunting and gathering band, but a settled one. The village covered 2,000 square meters. Each hut had a hearth, and child and infant burials were found under some of the floors. Three successive layers of 50 stone houses have been found at the same site, so it must have been a remarkably stable site for a settlement.

What was life like, once bands settled down? This was almost from the start a woman's world. She would mark out the fields for planting, because she knew where the grain grew best, and would probably work in the fields together with the other women of the band. There would not be separate fields at first, but, as the former nomads shifted from each sleeping in individual huts to building houses for family groups of mother, father, and children, a separate family feeling must have developed and women may have divided the fields by family groups.

Their fire-hardened pointed digging sticks, formerly used in gathering, now became a multipurpose implement for planting and cultivating the soil. At harvest time, everyone, including the children, would help bring in the grain. The women also continued to gather fruit and nuts, again with the help of the children. The children watched the sheep and goats, but the women did the milking and cheese making. Ethnologists who have studied both foraging and agricultural societies comment on the change in the way of life for children that comes with agriculture. Whereas in foraging societies they have no responsibilities beyond feeding themselves and learning the hunting and foraging skills they will need, and therefore they have much leisure, it is very common in agricultural societies to put children to work at the age of 3, chasing birds from the food plots. Older children watch the animals and keep them out of the planted areas (Whiting 1968: 337; United Nations 1974).

I am assuming that the pressure of needing more hands that is felt by agricultural societies today was a pressure that began to be felt early among the newly settled horticulturalists and that children were enlisted as auxiliary labor from the beginning. In the discussion that follows on the heavy work load that fell on farming women, it should be remembered that children too shared this work load. Whiting suggests that the more punitive child rearing that develops concurrently with giving serious responsibility to children for fields and animals accounts in part "for the reluctance of hunters and gatherers to change their ways and become part of the modern world" (Whiting 1968: 337).

Space does not permit adequate attention to the changing situation of children through time. Because children move in their mothers' life spaces up to the first 10 years or so of their lives, however, restriction in life space for the one is usually also restriction in space for the other. We will see how confinement, beginning with the mild confinement of the agrovillage, both increases the punitive quality of mother-child interaction and at the same time creates new opportunities for understanding human *growth* as human *development* as mothers watch children grow up. De Mause (1974), who takes a grim view of adult-child relations through most of history, suggests that the relationship mode in antiquity was primarily *infanticidal and abusive;* that this gave way in the fourth to thirteenth centuries C.E. to the *abandonment mode,* when children were primarily turned over to servants and there was much heavy beating; and that the fourteenth to seventeenth centuries represent the *ambivalent mode,* when parents became aware that children could be shaped but did most of it by beating. From the eighteenth century on, he sees the *intrusive mode,* involving control of children's minds; the *socialization mode,* involving training instead of conquering; and finally the *helping mode,* with parental empathy as the key to that helpfulness.

In my view, all six of these modes have coexisted from the time of the earliest agrovillages. The proportions, however, have changed over time. To the extent that women are confined with their children to very limited spaces, the abusive and abandonment modes will be present. All the same, loving children, playing with them for the sheer joy of it, and comforting them in distress, are traits to be found in the mammal world and are never absent in the human world.[4] I have gone into this amount of detail here because it is in the agrovillages that the more complex and ambivalent modes of mother-child relationship began to develop. With settled life, motherhood becomes a different phenomenon for women.

The agriculture practiced by these first women farmers and their children, producing enough food for subsistence only, must be distinguished from that agriculture that developed out of subsistence farming and that produced surpluses and fed nonfarming populations in towns. The first type is commonly called *horticulture* and is carried out with hand tools only. The second is *agriculture* proper and involves intensive cultivation with the use of plow and (where necessary) irrigation. In areas like the hilly flanks of the fertile crescent of the Middle East, horticulture moved fairly rapidly into agriculture as it spread to the fertile plains. As we shall see, trading centers grew into towns and cities needing food from the countryside. Women and children could not produce the necessary surpluses unaided, and, by the time the digging stick had turned into an animal-drawn plow, they were no longer the primary workers of the fields.

The simpler form of farming continued in areas where the soil was less fertile, particularly in the tropical forest areas of Africa. Here soils were quickly exhausted, and each year the village women would enlist the men in helping to clear new fields, which were then burned in the slash-and-burn pattern that helped reconstitute the soils for planting again. The slash-and-burn pattern of horticulture has continued into this century, because it is a highly adaptive technique for meager tropical soils. Where the simple horticultural methods continued to be used, women continued as the primary farmers, always with their children as helpers. In a few of these societies, women continued also in the positions of power described for the first agriculturalists in the pages that follow; these are usually the tribes labeled by ethnologists as *matrilocal*. Not many tribes have survived into the twentieth century with a matrilocal pattern, however, although traces of matrilineal descent reckoning are not infrequent.

The first women farmers in the Zagreb foothills were very busy. Not only did they tend the fields and do the other chores mentioned above, they also probably built the round stone or mud-brick houses in the first villages. The frequency with which women construct shelters in foraging societies has already been cited.[5]

Women also began to spend more time on making tools and containers. No longer needing to hold the family possessions down to what they could carry, women could luxuriate in being able to choose larger and heavier grinding stones that crushed grain more efficiently. They could make containers to hold food stores that would never have to go on the road. They ground fine stone bowls, made rough baskets, and, in the process of lining their baskets with mud, accidentally discovered that a mud-lined basket placed in the hearth would come out hardened—the first pottery. Sonja Cole (1963) suggests that pottery was invented in Khartoum in Africa about 8000 B.C.E., spreading northwest to the Mediterranean, but the same process probably happened over and over again as people became more sedentary.

The evidence from food remains in these early villages, 10,000 to 6000 B.C.E., indicates that men were still hunting, to supplement the agriculture and modest domestic herds. This means that they were not around very much. When they were, they probably shared in some of the home-base tasks.

Evidence from some of the earliest village layouts suggests that adults lived in individual huts, women keeping the children with them. Marriage agreements apparently did not at first entail shared living quarters. As the agricultural productivity of the women increased, and the shift was made to dwellings for family units, husband-wife interaction probably became more frequent and family living patterns more complex.

With the accumulation of property, decisions about how it was to be allocated had to be made. The nature of these agreements is hardly to be found in the archaeological record, so we must extrapolate from what we know of the "purest" matrilineal tribes of the recent past.

The senior woman of a family and her daughters and sons formed the property-holding unit for the family. The senior woman's *brother* would be the administrator of the properties. His power, whether over property or in political decision making, would be derivative from his status as brother (usually but not always the oldest) to the senior woman in the family. This role of the brother, so important in present-day matrilineal societies, may not have been very important in the period we are now considering, between 12,000 and 8000 B.C.E. Ascribing in imagination to these ancient times the more extreme forms of more recently observed matrilinies (see the section "From Egalitarian to Ranked to Stratified Society," below), I suggest the following scenario, assuming both matrilineality and matrilocality: When a new household was to be formed, a young woman would build her home, and a young man would come to live there somewhat on sufferance, bringing gifts. He could easily be sent away if he didn't please his wife or his wife's mother. Older men (and sometimes young men) would have a thin time if their wives sent them away and they could not persuade any other woman to accept them.

To visualize more concretely the kind of society that emerged in these first villages, it may help to picture actual village layouts, some of which are reproduced in this chapter. The layouts indicate that village development can be roughly divided into two stages, the second with several subdivisions:

Stage 1. The communal village, undifferentiated functions
Stage 2. The household and craft-shop village, differentiated functions
    a. local craft only
    b. "town" with craft shops and trading activities
        (1) unstratified
        (2) with administrative center and social stratification

I suggest that women reached their maximum of differentiated social participation in the local craft-shop village and possibly began to lose ground in the villages where extensive trading developed. What follows is a survey of "life-styles" in these different kinds of villages.

The Communal Village

If we study the diagrams for Eynan, Wadi Fallah, and Stage 1 of Beidha (Figures 4.1a, 4.1b, and 4.1c), we see they are remarkably similar: very small

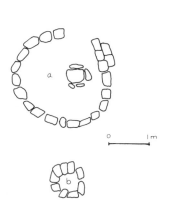

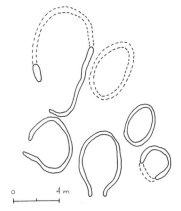

Figure 4.1a. Natufian Village of Eynan, 10,000 B.C.E.
NOTE: (a) house with central hearth; (b) storage pit. Redrawn by BB.

Figure 4.1b. Settlement at Wadi Fallah.
NOTE: Of the same type and period as early Jericho, 8000 B.C.E.; roundhouses were built on terraces. Redrawn by BB.

Figure 4.1c. Beidha, 7000 B.C.E., Level VI
NOTE: (a) dwellings; (b) storage area. Redrawn by BB.

round huts around a common center (which may contain a storage center or living hut). The huts are big enough for at most an adult and a child or two, not for family groupings. The village probably represents an extended family or clan group with a senior woman as head and husbands and wives living in separate huts. This pattern is still found in some parts of Africa today (Leonard 1973: 96), as may be seen in Cameroon (Figure 4.1d). Wives may or may not have cooked for husbands. Common activities and common food storage took place in the center of the circle. This type of village organization would be very efficient if the men were away a lot, hunting. There was a substantial increase in the number of personal possessions in a village like this, over what is found in nomadic base camps.

Women now had a variety of food processing equipment and all kinds of containers of stone, shells, reeds, and unbaked clay. They were also acquiring a store of ornaments and making clay figurines. Ocher, in use for burial sites since Neanderthal times, was an important part of the early "cosmetic industry."

The circular area in which women were spending much of their time when they were not in the fields or milking sheep and goats would lend itself to a great deal of cooperative and joint activity in the processing of food and in craft activities as well as in the care and teaching of children. It would also allow for joint planning of agricultural work, arranging marriage agreements for daughters and sons, allocating space for new houses, and deciding on distribution of property at marriage; for burials, decisions

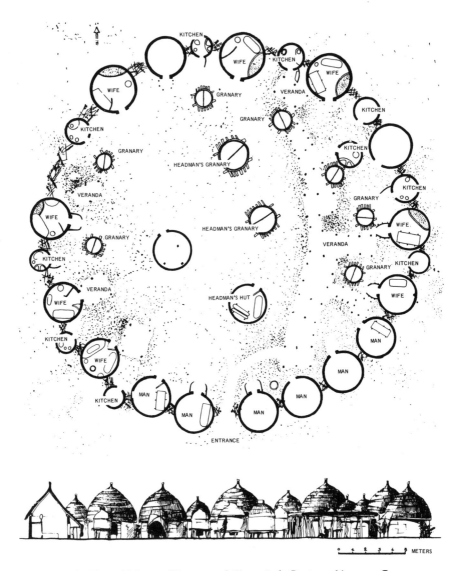

Figure 4.1d. Plan of Massan Homestead, Twentieth Century, Yagoua, Cameroon, Africa

SOURCE: Beguin et al. (1951); used by permission.

on what goods should be buried with the deceased would take place there. Ceremonial life may have been somewhat streamlined compared with Magdalenian times in Europe, because of the pressure of subsistence activities.

It is interesting that the oldest village, Eynan, shows signs of social stratification that we shall not see again until we find the more highly developed trading villages of Stage 2. At Eynan, a chief and his wife were buried in ceremonial gear in the center hut (facing the snowy peaks of Mt. Hermon— were they "homesick" for their previous nomadic existence?). Wadi Fallah's circular huts (Figure 4.1b) all have stone-lined fireplaces and show signs of the "mixed economy" transition from nomadism to farming; both agricultural and hunting implements and advanced polished-stone crafts are present. Jericho, for which I do not have housing drawings, was rather similar to Wadi Fallah in 8000 B.C.E., before the thick stone walls and towers went up around the former.[6] Jericho was an old nomadic camp site because of its ever-fresh spring. A stone shrine stood near the spring, long predating the village. Jericho gives evidence of having been an ancient main trading center for obsidian. Its circular huts all have goddess figurines, and at later levels a "trinity" of mother, father, and child appear in the figurines. Beidha (Figure 4.1c), like Jericho, has a shrine outside the town; in this case, a figureless monolith—a slab of stone. All four of these villages give evidence of specialist activities from earliest layers: the ceremonial function of "chiefing" in the central hut at Eynan, a "stone and bone" polishing hut at Beidha, and obsidian trade in Jericho.

The Local Household and Craft-Shop Village and the Trading Center

Stage 2 includes two kinds of villages: the individual household and craft-shop village, which made things for local consumption only, and the trading-center village. Jarmo and Hacilar are in the first category. Later levels of Jericho and Beidha, as well as Catal Huyuk, Arpachiyah, and Kherokitia, are in the second category. They all have certain things in common. Round huts were replaced by rectangular (often two-storied) houses large enough to shelter entire families, and there were individual courtyards opening into communal spaces, with hearths and ovens usually in the courtyards or communal spaces. There were specialty work areas for the manufacture of different products, generally pottery and baskets in the least differentiated villages. There were also shrines and often cult center buildings. Beyond this, the differences were considerable. Hacilar (Figure 4.1e) and Jarmo (Figure 4.1f), small villages with populations of from 100 to 150, obviously provided great scope for both individual and group activities. Women had extensive pottery and basket-making areas. With these new crafts, and perhaps improved agriculture and larger herds of

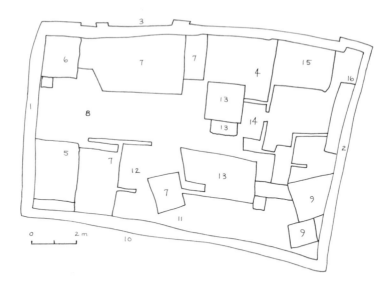

Figure 4.1e. Hacilar, 5700 B.C.E.

NOTE: (1) west wall; (2) east wall; (3) northwest gate; (4) north courtyard; (5) parching oven; (6) granary; (7) house; (8) small courtyard; (9) kitchen; (10) south gate; (11) south courtyard; (12) basket weaving area; (13) pottery workshop; (14) pottery courtyard; (15) shrine; (16) well. Redrawn by BB.

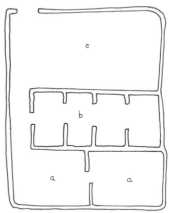

Figure 4.1f. Jarmo House, 6700 B.C.E.

NOTE: (a) living and sleeping quarters; (b) four storage rooms; (c) open courtyard; the village had about 25 such houses with alleys or courtyards between them. Drawing by BB.

goats and sheep, economic surpluses would be larger. Ceremonials would become more important again, in contrast to the very simplified life of the first villages, and more attention would be given to property exchanges through marriage agreements. Fields might be further away from the village, and larger. Milking, cheese making, and butchering took more time with the larger herds. Older children would have more responsibility for the younger ones, for herding, and for nut and berry gathering, as the women became busier. Special attention would be given to the making of figurines to be placed in the cult center building, and time would be spent caring for that building. Women also made figurines for their own homes.

Men continued to hunt and were also learning to tame the fearsome wild ox, the aurochs. The bull auroch began around this time to take its place alongside the mother-goddess in religious rites. Village herds of sheep and goats were growing larger, and it was probably the men who captured and tamed cattle. Cattle herds were looked after by the men from the very beginning.[7] Women were so busy at that time that they could not possibly have done so.

The trading towns like Jericho (not shown) had a different flavor than that of the craft villages. In Jericho, quarrying and trading brought in substantial surpluses, in addition to the agricultural and craft wealth produced by the women. The new rectangular houses that overlay the old round huts were made of cigar-shaped bricks—men's or women's activity now? The new houses were extensively decorated, and the women wove circular mats for their floors, perhaps in recollection of the old round houses of long ago. Walls and floors were painted, both in plain colors and in basket-weave designs. Pottery came late in Jericho—the women had made fine limestone bowls and plates for a long time and continued to do so while pottery was already being made elsewhere. Their agriculture and sheep-herding practices were similar to those of other settlements.

Life for men in Jericho was more varied than it was for women. It was based on quarrying and trading; going to the Dead Sea for salt, bitumen, and sulphur; dealing in obsidian from Anatolia, turquoise from Sinai, and cowries from the Red Sea. All these activities, like the taming of wild bulls and cows, were by-products of hunting days—discoveries made by men while tracking animals. Dealing in these products became more lucrative than continuing to track animals.

Beidha (Figure 4.1g) moved, in 500 years, from circular huts to rectangular houses in a pattern that indicates fantastically rapid economic and social development, complete with social stratification:

> Three large rectangular houses measuring 16 by 20 feet displayed interiors finely finished in plaster, equipped with hearths bordered by plastered sills. Set into the sills were stone bowls; food could have been boiled in the bowls by filling them with water and then dropping hot stones into them. These houses faced a large open space, like the central plaza of a Latin American town. Around them and across the plaza were much smaller rectangular houses. (Leonard 1973: 103)

If the big houses belonged to those who had grown rich by trading, the smaller houses would contain the craft workers' homes and workshops. The women in the poorer homes presumably did more agriculture and fewer crafts.

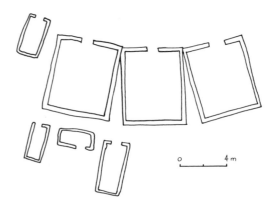

The fact that trading towns develop a character very different than that of agricultural towns with subsistence craft activities is further evidenced by Catal Huyuk (Figure 4.1h), which is in fact the largest Neolithic site in the Near East (Mellaart 1965). One entire acre of a "priestly quarters" has been excavated, and the cult of the bull as companion to the mother-goddess is everywhere in evidence. Homes are roomy one-story buildings with hearth and oven indoors.

Figure 4.1g. Beidha, 6800 B.C.E., Level IV
NOTE: Large fine houses and many smaller houses around a plaza. Drawing by BB.

Each room was provided with at least two platforms of which the main one was framed by wooden posts, plastered over and painted red. A raised bench was placed at the far end of the main platform. The [platforms] served as divans for sitting, working and sleeping and below them the dead were buried. (Mellaart 1965: 82)

Darlington says, "In Catal Huyuk . . . we are shown a society in which women are the masters. They even have larger beds" (Darlington 1969: 79). If he is

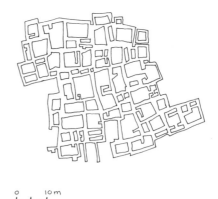

Figure 4.1h. Catal Huyuk, 6000 B.C.E., Building Level IV B. Redrawn by BB.

correct in his statement,[8] then the priestly quarters are probably priestess quarters. Reconstructions of cultic scenes by Mellaart (1965) also show priestesses conducting funerary rites. The preponderance of the evidence points to an all-female priestly class. There is much more to learn when more parts of the town have been uncovered.

Certainly, this was already a rich society. Next to two active volcanoes, both rich sources of obsidian, Catal Huyuk showed a wider variety of both import and export goods than any other town and also a wider range of foodstuffs:

> The standard of agriculture is amazing: emmer, einkorn bread wheat, naked barley, peas, vetch and bitter vetch. . . . [V]egetable oil was obtained from crucifers and from almonds, acorn and pistachio. Hackberry seeds occur in great quantities suggesting the producing of hackberry wine, praised by Pliny. (Mellaart 1965: 84)

The agriculture would be women's work. The standards of technology, except for pottery, were far beyond other Near East centers of the time, and Mellaart (1965) describes in eloquent detail the tools, stoneware, jewelry, woodwork, and textiles of Catal Huyuk. Wooden and stone vessels were executed with far greater mastery than the pottery.

More is known about the religion of Catal Huyuk than any other settlement because 49 shrines or sanctuaries have been excavated. They were built similar to the houses but were more elaborately decorated. The familiar human and animal fertility figurines were found only *outside* the shrines. Inside were the cult statues:

> The principal deity was a goddess who is shown in her three aspects, as a young woman, a mother giving birth, or as an old woman, in one case accompanied by a bird of prey, probably a vulture. Simpler and more terrifying aspects show her semi-iconic as a stalactite or concretion with a human head which probably emphasizes her chthonic aspects related to caves and underworld. (Mellaart 1965: 92)

A male deity appeared as a boy, son-lover of the goddess, or as an older god portrayed as a bull. Here, in 6000 B.C.E., were the most concrete evidences of the double life-and-death aspects of the mother-goddess that made her the terror and hope of the human race during the agricultural era and far into the age of the first great civilizations. There are also indications of a more assertive male identity, in the evidences of trade and cattle breeding. Arpachiyah (Figure 4.1i), a much smaller town, perhaps settled from Catal Huyuk, tells the same story of both agricultural and trade wealth, fine arts and crafts, a highly developed religious cult life, and distinctive, elaborate houses.

There is really no way to tell how much of the craft activity in these trading towns was carried on by the women. It seems likely that cultic activity was under their control. The tensions between the male and female may well have begun sharpening in these towns, with so many nonagricultural activities competing for attention, many of them by-products of the former hunting way of life. These activities were producing a substantial surplus of both goods and food, but the only evidence (as yet) of a stratified society is in Beidha. Apparently everyone lived well in Catal Huyuk. And, while administrative centers and houses of the rich may be revealed by further excavation, there was apparently no centralized planning and resource allocation. The cultic centers do not show evidence of being organized for or by administrative centers. In the absence of more information, we can only assume that women and men participated in the production and consumption of a variety of new kinds of goods and that the social and ceremonial life of these people, while dominated by women, was fairly fluid.

Figure 4.1i. Plan of a "Tholos" at Arpachiyah: Halaf Culture, Middle Chalcolithic Period. Redrawn by BB and HBR.

In the last Neolithic level of Beidha (Figure 4.1j), we find the "houses of the rich" were gone, and in their place was

> a house 23 by 50 feet, whose single large room was finished inside with burnished white plaster. . . . [O]utside this rather imposing structure stretched open courtyards, and beyond them an array of rectangular buildings in even rows. Each consisted of thick stone walls enclosing six small, cubicle-like rooms and a central corridor. Some of the cubicles may have been storerooms, but others were obviously workshops. . . . To judge from articles left in them, some of their proprietors were specialists in different kinds of stone, bone or horn work. One was a jeweler who made stone beads; another cut beads out of hollow bones. One shop with many animal bones and horned skulls may have housed a butcher, or possibly a supplier of bones and horns to other workers. (Leonard 1973: 103)

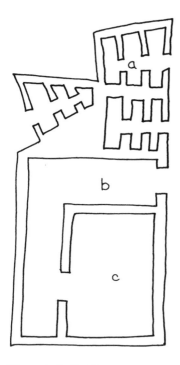

Figure 4.1j. Beidha, 6600 B.C.E., Level II

NOTE: (a) shops; (b) courtyard; (c) meeting house; living quarters were apparently on second stories. Redrawn by BB.

Families evidently lived in quarters above the workshops, which were apparently two-storied.

Beidha had become a rural industrial center, "supplying other villages with goods of its own manufacture and dominated by a management group whose headquarters may have been the large building with its red-banded walls and floor" (Leonard 1973: 103). There is no evidence that people lived in the "administrative center." The workshops do not reflect typically female crafts or even shared crafts, so it is possible that the women were specialized in agriculture only.

Our second example of an administrative center is Khirokitia (Figure 4.1k) on Cyprus. Although this town is more recent than any of the others described, culturally it is back in the roundhouse stage, perhaps because of prolonged isolation from other areas. It was near a major trade route from the Anatolian plateau to the Mediterranean, on a peninsula jutting out to the sea, and, because the people had seafaring skills, they were not totally isolated. The town was a trading center of a particular kind, accessible only to others with seafaring skills.

It is estimated that Khirokitia may have contained 1,000 houses and therefore a population of several thousand. The houses were comfortably furnished for complete families. There were paved stone roads, and houses ranged in size from three to eight meters in diameter. Some were dwellings, some workshops, and, given the size of the settlement, it may have had an administrative center in one of the larger domed houses. The organization of the town, with paved streets, roofed corridors, and ramps from the houses to the streets, reflects some type of planning. There is not much evidence of stratification; the differences in house size may reflect different uses rather than individual wealth. Larger and smaller houses are standing side by side.

The people specialized in beautifully polished stoneware, weaving, and jewelry and raised grain, sheep, and goats. There are schematized figurines with no sex indications, and apparently there were no cult centers.[9] Burials were inside the houses, and the rich burial gifts to women and men alike suggest that women and men were of equal status in this society. This town, while of a size that would need some organizing, seems to have the fluid characteristics of the villages like Hacilar and Jarmo. Khirokitia suggests that high population density, craft specialization, and trade do not necessarily lead to social stratification or to a male or female priestly class.

We have spent a long time on these villages. It has been necessary to try to present the most concrete data base possible for the discussions to follow on women's roles in the supposed "golden age of matriarchy" during the early agricultural, precivilizational era in human his-

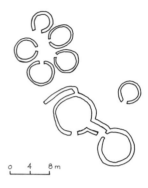

Figure 4.1k. Khirokitia in Cyprus, 5500 B.C.E.

NOTE: Houses and workshops are domed. Redrawn by BB.

tory. If women ever "ruled," it was at this time. The task of outlining the basic structure of daily life for the period is not made easier by the assumption by most archaeologists that all the activities for which they uncover evidence, except cooking (and sometimes pottery), were carried out by men. To achieve anything at all here, the evidence must be approached with an open mind and a lively imagination.[10]

I will pass over Stage 1 villages, where the egalitarian hunter-gatherer relationship between women and men translated into living separately in individual huts with minimal differentiation of activities, and sharing was confined to providing for needs of children and ceremonial activities. It is in villages belonging to Stage 2a that the special cultural elaborations of the agricultural way of life developed. There was enough surplus to make differentiated activities possible, but not so much that status differentials become important (with exceptions such as Beidha). The craft activities described above for women do not convey the variety of products actually made. A reading of the sections describing the technological achievements of the Neolithic in volume 1 of *A History of Technology* (Singer et al. 1954) is a corrective to the general tendency to assume that these early village products are rather crude. Woman's tendency to remain "Jane of all trades," to not specialize (will be discussed later), works against developing the high skill levels of specialist craft workers. The range of tools and equipment she creates is nevertheless impressive.

While the archaeological record is fragmentary at best, whatever it is possible to know about women in this era we will discover from these records. Stage 2b towns, with more differentiated skills, greater productivity, and larger surpluses, underline the nature of the challenges that new levels of productivity present. These trading towns provide clues about the transitional stage between town and urban center, but most of our information about the transition in terms of women's roles will have to come from the urban settlements themselves—discussed in the next chapter. Now we turn to the life of the villager.

The Daily Life of the Women Villagers

Women's activities can be described as falling into three spheres, the *hearth*, the *courtyard*, and the *fields*. (1) Hearth activities included cooking, feeding, and care of small infants. (2) Courtyard activities involved both *production processes*—(a) food, processing of foods to be cooked (sometimes cooking and baking also done in courtyard, combining items 1 and 2a), (b) *crafts*, sewing, weaving, basket and pottery making, stoneware and implement making, jewelry, production of cosmetics, and (c) *building activities*, houses, cult centers, and so on—and *social organization*—council meetings, ritual and ceremony preparations, teaching, general administration of the village. (3) Field activities included (a) gathering and collecting fruit and nuts; (b) clearing, planting, cultivating, and harvesting food; (c) caring for sheep and goats; (d) collecting fuel for hearth fires; and (e) collecting material for building.

One very distinctive feature of the women's culture is the omnipresence of children and the continuing nature of responsibility for infants and very small children. There is no moment of the day or night when this responsibility wholly lapses, although children may in fact receive highly variable amounts of care from one society to another. Additionally, pregnancy is a 24-hour-a-day "activity" and ought properly to be thought of as an activity, as the term *childbearing* suggests, because it requires energy and resources from the mother's body. Pregnancy merges imperceptibly into the continuing responsibility for infants after birth, a responsibility that really stretches from the moment of conception until the age of 3 or 4. The breast-feeding that begins after birth merges imperceptibly into the activity of preparing and serving food to children that extends for women to the activity of feeding all adult males in her household. There has never been a human society, to the knowledge of the anthropologist, archaeologist, or historian, where men have regularly performed the feeding role. The breeder-feeder responsibilities then form the backdrop for all other activities of women.

The activities that are hardest for us to visualize are the courtyard activities. We can extrapolate from twentieth-century kitchens to the hearth without difficulty, and we have all seen pictures of women working in fields. The courtyard, however, where women even today in many parts of the world spend most of their time, eludes us. This is where the special qualities of women's culture develop. Men's work, whether hunting, trading, stonework, or (after the plough is developed) agriculture, does not keep them in these open courtyards except in the evenings after the day's work is over.[11] For the Neolithic woman, however, the courtyard is the master-integrator of all other activities. The courtyard is her administrative base as well as the scene of much of her productive activity. Here is where the older women organize work routines for the community and teach or organize the teaching of the girls and of the boys under 10 years of age.[12]

What is taught? Genealogies, songs, dances, herbal medicine lore, and tribal rituals as well as the domestic crafts pursued in that village and some of the agricultural knowledge required in the field. Most, but not all, of the latter is probably taught in the field. It is during daytime courtyard sessions that new dances and songs are invented, later to be performed for ceremonial occasions.

> Such institutions [i.e., the courtyard] tend to develop women leaders whose authority often extends into the larger life of the community. As queen, chieftainess, priestess, prophetess, seeress, oracle, shamaness, magician, musician, and even as old wife who has experienced life, woman exercises a natural control over members of her society. If and when women celebrate jointly with men at religious ceremonies and games, they perform as an independent unit with their own leaders. (Drinker 1948: 9)

This description hardly fits all village societies, but it summarizes rather nicely the possibilities of courtyard life in those first villages of the Middle East.

Music is an important part of women's communal life and has been for a long time: Instruments were found in the caves of the Cro-Magnons in Europe. How soon women started singing we shall never know, because archaeology can provide no evidence for it. Women's choirs will be found, however—at worship, at work, and during all the ritual occasions of village life such as childbirth, puberty rites, weddings, and the reentry of a woman into society after childbirth—a long way back in history. (See the dancing women with flautist in Figure 4.2.) Drinker mentions archaic Greek figurines showing women bakers led by a woman flautist as a fairly sophisticated example of women singing at work (Figure 4.3). Tribal women have songs for every kind of rhythmic work, and a common saying is "a good singer is a good worker."

Singing has historically been a type of public participation of women. In addition to choirs, there have been individual wailers, historians, and

Figure 4.2. Women in Round Dance With Flautist in Center, Boetian, Sixth Century B.C.E. Redrawn by HBR.

singing storytellers; praise singers (in Africa today you can still pay a woman to do praise singing about you in public if your ego needs boosting); and party singers, who went through a village singing about a party someone was giving as a way of announcing it. A somewhat sharper use of song has been social criticism: Women still have the custom of singing their

Figure 4.3. Women Bakers Led by Flautist, Archaic Greece. Redrawn by HBR.

opinions of men in many societies. Wailing is a distinct art, separate from singing, used on special ritual occasions.

If ever there was a time in human history when women had free rein to develop their talents for singing, it was in these early agricultural villages. The association of women with the supernatural would give them a special role in the creation of music. Drinker (1948) points out that, when leadership roles in musical creation are assigned to men, women lose their creativity and become more stereotyped in their expression. She feels that it is only in women's groups unhindered by men that women fully express their musical genius and that the later male domination of all civilized societies "drove" women out of a field that had once been theirs. Unfortunately, there is no way we can re-create the religious music created by women in prehistory.

Women as Ritual Leaders

If the Neolithic woman was a priestess, what kind of goddess did she serve? The debate among scholars about mother-goddesses, and the relationship of fertility figures to mother-goddess cults, continues to rage.[13] We know from our examination of fertility figures in the last chapter that they were widespread and had many specialized purposes, including possibly serving as toys. There was no generalized woman-goddess figure (See Figure 4.4). The figures were always faceless. Some were beautiful, suggestive of Venus to our modern eyes, others were caricatures of pregnancy and the process of giving birth. The goddess figurines were rarely associated directly with animal figures until later. Early anthropomorphic figures related to the animal world were usually male. Catal Huyuk provides the first evidence of identification of women with animals in a cultic setting.

The cult statues in later villages begin to combine the female with a son-lover and to show her three faces—of youth (sexual attractiveness), life (giving birth), and death (the vulture nearby). The more terrifying semi-iconic versions suggest that, once the figurines changed from impersonal fertility symbols to representations of a goddess with female attributes, the resulting goddess was both beautiful and frightening.

Our one glimpse of the woman as priestess comes from the reconstruction of a funerary rite with priestesses disguised as vultures, from Catal Huyuk. Using this as a clue, we can imagine that these priestesses presided over three types of rites, corresponding with the three aspects of the goddess in the Catal Huyuk cult rooms: (a) the rite of marriage, in her aspect of goddess of youth and beauty; (b) the rite of giving birth, in her aspect of

text continued on p.119

Figure 4.4. Mother-Goddess Themes

NOTE: (a) Parthian goddess, 1st-2nd century B.C.E.; (b) Lileth, goddess of death, Sumer, 2000 B.C.E.; (c) Syrian fertility goddess, 8th century B.C.E.; (d) Belgian Congo mother and child. Redrawn by HBR.

Figure 4.4. Continued

NOTE: (e) Demeter and Kore, Greek (Thebes); (f) Kali the Devourer, northern India, 17th-18th century; (g) lower Rhenish or Mosan virgin and child, 14th century. Redrawn by HBR.

goddess of life—this would include two kinds of rituals, one in the village itself, focused on human procreation, and one partly in the village and partly in the fields, focused on fertility of the soil and planting rituals—and (c) the funerary rites, already mentioned, in her aspect of goddess of death.

The number of cultic objects, paintings, shrines, and so on indicates that a substantial amount of ritual activity was occurring and that the priestess possibly had a full-time occupation. If this is so, it is the first evidence of a specialized role for women in the Neolithic. Their daily activities were highly differentiated in the sense that they did many different things in the course of a day but were not specialized in the sense that each woman carried out certain tasks for everyone and benefited in turn from the specialties of other women. As far as we can tell, until the time of the active development of trade when there was a demand for the specialty role associated with elaborately decorated pottery, each woman did all the tasks assigned to women. The priestess role is the one exception; the amount of training women would need to carry out the range of ritual activities suggested would preclude their carrying a normal daily work load.

We do not know the belief systems that accompanied the ritual use of the goddess figures and the associated animal representations in the Neolithic. Many archaic religious myths, both of the ancient Mediterranean world and of contemporary tribal peoples, postulate a chaos figure, essentially neutral, who produces a mother-goddess who produces the world. Sometimes the chaos figure is female, but often not. While the mother-goddess is quickly surrounded by male gods in all the traditions of the Mediterranean, scholars generally agree that the goddess was the top figure first and that her son-lover (as in Catal Huyuk) only appeared later, gradually usurping her position. There has been some inclination to romanticize the goddess, with the suggestion that women taught the "pure" high god religion in the early Neolithic. According to this view, there was a later power struggle between women and men in which the goddess was dethroned and a whole galaxy of males took over; finally, the monotheistic religions of Judaism, Christianity, and Islam announced the victory of one top male god over all the other gods. It is perhaps more realistic to interpret the mother-goddess as an important early attempt at conceptualizing divinity, part of a long evolutionary process. In Christianity, the feminine element of the deity remains in the Virgin Mary—so there was no simple victory of god over goddess.

The trouble with romanticizing the "white goddess" or the "triple goddess," as Graves (1966) alternately calls her, is that she has so many grim aspects. Campbell makes the point that representations of men in the earliest prehistoric art are always clothed, while female figurines are naked, unadorned: "The woman is immediately mythic in herself and is experienced as such. . . . the mother is experienced as the power of nature" (1972: 31). The positive side of this is the mother, giver of birth. The negative side relates to the myth found in all ancient cultures of the Mediterranean, of the god who yields his body to be slain, cut up, and buried, thus providing for a good harvest:

> In the rites of human sacrifice common to all planting cultures, this primal mythological scene is imitated literally—ad nauseum; for, as in the vegetable world, life is seen to spring from death and fresh green sprouts from decay, so too it must be in the human. The dead are buried to be born again, and the cycles of the plant world become models for the myths and rituals of mankind. (Campbell 1972: 55)

That women as priestesses and representatives of the mother-goddess presided over human sacrifice of young men and children, culminating in the grisly mass sacrifices of the Phoenicians some millennia later, is indisputable. Just as we found scattered evidence for human sacrifice in the Paleolithic, so do we find traces of the same practice in the Neolithic, although the interpretation of findings of groups of skulls can never be clear. The group of baby skulls found under a basinlike structure in the earliest layer of Jericho (Mellaart 1965: 32) probably represents human sacrifice. The fact that such findings are infrequent suggests that the practice was not widespread and not a major religious theme. Systematically organized sacrifice is the product of "higher" civilizations.

The monster women associated in mythology with goddesses, who devour their children after giving birth to them, or suck them back up into the belly, or otherwise mutilate them, may have some basis in darkly remembered ancient ritual. Fontenrose's *Python: A Story of the Delphic Myth and Its Origins* (1959) gives a sample of the horror women have inspired in their priestess-goddess roles. In fact, the asides in Graves's *White Goddess* (1966), apparently a panegyric to the mother-goddess, have a nightmarish quality.

The theme of women as a source of terror is widespread enough both in ancient myths and in recurring bursts of antiwoman hysteria such as the witch craze of the Middle Ages to give the historian pause. Shades of the old hysteria are detectable in the outbursts of men against women in the current feminist struggle, not least in discussions on the issue of legalized abortion. The image of woman as sacrificer of children becomes linked sometimes with the image of woman as sex fiend. One ingenious theory about the fear men have of women suggests that primitive women were so highly sexed that they wore the men out completely and that the latter finally conquered and permanently suppressed them in self-defense (Sherfey 1972). This does not quite fit with the picture of village life we have just finished painting. The women were too busy to be sex fiends! Neither does the sex-war concept fit the earlier picture of cave life in the Paleolithic.

It is highly unlikely that there ever was a sex war or an overthrow of women. The infliction of savage constraints on sexuality, whether the constraint of the extremes of satiation or of abstinence, is probably a later phenomenon and associated with the strains of urbanization.

The Character of Matriliny

However we interpret the archaeological and mythic evidence, it does seem likely that women had a position of power in early Neolithic villages, and they probably frightened the men at least some of the time. This may seem like a far-fetched interpretation of data that on the whole point to a fairly egalitarian society. Let us back up a step from our question about women's roles as priestesses and look at their general economic and social position. During Stages 1 and 2 of the Neolithic village, as here character-ized, could the villages be called matriarchal? Given that they give no evidence of having chiefs, male or female (except Eynan), and given that *matriarchy* means "rule by women,"[14] this makes no sense. It would make sense, however, to think of them as matrilineal, as *tracing descent* through the mother's side of the family. With the emphasis on women's fertility, in a society organized primarily on the basis of access to land for farming, control over farmland, farm products, and sheep and goats, as well as control over house, tools, and equipment used by the women, might naturally be passed on through the women. Land ownership is not in question at this stage in social development but rights to use of land.[15] In the picture I am building here, it makes sense to suggest that these rights were controlled by women. It must be remembered, however, that the extent to which any of the patterns described here actually existed, includ-ing a system of matrilineal descent reckoning, is in dispute. There is no definitive evidence either way.

In villages where men did not develop trading activities, what did they do? They would have hunting and marginal farm work to do, tool making, and probably jewelry making. Women developed the pottery, weaving, and basketry as well as managed the food processing and cared for sheep and goats. When building needed to be done, men may have helped, as they would help at harvest time. When there were attackers, the men were the defenders, but in nontrading towns this was rare. Nomadic bands were usually content to trade peacefully with the villages. If the imbalance between women's and men's activities seems implausible, here is a list of Navajo occupations from a study by Aberle (1962a):

Males	Females
1. Cattle	1. Sheep
2. Agriculture	2. Agriculture
3. Silversmithing	3. Weaving
4. Ceremonial practice	4. Pottery
5. House building	5. Silversmithing
6. (There were hunting	6. Cooking
and warfare earlier	7. Child care
but now discontinued.)	8. House building

Even more dramatic evidence of the imbalance of women's and men's activities in subsistence agricultural societies has become available from recent studies undertaken for the Economic Commission for Africa (United Nations 1974) on relative inputs of women and men to daily agricultural work in Africa. Table 4.1 describes the results of the Africa study, showing work input in terms of the amount of women's work as a percentage of the total work done in a specific category. This is known as unit-of-participation analysis. According to Boserup (1970), this type of work imbalance is to be found in all subsistence agricultural societies that follow the "slash-and-burn" practice (see also Stamp 1989). The traditional role of the men in these societies is hunting.

To return to the Neolithic agrovillage: Except when out hunting, the men were probably together less and made a relatively smaller contribution than the women to the ritual life of the village. They did not have the equivalent of the courtyard for planning group activities during the day. Hunting expeditions were probably the occasions when they felt most important, and, if they could not find meat, even this activity would be more punishing than rewarding.

The society appears to have been essentially nonhierarchical. The older women may have acted as organizers, but they did not exert strong authority or withhold community resources to get special services performed. If they had, this probably would have shown up in different standards of housing and living styles. The resentments of the men may therefore have been rather diffuse. To speak of role deprivation on the part of the men is perhaps to say too much, because, to feel deprived, the men would have to have had some standard of comparison according to which their personal status was too low. Legends from the days of the great hunts, however, may have provided such a standard of reference.

TABLE 4.1 Participation by Women in the Traditional Rural and
Modernizing Economy in Africa

Responsibility	Unit of Participation[a]
A. Production/supply/distribution:	
1. Food production	0.70
2. Domestic food storage	0.50
3. Food processing	1.00
4. Animal husbandry	0.50
5. Marketing	0.60
6. Brewing	0.90
7. Water supply	0.90
8. Fuel supply	0.80
B. Household/community:	
1. Household:	
(a) bearing, rearing, initial education of children	1.00
(b) cooking for husband, children, elders	1.00
(c) cleaning, washing, and so on	1.00
(d) house building	0.30
(e) house repair	0.50
2. Community:	
Self-help projects	0.70

SOURCE: Data from the United Nations (1974).
a. Unit of participation is women's work as a percentage of the total work done in each category.

Men may especially have resented the relatively casual attitudes of women toward marriage. Marriage is never as central to the organization of economic and social life in a matrilineal society as it is in a patrilineal one. Although actual patterns of matriliny vary a great deal around the world, the house of the woman and her daughters tends to be an important stabilizing element. In the "pure" form (as opposed to the transitional form of matriliny, called *avunculocal,* in which a married woman may live with her mother's brother and men dominate through their sisters), the marriage bond is often weak and divorce frequent. It is often remarked by anthropologists describing matrilineal societies that these are high-tension societies. Some examples of tension in matrilineal societies, which may throw light on the family situation in Neolithic society, are provided below. All of the studies surveyed were undertaken in the twentieth century (Schneider and Gough 1962).

Man-Woman Relationships in Some Matrilineal Societies

Colson's Study of the Plateau Tonga

In a household census of two villages, it was found that, of 245 households, 32 contained no adult males and 31% of males and 26% of females were divorced. A divorcee or widow may prefer not to remarry but can retain her own household and property. In former times, she could be "headman," but no longer. There are stories of "amazons" who rid themselves of unwanted husbands, pairing up with daughters who have done the same, to live in all-female hamlets with some low-status male relatives around. "Old women chuckle happily at their independence; old men try desperately to find wives through whom they can once more establish a household unit catering to their wishes and giving them prestige and ritual potency" (Colson 1962: 68).

Aberle's Study of the Navajo

Two-thirds of the families followed a matrilocal residence pattern in the 1930s, when Aberle's study took place. There are few rules or ceremonies for marriage and a de-emphasis of the "bride price," which is not always given. "Marriage frees both partners for all subsequent marriages, in case of divorce" (Aberle 1962a: 126). Two females out of three are divorced and three males out of four.

Fathauer's Study of the Trobrianders

This is a tribe with matrilineal descent but male rule, in the avunculocal pattern. Husband and wife work together in agriculture, but each owns tools separately. The husband is important in child care but has no "rights" in the child. Divorce is "not infrequent." In marriage, women confer status on men, but not the reverse (Fathauer 1962).

Basehart's Study of the Ashanti

This is a matrilineal system with male chiefs nominated by a queen mother. Only 26% of the women were living with their husbands in one sample. Married women live with their mothers and sisters in matrilocal houses and may bring food to a husband in his house (his own or that of women in his family). There is little joint activity between husband and wife; each has an equal chance to be head of household, but men can usually obtain their own house at a younger age than can women. Husbands and wives work and produce separately; every adult earns her or his own living. There is a high divorce rate (Basehart 1962).

The Akan people of Ghana, of whom the Ashanti are one, have been referred to by Meyer Fortes, in the foreword to Oppong's *Marriage Among a Matrilineal Elite*, as follows:

Traditionally marriage was (and in village communities still is) the frailest of bonds and is secondary to the matrilineal kinship ties focused in the unbreakable natal bonds of brother and sister, and symbolized by the laws of "nephew inheritance." Spouses often resided apart, with their close maternal kin, on whom they had everlasting claims. (Fortes 1974: x)

Gough's Study of the Nayar

There is hostility among brothers in the matrilineal clan as well as between men of different generations. Men's affection goes into relationships with mother and with mother's sisters. Women live in their mother's home, and unsatisfactory husbands can be ordered dismissed by the mother. There is a first ritual marriage before puberty, then a series of "visiting husbands," with no limit on number although the range is usually between 3 and 12. There are casual unions in addition. All "husbands" visit their wives after supper, leave before breakfast, and never eat in the wife's home. The husband-wife relationship is very weak. The nuclear family—husband, wife, and their children—does not exist in Nayar society: No man has rights in one woman or one child; and no woman has legal rights in one man but in a group of men (Gough 1962a, 1962b).

* * *

I do not know of a systematic comparative study of divorce rates in matrilineal and patrilineal societies, but Mair's (1972) examination of the subject leads her to conclude that there is more divorce in matrilineal than in patrilineal societies. At the societal level, rather than at the level of individual families, Murdock's (1949) finding that societies move from matrilineal to patrilineal, but never the other way, can be taken as one more piece of evidence both for the instability of matrilineal family organization and for the instability of matrilineality as a form of social organization.

The instability of matriliny in the latter sense appears to be related to a pattern of small-scale social organization characteristic of early agrovillage life. This pattern is not sufficiently flexible to allow further differentiation, particularly in the nonagricultural sector, for its marginal (male) population.

A review of the conditions under which matriliny arises and the conditions under which it is likely to disappear, as outlined by Aberle (1962b) in his major study of the phenomenon, suggests that matriliny arises in situations where there are all-women work groups and where women control the residence bases. This is precisely the situation that I am suggesting obtains in the Neolithic agricultural village. Aberle describes matriliny as

> a special adaptation to certain production conditions, capable of surviving under other, but by no means all other, conditions. Matriliny itself is not a level of organization, but on the contrary, various levels of organization occur among matrilineal, patrilineal and bilateral systems. Its association with certain production systems, its incompatibility with others, and its incompatibility with extensive bureaucratization, imply that matriliny is largely limited to a certain range of productivity and a certain range of centralization—ranges narrower than those of either patrilineal or bilateral systems. Matriliny . . . cannot be viewed as a "stage" or "level" or generation of evolutionary development. (Aberle 1962b: 702)

The instability of matrilineal systems can be explained entirely in structural terms. Had women given more attention to spinoff activities with which they were not directly concerned, and had they adapted their communication patterns to encompass a wider range of happenings, matriliny might have adapted to a new scale of social operation. The fact that women did not do so should not be put in primarily biological terms, although their triple producer-breeder-feeder role may have put them at a disadvantage. An inspection of their daily work load compared with that of the earlier hunting-and-gathering era suggests that they were probably suffering from work overload and information overload and did not stand back to get the larger picture.[16]

In the discussion on the priestess role, I commented that this was evidently the only specialist role for women in the Neolithic village until much later, when a demand for elaborately decorated pottery in the trading villages finally produced a cadre of specialist women potters. Why didn't women specialize sooner? Men had begun to specialize much earlier, probably because they had more time to do so. Why didn't women reduce their own work loads substantially, giving themselves more time to think about that "larger picture"? They had the "power" to allocate their own time differently and presumably the men's time too. "Why didn't they . . . ?" is an old question in history. New social perceptions are slow to form, and we can only say that the women did not shift to the necessary new perceptions of their activities and of the total organization of village life soon enough to prevent loss of "political power."

Some readers might be inclined to argue the "traditional" conservatism of women as the reason for their failure to perceive the necessity for a new scale of social organization. An interesting study on the "sociology of pottery" (Foster 1968) suggests that conservatism is a trait that arises from an occupational basis rather than being associated with gender. Based on his own fieldwork in pottery villages in Mexico, and on his examination of data from other Latin American countries and from Tibet, India, Tunis, and Spain, Foster concludes that potters, whether male or female, "are more conservative in basic personality structure than are their non-potter villagers. . . . as a class, potters are more resistant to innovation of all kinds than are non-potters" (1968: 321). Drawing up a list of simple innovations in the Mexican villages and listing the names of the villagers associated with the innovations, Foster found practically no potters included although they constituted 60% of the population. He suggests why:

> The reason lies in the nature of the productive process itself which places a premium on strict adherence to tried and proven ways as a means of avoiding economic catastrophe. Pottery-making is a tricky business at best, and there are literally hundreds of points at which a slight variation in materials or processes will adversely affect the result. . . . economic security lies in duplicating to the best of the potter's ability the materials and processes he knows from experience are least likely to lead to failure. . . . this breeds a basic conservatism, a caution about all new things that carries over into the potter's outlook on life itself. (1968: 323)

Apart from the fact that, as far as we know, most early Near East pottery was done by women, the general situation of little margin for error leading to conservatism might apply to the whole range of activities carried out by women. Because they had so much to do, slight variations in care of farm or dairy products or pottery could lead to food spoilage, production failure, and a consequent increase in already heavy burdens. Care of children does not admit of much variation, particularly in feeding. Hunting activities, on the other hand, are often most successful for the risk takers.

Risk takers or not, the men certainly were the "free-floating resources"[17] of this society. As the "extra pair of hands" in the situation, they responded to the asymmetry in responsibility by inventing new patterns of social organization. The actual change process was, of course, far more complicated than this statement implies and could be the subject of an entire book in itself. For now it is perhaps enough to make this suggestive application of Aberle's thesis to the Neolithic matrilineal village.

From Egalitarian to Ranked to Stratified Society

The new scale of social organization moved Neolithic society very rapidly from egalitarian to ranked to stratified society, in Fried's (1967) terminology. The egalitarian society "is one in which there are as many positions of prestige in any given age- [and sex-] grade as there are persons capable of filling them" (Fried 1967: 33). Ranking implies that there are fewer positions of valued status than there are persons capable of filling them, but ranks do not necessarily have economic implications. The early priestly functions did not, according to Fried, carry economic advantage (1967: 140-141), for example. In those early village "rank" societies, everyone, including those with prestige status, participated to some degree in maintenance activities. Control over redistribution by prestige persons did not give them any personal advantage. With larger population densities and the growth of trade, there was a gradual withdrawal of high-status persons from basic maintenance activities, and these persons gained superior right of access to basic resources through administrative roles. Ranking, in short, is the "skeleton on which the musculature of stratification can grow" (Fried 1967: 178). Because women were not among those entering the redistribution roles, the narrowing of access rights to resources immediately began to diminish women's status and opportunities. The "ancient managerial revolution" that made the great hydraulic works of antiquity possible took place with women standing on the outside, even though their own lands were involved.

What did this mean for woman? In the ranked society, her place was still secure, for the ranked society is still built around the kinship system. Prestige derives from one's position in that system, and material resources are equally available to all. The stratified society, however, commands resources beyond the resources of any individual kinship system. Power holders in stratified societies use kinship-derived ceremonial bonds to develop a new resource distribution system[18] and in the process they develop centralized power. Women, according to our interpretation, were losing out in chances for administrative roles in the newly developed upper strata at the same time that their new status ensured their withdrawal from earlier productive roles. This left a newly created class with an increasing number of ceremonial and bonding functions and little power. For the ingenious woman, ceremonial roles could always be translated into administrative and decision-making roles, but it did not happen automatically. One might say that women were left behind in a ranked-society enclave within the new stratified society: They had prestige but also diminished command over resources.

Now that the decline of matriliny has been explained on structural grounds, what happens to the mother-goddess? Is it a phantom specter that can be exorcised, or does the mythology reflect a historical problem situation? I suggest that there was a problem situation and that it is one of the unlucky coincidences of history that the organizational failure of matriliny happened to coincide with the beginnings of nuclear family intimacy. (The Neolithic village provides the first evidence we have of mother-father-child dwellings.) Women's failure at that time to provide adequate role-differentiation opportunities for men, when the women were in a position of dominance due to the temporary primacy of their productivity skills, may have led to family tensions that were played out symbolically in the mythic and religious life of the community but never dealt with realistically at their source. The gradual shift from the more impersonal female symbols of the Upper Paleolithic to the naturalistically female mother-goddess of the early agricultural peoples, served by women in priestess roles and linked to the fertility of the soil, came, it could be argued, at a very bad time psychologically for the human race. According to this line of reasoning, the worship of the mother-goddess as the source of life flourished at the very moment, historically speaking, when women were also a source of role deprivation.

This proposition will not be explored in depth here, but the interested reader is urged to study Slater's *The Glory of Hera* (1968), which traces just such a connection in Greek society, at a later stage in evolution. Slater argues that Greek women were in fact dominant in the family and that the subsequent low status of women and the male terror of women were a vicious cycle set in motion by that dominance. The Greek boy lived in a female-dominated world until the age of 7 and was then thrown into the male world. The Greek father was an outsider in his house, unable to penetrate the domestic fortress ruled by his wife. The main thrust of the argument is that, under special conditions, maternal dominance produces male narcissism, which is a double time bomb in that it makes men unsatisfactory husbands and fathers and leaves the next generation of boys exposed to the dominance of frustrated mothers, ad infinitum. It also produces a high achievement need in the boys, along with self-doubt, libidinal repressiveness, and a tendency to prefer tomorrow's rewards to today's. This achievement drive is the motor for economic development, as is well documented by McClelland (1961) and McClelland and Winter (1969).

The type of dominance Slater describes is rather different than the dominance described for the Neolithic village. In the village, it stemmed from the nature of women's productive roles in the economy. In the Greek setting, it represented a subversion of an overt male dominance. Furthermore, the Greeks already held an army of gods on their side to protect them against women. Neolithic men only had one bull god, and he was invented rather late.

The Neolithic *dominance* of women, if that word is appropriate, was hardly conscious and intentional. Men may have sometimes been harmed through exclusion from needed resources. On the other hand, the structural framework supporting any possible maldistribution of resources would have been minimal and weak. The scales were soon tipping in the other direction.

The Neolithic in Africa, Southeast Asia, and Europe

Africa and Southeast Asia

To simplify the examination of women's roles in the Neolithic, I have discussed only the village life in the area known as the cradle of agriculture, the fertile crescent in the Near East. Agriculture probably began along the Nile at about the same time or soon afterward and also in what is now upper Kenya, on the shores of the Rift Valley lakes. The character of these villages would have been somewhat different than that of the fertile crescent villages, because the African villages bordered on lakes and rivers and fishing continued as an important supplement to agriculture (S. Cole 1963). It is usually assumed that women and men fished here during the Paleolithic and that therefore the transition to agrovillages would not involve the kind of role separation experienced in the Near East; women and men could continue to fish side by side after agriculture developed. This shared activity would make the "you hunt, I farm" division less sharp, although hunting certainly continued. There are hints of the importance of the "village goddess" as village life became more elaborated along the Nile, and a specialized priestess class to serve cult centers would certainly have developed. We see the evidence of this at the time when the first kingdoms of the Nile were consolidated, because each village goddess had to be formally assimilated into the "national" pantheon. This will be discussed more fully in the next chapter, but it is important to note that the basis for this pantheon was laid in the Neolithic villages.

By the time of the earliest political unification, there was probably a well-developed village life along the Nile as well as fine craft work. The women were pottery specialists as well as priestesses, and they may have been chiefs also. The roots of the woman-as-ruler and woman-as-administrator traditions of Egypt must lie in the Neolithic. Unfortunately, remains from this era are scantier along the Nile than elsewhere. Villages shifted sites frequently, and every Pharaoh built his own new capital on virgin land. We have little archaeological evidence on which to base inferences and must rely on the traces of earlier social usage in later practices. A scenario about the origins of agriculture alternative to the one offered in this chapter has been developed by Loeb (1960). He places it in the tropical forest setting, but he also proposes women as the inventors of agriculture and the matrilineal form of social organization as the cultural context. According to Loeb, "agriculture started in the tropical rainforests along the banks of small rivers, specifically along those flowing into the Bay of Bengal" (1960: 303), fanning to the east and west from there. This was a root-planting, rather than a seed-planting, technology. Seeds came later:

> The early root-planting culture was essentially a woman's world, since it was the women who performed the main work. A reconstruction of the culture on the basis of such evidence as is available indicates that the people lived on the banks of small rivers and lakes in elongated plank houses set on piles, each family having its own room in a communal house and its own fireplace for cooking. The inhabitants of a house were a matrilineal lineage, and several such houses formed a mother-right clan. The oldest woman in a house was the matron, but her eldest brother together with the other mature men of the house formed the village council. A mother, her brother or brothers, and her children, all inhabiting one room and using a single fireplace, made up the nucleus of the family. A man's nephews, not his sons, inherited his personal possessions, such as weapons and boats. Daughters inherited household goods from their mothers. Husbands came secretly at night to visit wives, and frequently wives changed husbands without ceremony. This form of society and manner of living are believed to have been decisive in the history of mankind. Except for the outrigger canoe and the blow-gun, women were responsible for most of the inventions of the period including the use of bamboo utensils for cooking and holding liquids, the steeping and beating of tapa to make cloth, the cultivation of root plants, and above all, the domestication of small animals as household pets. Early in the period the children caught young wild dogs and pigs and brought them home to the women to be nursed. Chickens and other fowl were added later to the list of household animals. Eventually chickens were used in divination and also in sports as fighting cocks. (1960: 303-4)

Evidence for matrilineality is given through archaeological evidence of the existence of matrilineal longhouses and by references to the continued use into the recent past of such matrilineal longhouses in Malaysia, Indonesia, the Malabar Coast of India, Japan, and in the American Northwest (Loeb and Broek 1947: 419; and Sauer, as quoted in Loeb 1960: 313). Loeb goes on to establish a connection between the matrilineal culture with its longhouses and the use of narcotics and intoxicants. While he does not suggest that women evolved the use of narcotics, he presents a variety of evidence in support of the position that they invented wine and beer in the Neolithic (1960: 305-11). The importance of his work lies primarily in the fact that he points out two different lines of agricultural development, both of which involved women: seed-planting culture and root-planting culture.

The penetration of agriculture into tropical forest lands in Africa, and a similar penetration into the forests of Asia and Oceania after the independent development of agriculture in Southeast Asia, were sometimes peaceful and sometimes not. Vayda (1961) suggests that peaceful expansion depends on the terrain, population density, and skills of social organization and exploration of the tribes in question. Given that all tropical agriculture is of the slash-and-burn variety, only skillful exploration and land use can avoid constant warfare. Warring tribes are a well-documented phenomenon in all tropical forest lands, but Vayda suggests that competition for resources is the primary triggering factor. The existence of head-hunting in some matrilineal forest tribes would then be associated with poor alternative technologies for exploration and expansion rather than with some uniquely bloodthirsty attributes of matrilineality.

Europe

Agriculture moved slowly into Europe. It took about 1,000 years for Neolithic agrovillages to spread into Italy, France, and Spain. Crete, Sicily, and parts of Greece were the first stopping points for migrants from the Near East. Crete in particular, with conditions most similar to those in the fertile crescent, developed a flourishing agriculture and went on quickly to develop a high village culture that laid the foundation for the later Cretan empire. As we will see in Chapter 6, it was in Crete that the ax cult, associated with a mother-goddess and priestess attendants, was born. Crete became known in the ancient world for the high status of women there, after this status had eroded for women elsewhere.

The conditions for the development of the new agricultural way of life in Europe, Africa, and Asia were very different than those of the Near East. Climatic differences were great; forests had to be cleared; different kinds of crops had to be tried experimentally. Perhaps most important of all, Neolithic immigrants were moving into already inhabited territory. Earlier inhabitants often continued a hunting and gathering way of life for centuries after their farmer neighbors settled in, adopting elements of the new economy but continuing their own system (Hawkes and Woolley 1963: 240).

The settlements northward into western Europe had a different character than those in southern Europe. The Danubian loess lands were so fertile, naturally well drained, and lightly forested that they made an obvious site for primitive agricultural methods. Soil exhaustion was an important factor in the continual migrations of the farmers and their spread throughout Europe. "Always virgin soil lay ahead" (Hawkes and Woolley 1963: 243). It has been estimated that a village moved about every quarter of a century, sometimes sooner. Hunting and fishing receded in importance, and agri-

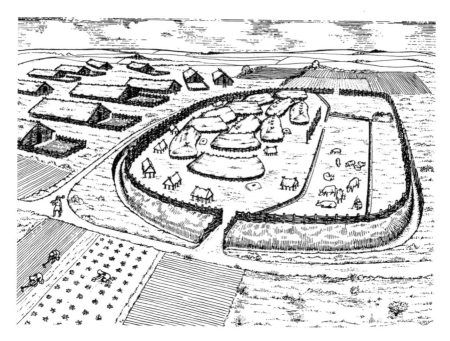

Figure 4.5. Neolithic Village of the Danubian Culture: Kölesson-Lindenthal (Reconstruction)

SOURCE: Hawkes and Woolley (1963); copyright © 1963 by UNESCO, reprinted by permission of Harper & Row, Publishers, Inc.

culture and cattle received a major share of the working time of the village. "Lack of chief's houses or rich graves suggests an egalitarian society, and the Danubians are generally assumed to have been a peaceable folk" (Hawkes and Woolley 1963: 244). The reconstruction of a Danubian village (Figure 4.5) gives some feeling for the different life-style the climate fosters. There is less emphasis on open-air work spaces and more on adequate sheltered places. The mother-goddess has traveled with these settlers along with the new Cretan religion, the ax cult. The ax cult must have had properties particularly helpful to migrating farmers, because it spread all over Europe. It seems to be associated with an egalitarian society and with equal status for women and men.

Engels ([1884] 1942) pictured a dramatic shift from matrilineal to patrilineal descent with the "overthrow of the mother right [as] the world historical defeat of the female sex." What he did not know was that what he conceived as the patriarchal "Great Family Community," or the extended family village, which he thought succeeded group marriage, was in fact a matrilineal community in many parts of the world. While none of the evidence presented in this chapter is conclusive, much of it seems to point in the same direction. The evidence does not, however, warrant establishing a "matrilineal" stage as an inevitable stage in social evolution. Other scenarios, involving different relationships between male hunters and female gatherers in the agricultural transition, could be imagined. The role of accidental factors, whether of the environment or of individual human personalities, or the vagaries of social drift in patterning social organization, could produce many variants of the transition I have described here from nomadism to settled life. The most tenable position to take is that, in some substantial number of tribal groups, women played a key role in the transition to agriculture. This key role was often associated with the reckoning of descent through the mother and with the allocation of land through the matrikin. We may remember here Wilson's statement, quoted in Chapter 2: "The key to sociobiology . . . is milk" (1975: 456).

We can also say that this transition involved the development of village life: the foraging band became the village. In all centuries, the most frequent pattern for human settlement has involved men and women living in villages and going out each day to farm surrounding lands. If a village got too crowded, a group of people might leave to start a new settlement, but rarely did a single nuclear family leave. Isolated homesteading requires very special social and environmental conditions. The clan-based pattern of village organization has in many parts of the world remained intact in spite of the rise and fall of surrounding empires. Nevertheless, change takes place with the development of trade routes and the passing through of groups and individual adventurers who eventually create new types of settlements or transform the character of old ones. The erosion of matrilineal organization within the clan-patterned villages is one of the consequences of this contact-and-transformation sequence. We will trace the dynamics of that process in the next chapter.

Notes

1. The following glossary is offered to aid the reader unfamiliar with kin-reckoning terminology:

matrilineal—reckoning descent through the mother

matrilocal—married couple lives with wife's family

matriarchy—sometimes used to denote the political rule of women, which is more properly called gynocracy

matrikin—all kin reckoned through the mother

patrilineal—reckoning descent through the father

patrilocal—married couple lives with husband's family

patriarchy—political rule of men

patrikin—all kin reckoned through the father

avunculocal—married couple lives with wife's uncle (associated with matrilineal descent reckoning)

It is important to note that choice of residence after marriage and system of descent reckoning are two separate and distinct sets of traits and may be combined in various ways; for example, matrilineal descent may accompany patrilocal residence.

2. The connection between good stands of wild grain and other plant food and the earliest agricultural villages was first made through some brilliant theoretical work by the archaeologist Robert Braidwood of the University of Chicago. His theories took him to the fertile crescent to dig for the first villages, and he did indeed find them where he had expected (Leonard 1973).

3. Not all nomads live in environments that require such short working hours.

4. See the comparative photographic studies undertaken by Hans Hass (1970) and Eibl-Eibesfeldt (1972) for illustrations of the universality of tenderness and helping modes in relation to children.

5. See Doris Cole (1973). Women still build adobe houses in the Southwest of the United States today.

6. Descriptions of Jericho are from Mellaart (1965: 31-42).

7. Margaret Mead sees the beginnings of patriarchy in this herding activity of men. They saw what one bull could do for a herd of cows!

8. He does not state the basis for his conclusion.

9. It is difficult to be sure about the presence or absence of cult centers from archaeological evidence. As Hawkes makes clear in her discussion of archaeological remains from the late Paleolithic and early Neolithic (Hawkes and Woolley 1963), one cannot always tell a kiln from an oven from a tomb from a cult center.

10. At the same time, anthropologist Peggy Sanday's warnings about the difficulty of predicting women's contribution to subsistence in the absence of knowledge of women's tribal organization must be borne in mind (Sanday 1973).

11. Tool making, unlike pottery making, leads very quickly to enclosed workshops.

12. To get some of the flavor of women's culture, I am drawing on the work of Sophie Drinker, whose study *Music and Women* (1948) brings out aspects of tribal women's activities that often are not mentioned.

13. See Pomeroy, *Goddesses, Whores, Wives, and Slaves* (1975), for some of this debate.

14. The correct term for rule by women is *gynocracy*, but *matriarchy* is often used in this sense.

15. Land as property is a by-product of city-state development. The king becomes holder of all state land in the name of the state god. To reward army leaders and merchant backers who help him in conquest and defense enterprises, he makes gifts of state land to them, which then become family rather than state property.

16. Reasons for the decline of matrilineal societies in the nineteenth and twentieth centuries are somewhat different than, though related to, the reasons for the early decline of matriliny in the transition from subsistence to surplus-generating agriculture. During colonization, there was pressure from the West, from both civil and religious authorities, to conform to patriarchal European patterns of social organization. At the same time, matrilineal organization represented a sharing ethic that interfered with the dynamics of modernization, which depended on accumulation by the male head of household for his own nuclear family to the exclusion in part of all other kin (see Oppong 1974, for an analysis of this).

17. This is a key explanatory concept used by Eisenstadt in his *The Political Systems of Empires* (1963).

18. This could not happen, of course, unless the society was also becoming increasingly productive.

References

Aberle, David F. 1962a. "Navaho." Pp. 96-201 in *Matrilineal Kinship*, edited by David M. Schneider and Kathleen Gough. Berkeley: University of California Press.

———. 1962b. "Matrilineal Descent in Crosscultural Perspectives." Pp. 655-730 in *Matrilineal Kinship*, edited by David M. Schneider and Kathleen Gough. Berkeley: University of California Press.

Alland, Alexander. 1962. *The Human Imperative*. New York: Columbia University Press.

Basehart, Harry W. 1962. "Ashanti." Pp. 270-97 in *Matrilineal Kinship*, edited by David M. Schneider and Kathleen Gough. Berkeley: University of California Press.

Boserup, Ester. 1970. *Women's Role in Economic Development*. New York: St. Martin's.

Campbell, Joseph. 1972. *Myths to Live By*. New York: Viking.

Childe, Gordon. 1963. *Social Evolution*. New York: Meridian.

Cole, Doris. 1973. *From Tipi to Skyscraper: A History of Women in Architecture*. Boston: I Press.

Cole, Sonja. 1963. *The Prehistory of East Africa*. New York: Macmillan.

Colson, Elizabeth. 1962. "Plateau Tonga." Pp. 36-95 in *Matrilineal Kinship*, edited by David M. Schneider and Kathleen Gough. Berkeley: University of California Press.

Darlington, C. D. 1969. *The Evolution of Man and Society*. New York: Simon & Schuster.

de Mause, Lloyd. 1974. "The Evolution of Childhood." Pp. 1-74 in *The History of Childhood*, edited by Lloyd de Mause. New York: Psychohistory Press.

Drinker, Sophie. 1948. *Music and Women: The Story of Women in Their Relation to Music*. New York: Coward-McCann.

Eibl-Eibesfeldt, Irenäus. 1972. *Love and Hate*, translated by Geoffrey Strachan. New York: Holt, Rinehart & Winston.

Eisenstadt, S. N. 1963. *The Political Systems of Empires*. New York: Free Press.

———. 1972. *Post-Traditional Societies*. New York: Norton.

Engels, Frederich. [1884] 1942. *The Origin of the Family, Private Property, and the State*. New York: International.

Fathauer, George H. 1962. "Trobriand." Pp. 234-69 in *Matrilineal Kinship*, edited by David M. Schneider and Kathleen Gough. Berkeley: University of California Press.

Fontenrose, Joseph. 1959. *Python: A Story of the Delphic Myth and Its Origins*. New York: Biblo and Tannen.

Fortes, Meyer. 1974. "Foreword." Pp. ix-xii in *Marriage Among a Matrilineal Elite*, by Christine Oppong. Cambridge: Cambridge University Press.

Foster, George M. 1968. "Sociology of Pottery." Pp. 317-28 in *Man in Adaptation: The Biosocial Background*, edited by Yehudi Cohen. Chicago: Aldine.

Fried, Morton H. 1967. *The Evolution of Political Society: An Essay in Political Anthropology*. New York: Random House.

Gough, Kathleen. 1962a. "Nayar: Central Kerala." Pp. 298-384 in *Matrilineal Kinship*, edited by David Schneider and Kathleen Gough. Berkeley: University of California Press.

———. 1962b. "Nayar: North Kerala." Pp. 385-404 in *Matrilineal Kinship*, edited by David Schneider and Kathleen Gough. Berkeley: University of California Press.

Graves, Robert. 1966. *White Goddess: A Historical Grammar of Poetic Myth*. New York: Farrar, Straus & Giroux.

Hass, Hans. 1970. *Human Animal: The Mystery of Man's Behavior*. New York: Putnam.

Hawkes, Jacquetta and Sir Leonard Woolley. 1963. *History of Mankind. Vol. 1. Prehistory and the Beginnings of Civilization*. New York: Harper & Row.

Lee, Richard B. and Irven De Vore, eds. 1968. *Man the Hunter*. Chicago: Aldine.

Leonard, Jonathon Norton. 1973. *The First Farmers*. New York: Time-Life.

Loeb, Edwin M. 1960. "Wine, Women and Song: Root Planting and Head-Hunting in Southeast Asia." Pp. 302-16 in *Culture and History: Essays in Honor of Paul Radin*, edited by Stanley Diamond. New York: Columbia University Press.

Loeb, Edwin M. and J. Broek. 1947. "Social Organization and the Long House in Southeast Asia." *American Anthropologist* 49:414-25.

Mair, Lucy. 1972. *Marriage*. New York: Universe.

McClelland, David C. 1961. *The Achieving Society*. Princeton, NJ: D. Van Nostrand.

McClelland, David C. and David G. Winter. 1969. *Motivating Economic Achievement*. New York: Free Press.

Mellaart, James. 1965. *Earliest Civilizations of the Near East*. New York: McGraw-Hill.

Murdock, George. 1949. *Social Structure*. New York: Macmillan.

Oppong, Christine. 1974. *Marriage Among a Matrilineal Elite: A Family Study of Ghanaian Senior Civil Servants*. Cambridge Studies in Social Anthropology 8. Cambridge: Cambridge University Press.

Pomeroy, Sarah B. 1975. *Goddesses, Whores, Wives, and Slaves: Women in Classical Antiquity*. New York: Schocken.

Sanday, Peggy R. 1973. "Toward a Theory of the Status of Women." *American Anthropologist* 75:1682-1700.

Schneider, David M. and Kathleen Gough, eds. 1962. *Matrilineal Kinship*. Berkeley: University of California Press.

Sherfey, Mary Jane. 1972. *The Nature and Evolution of Female Sexuality*. New York: Random House.

Singer, Charles, E. J. Holmyard, and A. R. Hall. 1954. *A History of Technology. Vol. 1. From Early Times to the Fall of Ancient Rome*. New York: Oxford University Press.

Slater, Philip E. 1968. *The Glory of Hera: Greek Mythology and the Greek Family*. Boston: Beacon.

Stamp, Patricia. 1989. *Technology, Gender and Power in Africa*. Ottawa: International Development Research Center.

United Nations. 1974. "The Data Base for Discussion on the Interrelations Between the Integration of Women in Development, Their Situation and Population Factors in Africa." Regional Seminar on the Integration of Women in Development, with Special Reference to Population Factors. Economic Commission for Africa, U.N. Economic and Social Council, Addis Ababa, May (mimeo).

Vayda, Andrew P. 1961. "Expansion and Warfare Among Swidden Agriculturalists." *American Anthropologist* 63:346-58.

Whiting, John W. M. 1968. Discussant in *Man the Hunter*, edited by Richard B. Lee and Irven De Vore. Chicago: Aldine.

Wilson, Edward O. 1975. *Sociobiology: The New Synthesis*. Cambridge: Belknap Press of Harvard University Press.

5

Megaliths and Metallurgy:
The Walls Close in on Women

In this chapter, covering roughly the period from 6000 to 2000 B.C.E., we will consider the consequences for women of two types of development that accompanied the transition from the nomadic to the settled life: the evolution of new skills of social organization and the discovery of the use of metals for weaponry as well as for tools. In tracing the history of this period, we will follow two migrant streams from the Near East to Europe and look at the peoples who remained behind in the Near East and moved from village and town to city life during these four millennia. The monument builders of Europe, who erected the massive assemblages such as Stonehenge, and the townspeople of the Near East represent very different kinds of cultures. Each group invented significant technologies of social organization during this 4,000-year period: The monument builders managed large-scale enterprises with a nonhierarchical, nonurban form of society, and the Near East townspeople developed the stratified city-state. Both groups were profoundly affected by the coming of metals and weaponry.

Traces of the matrilineal social order described in the last chapter remain, but the requirements of trade, territorial expansion, and warfare shift the focus away from the matrikin. Urban administrations devise new forms of land allotment, and old clan rights disappear. Because the transformations of scale are central to the process of erosion of the status of women, considerable attention will be given to the process, slow and gradual in its day-to-day impact on the folk of village and town, by which clan self-rule of women and men is replaced by the rule of chiefs, kings, and priests, assisted on the side by queens, princesses, and priestesses.

There are many archaeological remains for this period but few recorded legends concerning its peoples. The religious and social practices of the European megalith builders, in particular, remain hidden, making it difficult to do even a speculative reconstruction of women's roles for the megalith people. What is particularly intriguing is that the highly advanced skills of the megalith culture evidently developed in a minimally stratified and peaceful society. Metal smiths and traders arrived among these semi-agrarian village monument builders with something they had not had before: weapons designed specifically for fighting humans. With this new type of tool available, monument building faded away and wars increasingly absorbed the energies of women and men. Tribal organization continued to be strong, however; for the inhabitants of Europe, cities were still in the future.

In the Near East, which already had a head start on agriculture, social patterns changed more rapidly. The metal smiths had introduced their wares here first. Increasingly mobile and numerous, nomad traders pushed populations from the northern hills of the fertile crescent down to the river banks of the Tigris and the Euphrates. It was here that the large trading towns developed as well as the first city-states. Temples, canals, walls, and military skills developed apace in the new cities, as people, monuments, and wealth accumulated and had to be defended. By this time, the future belonged to the specialists: those who could produce monuments and artifacts, those who could administer their use, and those who could organize the countryside as a granary for the city.

Agriculture was also becoming more specialized. The plow was first used in the Near East about 3000 B.C.E. and shortly afterward in Europe.[1] With the pressure of increasing food needs brought about by the growth of towns, there was a premium on increasing production. Men, already specialized as the traders of the villages, would be the first to recognize the advantages of increased production. Because they also had the cattle in their charge, it is logical that the men should be the ones who figured out that, if they had an ox drag a hoe through the fields, the ground could be prepared much more quickly (Jacobsen 1960: 53). Design improvements produced the plow, and soil preparation was taken over by men working ever larger fields.

The shift in the status of the woman farmer may have happened quite rapidly, once there were two male specializations relating to agriculture: plowing and the care of cattle. This situation left women with all the subsidiary tasks, including weeding and carrying water to the fields. The new fields were larger, so women had to work just as many hours as they did before, but now they worked at more secondary tasks. Separation from preparing the ground for sowing was also separation from the age-old planting rite on which both the religious and the social structures were based. This would contribute further to the erosion of the status of women.

In what follows, we shall see what happened to women in Europe and the Near East as the new metal-using, production, and trade-oriented societies developed. To aid the reader in keeping time sequences straight, a chronology of the societies discussed in this chapter is provided in Appendix 5A. A world map is also provided, in Appendix 5B, showing the location of the first world civilizations in relation to the development of agriculture.

The Megalith Builders

The limited productivity of fields and pasturages and the increase in population density in the Near East meant that every couple of generations some families would move on from an overpopulated parent village. By 6000 B.C.E., families were moving along the shores of the Mediterranean and up European rivers either by boat or on foot. We know that they could move by water, for a wooden dugout dating from 6000 B.C.E. has been found in a bog in Holland (Edey 1972: 37). Much more sophisticated longboats with oars would also be plying the Mediterranean by this time. Women, men, children, cattle, seeds, and tools all moved together through the inviting forests of Europe as the damp and cold that were the still-lingering residue of the last ice age finally evaporated. The first villages the farmers built were unprotected by ramparts of any kind, so the migrants apparently mingled freely with the hunting-gathering peoples, the Azilians, who had stayed on in Europe after the fading away of the dynamic Magdalenian culture. The newly introduced farmers' tools and the traditional European hunter-gatherers' tools are found together in village sites.

As noted in the preceding chapter, freestanding, not wall-to-wall, housing suggests a greater emphasis on individual family units in the society. The character of these villages was very different than that of the Near East villages. The dense forests everywhere meant heavy work in clearing land and building houses. It is likely that women and men cleared, built, and planted together.

With plenty of land and wood available, these villages achieved a comfortable standard of living very quickly, as archaeological remains indicate. The groups that crossed the channel to the British Isles and those that settled in France found themselves near valuable quarries and developed sophisticated flint-mining operations. They also built great earthworks, called *causewayed camps*, which were apparently sites for large-scale communal celebrations. They were not fortifications (Wernick 1973: 87-90; Hawkins 1965: 35). We know that the monument builders, as they are sometimes called, had houses that were extremely comfortable and well furnished. This knowledge comes from the accidental uncovering of the small village of Skara Brae in the Orkneys, a third millennium B.C.E. village of this megalith culture. With no earth or wood on the island, everything was made of stone, including built-in furniture, beds, "dressers," tables, and so on. So well designed and efficient were the houses, by twentieth-century standards, that a local woman hired by the archaeologists at the site to work for them "moved into one of the prehistoric houses and lived there quite comfortably" (Wernick 1973: 81-82). Musical instruments have also been found in megalith villages: clay drums of varying sizes for different pitch levels, cow horns with holes in the sides that sound like trumpets, and several types of flutes (Wernick 1973: 83).

It is tantalizing to think of how little we know about the kind of society that produced these villages and built the great earth mounds and then finally the great stone structures.[2] Stonehenge is the best known, though perhaps not the most remarkable, architectural achievement. The monuments of stone that were being built in France, Spain, the British Isles, and Malta between 4800 and 1800 B.C.E. required a degree of engineering skill beyond any known in the world at the time. Although these stone structures range in size and complexity from simple freestanding stones (menhirs) from 2 to 70 feet in height to the towering 40-menhir alignments of Stonehenge, they have enough in common to be labeled as products of a megalith culture distinctively different than any other culture of that three-millennia period.

Many of the stone structures are associated with burials. The bulk of the burial evidence reflects egalitarian societies, with women, men, and children buried in group graves bearing no rank distinctions. Toward the end of this era, however, some individual tombs were constructed for prestigious people.

Because the menhir alignments are not themselves burial mounds, there have been many speculations about the possible religious significance of the monuments. Taking the measurements of Stonehenge is as popular a twentieth-century activity as taking the measurements of the great pyramid was in the nineteenth century. Engineer Alexander Thom of Oxford University and astronomer Gerald Hawkins of Boston University have brought the trained scientific eye and the computer to the problem. Thom makes it clear that the megalith builders worked out many of the concepts attributed to Pythagoras and geometricians of much later dates. They also developed a unit Thom calls the "megalithic yard." Hawkins presents convincing evidence that Stonehenge was used for advanced astronomical observations (Hawkins 1965).

If Stonehenge is in fact designed around sun-moon alignments that make it possible to "capture" eclipses, equinoxes, and other celestial phenomena, this points to a complex knowledge of calendars and cycles that must have continued to accumulate from the time of the Magdalenian record keeping we noted in the last chapter. Some of it must have developed in the Near East, and some of it may have been picked up in fragments from local Azilians by the more sophisticated newcomers. One can imagine that the women of the two intermingling cultures shared their knowledge with each other, and it is perfectly possible that the immigrant women "rediscovered" some lost knowledge that the Azilian women had kept in folklore and rituals.

The newcomers might have grasped meanings that their local teachers did not know they were conveying. In any case, the kind of knowledge that went into the building of Stonehenge, about 2775 B.C.E., had been accumulating for a very long time. The monument builders themselves, while they had a comfortable life, did not have the amount of leisure time, the degree of specialization, or the kind of population density that could have produced Stonehenge and other monuments in a sudden cultural explosion out of "nothing," as has sometimes been depicted.

In fact, the kind of large-scale assemblies implied by the megaliths and the causeways before them were a new social phenomenon. It has been calculated that the Avebury monument could have seated an audience of 250,000 (Wernick 1973: 11). In Malta, a megalithic catacomb tomb contained 7,000 bodies. The practice of periodically opening a community tomb and adding new bodies contributed to the large graveyard population. Because the villages themselves were small, there must have been a communication system and a priesthood of some kind that brought people together in large numbers for special occasions, such as summer and winter solstices.

Some relatively large-scale ceremonial gatherings, which developed the community of potential builders, must have been taking place over a long period of time before the megaliths themselves were built. As it has been estimated that 1,000 strong men (or women) would be needed to transport a single 50-ton stone, and as Stonehenge was built and rebuilt over a 1,200-year period, the populations of many villages must have cooperated in the building. The process would be something like the cathedral building in Europe in the Middle Ages, where entire communities turned out to participate in the hauling of materials and in the building process. The architect-priest-coordinators must have had many skills at their command.

Figure 5.1. Woman Washing Ore, 1556 C.E.
SOURCE: Woodcut from G. Agricola in O'Faolain and Martines (1973); used by permission.

It is hard for us to visualize large-scale nonurban social agglomerations engaging in sustained long-term cooperative activity at high skill levels, but this is precisely what was happening in the megalithic societies.[3] The fact that we do not (before the coming of the Bell Beaker people [1800-1500 B.C.E.]) find evidence of accumulation of personal wealth and power in tombs or houses suggests that the priests, architects, engineers, and overseers were not in a class apart from the ordinary villagers.

What part did women play in the building activities, the ceremonies, and the daily life of the megalithic societies? We do not know for sure. But in Chapter 3 we gave the evidence for both ancient and modern participation of women in construction work. They would hardly have been excluded at this particular moment in history. Certainly they farmed, fished, and made tools and pottery. They probably worked in the flint mines, at crushing rock and separating ore. Figure 5.1, a rendering of a drawing from the Middle Ages in Europe, shows a woman at work at a mine. Toward the end of the megalithic era, in Egypt, women worked as captives and slaves in the gold mines of Nubia (Knauth 1974: 12). Women may have made the small boats of sewn skins stretched over a wooden frame used before the era of the larger trading vessels. They might have made musical instruments, and certainly they worked at monument construction. Assuming there was a specialized priestess role, then the women would have developed engineering skills too. If they continued the observations and record-keeping activities we ascribed to them in the Paleolithic, they would certainly have been able to make the astronomical computations required to determine the placement of the stones at Stonehenge.

We know nothing of the nature of the religion the megaliths honored, except that both sun and moon played a central role in it. Ceremonials involving thousands of people gathered to greet the rising sun at the winter solstice must have created powerful and moving occasions and suggest the possibility of a highly evolved sense of the cosmic as well as a strong sense of community. The human sacrifices found associated with so many of the religions of the Near East are not found in the megalithic cultures.[4] Evidences of a mother-goddess are present, but sporadically. Stylized representations of the female figure, in the tradition of the fertility figurines of Stone Age Europe, are found at some European megalithic sites. The mother-goddess cult is much more strongly evidenced in Malta. In the Maltese temple monuments, the mother-goddess becomes the central cultic figure, as reflected in the statuary and arrangements of shrines (Wernick 1973: 21-22, 36-37). Meandering lines and hitherto undecipherable curves and tracings, similar to those studied by Marshack (1972) for the European Paleolithic, are found in many megalithic tombs. It is not known whether they refer to a mother-goddess. No cult objects are found in private homes, suggesting that worship was a communal rather than a private activity.

We do not have the same evidence here for a matrilineal society that we had in the villages of the Near East, but there are arguments by analogy from twentieth-century matrilinies as described in Chapter 4. If the society was in fact as fluid and egalitarian as I am interpreting it to be, then descent might have been traced through both mother and father. It seems reasonable to think that older fertility-ritual traditions remained as a background to new social developments.

The European megalithic culture appears to have been totally unique in human history, in its development of large-scale social enterprises with a minimum of evidence of social stratification and no clear evidence of military struggle. The nature of the transition to a more warlike society is not clear. There are scholars who maintain that the peoples already in Europe created battle-axes out of the stone hammers and axes they used as tools. There are others who maintain that the battle-ax peoples represented a different culture, coming with more recent migrants from the East (Hawkes and Woolley 1963: 253-54, 317-19, 322). In either case, the peaceful egalitarian society we have just described could not hold its shape in the face of an arms race heavily assisted by traders and metal smiths from the Balkans and the Caucasus. It was not destroyed; it simply armed itself and stopped building megaliths. Whether its ancient secrets were in fact taken into custody and perpetuated by the druidic priesthood that came later we shall never know, given that we know almost as little about the later druids as we know about the megalithic religion. Shadows of the mother-goddess flit in and out of this later religion too, as we shall see shortly.

The Metallurgists

From the Alps to the Persian Gulf, by the year 6000 B.C.E., folk were scrambling on their hands and knees to find metal—gold, silver, copper, iron—in mines, in river valleys, in whatever terrain had been recognized as yielding the new kind of wealth. They were also to be found sweating and stinking in front of hot fires, which gradually evolved into smelting furnaces.

Gold and silver were always for the rich. But copper and iron, used first for jewelry and ornamentation, showed their usefulness for knives and axes. The demand first for copper and then (after 3000 B.C.E.) for iron was immediate and widespread. Metal sickles harvested grain much faster than stone ones. Metal knives cut cleaner and faster than stone ones. Metal axes chopped trees faster, and so on.

Women have found their way into metal smithing from Assyrian times onward; but not many, however. Women's tendency not to specialize would historically have kept most of them out of metallurgy. Yet it might have been otherwise. They stayed with pottery, and eventually became pottery specialists, and the difference between pottery kiln and ore furnace was not so great in the earliest period. In fact, the smelting furnace evolved from the pottery kiln. But metallurgy has long been considered a man's work. A sixteenth-century Sienese writer warned:

> No one should practice it unless he is accustomed to the sweat and many discomforts which it brings. He must suffer the great natural heats of summer as well as those excessive and continuous ones from the enormous fires that are used in this art. . . .
> He who wishes to practice this art must not be of a weak nature, either from age or constitution, but must be strong, young, and vigorous. . . . [T]he

founder is always like a chimney sweep, covered with charcoal and distasteful sooty smoke. To this is added the fact that for this work a violent and continuous straining of all a man's strength is required, which brings great harm to his body and holds many definite dangers to his life. (Knauth 1974: 22)

The author was not trying to dissuade women from the field (he would not even have thought of women, probably); he was warning men that only the brawniest of them would make it.

Metal ornaments are found in Turkey from as early as 9500 B.C.E. (in the already familiar caves of Shanidar) and appear intermittently for the next couple of thousand years. Between 6500 and 5200 B.C.E., metal objects and tools spread all over the Middle East, far from points of origin in local metal mines. The metal smith was the first specialist whose profession determined a whole new way of life. Because of the tremendous demand for metal objects, and the scarcity of metal and metalworkers, the wandering metal smith who set up a little furnace wherever he found metal, and produced tools and jewelry that no villager could produce, became a common figure in the Near East, Europe, and Asia within a few centuries. Twentieth-century gypsies are the last of a social phenomenon 8,000 years old. The metal smith's wife developed a special set of craft skills of her own to complement her husband's, and the nomadic bands had their own kind of egalitarianism, as we will see in Chapter 7.

More was involved than wandering metal smiths, however. The keen demand for metal reorganized the use of labor in the Mediterranean. Towns organized large-scale mining and smelting operations, and soon there was a great demand for slaves to work the mines. Metal adorned, and metal enslaved. The first dagger appeared soon after the first earring, and, shortly after, much of Europe and Asia was armed. The extent of that arming process, however, is quite possibly exaggerated because of our attachment to the warrior tradition in history. Scholars tend to emphasize very strongly the connection between arms and metallurgy.

The Bell Beaker people were the first European metalworkers.[5] They settled among the northern Europeans, taught them their arts, and developed trading networks. They did make knives, but they were also peaceable folk and the emphasis on weaponry came later. The next migrants were metalworker-farmers who settled in the Carpathian Mountains, learned to make bronze, and further developed an international trade network. The graves of these and successive migrating groups, all skilled metalworkers, show increased social stratification and sometimes the practice of burying wife and children with an important chief. Above all, the dead were no longer buried with tools but with weapons. The Urnfield people (labeled from their practice of urn burials), pre-Celtic, seem to have spread by 1250 B.C.E. all over Europe with their weapons and superb bronze tools and seem to have used the former extensively. Did they fight to gain land, to conquer peoples they considered stupid and backward, or just for the fun of fighting? This was a new experience for the Europeans—the monument builders and all the others too. They bought plowshares and swords from the colorful newcomers—and used the plowshares to improve their farming and the swords to defend their farms from these quarrelsome people. Knauth writes admiringly of the "tremendous slashing sword that was the pinnacle of the Urnfield bronze smith's art. Heavily bladed, solidly anchored in its haft, the Urnfield slashing sword turned peasants into heroes for bards to sing about" (1974: 72). Because horses were being tamed in Central Asia by 2500 B.C.E., men on horseback, brandishing swords and spears and wearing helmets and armor, were also a part of the scene.

Now the idea was abroad in Europe of seizing wealth rather than creating it. This meant that every village had to build walls and learn to defend itself. Given the egalitarian society that existed in Europe, both among the monument builders and among the still transitional hunting and gathering peoples, women must certainly have owned and learned to use weapons. Burials do *not* reflect this, however, because only men were buried with their weapons.[6] The chief evidence that women were trained in the art of defense is the wide range of tales that existed by Roman times of tribal women fighting side by side with men on the battlefield and the early Celtic legends of women who conducted "military academies" where they trained men in the art of fighting. These materials will be discussed later.

The building of village walls and the new focus on defense meant a constriction of activity for both women and men, but more for women, who spent more time inside the walls. There is no evidence for the *confinement* of women, however, as is supposed to have happened in India after the Aryan invasions. In fact, we can assume that women sat in village councils as men did and continued their religious ceremonial roles, given that in the time of the Caesars they were still doing these things.

Much of what has been said about the megalithic and postmegalithic woman has been inference, because the evidence is so sparse. Now we are moving toward the historical eras, particularly in Asia and North Africa, although we will still have to turn a great deal to archaeological evidence. History and legend will also have to be disentangled, and this is not easy.

Near East Towns and Walls

The familiar picture of the development of the first cities in the Near East—through the seizure of power by a priest or king (or priest-king) who emerges as top dog in a previously tribal society (e.g., in Mumford 1961)—

appears to be oversimplified. The first fact that we have to face is that the agricultural village-trading town combinations we described in the last chapter were *not* the sites of the first cities. These towns were evidently an abortive urbanism. The first cities developed farther south on the banks of the Tigris and the Euphrates and on the Persian Gulf. Presumably, nomadic peoples north and east of the first agricultural settlements pushed the settlers south as a result of pressures from the steppe lands. Population pressure on the river banks pushed the development of canals so that more food could be grown to feed more people, just as it pushed the development of the plow. Apparently, agriculture, trade, canal building,[7] and the erection of temples all developed more or less concurrently.

It makes little sense to argue about which element is most important in the development of a city: location on a key trade route, agricultural surplus, population density, new technology, skills of social organization. If any of these by itself could produce a city, Jericho and Catal Huyuk would have been among the first cities, given that they were once important trade centers. Or the monument builders would have produced cities, because they had both skills of social organization and some significant population densities on which to draw.

What we are talking about in this chapter is not so much final, or "definitive," urbanization as "primordial urbanization," to use Lampard's phrase (in Hauser and Schnore 1965: chap. 14). *Primordial urbanization* refers to the coming together of diverse subcultures and subenvironments in such a way that symbiotic interaction eventually leads to "more productive modes of collective adaptation to physical and social environment." Peoples, skills, and resources came together in the region that was later known as Sumer.

The very notion of a symbiosis of subcultures implies a greater heterogeneity than was found in the first simple trading towns. The later towns became the meeting places of many cultures. Those who came to settle came for the most part in groups, during the early urbanization. Both the town-magnetized nomads and the agriculturalists in search of new land usually moved in extended-family groupings.

The towns grew in other ways too, because they were on the trade routes between Egypt and Arabia or between Palestine-Syria and Mesopotamia. The trade routes were already ancient by 2000 B.C.E.:

> Bedouins or merchants, messengers and mendicants, armies and refugees passed through the Negev, some staying permanently as peasants or soldiers or pilgrims or miners, striking roots in the soil, and together with their families and kinfolk building up civilizations which maintained relations with the places and cultures of their origins. (Glueck 1960: 48-49)

The new towns of antiquity, created at points on the trade routes, were therefore complex from the beginning. Older towns, growing more slowly, became more complex with time. These older towns were not simple tribal settlements or great family communities, though clan groupings must have been important. They probably represented inter-clan alliances from the start.

It was probably during this phase of town development that the shift from the matrilineal extended-family residences described in the last chapter to patrilineal extended-family residences took place. While Blumberg and Winch's study (1972) of contemporary ethnographic materials led those researchers to suggest that the conditions for development of large family systems sharing common residences would be in agricultural societies with towns having populations under 5,000, in the period we are describing many of these towns might still be matrilineal. With expanding population and the development of several levels of political hierarchy, another predisposing factor Blumberg and Winch propose, we are moving into patrilineal conditions and the likelihood of male-headed extended families. In any case, the number of families actually living together in extended-family households was probably small. Wherever we have records of such living arrangements, with some exceptions to be noted later, extended-family households tend to be associated with the upper classes and with the presence of women slaves as helpers. The phenomenon of generalized sexual availability of domestic slaves to the men of a household must have begun with this earliest urban slavery, adding one more push to the set of forces that were combining to lower the status of women in the city. The general expectation on the part of men that women in service roles were to be sexually available long outlasted slavery and continues into the twentieth century.[8]

The process of establishing rules to handle interclan transactions within the community and with seminomadic herders from the surrounding countryside would have been part of town development from the outset. In the Bau community of early dynastic Lagash, for example, out of a population of 1,200, there were 100 fishermen; 125 sailors, pilots, and longshoremen; and 100 herdsmen. The seminomadic herdsmen were especially important to the town's textile industry. They stayed free of urban roots but worshipped the shepherd god Dumuzi in temples erected for them in the town (Adams 1966: 49). These temples also held supplemental grain stocks for the use of the cattle and became administrative centers for the exchange of goods both for herders and for fishermen (Adams 1960: 30). The equilibrium between herders and townspeople was never an easy one, and, as the towns grew, herdsmen were given special roles in early administrative hierarchies, to try to keep relationships smooth.

In those early days, one of the major jobs of the town administrator was to see to the plowing of the lands belonging to the town. It was done by *corvée* (a labor tax) and *ensik*, the term for the head of the city-state, originally denoted as "the administrator who was in charge of plowed land." Originally, this position could well have been filled by a woman or by a man designated by a council of matrons.

Students of the first urbanization, such as Adams, Jacobsen, and their associates, emphasize strongly that these first towns-to-become-cities grew organically. In the early days, there were assemblies of townspeople, women and men, to deal with problems as they arose (Jacobsen 1960). Temporary officers would be elected to carry out decisions. When conflicts arose with other towns, as specialization in trade introduced rivalries or as hostile nomads began raiding the town or its surrounding fields, temporary "kings" would be appointed to lead in attack or defense. This kind of temporary war-king has been known in tribal areas all over the world. Only as the town grew in size and wealth, extending hegemony over an ever wider agricultural area including nearby villages, would the "king" take on more permanent powers—partly through his own ambition, partly through the disinclination of townspeople to spend so much time traveling to assemblies and making decisions. "Thus," as Jacobsen points out, "the expansion had the effect of overextending and breaking the pattern of primitive democracy on the top political level and replacing it with a new type of pattern: monarchy" (1960: 66).

The gradual differentiation in economic and political roles associated with increasing productivity and affluence, and the need to defend that affluence from others, created two new social phenomena that had not existed before: social distance and expectations of certain kinds of assistance. People who stopped going to assemblies saw the king acting on their behalf, raising armies, defending them. The same process that put distance between the people and their king operated first to put distance between the people and their priestesses and priests. Religious awe fostered the climate in which political combativeness developed. Because full-time priesthoods existed before full-time kingships, the temples in the growing towns were built first. Early administrative systems evolved there; palaces came later. The skills of the priest were only indirectly of use on the battlefield, however, and the independent power of the king grew from the battlefield, not the temple. Nevertheless, the town assemblies never forgot the old days before they had kings.

The process that produces power differentials, centralization, and stratification is a complex one. Our attention is more often drawn to the seizure of power than to the giving over of power. Yet there is a good deal of evidence that, historically, much power has been relinquished rather than seized in situations of early surplus or in the face of new needs for social coordination. The Book of Samuel gives a dramatic instance of such relinquishing of power, in a period just after the one we are discussing in this chapter. Some Israelites, impatient with their democratic system of tribal councils and judges in the face of complex military requirements as they tried to establish themselves in Canaan, went to their judge Samuel and said, "Now make us a king to judge us like all the nations." Jehovah advised Samuel:

> So Samuel told the people what the Lord had said: If you insist on having a king, he will conscript your sons and make them run before his chariots; some will be made to lead his troops into battle, while others will be slave laborers; they will be forced to plow on the royal fields, and harvest his crops without pay; and make his weapons and chariot equipment. He will take your daughters from you and force them to cook and bake and make perfumes for him. He will take away the best of your fields and vineyards and olive groves and give them to his friends. He will take a tenth of your harvest and distribute it to his favorites. He will demand your slaves and the finest of your youth and will use your animals for his personal gain. He will demand a tenth of your flocks, and you shall be his slaves. You will shed bitter tears because of this king you are demanding, but the Lord will not help you.
>
> But the people refused to listen to Samuel's warning. "Even so, we still want a king," they said, "for we want to be like the nations around us. He will govern us and lead us to battle." (1 Sam. 8: 5-20, translation from *The Living Bible*, copyright 1971 by Tyndale House Publishers, Wheaton, Illinois 60187; used by permission)

The principle of the giving over of power works in many different kinds of settings. It has been noted in Iraq today that, once the government has placed an engineer in an area to be in charge of a specific task such as irrigation works, the villagers will come to him with many other unrelated problems and give him a decision-making authority that he has not asked for (Fernea, in Kraeling and Adams 1960: 35-37). The widespread practice in the Arab world of seeking an outside mediator rather than the local sheikh when there is a serious controversy is an example of a largely unintentional giving over of power. The mediator is supposed to be disinterested but may of course use his position to further her or his own ends.

What this suggests is that the most elemental differentiation in authority, if it continues long enough to create social distance between locals and the one wielding authority, and if the need for authority is great enough, gives other kinds of authority to the power holder because she or he is seen as having superior problem-solving skill. This process creates two new kinds of power: political and religious.

The rise of cities thus presents to us a mind-boggling interplay of forces, as the original town assemblies alternately give and try to retract power, as kings and priests alternately seize or are handed power, each needing the other, yet each fighting to protect their separate privileges. The temple-palace administrations characteristic of Sumerian cities by 2000 B.C.E. were, then, secondary developments grafted onto the original towns. Memories of an ideal "town and temple" system stayed alive all through Mesopotamian history, according to Jacobsen (1960), and civic pride made it surface every time a ruling king violated ancient rights. Where royal decrees were recorded stating that the citizens of such-and-such a town did not have to pay taxes or contribute soldiers to the king's army, this was probably restitution to an aroused citizenry that had been wronged in some way. Over and over, kings appear to have been forced to the wall by rebellious civic assemblies. The founding of entirely new capital cities, as we find in Sumerian times, was often a king's desperate response to the noncooperation of his subjects. In a new town of his own founding, with no ancient rights to take account of, he could tax and conscript as he pleased. Recruits would come to live there through a combination of bribery and forced resettlement.

The very concept of the development of social distance involved in this "organic" model of the rise of cities lies at the heart of the problem of women's roles in the emerging urban scene. In one sense, all social bonds are distance bridging, whether they are kin ties or political ties. The distance bridging involved in kinship labeling, however, has a special immediacy about it that is associated both with the feelings about the kinship group as a solidary group and with feelings about the mother role as a key aspect of the solidarity. It is probably no accident, as Borgese points out, that collective nouns tend to be feminine and that "the typical, the generic, the non-individual, these are associated in our minds, and therefore in our languages, with the feminine, no less than the collective" (1963: 76-77). The feminine is associated with the aspect of the family that is dedifferentiating. The dedifferentiating aspect of kinship can particularly be noticed in such customs as adoption and blood brother ceremonies through which the stranger is made one with the group.

The distance of the *majestas*, the ruler, the lord, from his subjects is at least in part a distance that is first created, *then* bridged. Those who do best at administration and ruling have to have distance-creating skills as well as bonding skills. Distancing is necessary both to develop perspectives on the working of all parts of the system one deals with and to deal impersonally with conflicting wants and needs of persons inside the system. The claims of kinship or any other ties are not supposed to sway one's judgment about just allocation of resources in the polity.

A woman can perfectly well learn these skills, and we will see that she often has done so. There is, nevertheless, a set of situational determinants that work against women's development of distancing skills, related to their biological role. (The matrilineal society resolved this by creating a certain amount of distance in the mother-goddess role.) As long as women are operating within the land-linked clan structures, their administrative skills operate without deterrence, because little specialization is required. Women's problems arise at the point where clan structures begin to recede in importance while the public sphere, which by definition lies outside clan structures, expands. Once social differentiation has reached the point where political bonding must supplement and extend beyond kin bonding, a woman's nonspecialist position becomes a real handicap.

An example from the hypothesized development of the urban center of Susa in the Uruk culture of the Susiana Plain of Iran in the period 3500-3150 B.C.E. will make the woman's problem clear (Johnson 1975: 294-306). By the middle Uruk period, there were 52 settlements in the Susiana Plain, consisting of villages and small towns ranging in site size from 1 to 8 hectares, and two urban centers, one of 10 and one of 25 hectares (Choga Mish and Susa, respectively). Archaeological excavations have shown that pottery made at each settlement had its own distinctive characteristics. It has therefore been possible to study the distribution of each pottery type and thus identify a distribution network and emergent administrative system for the entire area, centered in Susa. While details of the interpretation of the data have been questioned (Adams 1966: 158-59), the main outlines are believable. Any kind of communication system linking one large urban center with 51 smaller ones would be operating with channels that crosscut kinship channels.[9] The skill to "work the system" would be a specialized skill standing outside the array of clan specialties. This was the kind of specialization that matrilinies did not develop.

Sumer

What we will see happening to women in the towns of Sumer and elsewhere is a progressive lessening of their participation in significant decision making as clan-based roles recede in importance. Their roles continue to have some visibility, but decreasingly so. While women's failure to specialize left them behind as trade and crafts became more important, they continued to have important public roles because of their traditional responsibility for allocating and working the land and for serving in the temples of the religious cults. When the development of the plow, as outlined earlier, put more of the agricultural process in the hands of men, women began to be faced with an increasingly difficult situation regarding control over resources and production processes. Not only were they being elbowed aside in regard to decisions about land, but in some areas they were also being pushed out of pottery making too. This process was hardly a kindly effort to relieve overburdened women but was the beginning of a very long-term trend involving relegation of all unskilled and miscellaneous tasks to women. Though we have no records describing the struggles that must have gone on as women resisted having valued roles taken away from them, we should not imagine that they quietly laid down their digging sticks and let men take over. Many centuries later, when the men of London forced the women out of one of their major occupations—brewing—we know that the women fought hard and bitterly against the loss of their occupation. But protests, petitions, and pitched battles were to no avail. And so it must have been in the Middle East, several thousand years ago.

Still, the force of custom and the need for their knowledge and experience must have kept women on the town councils for a time after this process started.[10] Certainly they held on to land rights as best they could as well as to matrilineal descent reckoning. So, while materials from early dynastic Lagash, a city of the Sumerian culture, make it clear that the descent of the elites was usually recorded in government records through the male, sometimes a woman is named and descent traced through her. Women sometimes appear in land deeds as heads of households and as donors and recipients of ritualized food offerings. They are recorded as doing long-distance trading under their own names, and they sometimes held administrative posts as wives of ruling husbands, as in the case of Baranamtarra, wife of the ruler Lugalanda (Adams 1966: 82).

Women's strongest position was in relation to the temples. In general, a female priesthood served the male gods, and a male priesthood served the female gods. The names of nearly all the high priestesses are recorded from the time of King Sargon forward. Harris, in her study of clay tablets recording business and legal affairs of the city of Sippar, has found the names of 10 women scribes out of a total of 185 scribes listed between 1850 and 1550 B.C.E. (in Claiborne 1973: 101). We do not know whether these women scribes were trained in regular scribal schools with men or whether they were taught inside the women's temple organizations. It is possible that women, like men, could choose between secular and religious training. In any case, many women would be needed to administer the large temple complexes.

Sumer had essentially three major centers of economic and political power: the palace, the temple, and private clan holdings (Diakonoff 1959: 77). Women participated in temple and clan administration but rather rarely in palace administration. The title "lasting ladyship" may refer to palace-conferred titles, but such titles are rare (Kramer 1963). The fact that the king of Sumer ritually married a representative of the goddess Inanna once every year helped sustain the power of the priestesses for a time at least.

In the earlier, more democratic era of Sumer, women carried out a variety of business activities and freely used the "street scribes" available to everyone. As the society became more stratified and specialized, the street scribes disappeared (Kramer 1963). Women workers lost their independent status. When we see them later in the textile factories in teams of three, spinning and weaving, it is not clear whether they were simply unmarried women, or slaves, or war captives.

Farming was increasingly in the hands of the men. A "farm manual" recently translated (Kramer 1963: 105-8) is written as from a father to his son, with no mention of female agricultural activities at all. Because we can be sure that women were actually working in the fields, the lack of mention of this fact in the manual is an indication of the rapid erosion of women's status as farm laborer. Lists of herbal remedies from a "pharmacopeia" (Kramer 1963: 93-97) may originally have been prepared by women herbalists for male doctors, as we know was the case later in Europe, but there is no hint of the fact in the existing records.

The various cities of Sumer differed from one another, of course. Erech, which was overrun by conquering nomad war bands in 3500 B.C.E., had a more patriarchal cast than Lagash; there seems to have been a complete absence of participation of women in public affairs in Erech. The same basic pattern of palace and temple, schools, a system of "law and order," and written records, however, were found in all towns. Stratification was increasingly rigid. The temple roster in Erech lists the following categories of persons in 2500 B.C.E.: upper-class scribes, ordinary scribes, teachers, city fathers, ambassadors, temple administrators, military officers, sea captains, tax officials, priests, managers, supervisors, foremen, archivists, accountants. No women are mentioned at all.

The nomadic warlord tradition imposed on Erech contrasts markedly with the Lagash tradition, which developed locally. Warlordism led to a degree of stratification not found in communities that did not have to absorb these alien elements. Old rights and privileges resisted erosion, everywhere, however. The fact that Hammurabi's code in 1751 B.C.E. contained 68 sections on family and women, 50 on land and territory, and 7 on priestesses indicates that women and clan rights were still a very important part of the Sumerian polity more than 1,000 years after the time we are discussing.

As Sumerian cities developed in the pre-Hammurabic millennia, the long process of redefining matrilineal clan rights to suit a newly evolving patrilineal descent system took place. As increasing stratification left all but elite women in privatized roles of domestic production, the battle to defend ancient rights on the part of women of the middle classes who still retained interests in agricultural land must have shifted from town council to palace courtyard. Kings emerge very early as administrators of justice. For some reason, women were never barred from the king's court of justice, although they were excluded from other public spaces. In all the ancient civilizations, and up to modern times, we will find women in the courts claiming their rights. While these rights have been severely reduced at times, it appears that the ruling class has to some extent always recognized the importance of the producer role of women and provided them with whatever protection the prevailing law allowed. The phenomenon of the court as the interface between the privatized life spaces of women and the public spheres of society must be considered in assessing the status of women in any period of history. An adequate understanding of the role of law in determining the participation of women in producer roles must await a systematic comparative study of all codifications of law, ancient and modern, with respect to provisions regarding women's marital status, inheritance rights, and rights to land and to capital for the transaction of business.

Codes of law were not initially the most conspicuous feature of new urban developments, however. The most visible aspects of developments in Lagash, Erech, and Ur centered on the emergence of complex temple-palace ceremonial centers and a powerful priesthood. Successive archaeological layers of these cities show an expanding *temenos*—the walled religious citadel within the town containing temples, palaces, and government buildings (Morris 1974: 7-11). Located on desert as well as water trade routes to Syria, Egypt, and India, these communities provided ample opportunities for king and priest to accumulate economic and political power. (In Ur, at one period, the high priest and king were brothers and continually struggled with each other for dominance.) When surpluses made armies possible, between harvest and seed time, nearby towns and villages were captured. Finally, there was intercity warfare and a series of "empires" depending on which city-state had most recently conquered its neighbors in war. The plum of governorship of a conquered town evidently was sometimes handed to a woman. King Dungi of Ur (2459-2401 B.C.E.), for example, made his daughter "lady" (apparently ruler) of Markhashi in the district of Elam. There was more monument building than warring, however, and in between warrior kings there were also peaceable ones. King Urukagina curbed the extortions of priests at funerals; prevented them from stripping the gardens of the common people of their fruit, "for taxes;" dismantled the army; and gave slaves "rights."

There is an amusing debate between the two Sumerologists, Kramer (1956, 1963) and Jacobsen (1960), about what the Sumerians were really like.

Figure 5.2. Arbela Today, Much as It Was in the Fifth Millennium B.C.E. Re-drawn by KH.

Kramer sees them as contentious, ambitious people always on the make, while Jacobsen sees them as relatively peaceable, family-loving, moral, and socially conscious people. They were surely both. The two-edged character of the *polis* as a people-shaping force, observed and commented on so frequently through history, is as evident at the birth of the city as in its later evolution.

After 2,000 years of intercity jockeying and warring, Sumer declined as the civilization-building dynamic shifted to Babylonia. What we can see of the remains of the 89-hectare walled city of Ur, population 35,000, gives us a taste, however, of the cities to come and of the life for the women in them. Figure 5.2, a drawing from an aerial photograph of Erbil (ancient Arbela), is of a city very much as Ur would have been; the patterns have not changed since the fourth millennium B.C.E. We get a strong sense of crowding, of lack of space. Children must have played in those narrow alleys; the earliest references to cities describe children playing in the streets, as in Zachariah,

Chapter 8: "and the streets of the city shall be full of boys and girls playing in the streets thereof." The women, however, saw little of the streets. The enclosed courtyard pattern that characterizes the Middle Eastern city pushed women of the middle class out of public life. The village houses of preurban Hacilar had courtyards, but they opened into one another. Women were able to gather together and carry out many of their activities communally. In the new cities, they were walled off from one another. With few public roles and few public gathering places, the walls were indeed closing in for women. Working women and domestic slaves continued to move about freely, as did the farm women outside the city walls, but there are no records of their lives. Among the elite women, there would be continued administration of family holdings outside of the city, as reflected in the Hammurabic Code. Rural holdings would continue to be important for women's roles in the upper classes right up to the industrial era. We do not know how important the priestesses were who administered the women's temple buildings excavated in Ur, but they had a substantial area inside the *temenos*. Here was their public arena, close to the center of power.

Clearly, Sumerian society had become increasingly stratified, and women lost ground even as their nice new center-courtyard houses were being built up around them. Nevertheless, as the center of power shifted from temple to palace, and the social dynamic shifted from peace to war, women held on to what they could. The shadow of the old egalitarian society did not totally disappear.

Egypt

Egypt, in all the long history of its classical period, never developed an urban infrastructure separate from the temple administration ruling the country on behalf of its pharaoh.[11] In predynastic times, every village had its own deity, and these were frequently female. None of these original goddesses was a "spouse" goddess, but were divinities in their own right. Later, gods and goddesses came to be listed in "companies," with complementary male and female divinities listed together. This later pairing, which linked the fate of the female divinity with that of the male, could not, however, take away from the fact that in early times female deities operated autonomously. The fortunes of a local goddess were intimately bound up with the fortunes of her village; when the village prospered, her rank and dignity kept pace; in times of defeat, she was abused. The total number of deities was gradually reduced as deities of certain villages gained special fame and were adopted by other villages. In the later process

Figure 5.3. Isis With Horus, c. 2040-1700 B.C.E. Redrawn by HBR.

of selection from which the "great gods" of Egypt emerged, the cards were stacked by political maneuverings of priests. By the time the god Amon-Ra had become top god, his priests had seized for him the attributes of all the other gods and goddesses (Budge 1904). But local memories were stronger than priestly maneuvers, and reflections of earlier matrilineal orientations on the fertile-crescent pattern are found everywhere.

Priests at the major temples consolidated their power by bringing village deities and their attendants to the "capital city"— which changed from pharaoh to pharaoh over the centuries. The continuance of the priestess role during this time in the face of deterioration of other aspects of women's roles can be attributed in part to the continuing power of the goddesses the women served. Neith, the great goddess of Sais, was one such powerful goddess. She was originally a local Libyan delta goddess, the uncreated source of all being. Traits belonging to Neith turn up in nearly all other goddesses, including Isis and Hathor. She was also a *theotokos*, mother of god, and produced a son by parthenogenesis. Statues of Neith-Iss-Hathor, with an infant at her breast, have been taken in the Christian era for the Christian virgin and child (Figure 5.3).

During the Old Kingdom epoch, all 22 of the Neith priesthoods were held by women (Murray 1908). During these centuries, priestesses performed a whole range of duties, from mummifying bodies, preparing funeral papyri, and serving as mourners (Figure 5.4), to maintaining temple buildings, copying manuscripts, and providing religious education for the community. Later, they were only allowed to sing and dance in temple choirs. Designating a woman as high priestess in early dynastic periods meant she *functioned* as a high priestess. In later periods, it was a purely honorific title with no duties.

Wenig's (1970) study of women's roles in ancient Egypt as portrayed in its art points to evidence from prehistoric times of a long-existing equality

Figure 5.4. Chorus of Professional Egyptian Mourners: Tomb Painting. Redrawn by HBR.

of rights between women and men. Women had their own separate tombs, as well furnished as men's, from earliest times; they had their own statues and tombstones when these became part of funerary custom. Social class, not sex, determined the quality of the tombs. Queens, princesses, court ladies, wives of administrators, and wives of workers all had tombs appropriate to their rank. Later, however, by the time of the great age of pyramids, queens' tombs were dwarfed by those of the pharaohs.

Old and Middle Kingdom references in later papyri indicate that the women had full competence and rights in law and business. A woman could

> dispose of private property, such as land, servants, and slaves, money or materials, and administrate it according to her own free and independent will. She could conclude any kind of settlement, appear as contracting partner in marriage contracts, execute treatments, free slaves, make adoptions, or officiate as a witness of records. . . she was even entitled to sue at law. (Wenig 1970: 12)

So independent was she in marriage that she could lend her husband money and charge him a stiff rate of interest. She could exclude her own children from her inheritance if she wished.

Queens and princesses and some upper-class women knew how to write, and there are mentions of women scribes. Nevertheless, while peasant and artisan-class women worked, upper-class women, apart from priestesses, had few public roles. What roles they did have were in a typically feminine sphere—a woman might be headmistress of the wig or weaving workshop, or of the women singers, or professional mourners (Figure 5.4), all associated with the temple or the women's section of the palace.

We can see outlined in Egyptian history the dual status of the woman of the elite, as we shall see it again and again in later periods. Stemming from an earlier, probably matrilineal, agricultural era when she did indeed exercise full decision-making power in her village council and in the village temple, her role in the rich, highly stratified society of Pharaonic Egypt kept, at the very highest level, some of the characteristics of that earlier time. She was educated and she was honored, and her "rights" were fully elaborated—but, like her Sumerian sister, she was gradually removed from significant decision making and exercise of power.[12] Reflections of that earlier status for women are seen in later Egyptian society to the extent that the fairly elaborate provisions for contractual relationships found in temple records continued to be applied to all who were educated enough to make use of them. (Then as now, of course, a poor, uneducated woman such as the corn grinder in Figure 5.5 would scarcely know how to make use of her "rights.") We will see in the next chapter how that basic level of elite education made possible occasional dramatic eruptions of powerful women on the public scene in Egypt.

India

India appears to have gone through a Near East-type sequence of scattered, self-sufficient agricultural villages in hill country followed by a shift to the Indus Valley and irrigated agriculture and the rise of larger, centralized towns and trading centers that dominated surrounding villages (Fairservis 1971, chaps. 4, 5). The archaeological record gives evidence of a considerable degree of social stratification in these central villages, in terms of type of housing, administrative centers, and cult buildings. There were craft specialists and priesthoods in these towns, and cultic remains of "goggle-eyed mother-goddesses." Imposing "planned cities" of 35,000 to 40,000 people of the Harappan civilization flourished from 2300 to 1500

Figure 5.5. Girl Grinding Corn, Fifth Dynasty (Egypt). Redrawn by HBR.

B.C.E. These urban centers owed at least as much to local developments as to the Sumerian traders, of whom evidence is everywhere in the major cities of this civilization (Fairservis 1971, chaps. 6, 7). The Harappan civilization is a voiceless one, however. Apart from as yet undecipherable seal inscriptions, no system of writing appears to have developed. The huge buildings inside the walled towns could be for baths, cultic worship, food storage, or palace administration—there is no way to tell from the remains. Because there is no record of the lives of the men, there is certainly none of the lives of the women.

It appears to have been a static civilization, never developing beyond the very earliest stage of the comparable Sumerian cities. It slowly faded away into a succession of smaller towns whose elaborate paved stone roads, monumental buildings in a raised central area of town, and megaliths erected in various arrangements between towns belied the apparent simplicity of the subsequent way of life (Fairservis 1971, chap. 9).

The invading Aryans, nomads from the Asian steppes who are supposed to have stormed the walls of Harappa (Wheeler, in Fairservis 1971: 310-11) and then settled down in India, gave rise to the literature of the Vedic Age. It is from this epic literature that we know something about the women of India. The Vedas are variously dated as being first composed as early as 2500 B.C.E. or as late as 1000 B.C.E., but they were certainly not written down until well on in the first millennium B.C.E. or even later. Because this body of literature was first handed down through oral tradition, the "facts" so recorded do not have the same weight as those recorded in historical eras. On the other hand, they contain history as well as myth and deserve at least as careful attention as the much studied later Homeric legends.

Given that the Vedas were composed after the Aryans had attacked the cities, we must suppose that the poetic tradition from which the Vedas sprang developed in these post-Harappan towns with their contradictory evidence of complex ceremonial observances and relatively simple, nonurban living. Were these towns the origins of the Panchayat tradition, the famous Indian village republics? Or does that tradition reach back to the centralized villages of pre-Harappan times? Fairservis (1971) does not mention the Panchayat, but he does speak of clan councils ruling the villages and of evidence that the pre-Harappan villages were all linked administratively to the centralized stratified villages. The Panchayat tradition may then go back to 3000 B.C.E. or further. A student of the tax records for the pre-British Indian villages has uncovered systematic evidence that local village councils in various regions themselves administered most of the taxes they collected, sending only 20% on to the rajah or king and making all kinds of disbursements to villagers for both practical and ceremonial services to the community.[13] But the British reversed the direction of flow of funds, leaving only 20% in local coffers, and as a consequence the picture of active village councils in the Panchayat tradition has been discounted by many contemporary scholars.

For our purposes, the existence of the Panchayat tradition is important, because the women participated in it. Scholars by no means agree on women's roles in the Panchayat, but the position taken in Barbara Ward's *Women in the New Asia* (1963), of a gradual decline in women's status from Vedic times until near the end of the first millennium B.C.E., is the one followed here. A. S. Altekar's ([1956] 1978) research on women's roles in India will be used in this section. (Of course, a more complete study would need to draw on many different sources.) Altekar writes: "There were democratic assemblies in the Vedic age. The marriage hymn expresses the hope that the bride would be able to speak with composure and success in these public assemblies in her old age" ([1956]: 190). Later, women were forbidden to attend these assemblies.

It appears that there was a very substantial deterioration in the status of women—which may have begun in the Vedic Age itself—from an earlier era of full participation in the public life of the village. The Vedas reflect this higher status. At the time of the Vedas, the women of the upper strata in the towns married at the age of 16 and apparently spent considerable time in Vedic studies before marriage:

> In prehistoric times lady poets themselves were composing hymns, some of which were destined to be included even in the Vedic samhitas. According

to the orthodox tradition itself as recorded in the Sarvanukramanika, there are as many as twenty women among the "seers" or authors of Rigveda. Some of these may have been mythical personages; but internal evidence shows that Lopamudra, Visvavara, Sikata Nivavari and Ghosha, the authors of the Rigveda 1.179, V. 28, VIII. 91, IX. 81. 11-20 and X. 39 and 40 respectively, were women in flesh and blood who once lived in Hindu society. (Altekar [1956]: 10)

Women students were divided into two classes, Brahmavadinis and Sadyodvahas. The former were life-long students of theology; the latter used to prosecute their studies until their marriage at the age of fifteen or sixteen. [Note: This would already be in a later era.] During the eight or nine years that were thus available to them for study, they used to learn by heart the Vedic hymns prescribed for the daily and periodical prayers and for those rituals and sacraments in which they had to take an active part after their marriage. . . . [W]hen writing came into general vogue, girls were initiated into the three R's as a matter of course. ([1956] 1978: 11)

Women scholars who specialized in a theological work called Kasakritsni

were designated as Kasakritsnas. If lady scholars in such a technical branch of study were so numerous as to necessitate the coining of a special term to designate them, is it not reasonable to conclude that the number of women, who used to receive general education, must have been fairly large?
     Education was mostly centered in the family; brothers, sisters and cousins probably studied together under the family elders. (Altekar [1956]: 11)

And, finally, my favorite item of information from the Vedic age: "We find one of the early Upanishads recommending a certain ritual to a householder for ensuring the birth of a scholarly daughter. Brih. Up. IV. 4. 18" (Altekar [1956]: 3).
     These paragons of scholarship were also active in a variety of occupations. They farmed, wove and dyed cloth, embroidered, and followed the teaching profession. Artisan women made weapons including bows and arrows. Lower-class women traded, though upper-class women did not. Every upper-class woman was also expected to carry out the ordinary domestic and hostess duties and to perform the Vedic rituals side by side with her husband, if married.
     Whatever the proportions of myth and history in these references, this is an interesting conception of a woman's life for 2000 B.C.E.! That there is something unusual in the Indian tradition will come out later when we look at Indian women warriors.

China

Not very much can be said about China in this period because the earliest archaeological evidence of town life to date comes from the Shang Dynasty in 1500 B.C.E. That evidence points to an already ancient culture, but, apart from Neolithic villages at the stage discussed in the last chapter, nothing has been found. We can suggest one thing about the role of women in this period, however. In emerging village and town life, women must have had important shamaness roles. In later centuries, there were frequent efforts to stamp out the Bronze Age shamaness tradition. It nevertheless cropped up repeatedly in historical eras in times of crisis. For example, an eighth-century drought impelled a high government minister to send shamanesses out to all parts of the realm to perform religious rites. They must have been around all along or he could never have found them. His successor, an unbeliever, had the shamanesses jailed or executed (Schafer et al. 1967: 65). There is also a tradition that the divine legitimation of ancient legendary kings of China derived from the mating with a beautiful "rain-goddess." A ritual mating of the king with a high priestess-shamaness is thought to have continued down to Chou times (Schafer et al. 1967). We noted this type of ritual mating of king and priestess in Sumer. This may have been a common practice in many early monarchies, giving evidence of earlier matrilineal days.

Women's Roles in Fact and Myth

It seems clear that urbanization in many ways "encloses" women. Mumford (1961) speaks of the city as the container; it contains all kinds of material possessions, and it *contains* women—but it seems to *launch* men. Social class moderates the containment. Among the elite, politically minded priestesses probably had a very interesting life, and the male workers, peasants, and soldiers probably were no freer than their spouses. Few women's voices were heard in councils of state, however. The palace complex was the terrain of the princess and the high priestess only.

The privatization of women's roles has begun. In the earlier, open-courtyard village, child care was much more of a community undertaking. Women worked in groups on a variety of tasks. For the lower classes, this was still true, to some extent, with urbanization, but the work was so hard that there was no margin for leisure or reflection, certainly not for more than reactive thinking about the state of the polis. Furthermore, the successive cramping and contraction of living space for the poor in the newly walled towns and cities cut down even further on the possibility that they might make constructive use of free hours. In a book like the *History of Urban Form* (Morris 1974), one can trace this gradual contraction and deterioration of living space for the urban poor from prehistory to the Renaissance, and the history is a grim one.

The life of elite women was never privatized, but it was gradually delimited. The increasing militarism of society diminished their palace roles and left them with increasingly ceremonial, nonpolitical functions. Settled agricultural societies have no traditions of military training for women. Some of the nomadics were to develop this, but it scarcely affected urban societies. A whole new set of cultural prescriptions for woman as a householder was about to develop, and we will follow this in the next chapter.

At the very moment that her roles were in fact being privatized, however, myth was at work in the opposite direction, creating a public image of woman as the creator of culture to an extent beyond what had ever (in all likelihood) existed in fact. We can deal with this at two levels. At one level, these myths are what Campbell calls facts of the mind (1972: 11), a way of ordering our own inward understanding of the nature of reality. At that level, these myths tell us about a profound reverence that men have for women. They are the "praise books" consciously produced by one sex for the other. At another level, they often present an elaboration, however fantastic, of certain historical facts. The effort to ground mythic figures in real-life persons cannot simply be dismissed by labeling it *euhemerism*. In fact, deification of ancestors was widely practiced in all the early civilizations. It was particularly applied to queens and kings who achieved special fame in their lifetimes. So, while we know perfectly well that Juno, Ceres, Minerva, Venus, Isis, and Europa are goddesses, maybe Boccaccio was not entirely wrong when, in his delightful *De Claris Mulieribus* (*Concerning Famous Women*) in C.E. 1359 (1963), he gave biographies of Queen Ceres of Sicily, inventor of many things associated with agriculture; Queen Minerva of Lemnos and Cyprus, who discovered the use of oil and invented spinning, armor, and numbers; Queen Isis, daughter of the first king of the Argives, who fled to Egypt, civilized that country, gave it laws and an alphabet; or when he described Queen Juno as a native of Samos who married King Jupiter, Queen Venus as a native of Lemnos who married King Vulcan, and Queen Europa of Crete as the mother of King Minos.[14]

In any case, a variety of goddesses, some of whom may have been based on flesh-and-blood queens, are recorded as having done useful things for humankind in the past. They have also been considered useful in this time for things as varied as childbirth and war. Beard comments on how often the early empires transformed one of their goddesses into a war goddess:

How commonly she was so transformed may be seen in a study of that attribute of her potency which is elaborated in the first volumes of the *Cambridge Ancient History* dealing with the rise and fortunes of great historic states. (1946: 287)

Diner ([1932] 1965), from a less scholarly stance, points out that a female deity is also frequently associated with the administration of justice—a role that, if it ever was hers, certainly did not translate into city life: "Demeter, Themis, Nike, Poine, Nemesis, Erinys, and Justitia are the bearers of an ancient order, never completely replaced by the later, man-made law" (1965: 18).

A third realm frequently associated with the woman-goddess is, interestingly enough, the alphabet. There are a whole series of woman-as-alphabet-giver legends, and, because these are less well known than those associating women with agriculture, war, and justice, I will mention a few here, culled from Graves's fantasy-rich *White Goddess* (1966) and other sources. Colleges of women priestesses are frequently associated with these legends as well as with queens and goddesses.

Carmenta, in one version, a Syballine priestess who presided over a college of maidens at a place also called Carmenta, is supposed to have created a Latin alphabet from the Greek. In another version, Carmenta is replaced by Queen Nicostrata of Arcadia, who helped found Rome. She is also known as a goddess and sometimes as an alternate form of Minerva, the goddess of wisdom.

Medusa of the Gorgons, a beautiful Libyan warrior queen whom Perseus, King of Argives, decapitated in battle, and who was later identified with the Libyan snake-goddess Lamia, is involved in giving the alphabet to Hercules; the Gorgon thus has the typical dual role in mythology of being both helper and fiend.

Queen Isis, already mentioned as a refugee from Greece in Egypt and giver of the alphabet to the Egyptians, is in the Archbishop of Seville's version of history (C.E. 636) credited with bringing the alphabet back from Egypt to Greece.

Bloodeuwedd is another priestess with a college of maidens, identified with Athena, goddess of wisdom. Her gift of wisdom was displaced by the new order of Apollo, so her 50 maidens jumped in the lake rather than being ruled by Apollo.

Samothea, a Briton, invented letters, astronomy, and science. According to some stories, she also ran the Hyperborean University in Cornwall, where Pythagoras is rumored to have studied. Pythagoras is also said to have learned the ancient alphabets from priestesses at a Minoan-Cretan college.

These priestesses turned the older hieroglyphics into an alphabet-syllabary. There is also the legend of a Vedic college where the priestess-goddess Kali invented the Sanskrit alphabet. The Egyptian goddess Safekh-Aabut was sometimes recorded as the source of the alphabet in Egypt, alternately with Isis, and had the role of "recording angel"; she was also in charge of literature and libraries. Sumer, too, has its legends about gifts of knowledge from women. Inanna, goddess of Erech, makes an adventurous trip to Eridu to the god of wisdom and tricks him into giving her the "100 or more divine decrees" that she brings back to Erech for her people against great odds. Nidaba is the Sumerian goddess of the alphabet and of accounts (Kramer 1963). And the list of legends continues.

How is one to interpret these legends? We know that women did have a hand in the development of agriculture. Did they participate, as well, in the administration of tribal justice, in a priestess or prophetess role? There is ample evidence for this, as we will see in the next chapter. Did they contribute to the development of the alphabet? The status of women in the period of the first systematic record keeping that we know of, in Sumerian temples, does not forbid such an interpretation, but neither does it support it. And, while we will see a number of warrior queens, the likelihood of women having played a key role in the initial development of the martial arts is almost nil. In fact, the general shift of power away from priestess-run temples to palace and male priesthood that seems to have taken place with the rise of militarism would be enough to put the alphabet into the hands of the men, if the women indeed had "had it first." The stories of mass drownings of colleges of priestesses hint at dramatic takeovers by the men. Endless speculations are possible, but unfortunately there are few facts.[15]

The invocation of woman as patron and/or inventor in spheres of major human activity over the next three millennia, precisely during the era when women are becoming less visible to the public eye, is certainly interesting. If the myths are not to be taken as having specific historical import, they at least point to the significance of women as the agents of symbolic reality construction in four major human activities: agriculture, war, peace (justice, order), and letters. While some of the myths originate as late as the first millennium B.C.E., the time period to which they refer lies somewhere in the third and fourth millennia or earlier. The use of the goddess as a legitimating authority for human enterprises as late as Greek and Roman times might be considered one kind of lingering evidence of an earlier, more public, role for women.

It is interesting to contrast this line of analysis, which focuses on the analytic-cognitive contributions of women to cultural development, with the Jungian analysis, which emphasizes that women's chief contribution has been through "moon thinking," that is, nonrational thought. Esther

Harding, a gifted and articulate student of Jung, has described this kind of thinking, which relates to Sophia, or divine wisdom, as

> the wisdom of that inner spark which speaks and functions of itself, quite apart from our conscious control. This wisdom was called the Divine Sophia. The Greek word sophos means wisdom and Sophia is a person- ification of wisdom, the Lady Wisdom or the Goddess Wisdom. She is the highest incarnation of the feminine principle, the Moon Goddess in her function of spirit, divine knowledge. (1971: 232-33)

Unquestionably, "moon thinking" refers to a profoundly important intu- itive capacity that Western rationalistic traditions have shunted to one side. It is doubtful, however, that the best way to redress the balance is now to elevate this capacity as something peculiarly feminine in the human con- dition. Jung and Harding use *masculine* and *feminine* in a more technical sense than does the layperson, to connote bundles of capacities that lie in each of us, but the danger is that more simplistic associations will be made. It is important to look at the full range of human capacities available to women and to men and to note and deal with the imbalance as they appear. This, in fact, is the goal of Jungian analysis.

* * *

We stand now at the threshold of the great primary civilizations, and the process has already begun of relegating women to the minor elite and interstitial roles in the urban areas where these civilizations are arising. The earlier fluidity of roles has gone, and the status of woman as householder, with all its strengths and all its limitations, is being consolidated. The stratification of urban society has produced the middle classes, that group of men and women who belong neither to the elite with its large landed estates, nor to the workers, whose only capital is in their bodies. It is the women of these classes who experience the most restriction with urbaniza- tion, as we shall see more clearly in the next chapter. Their household sphere has been vastly restricted and they have not the freedom of movement of richer and poorer women. They struggle to protect the resources at their disposal and use the courts to this end. It is the husbands of these women who fill the middling jobs of officialdom (such as those listed in the Erech roster of 2500 B.C.E., noted earlier in this chapter). These men are essentially the scribal class, and they bear the full brunt of the insecurities of their in-between roles. Hoffer (1964) has written forcefully about the alienation and insecurity of the scribal class through history. The wives of the scribal class have suffered doubly, through the insecurity of their husbands and through the far more severe constriction of their own social space.[16] This social group is tiny numerically but looms large in terms of pent-up social dissatisfaction.

The primary civilizations, with their new middle classes, are only one part of the unfolding social drama, however. While life in the cities was going one way, something quite different was happening in nomadic societies and in the nonurban forest civilizations. In the next two chapters, we will look at the situation of women in both types of settings.

Appendix 5A

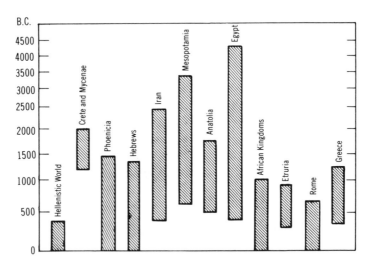

Appendix Figure 5A.1. Chronology of Societies, 4500 B.C.E. to the Common Era

Appendix 5B

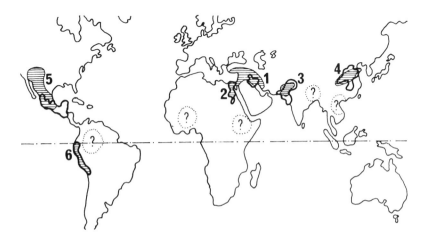

Appendix Figure 5B.1. Location of First Civilizations

SOURCE: Morris (1974: 3); used by permission.
NOTE: The first civilizations are shown in heavy outline. They are related to the location of the earliest known agricultural communities (shown in the hatched areas) and other early agricultural centers. Key: (1) Southern Mesopotamia (Sumerian Civilization); (2) Nile Valley (Egyptian); (3) Indus Valley (Harappan); (4) Yellow River (Shang); (5) Mesoamerica (Aztec and Maya); (6) Peru (Inca).

Notes

1. The first evidence in Europe, found in Sweden, is a rock painting including a plow, from about 1500 B.C.E. (Hawkes and Woolley 1963: 515-16).
2. It used to be thought that the Egyptian pyramid builders brought their skills to England. But the greatest of these monuments predate the pyramids.
3. Kaplan, in an analysis of monument building and political systems in pre-Hispanic Mesoamerica, concludes: "We have greatly underestimated the ability of many stateless societies, particularly chiefdoms, to engage in communal production on a fairly large scale, the notion apparently being that such production requires the direction of a powerful, centralized, coercive state" (1963: 407). He also adds supporting evidence for monument building in Oceania.
4. Or, rather, the evidence for it is very slight and highly controversial.

171

5. Because the spread of the brewing of beer coincides with that of the Bell Beaker people, it is suggested that they taught this as well as metalwork and carried their beakers with them everywhere, including to the grave, so they could always have a draught of beer handy.

6. The only mention I have discovered of burying women with weapons is a reference in Childe to the practice of burying Siberian women with their bows (1963: 84).

7. Wittvogels's thesis that irrigation works were the prelude to higher forms of social organization and provided a training ground in new skills has been superseded by the view that irrigation came afterward, in response to new needs (Adams 1960).

8. It will be noted that I am not offering a "grand theory" about the shift to patriarchy. I am suggesting instead, as in the discussion of agrovillages and matriliny in Chapter 4, that a very gradual shift in the balance of power took place as a result of changing social arrangements, with the superior trade-network knowledge of the male, the process of population concentration and the attendant development of political hierarchy, and the institution of slavery as key factors in the shift.

9. Clan organizations have in fact often served as the political infrastructure of both ancient and recent empires, most notably in China, but this could only work because interclan specialist roles were developed. This specialization came after the shift to patriarchy in China and elsewhere.

10. Mason Hammond (1972), in *The City in the Ancient World*, is the only writer I have come across who specifically refers to women on the town councils.

11. At least the evidence has never been found, although Egyptologists looking at the Sumerian sequence are beginning to wonder whether there are not as yet undiscovered (or undiscoverable) town and city traces in Egypt.

12. Exactly how much power Egyptian women had in earlier times, and how much they lost or gained through time, is a matter of dispute among scholars. An assessment of the relevant literature is not possible here, so what has been presented is the once-strong-but-now-fading matriliny view.

13. This is from my notes of interviews with Indian scholars in Delhi in 1970. I regret that the name of the scholar has been lost.

14. Another practice that causes confusion for scholars is that of a famous person having the same name as the place from which she comes—a practice common in tribal societies, as noted by Colson in Fried (1967: 177).

15. Alice and Polly Perlman (1975) have done an interesting analysis of goddesses as models of the exercise of social power, withholding interpretive comments. The classical scholar Sarah Pomeroy suggests that all roles assigned to goddesses in Greek and Roman mythology are "archetypal images of human female as envisioned by males" rather than reflections of any historical traces (1975: 8). See the essays in the section on the ancient world in *Hidden from History: Reclaiming the Gay and Lesbian Past*, by Duberman, Vicinus, and Chauncey (1989), for an interesting discussion of these myths; see also Judy Grahn *Another Mother Tongue: Gay Words, Gay Worlds* (1984). I prefer not to rule out the possibility that myth is the shadow, however distorted, of ancient social structures.

16. I am indebted to Sheila Johansson (historian, Seattle, Washington, personal communication, 1975) for pointing out the special constraints that wives of the scribal class would be living under in urban society. She suggests that much of the hate literature about women comes from frustrated male scribes who feared the competition of their discontented wives.

References

Adams, Robert McCormick. 1960. "Discussion." Pp. 24-34 in *City Invincible*, edited by Carl H. Kraeling and Robert M. Adams. Chicago: University of Chicago Press.

————. 1966. *The Evolution of Urban Society: Early Mesopotamia and Prehispanic Mexico.* Chicago: Aldine.

Altekar, A. S. [1956] 1978. *The Position of Women in Hindu Civilisation.* Banaras, India: Motilal Banarsidass.

Beard, Mary R. 1946. *Women as Force in History: A Study in Traditions and Realities.* New York: Macmillan.

Blumberg, Rae Lesser and Robert F. Winch. 1972. "Societal Complexity and Familial Complexity: Evidence for the Curvilinear Hypothesis." *American Journal of Sociology* 77(March):898-920.

Boccaccio, Giovanni. [1359] 1963. *Concerning Famous Women,* translated by Guido A. Guarino. New Brunswick, NJ: Rutgers University Press.

Borgese, Elisabeth Mann. 1963. *Ascent of Women.* London: McKibbon and Kee.

Budge, Ernest Alfred Wallis. 1904. *The Gods of the Egyptians.* London: Methuen.

Campbell, Joseph. 1972. *Myths to Live By.* New York: Viking.

Childe, Gordon. 1963. *Social Evolution.* New York: Meridian.

Claiborne, Robert. 1973. *The First Americans.* New York: Time-Life.

Diakonoff, N. M. 1959. *Sumer: Society and State in Ancient Mesopotamia.* Moscow: Academy of Sciences.

Diner, Helen. [1932] 1965. *Mothers and Amazons,* translated by John Philip Lundin. New York: Julian.

Duberman, Martin, Martha Vicinus, and George Chauncey, eds. 1989. *Hidden From History: Reclaiming the Gay and Lesbian Past.* New York: NAL Books.

Edey, Maitland. 1972. *The Missing Link.* New York: Time-Life.

Fairservis, Walter A., Jr. 1971. *The Roots of Ancient India: The Archaeology of Early Indian Civilization.* New York: Macmillan.

Fried, Morton H. 1967. *The Evolution of Political Society: An Essay in Political Anthropology.* New York: Random House.

Glueck, Nelson. 1960. "Discussion." Pp. 24-34 in *City Invincible,* edited by Carl H. Kraeling and Robert M. Adams. Chicago: University of Chicago Press.

Grahn, Judy. 1984. *Another Mother Tongue: Gay Words, Gay Worlds.* Boston: Beacon.

Graves, Robert. 1966. *White Goddess: A Historical Grammar of Poetic Myth.* New York: Farrar, Straus & Giroux.

Hammond, Mason. 1972. *The City in the Ancient World.* Cambridge, MA: Harvard University Press.

Harding, M. Esther. 1971. *Woman's Mysteries, Ancient and Modern.* Rev. ed. New York: Putnam.

Hauser, Philip M. and L. F. Schnore. 1965. *Study of Urbanization.* New York: John Wiley.

Hawkes, Jacquetta and Sir Leonard Woolley. 1963. *History of Mankind. Vol. 1. Prehistory and the Beginnings of Civilization.* New York: Harper & Row.

Hawkins, Gerald S., in collaboration with John B. White. 1965. *Stonehenge Decoded.* Garden City, NY: Doubleday.

Hoffer, Eric. 1964. *The Ordeal of Change.* New York: Harper & Row.

Jacobsen, Thorkild. 1960. "Discussion." Pp. 24-34 in *City Invincible,* edited by Carl H. Kraeling and Robert M. Adams. Chicago: University of Chicago Press.

Johnson, Gregory A. 1975. "Locational Analysis and the Investigation of Urok Local Exchange Systems." Pp. 285-339 in *Ancient Civilization and Trade,* edited by Jeremy A. Saboloff and C. C. Lamberg-Karlovsky. Albuquerque: University of New Mexico Press.

Kaplan, David. 1963. "Men, Monuments, and Political Systems." *Southwestern Journal of Anthropology* 19:397-410.

Knauth, Percy. 1974. *The Metalsmiths.* New York: Time-Life.

Kraeling, Carl H. and Robert M. Adams, eds. 1960. *City Invincible.* A Symposium on Urbanization and Cultural Development in the Ancient Near East held at the Oriental Institute of the University of Chicago, December 4-7, 1958. Chicago: University of Chicago Press.

Kramer, Samuel Noah. 1956. *From the Tablets of Sumer: Twenty-Five Firsts in Man's Recorded History.* Indian Hills, CO: Falcon's Wing.

————. 1963. *The Sumerians: Their History, Culture, and Character.* Chicago: University of Chicago Press.

Marshack, Alexander. 1972. *The Roots of Civilization.* New York: McGraw-Hill.

Morris, E. J. 1974. *History of Urban Form: Prehistory to the Renaissance.* New York: John Wiley.

Mumford, Lewis. 1961. *City in History: Its Origins, Its Transformations, and Its Prospects.* New York: Harcourt Brace Jovanovich.

Murray, Margaret Alice. 1908. "Priesthoods of Women in Egypt." Pp. 22-224 in *International Congress of History and Religions.* Vol. 1. Oxford: Oxford University Press.

O'Faolain, Julia and Lauro Martines. 1973. *Not in God's Image: A History of Women in Europe from the Greeks to the Nineteenth Century.* New York: Harper & Row.

Perlman, Alice and Polly Perlman. 1975. "Women's Power in the Ancient World." *Women's Caucus-Religious Studies* 3(Summer):4-6.

Pomeroy, Sarah B. 1975. *Goddesses, Whores, Wives, and Slaves: Women in Classical Antiquity.* New York: Schocken.

Schafer, Edward H. and the Editors of Time-Life Books. 1967. *Ancient China.* New York: Time-Life.

Ward, Barbara E., ed. 1963. *Women in the New Asia: The Changing Social Roles of Men and Women in South and South-East Asia.* Paris: UNESCO.

Wenig, Steffan. 1970. *Women in Egyptian Art.* New York: McGraw-Hill.

Wernick, Robert. 1973. *The Monument Builders.* New York: Time-Life.

PART II

Women
as
Civilizers

6

The Powerful and the Powerless: Women in Early Civilizations, 2000 to 200 B.C.E.

The New Urbanites

In this chapter, we are moving toward the historical "present." By 2000 B.C.E., Egypt is already old; King Sargon has created a united kingdom in Sumer; Byblos on the coast of Canaan is a great trading center; the Minoans are building the great palace of Knossos in Crete; and the nomad Sarai and her band are setting out for Palestine from the edge of Arabia. During the first few hundred years of our time span, as the new urban centers of civilization develop and expand, women are still fairly visible in each of the civilizations described. By the end of this period, the elite remain visible but the educated urban women of the middle classes find themselves hidden in cities not designed for public mingling of women and men.

That part of the world that centers on the Mediterranean was seething with political activity and trade in 2000 B.C.E. In the Indus Valley, the Harappan civilization, already tied into the Mediterranean trading system, was at its height. The Shang kingdom in China, however, was still 500 years away. In all the wide spaces between the city-states, kingdoms, and empires of the Near Eastern world, there was movement. Nomadic tribes moved in from the Arabian peninsula, from the Iranian plains, and from the Asian steppes. About 2500 B.C.E., the herdsmen of the steppes learned to tame horses, so they moved in and out of settlements with increasing swiftness when they came to the fertile crescent. Some came to make their own settlements; others "moved in on" prosperous city-states and set up their own warrior aristocracy government, as in the case of Lagash in Sumeria; others came to plunder and—later—discovered the benefits of trade.

The so-called Aryans—the Mitanni, the Hittites, the Scythians, and the Hurrians—swarming in from between the Danube and the Don at the beginning of the second millennium,

> retained for over a thousand years a remarkable similarity of character. Whether we think of the Homeric heroes in Greece, the heroic kings in Ireland or India, or the early patricians in Rome, there appears the same pattern of warlike masculine Gods, military prowess and patriarchal government. (Darlington 1969: 141-42)[1]

They set up their own empires, of which the Hittite is the best known.

The tribal-nomadic, tribal-settled, city-state, and nation-state—usually also a conquest state—sequence is best seen in the Syriac-Palestinian region, where it evolved after Mesopotamia and Egypt were already empires. In one common pattern, the trading town grows into the city-state—a kind of territorial state where the common bond is simply shared territory. Already an ethnic mixture from centuries of trading activities and gradual absorption of incoming nomads, these towns evolve slowly from town-council government with temporary leaders to wealthy city-states with hereditary kingship, still subject to the city council of elders (who may now be called nobles). This is the Tyre and Sidon pattern. In the pattern of Israel, an ethnic nomadic group moves in and keeps its ethnic identity; as it grows in wealth and power, it creates a nation-state that is not primarily territorial. We observed a similar double pattern in old Sumeria, in the contrast between the organically evolved city-state and the nomadic-conquest state. Women seem to do somewhat better in the organically evolved states.

By 1250 B.C.E., many of these city-states were well developed, and the Mediterranean world seemed relatively peaceful. It was true that Cretan civilizations had gone up in flames, but the Myceneans had taken over from the Cretans. The Canaanite port cities, including Tyre and Sidon, had developed into prosperous city-states with an active international trade. Egypt, Babylonia, the Hittite empire, and the Syrian city-states all had dynasties linked by political marriages: The king of Ugarit was married to an Egyptian princess; the daughter of the king of the Hittites was married to the Pharaoh Ramses II; a second daughter of the Hittite king was married to a prince of Amurru (Hawkes and Woolley 1963). There was a great deal of visiting back and forth between these states, and they all had multilingual and multinational diplomats. International law and royal treaties secured rights for traders. For example, a Hittite queen paid compensation for the sinking of a Ugarit vessel. In general, there was a condition of mutual tolerance, with no rulers wanting war. Except for slaves, there was, in general, opportunity for economic and geographic mobility and considerable security of contract. To what extent this was true for women we shall see shortly.

The year 1200 B.C.E. was the end of an era. By 1194 B.C.E., the migrations of the "Peoples of the Sea" set everybody moving again and the cozy little international club of the Mediterranean fell apart. The earlier nomadic groups were by now well settled and suffered as much as the older peoples of the Near East in the new turmoil of movement. No one is exactly sure who the "sea peoples" were; nor is it clear who were invaders and who were only refugees from invaders, moving frantically to what they supposed was safer territory. It is only agreed that the sea peoples came from the north.

If there ever was a period in history when the "domino theory" of international relations applied, it was this, but unfortunately nobody knows who pushed over the first domino or even which way they were falling. The first to be displaced by the invaders were the Anatolians: Danaans from Cilicia, Lycians, and Philistines. Here is an account of the newcomers:

> This was not an army but a congeries of peoples; some came by sea, skirting the coast; others marched overland with their womenfolk and children, traveling in heavy two-wheeled oxcarts, prepared to settle down in the conquered land; wherever they came they ravaged and burned and slew, and those that escaped the sword were enrolled in their ranks to the numbers of fighting men. (Hawkes and Woolley 1963: 394-95)

Some settled in Syria and Palestine; some, known as Etruscans, invaded Italy; others, known as Dorians, invaded Greece. Even Egypt was invaded, both by sea peoples and by neighboring Libyans.

Assyria, successor to Babylon, and the Phoenician city-states survived best: Assyria, by adopting the technology of the invaders; Phoenicia, by buying them off. In the middle of all the turmoil, the Israelites managed to set up a kingdom for 100 years, from 1020 to 930 B.C.E. At the end of the dark period, the Greek city-states emerged, about 750 B.C.E. After 200 more years, Cyrus the Persian established the first "world empire." Still another 200 years later, Alexander founded another, larger, "world empire," which eventually faded away after a takeover by Rome. By this time, the Mauryan empire was strong in India, and the Han in China. Olmec, Mayan, and Peruvian civilizations were developing in the new world.

This rather breathtaking romp through the history of the last two millennia before the Christian era has been necessary to provide the background

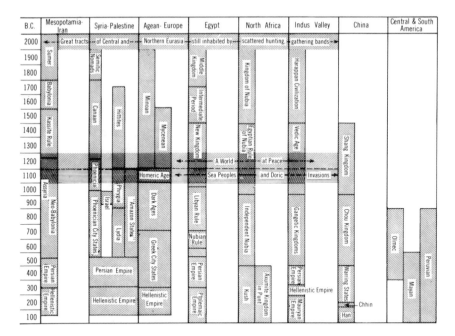

Figure 6.1. Chronology for Societies, 2000-200 B.C.E. Drawn by KH.

for an analysis of women's roles. We have moved away from that simpler world of the temple-palace trading partnerships of third-millennium Sumer and Egypt, a world in which traditional town councils still played a role, slavery and militarism were just beginning, and a relative social egalitarianism still prevailed. By 200 B.C.E., we are confronted with urban civilizations based on substantial concentrations of economic and political power, with complex diplomatic relations between centers of power, and with sharp differences between social classes. Figure 6.1 is a chronology for the societies discussed in this chapter, to help readers keep track of where we are.

Urbanization, the Rise of the State, and the New Conditions for Women

If there is something in the phenomenon "urbanism" that creates special constraints for women, it is important to understand exactly what urbanism is.

Students of early cities have given a good deal of attention to the problem of defining the concept "urban." When do we have a true city, or definitive urbanization, rather than the primordial urbanization described in the last chapter? Kluckhohn's definition is the simplest: There must be a population of at least 5,000, there must be a written language, and there must be ceremonial centers (Hauser 1965: chap. 14).

Conceivably, some rather simple population aggregations might slip into the category "urban" under that definition, given that there is no mention of diversity of population or specialization. Sjoberg (1960) adds the concepts of density of residence and the existence of a variety of nonagricultural specialists and a literate elite. Morris (1974) further adds that there must be a form of record keeping, evidence of social organization, and technical expertise. Adams includes the existence of class stratification, different degrees of ownership, and control of the sources of production; political and religious hierarchies; and a division of labor that includes craftsmen, servants, soldiers, and administrators of peasants (Morris 1974: 7; see also Adams 1966). Finally, Mumford would add the rise of secrecy accompanying the concentrations of power in the city along with the increasing segregation of the communication channels of temple and palace from the populace (Mumford 1961: 64). Here we have the beginnings of the "in" network that has through the centuries excluded all but the top elite as well as most women.

Women's fate in the cities lies at the intersection, one might say, of the systems of stratification and specialization. The failure of women to specialize when agricultural villages began to add new craft skills and trading activities to food production has already been discussed. As long as the society was an egalitarian one, women held their own in village and town councils. Their one major specialization—the priestess role—would help in this. Once significant differentials in control of resources emerged through the development of mining and metallurgy and associated crafts, through the expansion of accompanying trading activities, and particularly through trade in war captives, the whole situation was different for women. I have already suggested in Chapter 5 that, as administrative roles and centralized control over resources develop for men, the marital partnership takes on a special significance among the elite. The increased resources of the successful trader, and of the increasingly permanent warrior king-temple administrator alliance, are in some significant way shared with the spouse. In general, she receives an increasing share of the ceremonial functions but not of the decision-making ones, so that she remains behind in a microcosm of the earlier rank society while her spouse moves ahead into the new centralized power society.[2]

Ability could lead to an extension of a woman's role, however. Thus we sometimes find queens in the Near East civilizations acting as governesses of provinces their husbands have conquered and serving as high priestesses of the major temples, essentially a papal-type role. We find other women of the royal family and of families rewarded by the king for special service similarly playing prominent roles in temple culture, in the erection of public monuments, and in the international political life of the times. The roles are nearly always second-rung roles. Only in some tribal societies, which are still essentially rank societies, and in the exceptional interregnums of empires, do we meet reigning queens who do not derive their power from the positions of their husbands.

The urbanization, or resource centralization, of the trading town led directly to the development of the city-state in this period, so urbanization and the autonomous city-state were almost synonymous. The city-state extended wider and wider hegemony over surrounding agricultural villages, and more and more decisions about village resources and agricultural and other activities of the villagers were made in the city-state. Thus the village women, along with their spouses, lost out in decision making, while the upper strata of city women gained the ceremonial part of the power of their spouses, along with whatever else their ingenuity contrived.

It should be noted that women of the upper classes in Mesopotamia, Egypt, and India all received through private family tutors whatever education the men in the family received and, by virtue of their social position, they spent some part of their time in the public arena from adolescence on through their lives. They were prepared for responsibility, and they were expected to take responsibility. When women of the royal family didn't like the way the king was handling things, they might conspire to overthrow him and put the man of their choice in power or, more rarely, seize power themselves. We shall see this phenomenon frequently in subsequent history. They were also in touch with the international scene, because some women of each royal family married kings and princes abroad. We know from Egyptian papyri that the overseas women visited and corresponded with the family back home, so the women had an excellent private communication system.

The nonroyal elite, favored with gifts of land from the king, admitted women to a share in their power to a degree worth noticing. Royal gifts of land were often administered by women. The tradition of the matron ruling the country estate while also maintaining a household in the city can be followed from Mesopotamia and Egypt in 2000 B.C.E. right on through Greek and Roman times, through the "age of barbarism" in Europe, through the feudal era, and up to the time of the industrial revolution. Her role was not confined to management of household consumption; she supervised agriculture, manufacturing, and the trade in estate products. She had to be as good an accountant as the average temple administrator.

What I have been describing is certainly not "equality" for women. Military action became increasingly important throughout the second millennium, and each new arms levy, each new conscription of soldiers, and each new round of booty brought home from a successful war would enhance the power differential between women and men of the elite. The women's access to the new resources was far more limited than that of the men. Power was shared, but not shared equally.

Below the level of royalty and the elite, urbanism was a very different experience. We will look at the situation of the middle classes, the skilled and unskilled working classes, and the slaves. The two groups who physically suffered the most from urbanism were (a) the unskilled workers who did the maintenance work of the city and lived in dirty, crowded quarters with inadequate food, at a standard of living far below their hunter and farmer forebears, and (b) the slaves. Suffering was not sex linked for these folk. Among the very poor, then as now, women were neither veiled nor secluded but worked at the same range of unskilled jobs that men did. They would be found among the construction workers, the porters and haulers, and the petty traders.

Slavery became increasingly probable for women, as for men, during this period, chiefly due to the increase in warfare and to the demand for women slaves in temples, workshops, and private homes. There were more female slaves than male, due to the frequent practice of killing male prisoners of war and taking females as booty. Slavery itself antedated wars of conquests, however. One of the earliest cargoes that moved along the trade routes was *moventia*—slaves and cattle—mainly from nomadic raiding activities. The demand for slaves was a function of economic surplus and unused resources. Male slaves were particularly useful in mines, and they could also be useful wherever there were large-scale construction enterprises. Women could increase craft productivity. Slave women and men also worked together on a variety of maintenance tasks, as we can see from Nippur tablets showing both sexes at work together.

In ancient empires, the slave status was a highly fluid one. Today's princess could be tomorrow's slave. Skilled and highborn women were often given work commensurate with their background, though by no means always. In general, the woman slave was expected to render sexual services, whatever her other duties were, which made her situation different, though not necessarily harder, than that of the male slave. There would be an enormous difference between the living conditions of a woman who sold herself or her daughter into slavery through sheer destitution and those of the ex-princess. The term *slave woman* therefore cannot be considered to refer to any one simple status. Furthermore, every society stipulated certain conditions under which slaves could buy or be given their freedom. They frequently earned wages and could marry. Slavery was not, per se, associated with ethnic or racial characteristics.

The skilled free workers represented a class above the slaves and the unskilled workers. In this artisan class, the women often contributed craft skills to the production process in the domestic workshops, side by side with their spouses, or in the government workshops. We rarely read about this early form of craft guild available for women, but we see pictures of such women in antiquity plying skilled trades at home and abroad. These women would share the freedom of movement of the women of the unskilled classes but also probably the social limitations of that class. Schools were becoming increasingly widespread in the cities of the Mediterranean toward the end of the last millennium B.C.E., but the children of the artisan class, particularly girl children, would not be free to attend them.

The class for which status differentials for women and men showed up most sharply in the city of 2000 B.C.E. is precisely the class where they show up the most sharply today: at the level of the petty merchants, scribes, and lower-level administrators—the Near East equivalent of the middle class. It was the women of these groups whose lives were privatized by urbanism. The boys of this class were sent to the new city schools, but the girls were not. Neither were there family tutors to prepare the girls at home for public roles or landed estates outside the city for the women to administer. These women did not need to go out to work, as poorer women did.

The challenge of administering a shrinking household enterprise, hemmed in by high walls and cut off from public spaces, first came to middle-class city women about this time. Mesopotamia, like any modern city, had bakeries and restaurants and sold cloth and every type of domestic article. The women no longer *needed* to bake or weave or sew (Morris 1974). It is hard to evoke an image of these women in 2000 B.C.E. in their own homes. To what extent did they continue with their domestic craft work? References to women baking and weaving at home in urban settings continue for many more centuries. Then who purchased the ready-made products available in shops? Possibly the bakeries, inns, and cloth shops were primarily for the working poor, who had no time for their own domestic work.[3] But, even if middle-class women wove and baked at home, their work load would be much lighter than that of working-class women. Information we have about family size (de Mause 1974: 25) indicates that families were small and more than two children were a rarity. The average middle-class housewife also would have several slaves to help her with domestic work. Supervising and teaching slaves seems to have been an important activity for these women (Xenophon, in O'Faolain and Martines 1973: 21-23).

One area of expanded activity that can be imagined is the rearing of the children, however few in number. I have already suggested that, with urbanization, women spend more time with children. The preparation of little boys for the increasingly complex life outside the home would inevitably fall in part to the mother, because boys spent much time in the women's quarters at least until 10 years of age.[4] Possibly Mediterranean women of 500 B.C.E., by the time elementary schools were common, got some of their learning through rehearsing their sons in their lessons, just as Japanese women have done in the twentieth century (Boulding 1966). One way or another, they surely knew more about the world outside the *gynaeceum* than custom acknowledged. These years of mother-child interaction would foster a new concept of motherhood as an important role involving more than physical care for the child. In an imagined dialogue with his wife, Isomachus, as described by Xenophon, speaks of having chosen her to help make a home and raise children: "Now, if God sends us children, we shall think about how best to raise them, for we share an interest in securing the best allies and support for our old age" (O'Faolain and Martines 1973: 21).

It would be impossible for little girls not to benefit from the increased amount of guidance given to little boys, given that they shared the same domestic space. Also, the more elaborated the concepts of wife and motherhood became, the more teaching the girls themselves would receive. Sometimes there were educated slaves in the home who could supplement the education given by parents and school. Thus we find the phenomenon of increased literacy among women even though few of them were attending schools.

One piece of interesting external evidence for the increasing standards of care given by mothers to children is found in the gradual development of attitudes condemning infanticide and the sexual and physical abuse of children, phenomena apparently widespread in all urban societies of these millennia. The public evidence for the change in attitude does not come until Roman times (de Mause 1974: 42), but the beginnings of this shift are surely found in the new sets of shared experiences for mothers and children in the home spaces of increasingly self-aware societies. The double potential of those home spaces will be traced up to the twentieth century. On the one hand, to the extent that women were able to make creative use of their household resources and those spaces in the city that remained open to them (for example, cult associations), they were providing an enriched environment and education for young children. On the other hand, to the extent that women felt frustrated and cut off from society, they relieved their tensions by inflicting physical as well as psychological abuse on children. The latter situation could produce the power struggle described by Slater in *The Glory of Hera* (1968).

In any case, the fraction of the population represented by these middle-class mothers was very small indeed: 95% to 98% of the total population was agrarian. Of the 5% or less of women living in the cities, by far the largest number were working women and slaves. So less than 1% of the women could potentially experience the frustration of confinement of the middle-class housewife. Yet one may fantasize a historical continuity from 2000 B.C.E. to the current time and see the frustrated urban middle-class housewife generating periodic protest movements. Like her nineteenth- and twentieth-century counterparts, she dressed well, wore jewelry, went to shows, and was often bored. The tending of the sacred domestic hearth, which Fustel de Coulanges makes so much of in his *The Ancient City* (1956), comes well after 1000 B.C.E., and it comes in Greece. There were no sacred hearths to tend in the homes of the Near East. Attending temple rituals in the local shrines and temples distributed throughout the urban quarters for the householders' use was in the early days of cities the only "club life" and entertainment a housewife could find (Mumford 1961: 74).

Freedom of movement even for middle-class women varied considerably from one region and epoch to another, so the generalizations made previously must be modified. It was very different in 2000 B.C.E. than in 200 B.C.E., and even in 200 B.C.E. the situation for women in the cities of the Near East differed from that in the Greek city-states, which in turn differed among city-states. Some degree of confinement was common to all. It is one of the penalties of trying to write a macro history that one must frequently collapse time and space to draw the larger picture. As much as possible, I will try to draw attention to the differences among states in regard to the status of women.

Did the middle-class women of the second millennium develop an underlife, as I have suggested would happen in the absence of public roles? They did, and it was related to the various types of religious forms, associations, and cults developing in the urban areas from the late second millennium forward. These associations were essentially of two types: the secret societies and the mystery religious cults. Secret societies form around needs not being met by existing religious or secular institutions; Wach (1944) calls them an undeveloped form of a specifically urban form of association. They do play a special role in adaptation to urban life. We know the early urban form best from Greece, where the *orgeones* were associations of individuals devoted to a cult of special deities and the *thiasos* were clan associations to further common clan interests in the city. A third type of association includes many special-purpose variants of (a) the craft and professional type of association, under the protection of a special deity, and (b) mutual aid societies to assist members with births, marriages, and deaths. These latter would be of special importance to women, who always have some responsibility for arranging the marriages of the next generation as well as the funerals of all family members. Some of the craft associations were for men only, some for families, and some for women only. Some probably had secret women's branches. These associations had the double function of dealing with problems of relationship on a new scale in the urban setting and of giving expression to creative new insights in the religious domains that went beyond traditional experience. They therefore made a logical vehicle for women's participation in the new dimensions of social existence the city brought into being.

We know very little about women's participation in the secret societies, but we know that they participated actively in the mystery religion cults. It was a common complaint of the Greek husband that his wife was off at the temple, engaged in mysterious cultic activities. Given that, in some cities, that was practically the *only* place a middle-class Greek housewife was supposed to be, outside of the women's quarters in her own home, we can imagine she made the most of it. The mystery religion performs many of the functions of a secret society. It is found only in complex societies and represents more advanced concepts and doctrine, more elaborate ritual, and a stronger bond of solidarity between group members than were found in earlier cults. It invariably springs up in societies whose traditional religious base is weakening and frequently fulfills important political or economic functions. It also, however, represents an upwelling of religious impulses, of intuitions and understandings, that are reaching toward a new synthesis of the forces and counterforces experienced in the crosscurrents of the city of antiquity. The Eleusinian, Sibylline, and Mithraic cults originated in Asia Minor and Persia, and the Orphic probably in Greece itself. The full flowering of these cults came in Greece, Alexandrian Egypt, and Rome, toward the end of the period covered in this chapter.

Perhaps the real significance for women of the mystery cults, as of the world religions, is that the cults provided them with a powerful lever for wrenching themselves loose from exclusively household-centered ties. The cultic identity, like the identities provided by the world religions that followed, crosscut all other identities of sex, kin, and social class. The cult setting was the only one in which a woman could experience her full humanness. That cultic experiences could become pathological in no way detracts from the validity of this universalizing function. Cults also provided for some minimal amount of fluidity of role structure in an otherwise rigid society.

In general, role fluidity was reduced for women in the city. What fluidity remained, outside the cultic settings, was chiefly for the elite. The poor woman experienced the rigidity of poverty as did the poor man. The middle-class woman experienced the role rigidity consequent on the shrinking of the household productive enterprise and separation from economic and civic activities outside the home. The elite woman experienced the role rigidity related to almost total exclusion from military leadership. The relative contributions to the plight of the female of militarism and of her own failure to specialize during the transitional era between the agrovillage and the city are difficult to assess.

We will turn now to an examination of the actual situation of women in each of the major civilizations of the two-millennia period.

Mesopotamia

Peaceful Sumeria, culturally ambitious Babylonia, and militaristic Assyria succeed one another in the same general territory throughout these two millennia. The clay tablets from Sumer are philosophical and reflective; from Babylonia come ornamental stelae recounting the building of great monuments; from Assyria, stela upon massive stela record bloody victories. How did women function in this era of unfolding disaster? They began peacefully, and with self-assurance, in the earlier Sumerian tradition of extensive temple activity by women.

Although the temple is often woman's only public space and political platform, this does not mean that outward temple activities are not also reflective of that process of profound inner ordering of perceptions of self and cosmos that we first observed in the caves of Paleolithic Europe. The more complex the social universe becomes, the more urgent is that ordering process. To do justice to that inner ordering would take a different kind of book than this one, so an examination of the belief structure of ancient religions will not be included here.

Bearing in mind the range of meanings of temple activity, let us now examine the activity of Mesopotamian priestesses. An important part of that activity involved performing ceremonial music for special public occasions:

> There was elaborate music by women, under the direction of the queen and princesses as priestesses. Queen Shu-bad of Ur made music on harp and tambourine with her ladies in waiting or with professional musicians. . . . the word nartu, meaning "chanter," is feminine. . . . Lipushiau, the granddaughter of King Naram-Sin, was appointed player of the balag-didrum in the moon god's temple at Ur. . . . We can fancy this girl of 2380 BC drumming and making incantations to hasten the rebirth of the moons and then dancing and singing with her companions in the palace. . . . In Ishtar's temple at Erech, troops of dancing priestesses chanted their laments in a dialect used only when a female deity was supposed to be reciting. (Drinker 1948: 81)

Sargon's daughter, Princess Enheduanna, was high priestess of the moon god in the 2200s B.C.E. and a person of considerable consequence

Figure 6.2. Goddess Ishtar Receiving an Offering, Eighteenth Century B.C.E. Redrawn by HBR.

in her time. Her famous poem, "Exaltation of Inanna," has survived the millennia. Under her leadership, temple activities must have been lively indeed.

It should be remembered that there was a continuous influx of nomadic warrior elites into Mesopotamian ruling structures. Sometimes it was peaceful; sometimes it was violent. The process by which this happened will be discussed in more detail in the next chapter. The presence of new nomadic traditions of the participation of women in the old courts of Mesopotamia is sometimes important in explaining how a few individual women played very outstanding roles when most women were lost to view. King Sargon and his daughter Enheduanna were from such a formerly nomadic aristocracy.[5]

Some of the ex-nomadic women played innovative roles in their adopted society. The high priestess Nina may have been one of these; she seems to have been an important counselor to King Gudea, Sargon's successor. We find her interpreting to him the meaning of his dream about a temple in a time of drought. He is to build a temple, Nina tells him: Here is how he is to build it, and this is where he is to order materials; specifics follow. Presumably she draws the plans and supervises the erection of the temple. Later we run into a reference to schools for girls (for nuns?) beginning with

Figure 6.3. Assyrian Women in Headdresses, 3000-2500 B.C.E. Redrawn by HBR.

a palace school in 1800 B.C.E., a private house in Ur in 1780 B.C.E., and a temple school that operates continuously from 1400 to 539 B.C.E. It was presumably within these schools that the Eme-sal literary language, spoken by women to women, developed (Diner [1932] 1965).

We infer from these references that women of the elite were well educated and produced literature and that the talented ones participated in the major building programs of the Babylonian era. See Figure 6.3 for reproductions of aristocratic Assyrian women in their headdresses. They suggest very self-assured women indeed. (Note how similar the goddess in Figure 6.4 is to the women in Figure 6.3.)

It is very possible that the sibyl role developed out of a combination of the Sumerian women's temple culture and the influx of prophetesses from settlements of earlier nomadic elites. The role of the prophetess exists in all nomadic societies and in many settled societies. In the millennia we are now examining, there were prophetesses in Arabia and among the early Israelites. The Sibyl was a semilegendary seeress of unknown antiquity who gave her name to a whole tradition of prophecy and triggered a major intellectual tradition set in a religious context. Sibyls were at the height of their political power in the eighth to sixth centuries B.C.E., especially in the Greek colonies of Asia Minor, but there are persistent references to earlier Iranian origins. All the evidence points to a well-established communication

Figure 6.4. Water-Dispensing Goddess From Mari, c. 2040-1870 B.C.E. Redrawn by HBR.

network between sibyls at different locations. The development of a trained sisterhood across Asia Minor could best have been done out of Mesopotamia. Nomadic sibyls may somehow have connected with the city sisterhoods or with rebel members of the city sisterhoods who were looking for alternate power bases. This is sheer speculation, but the role of the sibyls as international figures advising kings and emperors at a time when few women were publicly visible invites some speculation.

The sibyls gave rise not only to a new social role and tradition but to a whole literature and system of interpreting history: the sibylline books. Sibyls and sibylline books continued to thrive right through the Middle Ages in Christian Europe (Hennecke 1963). In addition to the public political rule of sibyls, many sibylline mystery cults developed. I have already mentioned how these cults, along with the Eleusinian mysteries that originated in the Aegean, contributed to the underlife for women of urban Greek, Roman, and early Christian society.

I hope I have adequately indicated that the priestess role was a versatile one in Mesopotamia. Some strange things are written about priestesses, and they are often lumped together with temple prostitutes. The twentieth-century eye has difficulty appreciating a complex temple hierarchy of women. In the Mesopotamian temple system, there apparently were a high priestess and associated priestesses of elevated rank who only married under certain conditions; there was a second rank of virgin priestesses, the Naditu; and several ranks of women performing special services. One of these services was "temple prostitution." In Babylonia, as in Egypt and Phoenicia, the concept of rendering sexual services on a public basis evidently first developed in connection with temples, and intercourse with temple women was considered an act of worship. All fees for such services took the form of offerings to the temples (Henriques 1962). The women who provided the services were often of the middle and upper classes. Prostitution as a secular service came later. Below the rank of the special-service women was an intermediate service and maintenance class and, finally, the temple slaves. Slavery, like prostitution, was strongly linked with temple service in its earliest forms. There appeared to be room for women from all strata of society in the temple complex.

Women of the upper classes who were not involved in temple-related occupations continued to administer landed estates and were also involved in trade, as we may infer from the number of references to women's contractual rights in the Code of Hammurabi. Generalizations about women being the "property" of men—husbands or fathers—come from literal interpretations of the sections in law codes on marriage and family, with no attention to actual practice or to special stipulations. A description of the life of women in any society today, from tribal to industrial, based exclusively on a reading of law codes, would be most misleading.

According to the legal stipulations of many societies, it appears that a woman must always be under the rule of a father, husband, son, or other male relative. But, in fact, property rights of women under special circumstances are nearly always provided for in law. There are two reasons for this flexibility. First, no law can prescribe the personalities and abilities of women and men. If in an individual family the wife has an abundance of talent for the work required by the family enterprise, and the husband does not, then the wife is very likely to be the de facto manager of the family business. Second, no law can provide for all the exigencies of family life. There are many circumstances, including widowhood, that leave women with substantial properties to administer and no appropriate male available to assist her. We will see ample evidence in the chapters to come of women taking care of their own households and estates without male assistance.

In the case of Sumerian law, it has been suggested that the items recorded in the Hammurabic Code were in fact alterations of previous customary practice. According to this view, provisions that remained unchanged were not repeated. This is one possible explanation for the fact that many areas of customary law are not included in the code. The likelihood has already been mentioned that earlier rights of women to property, and older descent and marriage rules, were abrogated through the creation of the new code. This cannot be documented in the case of the Hammurabic Code, but it can be studied by comparing the Hammurabic provisions with the new provisions of the Middle Assyrian Laws, dated between 1450 and 1250 B.C.E. The Middle Assyrian Laws are not a code but a miscellaneous assortment of laws in the character of amendments, nearly all referring to women, on the subject of property rights and offenses to and by women (Driver and Mills 1935: 12). I have not been able to discover a definitive comparison of the Hammurabic and Middle Assyrian laws, but it appears that the second set represented a further limitation on the rights of women.

In general, it appears that women had less personal and sexual freedom than men did, once privatized family life began in the stratified urban societies. Both law and practice confirm a growing double standard from this point on through history, again applied chiefly in strata above the semiskilled working class. Limitations on property holding for women were perhaps due to a combination of the acquired patriarchal pride in the capacity of men to fertilize women and the need for a conflict-resolution device for keeping estates intact. The tendency to treat women as a private fertility bank was kept in check, however, by the institution of the dowry, and women made the utmost use of the courts to protect their access to this dowry—often their only capital.[6]

An area as confusing to the modern reader as the temple hierarchy of women is the palace hierarchy of wives. It is difficult from the records to make operational distinctions about different kinds of wifely status. There were wives who were queens and corulers; wives who were queens and ceremonial figures but not coregnant; wives who were uncrowned "chief wives" in a cohort of wives; wives who were secondary wives, but with recognized status and privileges; women who were concubines chosen for their beauty but with no special court status; women who were chosen from the concubine group to enjoy special consort status; and other classes of concubines with differential status and privileges within that minicourt, the harem. Furthermore, there was a certain amount of social mobility in these systems, and wives could move up or down the wife status ladder.

In an international system of negotiation and alliance by marriage, every important king would have a number of wives, and it would be perfectly clear to everyone at court at any given time what the status and function of each wife above a certain rank was, what particular regional diplomacy she had responsibility for, and so on. These marriages would not necessarily be sexual alliances, although they usually were, and the resulting offspring were a part of the international alliance system. Historians often distinguish only between queens and concubines, whereas the real significance of royal marriages lies in the large band of secondary wives, each one brought to court in relation to a specific diplomatic need. These are not called queens except in the case of a very important alliance (or, sometimes, in the case of a love match). Many Babylonian and Assyrian women, and women of surrounding kingdoms all the way to Egypt, entered active court life with well-defined roles within the marriage-alliance system during the era we are describing. They are mentioned so infrequently, however, that it is impossible to describe their activities except through extensive analysis of the papyri exchanged between kingdoms—a task that could only be undertaken by appropriately trained specialists. Egyptian papyri are the richest source for this kind of information.

In addition to court life, temple-related occupations, estate management, and trade, women ran taverns and inns. Houses for sexual services came later in the period and are associated, Henriques (1962) suggests, with the availability of an increased number of women slaves for use outside the temple-palace complex. Managing houses for sexual services became increasingly profitable for women as cities grew larger and has remained a lucrative business for women with few means and much ingenuity right up to the twentieth century.[7] Another group of women constituted the professional class: physicians, scribes, musicians, midwives, and healers. Some were associated with the temples but some were probably independent.

Working-class women and slaves labored in the large textile and craft workshops producing cloth and other materials for export. Such workshops might belong to the palace, a temple, or to a private merchant family. Slaves were also everywhere as domestic servants and sometimes as traders for their masters and mistresses.

While there were no open-space marketplaces in the old cities of Mesopotamia, there were plenty of niches in the narrow alleys of the bazaars. It was here that poor women could earn their pennies as vendors of local products. There were also women—from wealthy families—engaged in the international trade of the times. Babylonia had a premarket economy, using a network of trading posts located on the rivers in port towns, controlled by the temple-palace system. Polanyi calls this "no-risk" administrative trading. Risks there must have been, however, and individual families must have had their own way of figuring profit and loss (Polanyi et al. 1957). Women merchants appear in temple and palace records just often enough throughout this era in the Mediterranean to suggest that there were a number of them. Widowhood has always been a standard route by which women become independent merchants, and many of these women traders may have been widows.

The Assyrians

The first Assyrian records begin in 1300 B.C.E., introducing a long story of slaughter. Shalmaneser I describes how he dealt with the Hittites: He took 14,400 captives, captured nine strongholds and a capital city, leveled 180 cities, and slaughtered all the armies of the Hittites as well as their allies the Aramaeans. The *cult of frightfulness*, as historians call it, had begun. Often entire armies and town populations were chopped to pieces so that "the rivers and fields ran red with blood." Conquered peoples who were not slaughtered were systematically resettled in other towns, so that all of Mesopotamia became one vast ethnic mixture. Every conquered town that was not razed to the ground was assimilated into the central Assyrian government administrative system. Power was concentrated in the Assyrian capital as never before in history.

What happened to ordinary women during the cult of frightfulness? There is a long period when there is no mention of women in the histories that are my source. Some women were probably wiped out in the general slaughter. Those who were not killed or deported were probably either enslaved or married to soldier citizens of other towns (Figure 6.5). Rarely would families survive intact in the regions of military activity. Military activity, however, was not everywhere, so probably the vast majority of women survived this era as men did, keeping a low profile, paying tribute,

Figure 6.5. Captive Women and Animals Being Led Away by Assyrian Soldiers, c. 858-824 B.C.E. Redrawn by HBR.

and farming or trading as best they could. Because, in war-scarred regions, most women were left without men, those who escaped the fate of capture and forced marriage would have been a tough and hardy lot. The wiping out of the males could happen to both settled agricultural and nomad groups. It is from this period that we begin to get the tales of the Amazon bands and kingdoms. Amazons were women from nomadic bands whose men were exterminated or widowed women whose towns were burned and who became nomads to survive. The latter would have learned to defend themselves with weapons previously used chiefly by men. We will discuss these bands of women later, only taking note now of the setting in which they arose.

The women of the ruling elite fared much better; as members of the new aristocracy, they, too, had access to the resources that accrued to the increasingly powerful temple-palace-army coalition. Among men, there was considerable mobility in the post-1300 B.C.E. era, as the demand for military genius catapulted ex-slave soldiers into generalships and sometimes led to one of them being crowned king, to start a new dynasty. Whether there was a comparable mobility for women we do not know, but it is less likely. The court ladies probably married the climbers and "civilized" them. Occasionally, a slave girl would become a queen.

One unusual note is sounded in this era of increasing militarism. During the rule of the Kassites—former nomads who rapidly became acculturated and who revered the older Sumerian ways—there was a revival in Nippur of an ancient Sumerian tradition of bringing singers and scribes together for common training. This was in about 1200 B.C.E. The texts prepared by scribes were traditionally intended for chanting or singing by the Nardu, the professional women chanters mentioned earlier, but the training for writing and for chanting had gotten separated. The Kassites had ties with matrilineal nomadic tribes of the Arabian desert that sometimes had queens. The Kassites also arranged for Arabian princesses to attend the newly revived school for scribes and singers.

In the next century, many from the military class of the desert-dwelling Chaldeans entered the Assyrian military service as a kind of state corps, but they kept their desert ties active. This linking with the Arabian desert may have provided some persistent source of matrilineal influence through the succeeding militaristic eras.

The first outstanding Assyrian woman to emerge from centuries of bloody warfare is Queen Sammuramat (late ninth, early eighth century B.C.E.), who in the legend-making tradition became Semiramis, daughter of a goddess. Queen Sammuramat was the wife of one king and mother of another. A powerful queen while her husband reigned, she vastly extended that power after his death. Memorial stelae and inscriptions testify to her accomplishments and influences, both in monument building and in civic and military affairs. There are perhaps more legends about her, says Rogers (1915: 254-58), than about any other figure in Assyrian history. Consistent with the theory of close contact between matrilineal warrior elites from the Arabian desert and the Assyrian rulers (Klimberg 1949), she is supposed to have led troops in battle.

In the 730s B.C.E., we find the energetic Tiglath Pileser IV encountering two queens of Arabian tribes in succession as he pushes southward into the Arabian desert. Were the old friendly alliances of the 1200s forgotten? Neither Queen Zabibi nor Queen Samsi was inclined to bend the knee to the Assyrians, and they both seem to have led their troops in battle themselves. Zabibi agreed to pay tribute; Samsi refused—and got away with it. Given the character of the times, this says a lot for the mettle of Arabian queens. They already had a long tradition of autonomy behind them. For whom in Assyria were they role models, I wonder? Perhaps for Queen Naqi'a, also a semilegendary figure sometimes called Nitocris. She was wife of Sennacherib, the able but ruthless king who applied the "final solution" to Babylon by diverting the river Euphrates through it, a simple way to wipe out a population. Naqi'a seems to have been independent minded, for, when her son Esarhaddon became ruler of Assyria, she took leadership in the rebuilding of the flooded Babylon—a most exemplary task of reconstruction. This same son Esarhaddon befriended the very Arabian tribes

Sennacherib had fought, and they became his military allies. He seems to have negotiated for an Assyrian princess to marry into an Arabian tribe as coruler, not simply queen consort. How much of a "sisterhood" alliance there was between women of Assyria and women of Arabia is not clear, but it does seem that the Arabian queens had some continuing influence in the land of two rivers for a long time.

Indo-European migrations from the north pressed long and hard on Assyrian borders, and finally Assyria fell in a squeeze play of Medes and Persians. The result was the first world empire. The apparently sudden emergence of obscure tribes of Medes and Persians to establish a world empire is not as remarkable as it appears. It in fact provides a brief case study in advance of the interactions of nomads and settled peoples to be examined in the next chapter. Parsua and Mada were two mountain valleys north of Assyria inhabited in the 800s B.C.E. by nomadic tribes of horsemen who already had a highly stratified society and were growing rich by raiding Assyria. By the 500s, these nomads had become more settled people, but they were still living on their high mountain plateau away from the "softening" influence of the cities of the plains. Cyrus, an ambitious young vassal king of a tribe in the Persian federation, managed to unite under his rule one set of tribes after another—some by conquest, some by alliance. Finally, weak Assyria and Babylonia were absorbed into the new Persian empire, now known as the Achaemenid empire. The fresh nomadic blood of the warrior aristocracy of Cyrus's little kingdom became the new ruling elite.

The women of the warrior elite immediately began to play a major role in the development of the Achaemenid empire. There are frequent references in the history of this period to Atossa, who was the wife of a satrap of Cyrus and was known to promote Zoroastrianism as the state religion of the new empire. Atossa was also the mother of Cyrus's successor, Darius. King Cyrus himself was killed on the battlefield by a woman, Queen Tomyris of the neighboring Massegetai—a people also not far removed from nomadism. Another queen, Artemisia of Halicarnassus, later fought *for* the Persians under Xerxes in the famous battle of Salamis. A series of savage and not so savage queens intervened again and again in the succession of the Persian empire: Queen Pheretime of Cyrene; the queen mother Amnestris, wife of Xerxes; and many others, all duly recorded in Persian annals.

The significance of the Achaemenid empire for our purposes is that it signaled the end of a series of assimilations of peoples, the peoples of the Babylonian and Assyrian kingdoms. The great days of these states were now over, and their women and men settled down in what niches they could find in an entirely new world. To summarize the role of Mesopotamian women when these kingdoms were at their height, one might say that

Sammuramat and Naqi'a are notable exemplars of the capacity of women to take leadership in one of the most intensely militaristic societies known to date.

Some of the leading women of the period came from nomadic tribes that had traditions of women rulers, but there were others, whose origins, unfortunately, we can rarely trace. Because only military conquests are recorded, we know nothing of the roles, constructive or otherwise, of the other thousands of elite women of that society. The peasants and the urban poor survived as much as they had done in the pre-1300 B.C.E. era, with women assuming a greater variety of production roles due to war-induced manpower shortages. How the middle-class women traders fared we have no idea. They would have had to be tough to survive. By the end of this period, there would be an enormous increase in the number of slaves in the cities, and every household would have slave attendants. The gradual change in the character of households as slaves became important to the domestic economy would be interesting to trace, but we have no data on the slave-mistress relationship within families before Hellenic times.

In general, this would appear to have been an era of prolonged and slow constriction of social spaces and role opportunities for women. A few women must have survived in public roles in temple and palace enclaves, because we read of the school for priestesses, from 555 to 539 B.C.E., at the Nin-gal temple at Ur under the priestess Bel-shalti-Nannar, daughter of a king, and it is mentioned that this is a continuation of a school located in the same building since 1400 B.C.E. Revival of earlier educational practices for Assyrian women and Arabian princesses, as well as the continuation of a school for women through the holocausts of 1300 to 600 B.C.E., suggest the durability of well-institutionalized roles and services through rapidly changing times—and the durability of women. These are enclaves, at the most, however. In the public sphere, leadership roles, whether in temple or palace or marketplace or battlefield, went to the men who had risen through the military hierarchies of the preceding centuries.

Egypt

While Sumerian women suffered a 2,000-year attrition of status and role opportunities, Egyptian women held their own to a far greater degree during the same time period. They were not exactly ruling matriarchs, but they did continue to be visible in a wider range of economic, religious, and social roles in Egypt than in any of the other pristine civilizations. Why? We have already noted that goddesses were more firmly entrenched in ancient village Egypt than in the Near East and also that urbanization never developed in Egypt to the extent that it developed elsewhere. Moving the capital city was a favorite game of the pharaohs and kept any one city from accumulating records and power past a given dynasty. Few of the names of Egyptian capitals sound any echoes in the historical record: Hieraconpolis, Thebes, and Memphis we recognize, but not Ith-Taui, Tell el-Amarna, Tanis, or Avaris, the desert capital of the Hyksos rulers. In one sense, the mobility of the capital strengthened the position of the pharaoh, giving him highly privatized personal power that went where he and his divine-consort-sister went. It also left local temple administrators with a freer hand, throughout Egypt. When these administrators were women, it gave them a firm grasp on local resources. Another curious fact is that extended family groupings apparently did not develop in Egypt as in Mesopotamian and Indo-European cultures. There are no Egyptian terms for aunt-uncle, only for mother-father, wife-husband, sister-brother, daughter-son. Each household thus became a new household, and there were no Engelian Great Family Communities around which to build power centers (Mumford 1961: 139). In that context, the practice of sister-brother marriages to keep lines of descent clear becomes more understandable.

Women continued in the same range of roles mentioned in the last chapter but with an intensification of political activity. While most of this activity was beneath the surface and does not appear in historical documents, from time to time, an unusually forceful queen initiated activities that gave new life and energy to the "women's society" at court. The consequences were felt through several generations of women as the role model effect ran its course. One of the first women we read about is Tausert, who, as regent queen and mother of Pepi II, ruled under her own name as a pharaoh in the twenty-third century B.C.E. She was a "foreigner" and there was much unrest during this century. Palace revolts, revolutions, and throwing out invaders were among the activities in which palace women engaged. We do not know whether palace women were responsible for opening up secret archives to the public in the popular uprising that took place in the period in which Tausert lived, when "the lower orders had broken into the [temple] precincts . . . and captured knowledge that had been withheld from them" (Mumford 1961: 100). We know that palace women did make alliances with the populace and foment revolution in later times.

One of the most interesting periods of women's activity is between 1600 and 1200 B.C.E. Queen Ahotep, heroine of the liberation movement that threw the occupying Hyksos rulers (ex-Palestinian nomads) out of Egypt between 1580 and 1510 B.C.E., was herself already a second-generation revolutionary. Her mother, Queen Tetisheri, was the ancestress of a new dynasty and the harbinger of a new age of individualism in the Nile country. Queen Ahotep, the first to be named divine consort in the new-style religious tradition, had entered with her two sisters, Merit-Amon and Sat-Kamose, into a wife-trio relationship with Amenhotep. It was as a member of the wife trio that she laid the groundwork for throwing out the Hyksos. This was actually accomplished by the daughter of the next generation, Thothmes, with her spouse Amose. The fourth generation in this succession of political dynamite was the famous Hatshepsut (see Figure 6.6), the woman who ruled as pharaoh for 20 years while she kept her power-hungry son-in-law waiting in the wings for his turn. She gave Egypt a rest from military activity and engaged in large-scale works of domestic reconstruction. The angry son-in-law, Tuthmosis III, effectively curbed female power when he got to the throne. He stopped all reconstruction work and turned the country back to military activity. The same power sequence occurred again 100 years later, though not so dramatically. It started with the Cinderella-queen Tiy, the homely, brilliant commoner who married Amenhotep III and affected two generations of politics after her time, and it continued in the reform activities of her daughter-in-law, the beautiful Queen Nefertiti.

This is the same period in which the Mediterranean marriage-alliance system was at its height. Court women were well informed about international affairs. To understand women's roles in this alliance system, one must have an adequate picture of the court, the "harem," and marriage practices. It is unfortunate that the term *harem* is generally used to describe any type of arrangement associated with the polygamy of aristocrats. The word comes from the Arabic for *sanctuary* or *holy place* and refers in later Eastern traditions to the women's part of the house. It has no necessary connection with polygamy (Penzer 1935: 15). Whatever the Egyptians called their women's court, it was certainly not by a word belonging to another and later culture.

When the word *harem* is used in connection with a royal court, the historian means to signify the women's court. In certain times and places in history, this court has become an instrument for the complete

Figure 6.6. Hatshepsut (Thebes). Redrawn by HBR.

seclusion—in fact, imprisonment—of women. This pathological form of what may have originated as a separate and parallel government of women by women in the temples of the major priestesses should not be mistaken for the whole institution.

At some point in Egyptian history, the special women's government in the temples became associated with the palace and with the royal alliance process. After that amalgamation, every military or trade agreement with a foreign power brought into the women's court one or more ladies from the country concerned. When Amenophis III married Gilukheba, the daughter of a Mitanni monarch, the princess brought "persons of her harem, 317 women," with her. The term *harem* as used by the translator of those records clearly does not refer to women brought for the pharaoh's sexual pleasure. It rather refers to the entire retinue from the home court of each newly arriving princess or lady of rank. There was a special administrative bureaucracy that looked after women's-court affairs, including both married men and married women of high rank, living outside the palace. The court provided all kinds of special education and training, and the famous "harem" dancing girls and musicians were only a few among the many women trained there (Figure 6.7). Many of these women spoke several languages and engaged in trade as well as political activity.

There is no evidence to my knowledge that the women of the Egyptian women's court were secluded. Rather, they were part of an intellectual and cultural elite that administered cultural and political affairs both for their own women's section and for the government as a whole. Many centuries later, the royal harem of Siam was vividly described by an Englishwoman (Leonowens 1953), well after the custom

Figure 6.7. Egyptian Women, Eighteenth Dynasty. Redrawn by HBR.

of physical seclusion developed. These descriptions, though belonging to another time and place, give some clue as to the scale of operation of women's courts. In the Siamese harem, women physicians, judges, artists, scholars, and warriors all received the best education the country could give and administered a social and economic and political system including 9,000 women (1953: 11). Only a very small percentage of these women were the wives and concubines of the king. Talented young girls from poor families, both slave and free, could receive the same education as a princess, if a woman administrator decided they could be used in one of the orchestras, choirs, dance troupes, or theater companies of the court. There was always a certain risk of being noticed by the king and taken into the more secluded apartments of the concubines, which was in fact a lifelong imprisonment. It is probable, however, that the majority of women who worked in these settings, even in nineteenth-century Siam, lived "normal" lives, going home at night to husbands who lived in the city. The women's-court system lent itself to great abuses as the status of women declined, but a careful study of the women's sections associated with palace complexes in all the great civilizations would probably reveal a stronger women's culture than is generally attributed to that part of royal institutions.

To return to the Egyptian women's court, there is no lack of evidence of women's involvement in politics. From time to time, their involvement in domestic conspiracy, "only referred to by allusions, since one was afraid to let such incidents become well-known," surfaces. We have, for example, the report from the Old Kingdom that

> a high official named Uni was called upon, because of his especially trustworthy character, to conduct a secret case against Queen Weretkhetes, whose mistakes were concealed, however. . . . In the Middle Kingdom Instruction of King Ammenemes I, it was conjectured that the assassination of the sovereign was plotted in the harem. Some of the preserved trial reports tell us about a harem intrigue during the Twentieth Dynasty that took on greater proportions. It was directed against King Ramses III, who fell victim to this attempt on his life. (Wenig 1970: 38-39)

In the case of this particular intrigue, some conspirators of the women's court wished to take advantage of a situation of rising prices, declining food stocks, and the unwelcome presence of a large number of foreign workers needing to be fed.

> They were led by Tiy [not the Tiy mentioned earlier], a concubine of the king, who wanted to install her son Pentawert on the throne, and by the chief official of the harem. The reports of the proceedings show that they wanted to incite the people to rebel with the help of mediators. This is

rather unusual, since palace revolutions were generally limited to a small circle, and the people were not consulted. This time, however, they speculated on the people's desire to rise up against the king, who was the cause of their misery. The conspirators succeeded with their planned murder of the king, but their pretender to the throne was defeated by the man who had already been chosen as successor, Ramses IV. He then ordered proceedings to be held against the insurgents before two special committees of trustworthy persons. . . . The unfaithful persons were subsequently punished by cutting off their noses and ears, while most of the accused were sentenced to death. (Wenig 1970: 38-39)

Sometimes dowager queens tried to circumvent court politics and make their own international alliances, to keep power in their own hands. One such queen, Ankhesenamon, tried to get the king of the Hittites to send her one of his royal sons for a husband so she would not have to marry the choice of her own court party. The unfortunate prince was murdered by Egyptian nationalists on his way to the wedding, and she had to marry locally after all.

Both the successes and the failures of the politics of the women's court were kept secret for reasons of state, so we have no way of knowing how effective this kind of activity was. It was apparently dangerous. The "harem" could not properly be called the underlife of Egyptian society, at least not until its later, declining epochs; it was too much a part of the public arena. The women in it were trained for international roles, so it is not surprising that they engaged in the activity for which they were trained. The ladies of this group brought art, literature, music, scholars, and physicians from their home country with them when they entered a new court. They also visited one another from country to country. They certainly helped to promote the circulation of the scientific and cultural knowledge of the day.

Elite women did not confine themselves to politics. Administration of temple centers involved training women in a wide variety of skills. The Eighteenth Dynasty represents the high point, according to Drinker (1948), of the development of music by temple women. Large choirs and orchestras were organized, and training and performance in the arts absorbed the energies of gifted women of all classes. Eighteenth Dynasty Egypt sounds in some ways remarkably like nineteenth-century Siam.

Among the working class, women worked side by side with men, at similar jobs, as we can see from the wall paintings in tombs. The degree of specialization in Egyptian workshops was tremendous, as reflected in lists of workmen kept by temple scribes.[8] A large force was needed, and every temple city had its temporary camps for workers who labored at temple construction when they were not needed for farming.

The claims on women's labor would foster specialization in domestic services and the serving of food, so there must have been at least as many

women innkeepers in the temple towns of Egypt as there were in the cities of Mesopotamia. (The servant girl in Figure 6.8 may have been attached to such an inn.) Egyptian women apparently had somewhat greater sexual freedom than the women of Mesopotamia, and there seems to have been less emphasis on professional provision of sexual services, although this was certainly an important urban enterprise in Egypt, as everywhere. The frequently mentioned presence of a large number of foreign workers, both women and men, living without families, provided both the demand and the supply for organized sexual services.

As in the case of Mesopotamia, we are reminded that there are neighboring cultures with ruling queens that occasionally made themselves felt in Egypt. Ramses II mentions Mysian women fighting on horseback under the leadership of their queen (Diner [1932] 1965). A legendary queen of Cush-Meroe—Nicaula? Kandake? Candace? Queen of Sheba?—was supposed to be trying to influence Egyptian affairs during a time of troubles. These references are vague in the extreme. Another kind of note is sounded by the practice of Cush, during the tenth century when it ruled Egypt, of sending Egyptian women as slaves to Cushite temples. That was a new, and probably crushing, experience for Egyptian women.

Egypt's power gradually faded away in the last millennium B.C.E. When Ramses III said, "The foot of an Egyptian woman may walk where it pleases her, and no one may deny her," he was already whistling in the dark, both for himself and for women. The time of troubles was by then well under way. Women kept their temple and harem jobs, and the fact that Cleopatra of the Ptolemies could engage as effectively in international affairs as she did in the last century B.C.E. shows that the political tradition for women was still present. Cleopatra, an Egyptianized Greek with a genius for politics, has had a misleading

Figure 6.8. Servant Girl With Food Offering, Eleventh Dynasty. Redrawn by HBR.

press; she was less pretty, and far more intelligent, than she is generally given credit for (Harden 1971: 86).

The whole phenomenon of Alexandria under the Ptolemies offers an interesting case study in the rise of full-fledged urbanization in the context of an old, minimally urbanized civilization. Should Alexandria be considered Egyptian or not, and what part did women play in this great cultural center of the Mediterranean world for the last 300 years B.C.E.? In a way, it was an enclave city unrelated to its Egyptian setting, built by a foreigner—Alexander—for the cosmopolitan elite of his world. The scholars, artists, and scientists who foregathered there, sumptuously fed, elaborately housed, and attentively cared for by Egyptian servants, knew little and cared less about Egypt. The sailors, metallurgists, traders, and assorted wanderers from both barbarian and civilized lands, filling up the inns and taverns, scarcely "saw" Egypt. The farmers, the construction workers, the unskilled workers, the domestic servants—these were Egypt.

There had to be women among the Alexandrian elite—by this time, there were women mathematicians and poets in Greek civilization—but there is almost no mention of them until the next millennium. The native Egyptian women, whether part of the service infrastructure or not, performed one major function—they married and educated men of all classes from Greek elites to barbarian craftsmen and traders. Men rarely came to Alexandria with wives. They found them there. Egyptian women who entered into these marriages were free contracting agents and the terms of trade were on their side. There are a number of references in Egyptian documents to these marriages of Egyptian women with foreigners and also of foreign women to Egyptian men. Their rights are very clearly delineated. This is almost our only glimpse of Egyptian women of the Alexandrian age. They seem to have walked through that age with some dignity and freedom. Culturally and politically, however, they had no role, except in their own temple culture well outside the Alexandrian sphere.

If pre-Alexandrian Egypt represents the high point of political participation of women in the pristine empires—and in a way it does—the record is hardly overwhelming. A wider spread of jobs for women is not necessarily accompanied by a wider spread of power among women. Women of the middle classes had a better time of it in Egypt than elsewhere—most of the lawsuits in the endless papyri records are about them, showing that they had a lot of rights to protect. In the end, however, they and the women of the elite alike were overshadowed by the priesthood and the army. Egypt never became as militarized as other societies, just as it never became urbanized, so the loss of status for women was more gradual and never went as far as it did elsewhere. None of the foreign powers that have occupied Egypt since the Ptolemies—Rome, Islam, or Britain—have ever fully succeeded in erasing the tradition of an autonomous womanfolk.

Syria and Palestine

The gods of the Phoenicians and the god of the Israelites, peoples living side by side and bounded by desert and sea, are well known to the Westerner brought up on the Hebrew Bible. Competing traditions out of similar nomadic and herding origins produced very different patterns for these two peoples. There were progressive limitations on women's roles in both societies as they became sedentary. One is tempted to think that the women who stayed in the desert had better conditions; they at least had a long line of queens to point to, while their urban counterparts at the most kept their hands in with political intrigue.

As the Phoenicians grew wealthy through trade, orders of priestesses served Astarte, priests served Melqart, and both were related at the top level to the king. It was as tightly interlocking a network of merchant wealth, religious control, and political power as we will find anywhere, but women of the elite were well integrated into it. The fact that Princess Elissa (or Dido) could take off from Tyre with shiploads of goods, priestesses, and a male retinue to found her own city in 800 B.C.E. indicates the kind of resources that women could command. Her great-aunt Jezebel, who left Sidon to marry an Israeli king, did not fare nearly so well; she fought the sexist Israeli society all her life and died a courageous death when her side lost in a civil war. In Israel, Jehovah and male priests had the upper hand. Israelite women did not have a goddess-protector as the Phoenician women did.

What led to the loss of status of the Israeli women? When Sarai set out with her tribe from Ur of the Chaldees in the 1900s B.C.E., she was setting out from a matrilineal society.[9] True, the Israelites were already herders, but the woman's line was clearly recognized. Right through the records of the later books of the Hebrew Bible, from Judges to Nehemiah, there are the descent listings recording the woman's line, so common in manuscripts of the period. Perhaps the shift toward patriarchy started when the tribes were fighting their way into Canaan; a militaristic orientation works against a high status for women. Certainly the Israelites did not learn to look down on women in Egypt; in fact, Moses was dependent on the women of the pharaoh's family for his very life, for his education, and for his rise to power in the court. His ancestor Joseph married an Egyptian woman.

The memories of women's earlier roles, and a continued status for wise women, prophetesses, and judges, carried on for a long time after settlement in Canaan. Rachel and Leah, descendants of Sarai and wives of Jacob, are called "builders of Israel" in the Book of Ruth (4:11). Deborah was a judge of Israel in the days before Samuel was talked into appointing a king for the Israelites: "And she dwelt under the palm tree of Deborah, between

Ramah and Bethel in Mount Ephraim; and the children of Israel came up to her for judgement" (Judges 4:5). When she commanded Barak, one of the tribal leaders, to take an army of 10,000 men to fight the Canaanite Jabon's army under Sisera, he replied:

> If thou wilt go with me, then I will go; but if thou wilt not go with me, then I will not go. And she said, I will surely go with thee: notwithstanding the journey that thou takest shall not be for thine honor; for the Lord shall sell Sisera into the hand of a woman. (Judges 4: 7-9)

Not only did Deborah ensure the victory by her presence, but, when Sisera fled from the battlefield after defeat, she got the cooperation of Jael, wife of a commander of a tribe purported to be friendly to Sisera's people, in capturing him. Jael completed the battlefield slaughter by calmly inviting Sisera into her tent "for refuge," putting him to sleep, and then driving a stake through his head. Deborah and Jael were clearly part of a sisterhood. Deborah's war song (Judges 5) sings proudly of the victorious battle and of the sisterhood of Jael and her women. Judith could also have been a member of such a sisterhood. Delilah the Philistine, whose astute work as a spy defeated Samson, was still another, though of a later era. Even after the institution of kingship, women continued to be looked to for prophesy and guidance. The wise woman of Tekoa in 2 Samuel, chapter 14, helps the king out in a tricky diplomatic situation.

In addition to being leaders and advisers, women also managed to establish substantial individual enterprises independently of their husbands. The law of the levirate, providing that a man must marry his deceased brother's widow, is supposed to ensure that every woman is under the protection and rule of a man at all times in her life. The teachings about women as unreliable and lustful creatures give cultural support to the legal doctrines. Yet we find in the Book of Kings (2 Kings 4, 6, and 8) the story of the Shunammite whom the prophet Elisha liked so well that on his journeys he always stopped at her house for bread. She first got her husband's permission to build a special room for Elisha, but that is the last we hear of her husband. When in later years she is warned by Elisha of a famine and on his advice leaves the country for seven years, she manages on her return to get the king to appoint an officer to "restore all that was hers, and all the fruits of the field since the day that she left the land, until now." By this time, she is a woman of substance, and we hear no word about the males of her family.

The courage and humor of the women of Israel and Canaan come through again and again. King Saul, who earlier had had all prophetesses—

"those with familiar spirits"—exiled, becomes fearful before a battle and wants to consult one of the very women he has exiled. She first scolds him for his treatment of her profession, then not only gives him a consultation but also feeds and comforts him before packing him back to court. We have already mentioned Jezebel. When she knew she had lost in a protracted political power struggle (her husband was already dead), she dressed herself in her most regal attire, wore an elegant coiffure and a carefully made-up face, and went to an upper window to watch for her victorious enemy, Jehu. When he came in by the city gate, she called out a challenge and a taunt to him from her upper window before he could give the orders to the eunuch guards surrounding her to kill her (2 Kings 9).

These women were tough and not always admirable by any means. In a later round of the same power struggle in which Jezebel was involved, Queen Athaliah had all the royal infants murdered when the king died so that she could rule herself (2 Kings 11). It is not a surprise that she was overthrown after a couple of years. Bathsheba, who looked on with apparent equanimity while King David had her husband killed so he could marry her, saw to it that her son Solomon was crowned king when David was old and helpless in the hands of scheming courtiers.

King Solomon knew how to receive Sheba, a queen of South Arabia, as an equal and with respect. Solomon was an ambitious king and aspired to have an Egyptian-style women's court, hence his negotiations for women from the Moabites, Amonites, Edomites, Zedonians, and Hittites as well as for the pharaoh's daughter. He did not, however, have an adequate political infrastructure to support such negotiations, and he was also continually distracted by his predilection for love matches, which sometimes undermined the strategies of diplomatic marriage alliances. His wives in turn did not have the usual institutional mechanisms at hand for the exercise of power that women in well-established women's courts had. He did, however, lay the foundation for a political-alliance system for Israel, and his 700 wives and princesses and 300 concubines could be interpreted as a fair start toward an institutionalized harem court. The wives, according to the custom of the time, all brought their gods, goddesses, priests, and priestesses with them, to the great consternation of the conservative Israelites. There was a reaction against the cosmopolitanism of Solomon, and, under Ataxerxes, there was a great "putting away of strange wives" (Ezra 9, 10).

It is to the strange gods of the royal wives that we might look for specific political forces contributing to a decline in the status of Israelite women. The royal wives were often priestesses in their own lands. Jehovah already had only male priests, and prophetesses had been exiled. Had army leaders figured that the national strength of the Israelites lay in keeping a pure all-male devotion to the best battle god in the whole area? Jehovah had proved himself again and again. The other gods had done nothing for Israel but cause trouble. Foreign women were dangerous role models for Israelite women, with their political ways and priestess notions. We will see the same scenario played out again 1,000 years later, in the Christian church fathers' distrust of pagan women and their priestess tradition. The sexual seduction aspect of this struggle is, I suspect, a male rationalization.

The actual kingdom of Israel only lasted from 1020 to 930 B.C.E. From then on, Jewish communities settled all over the Mediterranean, sometimes by forced displacement, sometimes by voluntary migration. Many of them stayed on in Palestine and were incorporated into the other city-states and empires of the region. Sometimes they showed up in interesting ways in other parts of the Mediterranean world. The Jewish community in Alexandria is spoken of as an important force in the rapid rise of that city as a great cultural center. Queen Esther was the determined heroine of a story of the persecution of the Jews in what was probably Persia, under King Ahasueras, in the high days of Persian power. Ahasueras got angry with his queen, Vashti, because she didn't feel like being shown off to his royal guests on a special occasion. He sent out a call for women to be brought to the palace as a replacement for the recalcitrant Vashti. Esther was an orphan under the protection of her uncle, a Jewish merchant residing in the royal city, and her uncle sent her to the palace, warning her not to reveal that she was a Jewess. She pleased the king so he made her his crowned queen. She was a paragon of docility. Some time later, however, she risked everything to confess her origin when she discovered the king had signed a decree that all Jews should be destroyed as a favor to a scheming courtier. The story had a happy ending, and Queen Esther has become for all time the model of the obedient, submissive wife with a will of iron whose virtue triumphs in the end. Vashti, I am sorry to say, comes off with a totally undeserved bad character.

A study of the different types of female role models that come out of Hebrew tradition would be interesting. The Book of Ruth, which comes considerably before that of Esther, presents another and much subtler set of role models—this time for both men and women. The story of the interactions of Ruth and Boaz presents a picture of the kind of finely tuned mutual adjustment and consideration of the other that comes close to the concept of egalitarianism used in this book, in spite of a setting filled with tribal obligations and the concept of the levirate.

After the dispersion, a new conception of Jehovah as teacher, lover, and guide, one who yearns over his children and over the entire human race, grew in the hearts of the dispersed people alongside the old image of the battle god. The psalms provide a picture of the transformation of their own battle-happy heritage into a joyous love for God and creation through the experience of suffering imposed by the Assyrian cult of frightfulness. There the entire gamut of emotions generated by the tribal experience of the Israelites is recorded, from triumphant battle cry to brokenhearted repentance to tender love song. Israelite women could hardly fail to recognize their part in their own history, given that it was preserved in the records.

In the end, they accepted the new male-dominated priesthood, but we shall never know what struggles the Deborahs among them went through to try to preserve ancient authority. Also, we have no idea what their relationships with the alien women and their goddesses were. It is not impossible that the expulsion of foreign wives represented a campaign to break up an alliance of Jewish and gentile women against the Israelite priests and military leaders.[10] What remains today of earlier power is the special role of Jewish women in the remembering and retelling of Jewish history on ritual occasions within the orthodox family. Until the founding of the Jewish state of Israel in the twentieth century, their political roles had been drastically limited for centuries.

The Canaanite neighbors of the bellicose Israelites must have often puzzled over the fuss the latter made over their male god. He hadn't done *that* well by them. The inhabitants of the coastal city-states of Byblos, Beirut, Sidon, and Tyre, all strung along a 100-kilometer line along the shores of the Mediterranean, had long since lost any sense of tribal identification. Byblos was a prosperous trading city appearing in Egyptian records as early as 2500 B.C.E. The city-states evolved slowly, organically, and the rulers and the councils of city elders came from the leading merchant families. It was a socially mobile society, with many rags-to-riches stories. Somewhere around 1500 B.C.E., the Phoenicians became differentiated from the great mass of Canaanites, but they never developed centralized kingdoms. Always they remained a loose confederation of cooperating city-states. They were good at making money and took a pragmatic approach to life. Solidarity was a result of common residence, not ethnic bonds. Rulers were supposed to see that order was kept so that business could go on and to "render justice to orphans and widows"—a necessity in a non-clan-oriented society.

The Assyrians were a problem to the Phoenicians. The Assyrians wanted the Phoenician wealth, and the Phoenicians did not want to give it away. Neither did they want to waste their time on bloody wars they were bound to lose, not being warriors. So, sensibly, they bought the Assyrians off each time they could, fighting only when there was no other recourse. One way of controlling the relationship was through negotiation by marriage, and there are a number of records of Phoenician princesses going to Assyria— one whole set of them to marry Ashurbanipal. These princesses probably had their hands full, given that this was at the height of the period of Assyrian military activity.

From a variety of evidence, we may infer that women were active in trade as well as in the priesthoods. A common motif in Phoenician ivory carvings is the "woman at the window" (see Figure 6.9). It is not possible to tell whether she is goddess, priestess, or citizen, but she is looking out of an upper-story window of a typical Phoenician house. Apart from Jezebel and Elissa, no characterizations of individual Phoenician women are available. Elissa was very enterprising. After she landed at the site of the future Carthage, she is supposed to have bought land from the local Libyans by

Figure 6.9. "Woman at the Window," Assyrian, c. 900 B.C.E. Redrawn by HBR.

means of the old "as much land as an oxhide will cover" trick. Cut into thin strips, it will cover quite a lot. The Dido and Aeneas story is pure myth—the timing is all wrong in relation to the Aeneas chronology. It was probably a way of diminishing Elissa's stature as a political figure. Another story has it that, when an "uncouth" neighboring Libyan chieftain asked for her hand, she built a funeral pyre and immolated herself rather than marry him. After everything else she managed, that story is hardly credible, but women founders of cities are bound to have their detractors.

The Phoenicians can be admired—they are real "yankee traders"—but it is hard to love them. The practice of child sacrifice that roused so much loathing in their neighbors has been irrefutably confirmed by archaeological evidence. In the precinct of the goddess Tanit at Carthage, "thousands of urns containing the cremated remains of small children, some as much as twelve years old, but mostly under two, and sometimes of birds and small animals as substitute sacrifices, have been found" (Harden 1971: 86). Evidence of devices to soothe frightened children about to be sacrificed somehow don't help to soften very much our feelings toward the Phoenicians. It is clear that priestesses were equally involved with priests in placing the infants in the dreaded mechanical arms of the hungry deities. Powerful priestly families dominated this society, sometimes for as long as 17 generations in a single line; priests and priestesses married each other. Sometimes the kings and queens were also of the priesthood, although not always. A hard-boiled merchant state that is also a theocracy and practices child sacrifice is hard to visualize—but it existed.[11]

The gap between rich and poor widened rapidly after Carthage (Phoenicia West) became wealthy, and the concentrations of power in temple-palace-warehouse soon came to require increased military defense. Carthage became a militarized society, increasingly divorced from the realities of its own poor and on very bad terms with surrounding native Libyans. Perhaps it all started because Elissa did not marry the neighboring chieftain. We all know about the final destruction of Carthage, but it was a sick society long before the confrontation with Rome. The fluidity and mobility of the early mercantile society of the Syrian seaport states did not last, and the women of the elite joined the men in a ruthless exploitation of their own society as well as of their environment. Goddesses are historically rarely gentle, but Tanit, spouse of Moloch, does seem to have been unusually bloodthirsty. What a band of priestesses Tanit must have had!

In this review of Syria and Palestine, we have looked at old, settled, merchant city-states that have lost all vestige of attachment to tribal life as well as at nomads who settled down and formed a kingdom, only to be dispersed to the world's cities. In the next chapter, we will look at nomadic desert tribes who never settled down at all yet whose fate was closely linked to that of the settlers. The early Israelites, like desert tribes, were ranked societies, and women appear as tribal leaders, prophetesses, and judges in both. In the stratified merchant states, women belonged to the priestly elite, and some middle-class women presumably participated in trading and the mobility that trading offers. Of the Phoenician poor, we know nothing except that the cities required numerous service workers. As traders, the Phoenicians would be among the first to have widespread use of domestic slaves. The Israelites, under less likely circumstances, also kept women slaves. It is difficult to reconstruct the Phoenician underlife society for women, although it probably existed. For Israelite women, our imagination has more materials to use.

The description of the day-to-day life of the women of the upper middle class in both Israel and the Syrian city-states that comes to us through the famous passage from Proverbs gives an interesting glimpse into the relative roles of women and men:

> If you can find a truly good wife, she is worth more than precious gems! Her husband can trust her, and she will richly satisfy his needs. She will not hinder him, but help him all her life. She finds wool and flax and busily spins it. She buys imported food, brought by ship from distant ports. She gets up before dawn to prepare breakfast for her household, and plans the day's work for her servant girls. She goes out to inspect a field, and buys it; with her own hands she plants a vineyard. She is energetic, a hard worker, and watches for bargains. She works far into the night! She sews for the poor, and generously gives to the needy. She has no fear of winter for her household, for she has made warm clothes for all of them. She also upholsters with finest tapestry; her own clothing is beautifully made—a purple gown of pure linen. Her husband is well known, for he sits in the council chamber with the other civic leaders. She makes belted linen garments to sell to the merchants. She is a woman of strength and dignity, and has no fear of old age. When she speaks, her words are wise, and kindness is the rule for everything she says. She watches carefully all that goes on throughout her household, and is never lazy. Her children stand and bless her; so does her husband. He praises her with these words: "There are many fine women in the world, but you are the best of them all!" Charm can be deceptive and beauty doesn't last, but a woman who fears and reverences God shall be greatly praised. Praise her for the many fine things she does. These good deeds of hers shall bring her honor and recognition from even the leaders of the nations. (Prov. 31: 10-31, translation from *The Living Bible*, copyright 1971 by Tyndale House Publishers, Wheaton, Illinois 60187; used by permission)

For women, there is a clear portrayal of the delicate balance between being anchored to the household and engaging in modest trading enterprises outside the home, characteristic of propertied urban women in all the early civilizations. The extent of a woman's autonomy and authority is revealed. Any sense of mother-child relations is strangely absent in this passage except for the bald statement toward the end that her children will bless her. Perhaps mothering really is a new development in these millennia.

For men, the passage shows an absorption in political roles and very little involvement in productive or domestic activity. Although excluded from political roles, the women of this class appear to have a wider range of activities than do the men. To some degree, this description will hold for propertied women right up to the industrial revolution.

Goddesses and Amazons in the Aegean and Greece

Crete, the Cheerful Island

In legend and myth, Crete is the home of matriarchy, the mother-goddess,[12] and the Eleusinian mysteries. It is also the source of the double-ax cult that became the symbol of all the "Amazonian" kingdoms of the Mediterranean time of troubles. Whether Crete represents a civilization comparable to the pristine civilizations of the Near East is something like the question of whether Egypt ever had true urbanism—it depends on how you define it, and this issue is still debated by scholars. Certainly Crete was an active trading center with protourban communities not unlike those of Sumer in 3200, and, by 2000 B.C.E., it had a flourishing palace economy and a vast international trade.

The Cretans appear to have been a remarkably cheerful and secular people. Woolley describes them as gay, picturesque, humane folk who approached god through dancing and feasting (Hawkes and Woolley 1963). The archetypal mother-daughter myth comes from Crete—Demeter (De Meter, mother of grain, Ceres in Roman form) in search of her daughter Kore (Gaia or Ge, earth). The basically positive themes of death and rebirth, winter and summer, separation and reunion, which run through these stories, are later overlaid with more somber themes. Zeus, the god in search of power, is also supposed to have been born in Crete, in a cave on Mt. Dikte.

Figure 6.10. Cretan Women in Round Dance With Lyre Player, Late Minoan. Redrawn by HBR.

His struggle with his father Chronos, which ends with Zeus throwing Chronos into Tatarus, the ancient hell, could be seen as the seal and judgment of the stern patriarchal society placed on the gayer, more casual matriarchy. That overthrow of the matriarchy already represents the Mycenean conquest of Crete. Another version of the stern succession of patriarchy is the Europa and bull story. The bull cult comes to represent male dominance.

The ax symbol, and the cult it represents, is a problem to scholars. The basic single-bladed ax goes back to the Paleolithic as an all-purpose tool. The double-bladed ax may have been independently invented by several peoples and traveled to Europe with warlike nomads characterized as "battle-ax cultures."[13] The ax of the Cretan ax cult (Figure 6.11) is also a double-bladed ax, but it was not used as a weapon, unless possibly for child sacrifice, in connection with the archaic harvest rites suggested by the Demeter/Kore story. This makes the Cretans appear somewhat less gay. When prosperity came to Crete, cultic headquarters were apparently located in the snake-goddess shrine in the palace at Knossos. The double-ax symbol carved all over the walls of this shrine gives little information on meanings, however. The ax is never seen in connection with a male god, only with a goddess. The wide distribution of the cultic ax throughout Europe is probably associated with the fact that Cretans were seafarers and

Figure 6.11. Double Axes, Middle to Late Minoan. Redrawn by HBR.

traders. It is an interesting fact that the curved double ax was in a later era the battle weapon of the Amazons, the warriors widely recorded in the literature of antiquity. Known as the *labrys,* it has in modern times become a symbol of lesbianism (*Alyson Almanac* 1990: 56, 57).

How many of the Cretan cults actually were mother-goddess cults, and what significance they had at the time, we do not know. That they had immense significance for later peoples and were the source for later legends about a golden age of matriarchy, we shall see shortly.

Whatever the Cretans believed, they appeared to enjoy life and to love to dance. Their pictures show us this. As Jane Harrison (1912) says, dancing is the vehicle through which many peoples have taught their tribal lore and learned to separate themselves from and reflect on the experiences they are re-creating through dance. Through dancing, concepts of order, leadership, and religious projections are developed. The Cretans danced their way into culture and civilization, and their dancing figures still delight us today.

There is little evidence of a formal priesthood in this society, although dance leaders may have been priestesses. There are no temples, only minimal shrine sites and sacred caves. It seems to have been a very egalitarian society, although the representations of the mother-goddess holding the famous double ax may have given rise to later conceptions of an authoritarian matriarchy. The little folded-arms figurines found everywhere are apparently not cultic but simply figurines to delight the eye.

Knossos was apparently not very impressive as a city—the palace-dominated center and surrounding settlements did not cover more than 12 acres compared with the Mesopotamian towns that averaged 25 acres. The settlements were open; there is no sign of fortification until after the holocaust in 1400 B.C.E. The Mediterranean triad of wheat, olives, and the vine were all cultivated here, and wine and

Figure 6.12. Snake Goddess, Middle Minoan. Redrawn by HBR.

one-handled cups for drinking spread out in waves from Crete to the entire region. When women were buried, wine vessels and sewing equipment were buried with them. It is doubtful that the Cretans "invented" wine, but they are credited with inventing the dagger and with developing a process of alloying copper to make the metal harder.

We have a very interesting set of contradictory images of the Cretans. On the one hand, there are the cheerful, peaceable people who love to dance. On the other hand, their goddesses' double ax may be dripping with the blood of child sacrifice; and, in inventing the dagger, the Cretans produced "a military threat which could be answered only by equipping oneself with similar weapons. . . . every man needed a dagger during the bronze age" (Renfrew 1972: 320). While Crete had a variety of craft specialists attached to the palace culture, Renfrew suggests that the civilization was something between tribe and state—a redistributional chiefdom coordinating economic, religious, and social activities. There appear to have been no "peasant masses" and no private concentrations of wealth. It would be a ranked society on the verge of stratification, perhaps. We have no images of women householders from this society.

The Fall of Crete and the Rise of the Amazons

By 1200 B.C.E., the whole Cretan phenomenon was over. Homer's pompous heroes had helped to create disorder in the whole Aegean, although they did not do it alone. Even the serious and warlike Myceneans, who took over the island of Crete and its trade, could not cope with the general increase in piracy and unrest. Large-scale population movements in the area finally destroyed the Myceneans too. During the time of troubles, many of the inhabitants of Crete left the island and settled elsewhere. Out of this era came the myths of Amazons and matriarchies; Lycians, Carians, Lydians, and Mysians, all Cretan-related settlers on the coast of Asia Minor, are all supposed to have had similar matriarchal (in fact, matrilineal) systems.[14] Herodotus and a host of writers after him wrote of the custom of these people of taking the name of the mother and of property going to daughters. They also write of the absence of formal law. Bachofen, the apostle of the matriarchy theory, says:

> [Women] bore within themselves the law pervading all matter. Justice speaks out of their mouths without pervading self-consciousness and with certainty in the manner of conscience. They are wise by nature, prophetesses proclaiming Fate, Sybil or Themis. Therefore, women were considered inviolable bearers of jurisprudence and sources of prophecy. The battle lines drew apart at their command and they arbitrated the

disputes of the nations as sacerdotal umpires; religious foundation on which gynocracy immovably rested. (Diner [1932] 1965: 233)

While Bachofen cannot be treated as a scholarly source concerning tribal jurisprudence, the image of the tribal setting for the administration of justice that his passage conveys reminds us of the problems of scale that face matrilineal societies with growing population densities. Sacerdotal umpires are all very well in small communities but do not serve large city-states or kingdoms very effectively. The Lycians, Lydians, Carians, and Mysians are not mythical peoples. They will be found on maps in all the classical atlases. The Carian Queen Artemisia is a documented historical figure and did lead both a land army and a naval battle under Xerxes during the Greco-Persian War (Edey 1974: 50). To describe the capital of matrilineal Lydia as the Paris of Asia Minor (Diner [1932] 1965: 236), exporting finery and horoscopes to the Mediterranean world, may be an exaggeration, but Lydia does seem to have participated in the general Cretan tradition of craft, skill, and beauty. Oddly, there is little mention of craftswomen—mainly of queens, priestesses, and astrologers. Who did the work of production? What the proportions of ruling kings to ruling queens were over a several-hundred-year period in these matrilineal kingdoms I do not know, but it is doubtful that they were ever pure matriarchies. They certainly had substantial kingly rule by the time of the rise of the Greek city-states.

The relatively peaceable movements and activities of the matrilineal societies in the Aegean coincided with other more violent movements of barbarian nomadic tribes and a general period of bloodiness in Mesopotamia. The matrilineal societies probably have contributed to the formation of the Amazon bands that appear in classical history. The Black Sea region around the Thermodon River seems to have been for a time an area of settlement for such women's bands, but these women are usually described as Scythians from the Caucasus. The "classical Asiatic Amazons" are reported from Scythia, Anatolia, around the Black Sea, Asia Minor, India, and Central Asia (Cavin 1985). They were probably from nomadic tribes, as suggested by mentions in Greek literature of their being horsewomen and herders living on mare's milk and blood, as many herding peoples do.

That there should have been major pitched battles between women's and men's armies seems a little unlikely. There must, however, have been some armed confrontations to account for the widespread myths about these battles and to account for the very large number of sculptures and paintings of "dying Amazons" now spread throughout Europe's museums. Figure 6.13 is a reproduction of one of the famous dying-Amazon statues, and Figures 6.14 and 6.15 are reproductions from a longer series of some schematic representations of the battle postures in which Amazons are represented in Greek art from 500 B.C.E. forward. The preoccupation of Athenian artists with the theme of women as soldiers is in itself significant, even if there had been no battles. Given that it is such a strong Athenian theme, the possibility should not be discounted that a couple of Greeks (probably not gods, as storied!) kidnapped a young girl from an Amazon camp and carted her off to Athens and that angry Amazons followed them to Athens and gave them a good battle before being driven away. We certainly know that women fought in some of the major battles of the Persian wars, although not necessarily as all-women's units. We also know, from much later accounts of Roman soldiers confronting Germanic women warriors in the forests of Europe, that is unnerving to men to have to fight women in hand-to-hand combat. In other words, there could be a variety of experiences giving rise to the Amazonian theme, which appears again and again in history. Cavin (1985: 72), modifying an earlier statement by Bachofen (1967), states that "Amazonism is interwoven with the origins of many peoples across 5 continents, ranging in time from prehistory to the Old World Exploration of the New World."

Figure 6.13. Wounded Amazon
SOURCE: Reproduction by Allen Barr.

Figure 6.14. Amazons Fighting a Greek. Redrawn by HBR.

Figure 6.15. Amazons in Battle. Redrawn by HBR.

Athens: New Consciousness and Old Rigidities in the Greek City-States

The Greek city-states were legion, and to discuss adequately the role of women in them is an impossibility. As Tarn says, the spirit of particularism was the curse of Greece ([1927] 1961: 66). Each city was insistent on its autonomy, and yet threats from the rest of the Mediterranean continually drove the cities into one type of alliance or another. Their political systems were not complex. They had only one word, *koinon*, to cover every type of association from the village sports team to an intercity league. Some leagues, such as Aetolia, were simply a collection of villages. Aetolia's federal center in 280 B.C.E. was a temple of Apollo, and its assembly consisted of "every free Aetolian under arms"—male, of course. By 220 B.C.E., so many towns had joined it that it stretched across Greece. Representative government in this context developed to keep the masses out of government and public affairs in the hands of the well-to-do.

Given the tension between particularism and the need for integration into larger wholes both for trade and for military protection, cities developed all kinds of systems for extending rights to residents of other cities. Sometimes a city decreed citizenship en masse to all the inhabitants of another city; other times it gave citizenship selectively; and sometimes it simply put up citizenship for sale.

The three most important institutional devices of the Greek cities from our point of view are the rights of citizenship, the development of free elementary schools, and the development of clubs—religious, occupation-centered, and extended-family associations. They all represent potential public spaces for women. Except in cases of special honoring, women were generally excluded from citizenship probably because citizenship was associated with arms bearing. Macedonia, which had an aristocracy, was different, and we shall see later that the influence of politically active Macedonian princesses was felt in all the Greek states.

Educational institutions were more flexible. In Ionia, Teos, Chios, and Sparta, girls and boys were educated together during elementary school. In the other city-states, they were educated either in separate schools or at home. A few women went on to the gymnasia in the four cities named above; we do not know what access women had to the gymnasia in other cities, but we do know that exceptional women found their way to an education. Toward the end of the last millennium B.C.E., we find that the age of private libraries has begun; Aristotle is considered to have had the first private library on any scale in Greece (Tarn [1927] 1961: 269). Therefore we may deduce that women could have access to learning in the private spaces of the home.

Religious clubs provided the most important public spaces for women. There were mother-goddess clubs in all the cities of Hellenic culture, both in Greece and in Asia. While mother-goddesses were losing out to male gods during this period, even as late as Roman times, Hellenized Lydia had 112 mother-goddess-with-son cult inscriptions out of a total of 237 cult inscriptions examined. Earlier, the proportion of mother-goddess cults would have been larger. Tarn points out how important the mother-goddess was in the Hellenic pantheon:

Of all the deities of Hellenism, Isis of the Myriad Names was probably the greatest. She was identified with practically every goddess and deified woman of the known world. . . . All civilization was her gift and in her charge. [Furthermore] she was the woman's goddess. Half the human race had been badly off for a friend at the court of Heaven. Athena was uniquely a man's goddess. . . . Isis is the "glory of women" who gives them "equal power with men." "I am Isis" runs her creed, "I am she whom women call goddess. I ordained that women should be loved by men; I brought wife and husband together, and invented the marriage contract. I ordained that women should bear children, and that children should love their parents." ([1927] 1961: 357-59)

Isis was different than the chtonic goddesses of Catal Huyuk. Something had been happening under the Mediterranean sun. "Her statues portrayed a young matron in modest dress with gentle, benevolent features, crowned with blue lotus or the crescent moon, and sometimes bearing in her arms the babe Horus." In Christian times, some of her statues were to be relabeled as Mary, and these are known in Europe today as the Black Virgins (Tarn [1927] 1961: 360). Isis indeed represented new understandings of motherhood and family life; she provides suggestive evidence for a changing conception of parent-child relations.

The religious associations, or "cultic clubs," were the only activity outlet for women in the public arena that could be found in every city-state and kingdom. For the rest, there was enormous variability in the freedom and opportunities allowed to women from state to state. This makes it all the more ironic that it is Athens, where women had perhaps the least freedom of any of the cities, that has magnetized the historical imagination of the West. In Macedonia, queens led armies on horseback. In Sparta, women wrestled naked in the arena. In Ionia, Teos, Chios, and Sparta, they went to school with boys. In Athens, however, women were supposed to stay in the *gynaeceum*, the women's quarters. Yet Athens is our "heritage." Even more, it acted as a magnet in its own times. Women scholars and artists and traders from all the other city-states came to Athens, introducing an intellectual leadership of women that could not have found expression through Athenian culture alone.

Because Athens was the most articulate focal point for Greek culture, much of the discussion in this section will center on the situation of women in Athens. It must be remembered, however, that the context of the Athenian drama was the dynamic interplay of civic, cultural, and economic activities among all the city-states of Greece and also of Hellenized Asia. Many forces were at work in the consciousness of women and men in the Hellenic world during this last quarter of the millennium transition period. The relative self-containment of the early civilizations was gone, and the shift toward more complex, internationally linked kingdoms and world empires had to be endured. These empires were beginning to be a major force as the time of troubles sorted itself out, and the Mediterranean reached toward a new equilibrium by the middle of the first millennium B.C.E. New concepts of social relationships and new ideals of humanness were developing, but the prolonged period of militarization and centralization of power that the Mediterranean people had experienced tended in the main to squeeze women to the sidelines. It was not easy for women and men to explore these new ideas together.

What we see most strongly in the myths and legends about Amazons, about an ancient rule of women, and about mother-goddesses is a strong undercurrent of male uneasiness. Something is wrong that cannot easily be articulated. The negative husband-wife, mother-son dynamic analyzed by Philip Slater—that of contempt for and fear of the woman by the man, reinforced by the woman's frustration in the face of that contempt and fear—which was discussed first in Chapter 4, would certainly be well under way by now. Thus we have the paradox described by Slater:

> On the one hand one is usually told that the status of women in fifth- and fourth-century Athens achieved some kind of nadir. They were legal nonentities, excluded from political and intellectual life, uneducated, virtually imprisoned in the home, and appeared to be regarded with disdain by the principal male spokesmen whose comments have survived. . . . On the other hand, as Comme points out: "There is, in fact, no literature, no art of any country, in which women are more prominent, more important, more carefully studied and with more interest than in the tragedy, sculpture, and painting of fifth-century Athens." (1968: 4-5)

The explanation of this paradox, says Slater, is that the exclusion of women from political power leads to excessive accumulations of power by women in the home, because power does not follow deference patterns and a sizable power differential between sexes is not possible. Men facing this enormous accumulation of power at home are indeed miserable and don't know why.

I do not accept the notion of a fixed balance of power between the sexes that will be maintained by overt or covert means—I think social values can induce people (of either sex) to give up large amounts of "power." It is true, however, that the possibilities for the exercise of power must be commensurate with perceived opportunity within the total structure. The whole notion of "relative deprivation" is based on perception of opportunity, not actual opportunity. In that sense, Athenian women were suffering from relative deprivation. They had participated to some significant degree in the developments that made the Athenian city-state possible, and now they were pushed into the home and out of the new social space that was to mean so much to the men—the agora. There was a very unfortunate combination of a major new constriction of social space for women and an enlargement of social space for men.

The significance of Aeschylus's treatment of the Orestes legend lies in the attempt to articulate the "unconscious" suppression of women in fifth-century B.C.E. Greece. Put in the stark terms of the replacement of an earlier matriarchy by a patriarchy—"you ran things before, now we will run them"—the play presents the classical dilemma of the power struggle. Someone must win. Orestes has killed his mother to avenge his father, and by matriarchal law that is the unforgivable sin. Apollo advocates a new patriarchal law: "The mother is not the parent of the child, only the nurse of what she has conceived. The parent is the father, who commits his seed to her, a stranger, to be held with God's help in safe keeping" (Aeschylus 1954: 89). Athena, the "motherless daughter of Zeus's head, the even daughter, the trembling lightning of her father," has to break the tie because the judges are equally ranged on both sides of the issue: "The final judgment is a task for me; so for Orestes shall this vote be cast. No mother gave me birth, and in all things save marriage, I, my father's child indeed, with all my heart commend the masculine" (Aeschylus 1954: 91). The furies (Erinys) respond to this crushing of the matriarchy with a curse:

> Oho ye younger Gods, since ye have trod under foot the laws of old and ancient powers purloined, then we, dishonoured, deadly in displeasure, shall spread poison foul through the land, with damp contagion of rage malignant, bleak and barren, blasting, withering up the earth, mildews on bud and birth abortive. Oh! Venomous pestilence shall sweep this country with infectious death. (Aeschylus 1954: 93)

The furies later modify the curse, but the damage is done.

The reader will see that I have presented the city-state pattern as the basic pattern of evolution of all societies. In its early stages, I have suggested that there is an egalitarianism that stems from a minimum of occupational differentiation, somewhat modified by various ceremonial statutes. Athens fits the early Sumerian pattern nicely, except that in Sumeria women participated more fully in the ceremonial life and had less limitation on their movement. The fact that it was Athens, rather than another Greek city, or a Sumerian one, that was imprinted on the Western mind has had confusing consequences for the understanding of women's roles ever since.

Athens is presented to us as a trick with mirrors. Most historians write as if Athens invented democracy and an incredible new way of life in which individuals participated in the shaping of their personal lives as well as in that of the polity. Yet the same historians assure us that Athens had no place for women but the *gynaeceum*, or the women's quarters in the home. The question is this: Did Athens have something unique that Sumer did not? If it did, how did women come to be excluded from the "glory that was Greece"?

The answer to the first question is yes, Athens did have something unique: the agora, the public social space in which all transactions mingled—trade, social intercourse, education, the making of laws, and the making of political decisions. The only thing that was not done in the agora was the worship of gods, who were kept up on the hill, in the acropolis, out of the way.

Compare the city plan of Priene in Figure 6.16, a city similar to Athens, with that of Arbela (Figure 5.2 in Chapter 5). There are no public spaces in Arbela. Picture the bustling open space in the heart of cities like Priene and Athens: "In the agora stood the stoa, the open-sided markets where the

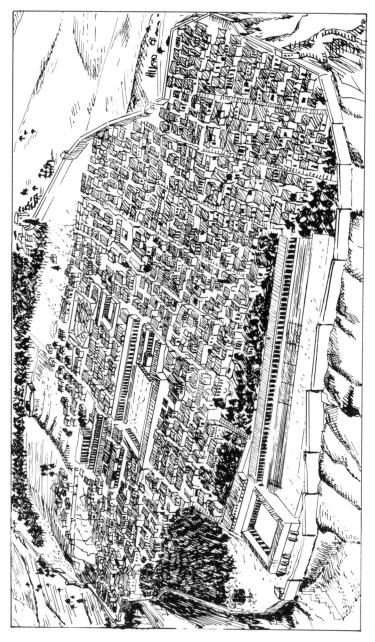

Figure 6.16. City Plan of Priene, c. 350 B.C.E. Redrawn by KH.

philosophers taught; the Boukuterion, where the 500-man council met; the mint; courts; and the Strategion, or military headquarters" (Bowra 1965: 106-7). The full assembly of the men of Athens had to meet on a neighboring hill, the Pynx. The agora could not hold them all.

If we contrast the agora as a civic institution with the walled temple-palace compound of a Near Eastern city-state, we see here the conscious re-creation of the concept of public interest. The council of the agricultural village had it—the sense of the civic good extending beyond kinship lines—for these villages were already ethnic mixtures in the posttribal stage. When the civic good was walled up inside the palace-temple compound, however, the consciousness of public interest disappeared. The citizens of Mesopotamian cities could worship in the temples and buy at the bazaars, but they could not enter the trading complexes belonging to palace, temple, or merchant families except as professional traders; they could not enter the palace on government business except as the king's officials.

How was Athens able to break apart the walled secrecy of the Mesopotamian city-state? The answer is not difficult. Athens was small. The average Greek city-state had a population of 5,000. Athens was one of three that had 20,000. The city-state of Ur, in contrast, had an estimated population of 250,000. Greek land was sparse and unfruitful and, with the existing technologies, could not support a larger population. This environmental poverty was Athens's best resource, leading it to specialize in the productive intellect. The partial sex segregation involved in the development of women's quarters in the households did not lead to the population explosion one might have expected but to a stable city size. This may be due partly to the cultural emphasis on male love relationships[15] and to birth control practices including late marriage, abortion, and infanticide. Were there comparable emphases on female love relationships? There may have been (Cavin 1985: chap. 2; Pomeroy 1975) and evidence of it destroyed, as most of Sappho's poetry was destroyed. This too could have kept the birthrate low.

Few families reared more than one daughter, and two sons were considered an adequate number (de Mause 1974: 25). De Mause's emphasis on the severe beatings of children, combined with practices of sexual abuse, can create an unpleasant picture of Greek family life and a particularly unpleasant picture of Greek motherhood. While de Mause's view of high levels of child abuse in Greece may well be correct, I believe that further study of life in the gynaeceum will uncover tenderness along with cruelty. It is true, though, that both child-rearing and pedagogical practices do seem to have relied on the rod as the shaper of the child, according to the records generally quoted. If urbanism were unkind to women, it was far worse for children.

In spite of small families, and the abuses inside them, the household and its hearth were important in Greek culture. The geographic isolation of many of the Greek city-states meant that Athens, like the other states, was characterized by an ethnic homogeneity and legacy of preexisting tribal structures that had long since disappeared in the Mesopotamian cross-roads. All these features led to an emphasis on the clan-linked household units. The traditions regarding the sacred hearth and sacred clan bound-aries come from tribal roots. Kin and tribe were still in the early city-state days meaningful units, and women entered a new kinship group on mar-riage to become its servant. The daughter of another man's hearth, con-tracted for and set to serving one's own sacred hearth, could never be fully trusted. She had been born under different gods and remained in one sense always a stranger.

It is not clear why Athens, the city that developed the most sophisticated public institutions of all the city-states and generated the greatest cultural flowering of Hellas, was also the city that inclined toward the greatest privatization of women's roles. Apparently it applied the ethics of tribalism to women and the ethics of universalism to men.

The concept of the *oikos* was made to serve the ethics both of tribalism and of universalism. The oikos was the household and served as the basic unit of the *polis*, the city. The father ruled the oikos and represented it in the polis. The continuation of the male line so that the oikos could be continued, in this relatively infertile population, was of crucial importance. Therefore all legal cases relating to the family were classed as public affairs. Any citizen (male) could become involved in these affairs on behalf of the public interest. Under these circumstances, it is all the more striking to find a variety of records that indicate that women, privatized as they were, could and did fight in the courts to protect the freedom of their persons and their property. They were not infrequently successful (O'Faolain and Martines 1973: 9-25). The confinement to the gynaeceum was therefore not complete. The rule that women were not to appear at their own dinner table if there were guests in the house may well have been more honored in the breach than in the observance.[16] The women had a vigorous underlife, and it is this underlife that erupts both tragically and amusingly in Greek theater, Greek literature, and the courtroom.

In fact, the number of women actually confined to the women's quarters must have been rather small, when one stops to consider the categories of women who were free to move about: (a) the older, high-status women; (b) the poor who worked at the same variety of crafts and trades at which poor women everywhere work; (c) the slaves;[17] (d) the foreign born, including women traders; and (e) the hetairae and intellectuals, also frequently foreign born.

Women over 60 performed public ceremonial functions and acted as message bearers for younger women living in seclusion. Poor free women

> were engaged mainly in retail trade, and seem to have had, if not a monopoly, at least a privileged position in the market place; the soldier's wife plaited and sold garlands; the mother of Euxitheus [a court orator who apologized profusely for having a mother known to work] sold ribbons at one time, and worked as a wet-nurse at another. . . . All kinds of comestibles were sold by women, both retail and as cafe or inn-keepers. (Lacey 1968: 171)

The innkeepers had the usual bad reputation. Workers in wool were more respected as were women vase painters. Lacey points out that

> it used to be argued that trade was not possible for citizen-women, since the limit of their contractual competence was the value of one medimnos of barley; it has, however, now been shown that this was not a paltry sum, but equivalent in value to more than a poor petty-trader's stock-in-trade, and enough to provide food for a family for several days. (1968: 171)

It is clear that both the poor and some enterprising middle-class women traded. Probably only women of the upper middle and upwardly mobile classes really kept to the confinement practice, not even going shopping. The woman entrepreneur was always wide open to the accusation of being a prostitute—an accusation frequently made against women. Table 6.1 lists occupations open to women in Athens, adapted and expanded from Evelyne Sullerot's *Histoire et Sociologie du Travail Féminin* (1968).

The slaves and some of the foreign-born women who moved about in public were the entertainers, "such as flute-girls and courtesans, who provided the female company at men's dinners and riotous parties" (Lacey 1968: 172), and the prostitutes: "The successful were able to obtain their freedom, retire and keep brothels or schools to train other courtesans, and we hear of one who acted as a go-between in business deals of men" (Lacey 1968: 172). Other freed women were wool workers, nurses, and retainers—and "one cobbler."

The fifth group of Greek women who moved freely in public spaces is hard to classify. They were intellectuals—philosophers, mathematicians, physicians. There were poets and poet-musicians. Some have been coupled with the names of famous men, with circumlocutions—such as "she was said to be the wife of" or "evidently she was the wife of"—used to describe their status. Some were foreign born—from the more sex egalitarian of the neighboring city-states and elsewhere in the Mediterranean—and some native, but none of them seems to have followed the rules of behavior of

TABLE 6.1 Women's Occupational Roles in Athens in the Age of Pericles

---

I. Occupations for women slaves (there were an estimated 90,000 women slaves in Athens in the fourth century):

    A. Food processing: threshing grain, grinding flour

    B. Mining: gold and silver mining; separating metal from slag, washing metal; transporting ore from underground corridors of mines to the surface

    C. Textile workers: all operations connected with carding, spinning, and weaving carried on by women in workshops (no indication whether these were state owned or privately owned); weaving also carried on as cottage industry in private homes

II. Occupations open to free women:

    A. Agriculture, unspecified except for "fieldwork"

    B. Textile work as above

    C. Trade: selling of vegetables, processed foods, baked goods, other home-manufactured products, unspecified; selling of cloth, garments, headdresses

    D. Innkeeping

    E. Prostitution

    F. Running schools for courtesans

    G. Midwifery, nursing

    H. Music

    I. Dancing

    J. Vase painting

III. Occupations specifically forbidden to women:

    A. Medicine (there are records of illegal practice and punishment of women practitioners)

IV. Occupations possible but not encouraged:

    A. Scribe—schools for women rare (Sappho's school was an exception) but, if a woman could write, she was not forbidden to exercise her skill

---

the respectable Greek married woman. They are variously referred to as courtesans, hetairae, or high-class prostitutes, in spite of the fact that many of them do not appear to have sold sexual services. They appear to have been a group of women who had an independent status outside the oikos system. Some of them were, in fact, married, although most of them were not. It has been difficult for later Western cultures to conceptualize educated, socially productive women standing entirely outside the legal and cultural system of male domination. Yet they were well thought of enough at the time to be widely written about by their male contemporaries. We know about them mostly through the writings of these male contemporaries and sometimes through surviving fragments of the women's own writings.

We will discuss these independent women who participated in the intellectual and public life of Athens in three categories: first, the Pythagoreans, belonging to a group that was "ideologically committed" to the intellectual equality of women; then the poets; and finally those known as hetairae. The Pythagoreans were partly a school, partly a community, and partly a philosophical-mystical "order" in which women were active. A history of women philosophers published in 1765 lists 28 Pythagoreans (Beard 1946: 321). First and foremost is Theano, who "appears" to have been the wife of Pythagoras, "devoted to medicine, hygiene, the arts of ethical living, physics and mathematics, a commentator on the art of healing and a writer on virtue in its large Greek meaning" (Beard 1946: 321). Some of her writings are still extant. There is Perictione, pupil of Pythagoras and author of *Wisdom* and *The Harmony of Women*. Then there is Diotima, priestess of Mantinea and also thought to be a Pythagorean, who taught Socrates and is mentioned by Plato in this regard (she is also thought by some to be only an imaginary person). Schools that were offshoots from Pythagoreanism also had women active in them—63 women are named in a list by Menage.

> Some became heads of philosophic schools, notably Arete of Cyrene who had urged her father Aristippus to set up a school at Cyrene and who conducted it after his death. She was interested in natural science and ethics and like her father she was concerned with a "world in which there would be neither masters nor slaves and all would be as free from worry as Socrates." (Beard 1946: 326)

Sappho was head of a girl's school on the island of Lesbos and one of the most widely renowned poets of her time. The surviving fragments of her vividly erotic love poetry addressed to other women have lifted a tip of the veil drawn over lesbian love by historians of every age. (All known copies of her love poems are supposed to have been burned by ecclesiastical authorities in Constantinople and Rome in 1073 C.E., according to the *Alyson Almanac* 1990: 12.)

What little we know about Sappho and her circle reveals a passionate women's culture that existed unrecorded side by side with the widely described and possibly less interesting gay culture of Greek males. In most history books, she appears on a lonely mountain peak of women's achievement, but this is because historians have chosen her as their token woman and

Figure 6.17. Sappho Honored by Pupils. Redrawn by HBR.

have not looked further. Sappho was one of the "nine terrestrial muses" celebrated during what we now call the classical period of Greek culture. The other eight were Erinna, a pupil of Sappho—called by the ancients the equal of Homer—who died famous at the age of 19; Myrus; Myrtis; Corinna of Boetia, Pindar's teacher, who "won five times over him in a poetic competition" (Drinker 1948: 103); Praxilla of Sicyon, famous for her drinking songs and epics; Telesilla of Argos, writer of political songs and hymns; Nossis; and Anyta. The list, however, leaves out Gorgo, Andromeda, and Danophila, the Pamphylian. These women belong to a much longer list of 76 poets of that period, acclaimed as great at the time. It will be noted that, where origin is indicated, none of these women is mentioned as an Athenian. The rich lesbian culture, which gave rise to this extraordinary creativity in an era when women were generally held in low regard, is one that deserves its own history—one that I hope will be written before too long.

There were at least two outstanding husband-wife teams in the public life of Athens, all philosophers: Crates and his wife Hipparchia, and Leon and his wife Themista, who was called the *solon* ("law-giver") of her time.

Following is a list of the leading hetairae of Athens and the men they companioned:

Aspasia	Pericles
Leontium	Epicurus
Danae	Epicurus
Glycera	Menander
Metaneira	Isocrates
Herphyllis	Aristotle
Archeanassa	Plato
Lais (1)	Aristippus
Lais (2)	Diogenes
Lais (3)	Demosthenes
Phrybe	Hyperides

The three Lais are three different women; this was a common name in Greece. We know most about Aspasia of Ionia, often called "the first lady of Athens" and the acknowledged teacher of Socrates. Together with her companion Pericles, she created a remarkable civic culture in her lifetime, through her work as both a scholar and as a stateswoman. She supported the education of Athenian housewives and had them included in social occasions whenever possible. She also visited and taught among them herself.

The hetairae from the city-states of Ionia and Aetolia were considered the most brilliant. All hetairae, from whatever city, could attend the Academy and the Lyceum and participate in lectures and discussions on an equal footing with the men. Two of Plato's best known pupils were Lasthenia of Mantua and Axiothea.

The women scholars from the various Greek city-states who congregated in Athens influenced the entire Mediterranean world for centuries to come, particularly the urban cultures of Alexandria, Constantinople, and Rome and later the Moslem centers of scholarship. The thread of influence was broken for the Western Christian world with the decline of Rome. With the rediscovery of antiquity in the early Renaissance, numbers of books were written about these lady scholars and poets of Greece. Little, however, of the original writings of these women survived the various library burnings of Christian and Moslem zealots.

The second revival of interest in women's writings took place in the 1700s and 1800s, with books like G. L. Craik's *The Pursuit of Knowledge Under Difficulties, Illustrated by Female Examples* published in 1847. Such books, unfortunately, can only refer to earlier secondary publications on women scholars and to manuscript fragments of the originals.[18]

Obviously, not all hetairae were scholars and leading public figures. Probably the vast majority were in the better known courtesan tradition of being skilled entertainers with varying degrees of education and cultural interests. One little known aspect of the hetaira's life in any society in any age is the task of accompanying her companion to war. On the battlefield, she is cook, nurse, and sometimes companion-in-arms. In Xenophon's famous account of the "Retreat of the Ten Thousand," that odyssey of human bravery and ingenuity in a leaderless army finding its way home over thousands of miles, he neglects to mention the simple fact that there were actually 20,000 and more persons in that retreat. The warriors "all had their hetairae, or camp-ladies, the majority of whom were free-born and were attended by slave-women attached to their service" (de Beaumont 1929: 65). Probably it was the woman slaves of their hetairae who did most of the scouting for food and the pathfinding on the journey home!

We know even less about the political activists, the Lysistratas, than we do about the scholars and the courtesans. We do know, however, that "both in town and country the women knew enough about the other women of their deme[19] to elect a president for the Themophoria" (the annual festival of Demeter and Kore) (Lacey 1968: 173). In other words, there were functioning demewide communication networks for women.

Keeping this array of women in mind, as well as the spoof item in the laws of Zaleucus, "a free woman may not have more than one girl escorting her unless she is drunk, may not leave the city at night except for adultery"

(Lacey 1968: 228),[20] it is clear that many women did find their own way into the public and nondomestic spaces of Greek society. What is more, some of them found their way as lesbians, not as wives or companions of men. They had considerably more to do with *creating* Greek culture than is generally recognized. Their male contemporaries admired, praised, and interacted vigorously with them but were also understandably ambivalent about the role of these women. They were in a plight similar to that of many liberal male university professors today: wanting to recognize the abilities of their women colleagues but needing reassurance that their own wives would stay at home to keep the established order of things running smoothly. Plato could not properly be called a feminist, in spite of the fact that he did acknowledge women as both his teachers and his students. He was, however, responding in a rather logical fashion to what he saw happening around him when he proposed in *The Republic* that women should have the same education as men because they also participated in the shaping of society. He had just witnessed the defeat of Athens by Sparta, and Spartan sex egalitarianism was becoming fashionable.

That the reinvention of the concept of free, open, and public decision making in the context of the city-state should be so fraught with difficulties in terms of the participation of women should not surprise us, having seen the difficulties that urbanism presents to the social participation of women in general. The concerns of the Pythagorean women, and of the politically oriented women, all seem to have been in the direction of egalitarianism. Following their own independent paths, and excluded from the usual derivative power base of women of the elite in other societies, they were thinking through the very same questions as the male citizenry.

One might say that the exclusion of women was a "social invention" for dealing with problems of scale, given that only half as many people had to be taken into account in decision making. The exclusion of slaves and the foreign born from civic life similarly made the political process more manageable. The doctrine of *included interest,* articulated by Mill senior (J. S. Mill's father), in the nineteenth century (Mill 1824), began to take shape in the framework of Athenian democracy. The interests of women, children, and slaves were included in the interests of the male head of household. The concept was sufficiently useful to survive for another 2,000 years.

The tensions in male-female relationships that underlay this "exclusion through included interest" may have been very ugly. We see the amused and self-confident male view through the literature of the time. One wonders what the Pythagorean women, who wrote on civic problems in manuscripts that no archivists of the time thought worth keeping, were thinking about the exclusion process. They may have had insights about participatory roles for the individual in expanding societies that under other circumstances might have changed the course of political events. They might have contributed to the improvement of the deplorable international relations among the city-states of the Greek language. We can only guess at the intensity of some of the sex-role conflicts that arose in Athens because able women with political ideas were not heard.

This discussion of the Mediterranean world should not close without some brief mention of the role of women in the founding of the first world empires. We have already briefly mentioned Atossa, wife of Darius. It was under Darius and Atossa that the Archaemenian empire was extended all the way to India. The only legal claimant to the throne of Cyrus, Atossa was legally coregnant with Darius. In addition to furthering Zoroastrianism as a replacement for the demonic tribal religion of the Persians, she was considered a great stateswoman and helped develop the political and economic infrastructures that Xerxes was to take over but not able to maintain.

The Archaemenian empire fell in its turn to the Greeks, who set out to liberate the world from Persian oppression. Philip of Macedonia, who started the crusade for liberation from Persia, died at the very start of his career. His wife Olympia, who was very much a partner in this enterprise, had in the meantime been preparing her son Alexander to take power. She was well known in her own time as an astute and ambitious woman. She was also ruthless and cruel. Many Macedonian women seem to have had a zest for politics.

It has been thought that perhaps Macedonia had a unique tradition of the participation of women, when compared with other Greek states, because such leaders as Olympia, Arsinoe II, and Cleopatra of Egypt—all Macedonians—have played such active and often aggressive roles on the international scene. An interesting study of this question (Macurdy 1932) brings out no evidence of a traditionally active role for Macedonian women but pinpoints the introduction of a new and more daring role model into Macedonian history with the marriage of Amyntis III in the late fifth-century B.C.E. to Eurydice, an Illyrian barbarian out of a tradition where "queens fought and hunted like men." Eurydice is famous not only for political activity and ruthlessness on behalf of the throne but also for having learned to read and write late in life and for a dedication to humane causes that alternated with her ruthlessness. She evidently set a whole new tone for Macedonian queens, and Olympia appears in that new active role. The historical research on this is not definitive, but, if current evidence is confirmed, it provides an interesting example of social learning from barbarian traditions on the part of women elites. Certainly the concept of Macedonian princesses as role models for the rest of Hellenic civilization has become part of the historian's lore (Tarn [1927] 1961: 98).

Whatever the source of the new behaviors, Macedonian women were an important part of the international system from Olympia's time forward. The activities of the international women's circle that centered on Athens seems modest by comparison, but both sets of women were trying to find ways to deal with new levels of social interaction and new levels of awareness of the larger world community. One worked from a position of isolation, the other from a privileged position at the hub of the social universe.

The Significance of Structures of World Empire: A Glimpse of India and China

With apologies for the unceremoniously scanty treatment of civilizations that represented half the world's population by 200 B.C.E., I wish to discuss the issues of scale in empire building, and women's roles in the new empires, with reference to India and China. The time demands involved in the adequate mastery of the history of Asia are insurmountable for the purposes of this book. To ignore half the world seems even worse. What follows should serve as a reminder of the need for making the history of Asia more accessible to the nonspecialist scholar.

The drawing of India into a world empire first under Darius of Persia and then under Alexander introduces a brand-new problem of scale into human history. The new kinds of resource use and resource distribution that this kind of empire building made possible are hardly hinted at in the early period of expansion. The first effects are chiefly felt in the gradual extension of the world trade routes, bringing both China and India into the world trading community. These "new" trade routes were in fact sturdy tracks already beaten firm by nomadic traders for several centuries before Alexander arrived on the scene. Alexander was already following a highway of sorts when he went to India, and much of the credit for the feat of conquest goes to traders and to the innkeepers and entertainers, women and men, who kept stations open on the trade routes. Alexander's contribution was a firming up of already existing communication and organization patterns that could integrate India with the Mediterranean world, but even so his own empire crumbled rapidly.

Only 27 years later, the Mauryan empire was founded in India by another international entrepreneur, Chandragupta, who made extensive use of the trade networks to build up a centralized system of government such as India had never known. Greek women played an important part in Chandragupta's court, as skilled slaves contributing to court culture, as a well-muscled Amazon bodyguard (were these Spartan women?), and as wives of the aristocracy. Chandragupta himself had a Greek wife, although she was secondary wife to his coruling consort, an Indian queen. The Greek Amazons who served both as personal servants and as a bodyguard "armed to the teeth" when the somewhat unpopular monarch rode abroad (Rawlinson 1916: 47-48) may possibly have served as the prototype for the pattern adopted by Indian kings of using women mercenaries for a standing army.

The significance of Greek women for empire building in India is a topic that might be further explored. We know that some of them came freely over the trade routes as entrepreneurs and entertainers; some of them were imported as slaves; and some of them came as part of the Mediterranean marriage-alliance system. The great unifier of India, Asoka, who came several decades after Chandragupta, must have relied on them for a variety of purposes. Nevertheless, the times of which we write appear to be a period of contracting roles for women, not of expanding ones.

In India, as elsewhere, the growing infrastructure of empire squeezed women out of public roles. Nevertheless, the heritage of the great women philosophers remained in the songs and rituals of the Vedas. The laws of Manu represented the culmination of a concerted effort by the Brahmin caste to replace all earlier traces of matriliny with strong patriarchal structures. These laws prescribed child marriage and eliminated almost all formal education for women. In terms of our thesis of a society needing ever-new techniques of resource use as the population expands, it is hard to explain the Indian development. Presumably the work load of Indian society was increasing and it was advantageous to have more hands at work in each household; the sooner a bride entered her new household, the sooner she could be put to work. One way to think of child marriage is as a regressive approach to work load problems.

It is interesting that the one caste that held out against child marriage and the "diseducation" of women was the Kshatriya, the warrior caste. There were women scholars in this caste longer than in any other. Chandragupta and Kumaradevi, Kshatriyan founders of the Mauryan dynasty, united two separate kingdoms as coregnant king and queen. All royal women received military and administrative training. In pre-Mauryan days, when Alexander attacked India, the Queen of Masaga was one of those on the battlefield directing the defense of her kingdom.

At the close of the first millennium B.C.E. in India, then, there were highly educated and politically active Kshatriyan women in the public spaces of power; there were lower-caste women doing all the types of maintenance, craft, and trading work they had been doing all along; and there were women of the middle castes confined to the "home workshop." Full *purdah*, however, came only with Moslem rule, after C.E. 700, and the

Brahmin caste never fully succeeded in imposing the new restrictions on its own women; old traditions remained, including traces of old matrilineal customs. The educated Brahmin women developed their own kind of underlife. Further, all these developments are only true for northern India. Southern India had had matrilineal tribal and village patterns from Neolithic times, persisting up to the twentieth century. The Nair, described briefly in Chapter 4, are the best known example today.

In China, the period of warring states was drawing to a close, and the great unifiers of China, first the Chin and then the Han, were at work. This unification process also acted to reduce the range of roles that women could play, while leaving a prominent place for royal women and for the institutions associated with the women's court. In Shang times, for example, we hear of (legendary?) Queen B'iug-Xog of Miwo-Tieng, who contributed 10,000 troops to an expedition against a hostile northern tribe (Wheatley 1971). When we read of an all-women's army in the state of Chao, this sounds like a product of a woman's court. Battalions of soldiers are described as clad in sable furs, wearing golden rings, and carrying bows painted yellow. Chao also had all-women orchestras—another woman's-court institution (Schafer et al. 1967: 40). Empress Nee Lu, the widow of the first Han emperor, ruled in her own name after her husband's death and then again after her son's death. She was evidently powerful and tried, unsuccessfully, by sending an invading army, to prevent the kingdom of Yueh (Vietnam) from engaging in the iron trade.

While reigning empresses are few and far between, the ladies of the court were as active in Chinese politics as in that of Egypt. The institution of court eunuchs was well developed during the Han period, and a system of alliances between the court eunuchs and the family of the current empress developed that for centuries provided a power base for women of the royal family in Chinese affairs. Another factor that strengthened the position of women in the upper strata was the

> triumph of Confucianism, with its doctrine of the duty of favoring one's own family and relatives. . . . [It] brought about the custom of distributing the highest posts to the family of the empress. All this led to those bloody palace revolutions which recurred so frequently at changes of reign in later times. (Needham 1954: 106)

By Han times, Chinese princesses were being specially groomed for the international diplomatic role they were already performing in relation to the barbarian nomad tribes that were always at the kingdom's gates. When the Han emperor married off a "female relative" to a barbarian king in return for 1,000 horses, one suspects that more than horses were at stake.

Buddhism provided another arena for women's activities. In Gautama's lifetime, a substantial education and communication network for women of the middle and upper classes had already been started, and there were thousands of nuns in Buddhist monasteries. Buddhist women's orders will be discussed more fully in the next chapter. In a later power struggle between Buddhists and Confucianists, the Confucianists won out, and the monastic avenue to participation in at least quasi public life was closed to women as the monasteries were liquidated. Trading, however, remained open to women. As in Mesopotamia, great merchant families expanded as China expanded. The widow of a great merchant could herself take over the business when her husband died. Sometimes poor women, starting out as petty traders, could amass considerable wealth. The widow Ching in late Chou times became so wealthy through the sale of cinnabar cakes that the emperor entertained her and built a terrace in her honor (Wheatley 1971). Every Chinese town had a market quarter. This quarter was not developed to fulfill the functions of the Greek agora, but it had a spaciousness that Near Eastern bazaars did not have. Thus it fulfilled some of those agora functions and was a public space in which women were free to move about.

Women's old roles of ruler, shamaness, and ritual leader lessened in importance during Han times, but all these roles filtered into the social organization of the masses and gave the peasant women in China a higher status than in other central empires. Nevertheless, when the central Chinese civil service was instituted, we do not read of women sitting for these examinations—though we know there were women scholars. The woman peasant and the woman trader stayed in touch with reality, while the mandarin class lived in its own insulated world. While matrilineal descent groups gradually lost their distinctive character, peasant activist traditions kept producing women leaders in a history that is pointed to with pride in contemporary China.

Along with the development of world empires came world religions. A great flowering of new moral teachings, some of which were destined to evolve into world religions, began as early as three centuries before Cyrus of Persia's conquest of Babylonia prepared the way for the first world empire. Prince Parshva of Varanasi taught the first Jain-type doctrine in India in 800 B.C.E., and Indian princesses abandoned everything to follow his teachings in his lifetime. Confucius, Lao-Tse, Buddha, and the founder of Jainism all began teaching in the sixth century B.C.E. Mencius was born 200 years later, and Jesus another 200 years after that. All of these teachers found women as well as men among the throngs pressing to hear their teachings. The need for a new mental map of the world social order was great.

The eagerness of women disciples for all these teachings is particularly significant in light of the fact that each religion was working with the problems of conceptualizing new kinds of bonds, new kinds of social and moral unities, beyond family, tribe, and state. The context for this reconceptualization, however, was a rejection of the by-now oppressive bonds of the major urban centers of the known world. Buddhism, Christianity, and, later, Islam, were all in a sense antiurban movements aimed at destruction of the corrupt structures of the old civilizations and rebirth into new charismatic communities. The new, small, egalitarian communities "of the holy spirit" were not, however, retreating into a rural past but forging new kinds of intercommunity links that were to make it possible for each to spread far beyond its point of origin. Women instinctively found their way to these communities, whether Jainist, Buddhist, Christian, or Moslem, and played similar roles in each of them. At the threshold of the agricultural transition, 10,000 years earlier, it was the men who had had the "spare time" to reflect on new demands and initiate new levels of social organization, while women were too burdened with their daily work load. Now, toward the close of the first millennium B.C.E., there were urban middle-class women who had the "spare time" to reflect on new demands and to initiate new ventures. Much of their work in the development of these new communities and of the networks that linked them together has been deleted from the history books. We will see in the next chapter how they began building the new society within the shell of the old, using new concepts of scale. We will also see how they were ruthlessly dismissed from all but a few niches of the new society.

Notes

1. There is no one-to-one correlation between nomadism and patriarchy, however, as we will see in both this chapter and the next.
2. The chapter on "Marriage and the Family" in Gideon Sjoberg's *The Preindustrial City* (1960) makes it clear that, in relation to marriage arrangements, there is if anything a tighter control over urban than over nonurban woman. It might be said that she trades freedom for ceremonial privileges.
3. We will find cook shops for the working poor much later in medieval London.
4. See the interesting theoretical discussion in Goody (1968: 8-13) of the years of the domestic life cycle children spend in their mother's social space. The significance of this for the status of women and the socialization of boys has not received adequate comparative study across societies of different degrees of complexity.
5. The women's mourning chorus mentioned by Drinker in the following passage may have been lamenting the oppression of their people by newly arrived nomadic women: "When the Sumerians and Akkadians were being oppressed by their Gutian conquerors during the third millennium, the women of several towns assembled to mourn their fate. Dividing into two choruses, they gave the lament antiphonally, each group singing, in alternation, appropriate verses" (1948: 81-82).

6. The extent to which monogamy prevailed in the privatized household is not clear. Plurality of spouses in rural areas is associated with the organization of production in agriculture. In the city, polygamy is always plurality of *wives* and is associated with the institution of slavery and affluence rather than with production. The privatization of the household is a phenomenon independent of the number of wives in the household. The protection of the courts, however, would be less available to other than the senior wife in a polygamous marriage.

7. It has also been a lucrative business for men. The line separating economic opportunity from economic oppression in the arena of sexual services is not an easy one to draw.

8. In mining alone, for example, "there are over 50 different qualities and grades of officials and laborers named in the mining expeditions" (Mumford 1961: 104).

9. The matrilineality of Israeli and Arab tribes is still a matter of dispute among historians. There will be a further discussion of this issue when the matrilineality of the Arab tribes is discussed in the next chapter. In the absence of decisive evidence one way or the other, I am taking the position that the Israeli tribes were originally matrilineal, because this fits my general reading of the history of this period.

10. Sheila Johansson (historian, Seattle, Washington, personal communication, 1975) points out that, at the time of the Babylonian captivity, there are references to the Israelite women being denounced by the prophets for returning to the worship of fertility goddesses.

11. de Mause (1974: 27) suggests that the practice of child sacrifice, a special form of infanticide, was widespread at this time in the Mediterranean. The Phoenicians may be receiving an undue share of the blame for it because they organized it so efficiently. The Egyptians, the Moabites, and Ammonites, and some Israelites, all practiced it, along with Celts, Gauls, and Scandinavians, says de Mause.

12. As was said in Chapter 3, the female fertility figurines, known from Neolithic times, are not to be considered the mother-goddess proper, source of life and death in all its possible meanings. It is by no means clear that the Cretans can be called originators of the mother-goddess, but many legends have it so. See Pomeroy (1975: 13-15) for a discussion of the controversy.

13. See Chapter 5 of this book for more on this, in the section "The Metallurgists."

14. Again, the existence of this matrilineality is now in dispute among historians.

15. Johansson (personal communication, 1975) suggests that homosexuality among adult males may have been exaggerated—possibly a fad of the literati. Certainly the Lysistrata plot assumes that males preferred female partners.

16. That the confinement was real enough, however, is attested to by the fact that among surviving law court speeches are two "in which the orator brings evidence to prove that a woman who had married and borne children had actually existed" (Lacey 1968: 168). The seclusion pattern was in some respects similar to that adopted much later by some Moslem societies.

17. Freedom of movement for slave women appears to be a contradiction in terms, but in fact mistresses sent slave women on errands to all the places they themselves could not go. This meant that enterprising slave women could get to know the city well and develop some projects of their own on the side.

18. Other eighteenth-century publications on women writers of antiquity include *Remains of Greek Poetesses* (n.d.) by Johann Christian Wolf (which includes 130 to 140 titles); *Greek Female Writers in Prose*, by the same author, published in Hamburg, Germany, in 1735 (which contains a 200-page catalogue of women writers from the earliest times to the sixth century C.E.); and *Historium Mulierum Philosopharum* (n.d.) by Menage, which concerns 65 women philosophers, mostly Greek and Pythagorean. Count Leopold Ferri of Padua, who died in 1847, left a library of 32,000 volumes, all by women. Does it still exist? I don't know.

19. *Deme* refers to a territorial unit of political organization.

20. It should be noted that these laws are said to have been attempts by ridicule to stop ostentation and immorality.

References

Adams, Robert McCormick. 1966. *The Evolution of Urban Society: Early Mesopotamia and Prehispanic Mexico.* Chicago: Aldine.
Aeschylus. 1954. "Eumenides," translated by George Thomson. Pp. 69-100 in *An Anthology of Greek Drama,* edited by Charles A. Robinson, Jr. New York: Holt, Rinehart & Winston.
Alyson Almanac. 1990. Boston: Alyson Publications.
Bachofen, Johan Jacob. 1967. *Myth, Religion and Mother Right: Selected Writings,* translated by Ralph Manheim. Princeton, NJ: Princeton University Press.
Beard, Mary R. 1946. *Woman as Force in History: A Study in Traditions and Realities.* New York: Macmillan.
Boulding, Elise. 1966. "Japanese Women Look at Society." *The Japan Christian Quarterly* 32:19-29.
Bowra, C. M. 1965. *Classical Greece.* New York: Time-Life.
Cavin, Susan. 1985. *Lesbian Origins.* San Francisco: ISM Press.
Craik, G. L. 1847. *The Pursuit of Knowledge Under Difficulties, Illustrated by Female Examples.* London: C. Cox.
Darlington, C. D. 1969. *The Evolution of Man and Society.* New York: Simon & Schuster.
de Beaumont, Edouard. 1929. *The Sword and Womankind.* New York: Panurge.
de Mause, Lloyd. 1974. "The Evolution of Childhood." Pp. 1-74 in *The History of Childhood,* edited by Lloyd de Mause. New York: Psychohistory Press.
Diner, Helen. [1932] 1965. *Mothers and Amazons,* translated by John Philip Lundin. New York: Julian.
Drinker, Sophie. 1948. *Music and Women: The Story of Women in Their Relation to Music.* New York: Coward-McCann.
Driver, G. R. and John C. Mills. 1935. *The Assyrian Laws.* Oxford: Clarendon.
Edey, Maitland. 1974. *The Sea Traders.* New York: Time-Life.
Fustel de Coulanges, Numa Denis. 1956. *The Ancient City: A Study on the Religion, Laws and Institutions of Greece and Rome.* Garden City, NY: Doubleday.
Goody, Jack. 1968. "Introduction." Pp. 1-26 in *Literacy in Traditional Societies,* edited by Jack Goody. Cambridge, UK: Cambridge University Press.
Harden, Donald. 1971. *The Phoenicians.* Rev. ed. Harmondsworth, England: Penguin.
Harrison, Jane Ellen. 1912. *Themis: A Study of the Social Origins of the Greek Religion.* Cambridge: Cambridge University Press.
Hauser, Philip M. and L. F. Schnore. 1965. *Study of Urbanization.* New York: John Wiley.
Hawkes, Jacquetta and Sir Leonard Woolley. 1963. *History of Mankind. Vol. 1. Prehistory and the Beginnings of Civilization.* New York: Harper & Row.
Hennecke, Edgar. 1963. *New Testament Apocrypha.* 2 vols., edited and translated by M. L. Wilson. Philadelphia: Westminster.
Henriques, Fernando. 1962. *Prostitution and Society.* New York: Grove.
Klimberg, H. 1949. *Von Frauen des Altertume.* Münster, Germany: Aschendorf.
Lacey, W. K. 1968. *The Family in Classical Greece.* Ithaca, NY: Cornell University Press.
Leonowens, Anna H. 1953. *Siamese Harem Life.* New York: Dutton.
Macurdy, Grace H. 1932. *Hellenistic Queens: A Study of Woman-Power in Macedonia, Seleucid Syria, and Ptolemaic Egypt.* Johns Hopkins University Studies in Archaeology 14, edited by David M. Robinson. Baltimore, MD: Johns Hopkins Press.
Mill, James. 1824. "Article on Government." 1824 supplement, *Encyclopedia Britannica.*

Morris, E. J. 1974. *History of Urban Form: Prehistory to the Renaissance*. New York: John Wiley.

Mumford, Lewis. 1961. *City in History: Its Origins, Its Transformations, and Its Prospects*. New York: Harcourt Brace Jovanovich.

Needham, Rodney. 1954. *Science and Civilisation in China. Vol. 1. Introductory Orientations*. Cambridge: Cambridge University Press.

O'Faolain, Julia and Lauro Martines, eds. 1973. *Not in God's Image: A History of Women in Europe from the Greeks to the Nineteenth Century*. New York: Harper & Row.

Penzer, N. M. 1935. *The Harem: An Account of the Institution*. Philadelphia: J. B. Lippincott.

Polanyi, Karl, Conrad M. Arensberg, and Harry Pearson, eds. 1957. *Trade and Market in the Early Empires: Economies in History and Theory*. Glencoe, IL: Free Press.

Pomeroy, Sarah B. 1975. *Goddesses, Whores, Wives, and Slaves: Women in Classical Antiquity*. New York: Schocken.

Rawlinson, H. G. 1916. *Intercourse Between India and the Western World from the Earliest Times to the Fall of Rome*. Cambridge: Cambridge University Press.

Renfrew, Colin. 1972. *The Emergence of Civilization: The Cyclades and the Aegean in the Third Millennium, B.C.* London: Methuen.

Rogers, Robert William. 1915. *History of Babylonia and Assyria*. Vol. 2. Nashville, TN: Abingdon.

Schafer, Edward H. and the Editors of Time-Life Books. 1967. *Ancient China*. New York: Time-Life.

Sjoberg, Gideon. 1960. *The Preindustrial City: Past and Present*. Glencoe, IL: Free Press.

Slater, Philip E. 1968. *The Glory of Hera: Greek Mythology and the Greek Family*. Boston: Beacon.

Sullerot, Evelyne. 1968. *Histoire et Sociologie du Travail Féminin*. Paris: Société Nouvelle des Editions Gonthier.

Tarn, W. W. [1927] 1961. *Hellenistic Civilization*. 3rd ed., revised by W. W. Tarn and G. T. Griffith. Cleveland: World.

Wach, Joachim. 1944. *Sociology of Religion*. Chicago: University of Chicago Press.

Wenig, Steffan. 1970. *Women in Egyptian Art*. New York: McGraw-Hill.

Wheatley, Paul. 1971. *Pivot of the Four Quarters: A Preliminary Inquiry into the Origins and Characters of the Ancient Chinese City*. Chicago: Aldine.

Wolf, Johann Christian. 1735. *Greek Female Writers in Prose*. Hamburg, Germany.

———. n.d. *Remains of Greek Poetesses*.

7

Those Who Dwell in Tents, or the Woman's View From the Road

Human history is written from the perspective of the male city dweller. What does he see of the human landscape, imprisoned within city walls? He is much freer to move about than the city woman, whatever her status, but actually both move in very restricted spaces compared with the nomad, man or woman. What does the nomad see? The nomads leave few records, because most of them are nonliterate.[1] Furthermore, they must travel light, and records can become heavy. The wisdom of nomads is not in books but in their heads. Their libraries are the minds of the gifted scholars they attract, by force or otherwise, to travel with them.

The view from the road is a very different view of history than the view from the city. How different is life for women on the road? And what do they see that their city sisters do not see? Do they share the greater freedom of their men, or is the nomad's caravan a new way of imprisoning women? In this chapter, we will be looking at the underside of history in a double sense: We will look at nomads as the swarming underlife that appears when we peek under the solid settlements in the historical landscape; and we will look at the part that nomad women play in this swarming society, in contrast to their stay-at-home city sisters.

Who are the *nomads*? The word comes from the Greek for "cattle driving," according to Toynbee. In his well-known treatment of nomads in volume 3 of *A Study of History* (1935), he keeps to that definition, dealing only with herding societies. I propose to broaden that definition and treat as nomads all those who do not live regularly in settled abodes but move from place to place in pursuit of their livelihood, traveling in complete households. The movement may be a perfectly regular one as between summer and winter pastures, a herding practice known as *transhumance*. It may be the irregular movement of hunting and gathering peoples through a relatively limited terrain where there are familiar camp sites revisited periodically. It may be the movement without destination of the Gypsy, traveling from continent to continent to follow roads without end. It may also be the wandering of the seafarer, although movements of sea peoples tend to be migrations in search of new farmland to settle. The migrant, looking for a place to settle, is not a nomad in this definition. Neither is the fisherman who goes off to sea and returns home at regular intervals. They do not carry their households with them. The term *nomad* for us here represents households more or less continually on the move. Because the woman in settled societies is often bound to her household in ways that the man is not, the situation of women in societies where the very household is on the move will be of particular interest to us.

One could argue that the social organization and patterns of movement of the nomads, for all their fluidity, have provided the true infrastructure of history. Perhaps cities and states are the "debris" and nomadism the actual social development of the human race. In any case, the beginnings of settled agriculture mark the point at which traditions of human adaptation to environments sharply diverge. As pointed out in Chapter 3, we were all hunters and gatherers once. After the development of agriculture and the concurrent domestication of animals, there were three options open to human groups: to continue the hunting-gathering life, to settle down on the farm, or to move with the herds, summering in one place and wintering in another. In fact, there was a fourth option—to wander from settlement to settlement in pursuit of trade. For women and men alike, the choice between nomadism and settlement implies very different adaptation patterns. The sex role adaptation itself is rather different in the two life-styles, although there are features common to both types of societies, as one would expect.

As a background to the analysis of women's roles in nomadism, it is necessary to say something about the function of nomadism in human history. We tend to think of nomads as marginals—people pushed off to undesirable fringe areas. If this were true, we would expect women to be even more marginal. Research on nomadism since the 1930s, however, has made it clear that the transition to a herding way of life, whether it is directly from hunting, or after a period of engaging in settled agriculture, is a choice made by preference. Nomads in every age of history have felt contempt for farmers and city dwellers. At the same time, the farm and the city produce goods useful to the nomads, and so they find various ways to procure these goods. Historically, perhaps as much as 90% of all nomad-settler contact has been peaceful, involving exchanges of goods or services between nomads and settlers. (Ahmed 1973: 75 ff., and Mohammed 1973: 97 ff., confirm the peaceful relations of nomad and settler in contemporary society.)

Herding societies develop characteristics very different than those of settled societies. There is an egalitarianism of steppes and desert that is different than the egalitarianism of the village. At the same time, the taming of horses (after 2500 B.C.E.) modified nomad egalitarianism. There is a tendency to develop an aristocracy on horseback and a warrior class, at least in areas like the Asian steppes, where people can ride great distances at great speeds without any barriers of nature or human habitation to slow them down.[2] (Did horses teach men to become warriors?) This produces a three-layered society: the chief family or families, the people of the tribe, and slaves captured in raids. In less open terrains, or with few horses, nomads remain more peaceable and more egalitarian.

It has been suggested that "most higher societies with a nobility as leading elite, and therefore, most classical and modern urbanized and industrialized societies, are the result of military conquest or peaceful penetration by nomadic groups" (Eberhard 1967: 279). In other words, peaceable or warlike, people who come into the city from the steppes or desert come in feeling superior and manage to achieve the ruling positions in the societies they penetrate. If it is the view from horseback that has caused all the concentrations of power in successive civilizations, horses have a lot to answer for! Reality, of course, is much more complex than that. It is interesting, however, that stratification may have a basis in the matter-of-fact experience of physical elevation.

The very fact of the distances that nomads cover in their daily lives, year after year, gives them different perceptions of society than people can arrive at who live inside walls and boxes. Seeing any one city or state in the context of other cities, and other states, makes it possible for the nomad not only to act as social organizer and living communication network but also to perceive possibilities of alternative modes of exploiting environmental resources over wide geographic areas.

Nomads have developed a unique set of adaptations to problems of increasing scale of social interaction from the time of the first major human settlements. Some nomads have remained outside the "social order problem" entirely by finding micro niches that will seal them off from contact with other populations, using resources not desired by those populations. Within their niches, they can have autonomy. This is the hunting and gathering adaptation that has survived all the way into the twentieth century. The more common adaptations involve establishing some sort of relationship with a settled society while retaining a degree of autonomy and freedom of movement that settled societies do not have. Among themselves, nomads have developed a segmentary model of society (Nelson 1973: 3-7) that maintains order and communication without hierarchy, diffusing power through the whole social structure. The segmentary model of nomadism is a political, not just an economic, model. Such segmentary tribes may develop a series of beachheads in cities, establishing formal or informal contractual relationships that permit them not only to transport what they need out of the city but to play leadership roles among the settlers. They may even assist in the federation of formerly separate cities. Their skills of nonhierarchical coordination would be very important in the federation process. Arabs, Turko-Mongolians, and Indo-Europeans have all played such roles, probably from the beginnings of the first pristine civilizations in Egypt and Sumeria.

When tribal federations are very strong, the emphasis shifts away from contractual nomad-settler relations to a highly selective "mining" of the human talent and physical resources of the cities by the nomads. During the period when the steppe empires were at their height, the khans were experts at this kind of mining, incorporating city resources into their own nomadic infrastructure. That this was an infrastructure of no mean proportions can be seen from the fact that, when Genghis Khan became khan at the age of 44, he ruled over 31 tribes with a population of 2 million persons. We know this because he had a census taken.

These empires had vast retinues of skilled crafts people, artists, philosophers, and scientists traveling with them and had fast transcontinental Eurasian "pony express" systems for information purposes. Their traveling retinue and accompanying knowledge stock and communication systems were the most valuable assets they had.

Nomads also conceive space, possession, and boundaries differently than settled people do. The people who dwell in tents are at home everywhere. Everything "belongs" to them. The world is their pasture. Gypsies exemplify this well. They are essentially hunters and gatherers, not herders, and sometimes their gathering is "misperceived" as stealing. They follow the most ancient means of livelihood of the human species.

Both nomads and settlers attribute an independence, an autonomy and freedom, to nomads that settled people do not have. In fact, the environmental constraints and physical handicaps of the nomads are often far more severe than those of settled peoples, yet the admiration for and envy of the unconquered fierce ones of history (whether fierce or not, they are thought to be so) is a continuing theme among settled folk, along with the fear and horror that nomads also evoke. The nomads themselves unquestionably feel far freer than city folk. What makes a people feel free is always an interesting question, and it is particularly interesting to note that nomadic women share with the men the feeling of greater freedom. What the bases for this greater feeling of freedom are, we will try to discover in the following pages.

The fact that nomads perceive, move through, and use space differently than settled peoples means that their behavior from time to time has the effect of shifting the political balance of power among settled peoples. Given that history records chiefly the doings of kings and generals and battlefield exploits, we are aware of nomad incursions chiefly as bloody events. The long, peaceful periods of interpenetration that eventually bring ex-nomad chieftains to kingship in Mesopotamian cities go unrecorded. The underground developments that undergird power shifts are noted only at moments of dramatic surfacing of new political alignments.

One of the greatest difficulties in studying the nomads has to do with the lack of archaeological remains of a nonbuilding, nonliterate, non-record-keeping society. Because they had no cities, they had no ruins. We only read about them through the eyes of the city dwellers and then usually only in periods when the nomads are responsible for reducing cities to ruins. This penchant of the nomads for clearing the plains of walls and buildings so there can be more pasture land, a reflection of their feelings about the uselessness of cities, gives us a one-sided view of their activities. In what follows, I shall try to reverse the perspective as much as possible and present the nomadic life from the point of view of, if not the nomads themselves, at least a friendly observer. Our focus will be a double one: on the internal character of the nomadic life and its role structure for women and men and on the function of the nomads as social organizers who developed a regional approach to resource use at a time when city-states had only a rudimentary knowledge of their own local environments.

Historical Overview of Nomadism

If nomadism is indeed the infrastructure of history, as I have suggested, then a look at nomadism between 2000 B.C.E. and C.E. 1500, from the period of pristine civilization through classical civilization, will give us a better basis for examining sex role structures than we could otherwise have. The three main types of nomadism appear to be (a) hunting and gathering nomadism, (b) herding nomadism of steppe and desert, and (c) craft and trade nomadism.

Hunting and gathering nomadism is the oldest, with 3 million years of human experience behind it. Today it represents in one way the most highly evolved approach to resource use in submarginal land of which we know. The Kalahari bush people, for example, survive in what is for them comfort under conditions in which other human groups would quickly starve to death. The fact that such societies survive in the twentieth century is a testimony to the skills involved. This is niche nomadism, which depends for its survival on *not* interacting with other forms of social organization and land use.

Herding nomadism of steppe and desert evolved contemporaneously with agriculture. Early farmers with growing herds retreated with their herds to less fertile regions, as the need for food led to the more intensive use of local land. This was the beginning of the competition between the desert and the town. Three major groups are known to us: the Bedouins of the Afro-Arabian steppes, the Turko-Mongolian groups of the Eurasian steppes, and the Indo-Europeans clustered more toward the European side of the Eurasian steppes. Bedouin and Asiatic herding nomadism continue up to the current time, but European herding nomadism has disappeared except in enclaves such as the land of the Lapps in northern Scandinavia. All three of these herding groups had profound effects on the evolution of urban society in the Middle and Far East and in Europe. This was partly through their special relationship with the craft and trading nomads and their superior knowledge of the world's trade routes and partly through direct involvement with the internal politics of major city-states and kingdoms. It was the long series of negotiations between chiefs and queens of "border tribes" and center cities that provided the nomads with the political skills necessary to organize empires once they had power bases inside the cities. Neither Darius and his partner, Atossa, nor Alexander and his partner, Olympia, would have been able to build their world empires if they had not followed the well-trod paths of the nomads. Much of the leadership for those empires came from ex-nomad chieftains and princesses. The role of the Celts, the Huns, and the Goths in the development of a fresh new European society on the ruins of the crumbled imperialism of Rome is perhaps a better-known example of this process, although the barbarian invasions of Roman Europe are still apt to be described as a disaster rather than a social blessing. Some contemporary historians are now inclined to describe the barbarians as more humane than the Romans; at the least they were more egalitarian.

The craft and trader nomads are in a special category by themselves: the Gypsies, who originated in India and developed a complementary role to that of the Turko-Mongolian hordes, traveling with them and "servicing" their almost craftless societies; the Bedouin peoples, who shifted from herding to trading and are best known in history as the intrepid Moslem traders who penetrated everywhere in the Mediterranean world; and the Bell Beaker folk of Europe, who brought the products of the Mediterranean civilization to a more backward agricultural Europe. These groups all live on in the twentieth century, most easily recognized in the Gypsy caravans of Europe, the Middle East, Africa, and the Americas.

One other set of peoples, the Vikings, will be included in our overview of nomads, although they are not true nomads at all. The Vikings are exceptions to all nomadic patterns: they moved by sea, while all true nomads hate water; they had behind them thousands of years of settled agriculture in the Northlands when they took to the sea; and, when they traveled, it was always in search of new areas of settlement. For the period between 600 and 1000 C.E., however, they were so constantly on the move—through Russia to Constantinople, along the Atlantic coast of Europe, and across the island-dotted reaches of the northern seas extending all the way to North America—that they performed all the functions of nomadism listed earlier: They were the social organizers of the North Atlantic, with outposts on the Mediterranean; they discovered new environmental resources; and they completely changed the balance of power in Europe. Also, they would have been helpless without the women who traveled with them.

The most visible archaeological traces of all these groups of nomads are the great sets of walls extending from the Roman *limes,* which fortified the Rhine-Danube frontier bounding the western reaches of the "known world," to the Chinese Great Wall bounding the northeastern reaches of the "known world." The walls, of course, were built by the settled peoples to keep the nomads out. They functioned as gates instead, inviting the nomads to destroy barriers and unify ever larger geographic territories.

In general, there was a continual pressure of nomads on settled land because they, like the settlers, were also rapidly expanding populations. Only the hunters and gatherers, who remained on foot, maintained zero population growth. All the other nomads multiplied and carried their families and possessions in wagons wherever they went. In times of drought, the pressures of herding people on agricultural land would be especially severe. It would be a mistake, however, to see the movements of nomads as only climatically triggered. The nomads came to the cities because they enjoyed them, even while they had contempt for them. The city was a challenge to which the nomad responded. Ibn Khaldun (1969), in *The Muqaddimah* written in 1377, describes the softening process that went on as one group after another became absorbed in city life and lost both the skills and the hardiness of their nomadic heritage. Nevertheless, given the population growth of the nomads left on the steppes and deserts, there was always a fresh supply of nomadic peoples for new leadership in the cities.

Sex Roles and Social Structure Among the Nomads

While nomadic societies differ considerably from one another in structure and role patterning, there are some characteristics that are found among nearly all nomads. Before going on to look at individual societies, we will examine some of these general characteristics.

The Family

One of the most widely recognized features of herding societies is their patriarchal structure. The herding mentality and culture have sometimes been blamed for the overthrow of the "Golden Age of Woman" and for her subsequent subjection. Yet, one of the most consistent features of each of the herding societies we will look at—the Arab Bedouin, the Turko-Mongolian, and the Celtic—are persistent traces of matrilineality and of significant public roles for women. There are tribal stories of a time when women remained in their own tents after marriage and received visiting husbands. Tribal genealogists mention the name of the king's mother as well as father in far more instances than we would expect if the mother were of no importance. When the head of a tribal group dies, whether chief, khan, or king, his mother and his widow play a very important part in designating the next ruler. Mothers and wives of chiefs continue to play an important role in nomadic tribal societies in Africa today. While a king or khan usually has more than one wife, there is never any question as to who the "ruling wife" is and who plays the chief political role in the tribe.

The man "heads" the family, but, when there are plural wives, each wife has her own tent and her own herds. A woman's relationship with her husband has many of the characteristics of a herding partnership, although men do much of the physical tending of the cattle. Women care for goats and sheep and frequently milk the cattle. Among pastoral nomads, only the well-to-do warrior-aristocracy tribes practice polygamy. The average pastoral nomadess and her husband would find partner-wives an economic drain.[3]

The rate of population growth in a nomadic tribe depends on the resources available to the tribe. Tribes with few pack animals and no wagons may keep close to zero population growth, using infanticide as the ultimate means of birth control. Tribes with substantial wagons and draft animals have no problem in transporting children and are less inclined to practice infant exposure, although there may be some attempt to keep down the number of girl babies raised. Girls cannot be used for herding, which is as physically rigorous an occupation as hunting and often requires long absences from camp.

Nomads tend to be sexual puritans, whether Gypsies, Mongols, or Arabs, and punish both women and men for adultery. Marriages are usually arranged, and, if there is divorce, there are usually rights to divorce on both sides. Property rights of both sides are protected in divorce. In general then, within the family, there is an egalitarian husband-wife relationship and an economic partnership based partly on individual ownership, partly on shared holdings.

Political Structures

The tribal chief, *khan*, or king, usually has a *khatun*, or queen, as coruler; the two are usually advised by a council of elders. The council of elders is not a mixed group, but there is usually at least one woman who serves as senior adviser to the council; she has partly the role of political adviser and partly the role of forecaster. Sometimes these roles are separated. The khatun rules until the next khan is designated and acts as regent during the minority of the next designated ruler, when necessary. In rare cases, as during the height of the Mongol empire, the institution of the harem appears. When it does, it has all the characteristics of a woman's court, with diplomatic retinues in attendance. Women are important as conductors of ceremonials. In some nomadic societies, only the women chant and sing, never the men.

We have seen that women of the elite also play important political roles in settled societies. It is difficult to compare the two peoples, given that records on nomadic societies are even more scarce than those on settled societies, but political participation of women appears to be more formalized in nomadic societies. Among the Mongols, the khatun *always* rules between khans, as a matter of tribal custom. In most nomadic groups, there are traditional spheres of authority allotted to women as corulers, advisers, regents, and participants in the choice of successor rulers, whereas, in general, women of the urban Middle Eastern elite who got into political action had only one formally recognized position to work from: that of priestess. Other activities depended on their own wits rather than on a tradition of participation. As mentioned in Chapter 4, there is some evidence that the most outstanding women who appear in the Mesopotamian chronicles are second-generation nomads. When nomadic elites entered cities, the women both activated the traditional priestess roles and generally expanded the sphere of women's political participation in the city.

Economic Roles

There is a sex-based division of labor in nomadic societies, but it is not as rigid as often appears. While men usually follow the herds, sometimes the men do the milking, sometimes the women. If war can be thought of as an economic activity (a type of hunting and gathering), then men are more engaged in fighting than are women. Because war is often fought as the entire tribe is on the move, however, the campground becomes the battle-field. The women fight also and are trained for this. Among the Gypsies, women and men are both craft workers and traders but specialize in different products. In general, women have more camp-based activities than men do, because women rarely engage in herding or raiding. Camp-based tasks, however, have a different social setting than the home-based tasks of the sedentary woman. Breaking or setting up camp, the woman's task, is a very frequent activity and is always done in close company with other women. Preparation of food, garments, and containers from wool and skins goes on in the spaces between tents as well as inside. There tends to be women's space versus men's space rather than private domestic space versus public space. On ceremonial occasions, women's and men's spaces intersect, although there are also all-women's and all-men's ceremonials. The community of women and girls and boys under 12 can be a strongly knit community that can make inputs into the men's community via the woman elder. Nelson (1973: 43, 48-49) is emphatic about the power of nomadic women in policymaking and in judging the conduct of men. She also notes the autonomy the women feel. "What do [men] know about what their women do?" queries one amused informant.

Religion

All types of nomad societies seem to have a deep religious strain, but it is a generalized religious responsiveness that can fit a wide variety of institu-tional forms. The Mongols were extraordinarily tolerant of all religions, having Nestorian Christians and Catholics, Buddhists, Zoroastrians, and Moslems in their courts. The Gypsies adopt the religion of the country or region they are in at the moment. Their religious fervor is matched only by their openness to highly diverse ways of expressing it. It seems to be particularly the women's job to identify and support the appropriate variety of cults in a given setting and to "take in" new religions. The underlying faith is shaman-istic. The tribal shaman may or may not outrank the prophetess.[4] To the extent that ceremonials reflect the basic belief structures of the society, however, the leading role of women in ceremonials belies the formal prominence of the shaman. The rites of childbirth, of baptism, of marriage, of death, and of the crowning of a king are often women's rites.

The nomadic life, then, does tend to create a man's world and a woman's world, accentuated by the need to provide protected space for childbirth and for children in a camp environment that does not readily allow for protected spaces. Women's participation in the total life of the society, however, is not less—and, more probably, greater—than that for women in settled societies. The common orientation of both sexes toward the "world as one's backyard," and the common experience of living out of the nomadic equivalent of a suitcase, is probably a more powerful bond between women and men than the separateness of their tasks would indicate.

We will now turn to an examination of the role of women in individual nomadic societies, beginning with a further examination of the hunting and gathering bands already discussed in Chapter 3.

Hunters and Gatherers of North America

Our earlier discussion of hunters and gatherers referred to bands in the African and Eurasian regions. Here we will focus on North America. The sheer historical diversity of hunting and gathering cultures in North America is overwhelming. There have been more than 500 languages spoken, some as different from each other as English and Chinese; every type of religious system known to humankind; many types of political organization and descent systems coexisting; and more than 2,000 kinds of plant foods used by various groups. Peter Farb's *Man's Rise to Civilization* (1968) makes it possible to conceptualize this diversity of hunting and gathering cultures in such a way that relevant aspects of women's roles can be distilled for the purpose of this study.[5]

First, some background information: Nomads wandered over to Alaska from Siberia, perhaps about 35,000 B.C.E., during the last ice age.[6] When they found themselves in North America amidst melting snows, they were suddenly exposed to an undreamed-of hunting wealth, and the archaeological record tells us they exterminated all the large mammals from Alaska to Cape Horn, including horses and camels, by about 5000 B.C.E. This is an incredible example of the mining of environmental resources, only equaled again in the twentieth century by industrial societies. The same hunting to extinction did not take place in Eurasia or Africa, Farb suggests, because bands of humans and the big mammals coexisted from the earliest hominid times. Overhunting took place after the last ice age with the pressure of expanded populations, but there was never hunting to extinction. Eurasian and African hunters knew their total terrain, and understood the ecological system within which they lived, well enough to move to the herding and breeding of animals when supplies ran low.

When we meet the North American hunter-gatherers in the historical record, they too have achieved familiarity with their environment and

learned to use it in ecologically sound ways, forced to this by the disappearance of big game. We find three main types of adaptation: the arctic Eskimo
culture, the desert culture, and the forest culture. An incipient steppe
horseback and herding culture began developing on the Great Plains in the
eighteenth century after the Indians acquired horses from the Spaniards,
but the conditions created by the invading Europeans were so catastrophic
that it was crushed before it could fully develop.

The view of the world from on foot is very different than the view of the
world from horseback. Bands moving on foot became familiar with a series of
micro environments across the continent. As in Eurasia, when the big game
disappeared, the women's scanning skills once more became primary. The
frequency of matriliny in the forest civilizations is possibly a reflection of the
importance of women's cooperative efforts in food gathering. In the harsher
environment of the arctic and the desert, the relationship is simply egalitarian,
neither matrilineal nor patrilineal, and bands are very small indeed.

In the arctic, each pair of hands is needed to the utmost, and there is a
complex system of husband-and-wife-borrowing to ensure that each man
who goes out on prolonged hunting trips has a female partner to handle
the closely interdependent division of labor necessary for arctic environmental use. Women who are pregnant cannot safely make such trips, so the
remaining women divide such responsibilities. Because this practice is
described for the most part by male anthropologists, it is described as wife
swapping, or wife borrowing. It would make as much sense to say husband
swapping or husband borrowing, given that the temporary hunting partnerships thus formed are equally necessary to women and men.[7] Much of
Eskimo culture can be interpreted as flexible social-bonding arrangements
that enable women and men to draw upon helpers from their own and other
bands in times of need. Everything depends on this being done as part of
mutually agreed upon arrangements within and between bands. What
causes jealousy and conflict is when certain individuals begin making
unilateral arrangements without full consultation with all the other marital
partners involved. The ad hoc man-woman pairings of the Eskimo are
public, not private, matters. When treated as private matters, they can result
in murder.

Under the arctic conditions, there are few "men's spaces" distinct from
"women's spaces," little accumulation, and no stratification. Under the circumstances, women are hardly excluded from decision making. The famous
nomad-style communication network is seen at its best among the Eskimo.
Tell a joke in Alaska and you will hear it next year in Greenland (Farb 1968:
35). No one to my knowledge has mapped that communication net!

In the desert, the Shoshone, with her digging stick, lives much as her
sister in the Australian desert.[8] These women and their spouses live in a

nonstratified leisure society (i.e., they have lots of free, unprogrammed time), moving from site to site in the familiar desert and putting up twig shelters in all their favorite spots. They know where to find the tastiest foods in the sparse land. The same complex elaboration of marriage alliances, combined with small families and much individual freedom, is found in both societies. In the desert, there is much more of a separation between women's and men's cultures than in the arctic, because women and men work at hunting and gathering in segregated groups, but decision making involves input from both groups.

The most famous of the forest cultures is the Iroquois, a matrilineal society that initiated the formation of an intertribal league made up of various Iroquois groups and neighboring tribes in 1450 C.E. (Morgan 1901). The league held together with remarkable skill and adaptiveness during the white man's invasion but finally disintegrated about 1850. The Iroquois had strong sisterhood institutions. The headwoman of each of the five tribes was responsible for choosing the male *sachems* who attended the league council meetings. They checked the sachems' behavior and decisions closely. When a sachem did not perform satisfactorily, the sisterhood removed him. This matriliny, however, was related to an already settled mode of existence. The Iroquois had taken up agriculture by the 1400s and were no longer true nomads. Their village life and social organization might be most comparable to that of the earliest agricultural villages of the Middle East.

The Indians on horseback—Farb (1968) calls them, somewhat unfairly, "make-believe Indians"—on the plains are a consequence of the Spaniards' reintroduction of horses to the continent. In the 1600s, Indians began to acquire numbers of horses (through both raiding and breeding), and by 1750 there were Indians on horseback along the eastern slope of the Rockies all the way from Texas to Alberta and all over the plains. The plains were a melting pot, and the tribal groups that roamed them were all composite tribes, made up of many different ethnic elements. These tribes developed almost overnight the warrior aristocracy we shall see on the Mongolian steppes. It all happened so fast, and the records are so battle oriented, that it is hard to say much about the women in this "overnight" society. They must have been extraordinarily adaptable, and they certainly had to work hard keeping up with sudden accumulations of goods in the absence of patterns for dealing with such accumulations. If they had been given more time, perhaps a more patterned stratification and reasonable use of accumulated resources would have evolved in this horseback society. Imagine the evolution of these tribes, had not the killing off of all the larger animals occurred by 5000 B.C.E.: The plains might indeed have been steppe country with a horseback society. In such a scenario, the European invaders would have had a very different kind of native society to reckon with, and North America might look very different today.

As it was, the plains warriors accumulated horses and weapons and power without any clear sense of direction and purpose. There was no time for the slower evolution of new social technologies and adapted social goals. The Indians were crushed by the superior accumulation of horses, weapons, and power of the invaders. There was no time for sisterhood between the independent pioneer women and the independent Indian women to develop.[9] That would have been another possible scenario, in a slower-moving play.

North American Indians were not lucky in their adaptations to problems of scale. They wiped out the mammal resources of a new continent before they discovered those animals' worth and, by the time they had created a viable new set of hunting/gathering/agricultural adaptations, they were confronted with a society operating on an entirely different scale, a society that could use the continental resources in totally new ways and mine them as ruthlessly as the ancient Indians themselves had done. If one is pessimistic, one could imagine a day when only the Shoshone with their desert digging sticks will have the necessary know-how to make a "decent living" from what is left of the continent.

The Bedouin Arabs and the North African Berbers

Now we will move back from the New World to the Old World, where "social time" moved more slowly. We begin by looking at the deserts.

The Bedouins of Arabia, part of a larger Afro-Asian steppe culture that covers all the drier parts of North Africa, live in one of the most unprepossessing—to the outsider—micro environments that the planet has to offer: the central deserts of their peninsula. Back in 2000 B.C.E., there was still plenty of space to choose from for settlement in that part of the world. To the contemporary historian, the choice of these deserts seems an improbable one. Therefore it has been assumed that only those forcefully driven out of more hospitable environments would ever live there. Arabia offers very pleasant places to live along the high, fertile plateaus bordering the Persian Gulf and the Indian Ocean. In the second millennium B.C.E., it had cosmopolitan trading ports on all three coasts of the peninsula, including the Red Sea side facing Africa. There were land routes to Egypt and a series of trading towns running north to south along the wadis (dry riverbeds), connecting Syria and Mesopotamia with the seaports that led to India and Egypt. These towns, strung out like sculptured beads on a famous old incense-trading track, were an important part of the infrastructure of the earliest trading routes in the ancient world.

But the Bedouins did not live in any of these places, and it is now agreed that they *chose* not to live in these places. They lived in the desert—and continue in the twentieth century to live in the desert—because they love it. It is perhaps by looking at the first Bedouins, the most incomprehensible of all nomads to the comfort-loving city dwellers, that we will get some understanding of the meaning of the nomadic way of life. Sargon II described them as "those who dwell in the desert, who know not governors or overseers, who have never brought tribute to kings." Sennacherib wrote of Adummatu, a place in northern Arabia that keeps turning up in old chronicles, as a place "in the midst of the desert, full of dirt, where there be neither food nor drink." This same Adummatu was, in fact, a nomadic camp site. It was home base for the Arabian queens—the queens of the Aribi that had such long contact with the Assyrians. It was from here that the Hyksos invaded and ruled Egypt in the 1700s B.C.E. and that Bedouins, Berbers, and Assyrians launched separate and joint attacks over succeeding centuries until Egypt finally came under Ptolemaic rule. Women warriors were from time to time leaders in these invasions.

In the old silent films of my childhood in the 1920s, the women of Arabia were always shown in harems, being carried, helpless captives, from one harem to the other. This hardly squares with the image of warrior queens at the head of their desert troops. What was the life of these tribes really like, how did women get to be queens, and why are there so many references to them in Assyrian chronicles?

A look at family structure and tribal organization may answer some of these questions. Given that the Bedouins and the Israelites are of the same Semitic stock, originating in the same Arabian deserts, the patriarchal structure described for the nomadic Israelites in the last chapter is the same structure found among the Bedouins. The traces of an earlier matrilineal descent system are also present.

In old Arabia (already old in 1000 B.C.E.), tradition has it that husbands were visitors in the tents of their wives—a desert version of the Nair (Nayar) form of marriage described in Chapter 4. Prototypical for this earlier era is the semilegendary Omm Karja, who contracted marriages in more than 20 tribes but sent her husbands home and lived in her own camp surrounded by her children. In those days, there were women judges, and a list of these women from ancient times is extant. This information comes from the research of W. Robertson Smith (1966: 126), who worked on kinship and marriage systems in Arabia in the 1880s, influenced by Bachofen's work on mother right. Smith's work has been discredited along with Bachofen's, but a reexamination of the data is perhaps in order. Smith, himself, points out that later marriage records are confusing and full of inconsistencies. This is because several different traditions evolved in Arabia, some keeping to the old matrilineal ways, others moving far from them. Every Arabian marriage contract to some extent represented a new negotiation between representatives of different sets of customs. Among the four major marriage patterns described by Smith, there is great variation in the amount of property and power reserved for the woman.

Spencer (1952) uses this variability to argue against the possibility that a matrilineal reckoning ever existed. One of the fascinating aspects of a study of marriage-contract literature for Mediterranean civilizations is how many ways in which marriage contracts were written. This simply tells us that there has always been a lot more room for bargaining in marriage contracts than social scientists of the structural-functional school of analysis would like to admit.[10] One does not have to postulate any grand evolutionary scheme to suppose that many societies began that bargaining process from a matrilineal descent-reckoning system.

For those who chose the Bedouin way of life, the matrilineal tradition remained much stronger than it did among the settled folk. "She walks with her head held high"—a saying about Tuareg women today—would certainly have been true of the women of the Aribi. In fact, all Bedouins walk with their heads held high. They recognize no authority or social organization not based on kinship structure (Buccellati 1967: 87). In 2000 B.C.E., this would have been in marked contrast with their settled fellow tribes to the south, whose lives in the port cities were already tied up with stratification systems and carefully contracted rights.[11] Such differences in social patterning in an ethnically homogeneous area with no alien tribal infiltration underlines the significance of the choice of the nomadic as contrasted with the settled existence. Each family roaming the desert is an autonomous unit, and "tribal society is held together by a delicate balance of powers, rather than by strict subordination" (Buccellati 1967: 88). The nomads who wandered toward Canaan were the same. The Book of Judges reflects the pattern: "In those days there were no kings in Israel; everyone would do what was right in his eyes" (21: 25).

Family units within kin groups formed and reformed into bands of continually changing composition, and there was no guarantee that common kin ties would prevent the start of blood feuds between bands that got in each other's way. The harshness of the environment, and the fierce clinging to autonomy, meant that tribal federations were of the loosest, and the authority structure was fragile. Yet structure did exist. The roles identifiable in that structure include the *sajjid*, the speaker, one who had moral authority alone (this was not a hereditary post, nor were any of the other positions); the *ra'is*, military leader in war; the *hakam*, judge in time of peace;

and the *kahin*, priest-diviner. Then there was a *maglis nadwah*, assembly of nobles. The Bedouin would appear to be a ranked, rather than a stratified, society, with nobles holding ceremonial responsibility but not having differential access to resources. Therefore the term *queen*, applied to the women with whom the Assyrians negotiated, and the term *princesses*, applied to the young women sent to Assyria to school, are misleading. It is the typical bureaucratic response in dealing with a less differentiated society to give rank and titles to those with whom one deals as if there were a counterpart structure to that of one's own society. The colonialist expansion of the West into Africa and Asia from the 1600s on is replete with examples of this. The queens, when leading troops in battle, were acting as ra'is; when negotiating with the Assyrians, they would be acting as sajjid or hakam. Whether they were also members of the assembly of nobles, the maglis nadwah, we cannot be sure. We will see many examples in nomadic society of women having special authority roles without counterpart representation in tribal councils. This may be due to the shift from matriliny to patriliny, because men sit on tribal councils as heads of families rather than simply as men. Women have authority as competent individuals and also by right of seniority. Men have authority given them by the role structure.

When the Aribi women were acting as tribal leaders in negotiations with the Assyrians, we can be sure that they acted with the same fierce dignity and self-assurance as the men and won the full respect of those with whom they dealt. In fact, they were probably dealing with their own kin, or persons from tribes well known to them, because we know that some Bedouins began settling in Mesopotamia from earliest times—Sargon, for example, was a second-generation nomad turned settler—and each new Bedouin immigrant in turn played an active role in contact between her newly adopted city and the tribes back home in the desert. Probably the leading temple priestesses in the cities had active contacts with their sister priestesses in the desert; in fact, the Aribi tribes were often referred to as the "confederation of the worshippers of Ishtar." Because each kin group worshipped its own goddess, in addition to recognizing Ishtar, the women played the role we shall see in many nomadic societies, that of linking old and new religions and cults.

The old aristocracy of Babylonia and Assyria probably welcomed the arriviste nomad leaders who settled in town, even while they resented them, because they needed help in dealing with the nomads who stayed in the desert. These desert tribes were respected because they were impossible to subdue; the Assyrians, Babylonians, and Persians all tried to restrain them, and all failed. The nomads lived in tent cities that could be moved at a moment's notice. So swift were they in their movements that none of the Mesopotamian troops had a chance at any kind of battle when the Aribi were on their home ground. They could only be defeated if caught off the desert, which happened very rarely. Furthermore, the defeat was highly temporary.

The Bedouin women who dealt so effectively with the Mesopotamian army and palace-temple complex were partly trained for their work by the Assyrians themselves, as we know from the accounts of Arabian princesses going to school in Assyria. This means they were to some extent an elite, and yet all the evidence we have about the desert Bedouins indicates a minimum of stratification and accumulation of wealth. All the women and all the men probably had to work hard to survive in the scanty desert-steppe feeding grounds. It is hard to visualize family life and child care in that setting.

Maysun's poem, at the end of this section, gives a clue as to the feeling of freedom and relatedness to their environment that the women of the desert had. Children probably learned to be self-sufficient at a very early age. Chroniclers of the Assyrian times comment on how healthy the Bedouins were compared with the city dwellers. Probably the infant mortality rate was high, due both to infanticide and to early childhood mortality, but the children who survived were sturdy. The diet of cattle blood, meat, and milk seems to be an adequate one for steppe dwellers. The desert steppe is a harsh mother but will feed a carefully limited population well. Given that nonurban women everywhere, nomadic or peasant, develop efficient baby-toting skills, we can assume that the women among the Aribi did not feel confined by their babies. When necessary, they went to battle with their babies on their backs, as nomadic women everywhere have done, including the barbarian women who fought Caesar's troops in Gaul.

Not all of the Bedouins were herders. Some followed the trade routes and, of those, some made their way across the Red Sea to what is now Ethiopia. Once the trail was blazed, both traders and herders followed it, and the Ethiopian highlands today shelter nomadic tribes that once traveled the Arabian deserts. Due partly to the nomadic women's tradition of supporting a variety of religious practices, one can find today in Ethiopia three major religious traditions: Judaic, Christian, and Islamic.

Some of the Berbers who have guarded and used the North African desert steppes from earliest recorded times and well before then may well have been Arab Bedouins who made their way across the land bridge to Egypt or across the trade routes of the Red Sea. Other Berbers came up from the Saharan steppes, further south, during the period when the steppes went from grassland to uninhabitable sand, well before 2000 B.C.E. In ensuing centuries, the Phoenicians, the Romans, and the Moslems had to deal with these Berbers. Some of the Berbers continued a herding existence. Others were traders, and others settled on the outskirts of invading civilizations to provide a buffer between the nomads and the settlers.

The Phoenicians tried to make alliances with the Berbers, without much success. The Romans built *limes* and fortified settlements, to keep them out. The Moslems converted them. But no one in three millennia has succeeded in assimilating them.

> They remained . . . a separate element in the population, with a different language, social organization and way of life. Even after the conversion to Islam, they retained their separate identity, and not infrequently came into conflict with their Arab co-religionists. (Oliver 1968: 31)

All the great African empires of the first millennium C.E. depended on the Berbers for trade and communication skills.

Today, in spite of steamship, railway, and airlines, the Berbers still to some extent operate their traditional Saharan trade routes. When all the oil wells have dried up, they will probably still be plying their old routes.

While the Arab Bedouin and the North African Berber today are separated by many twentieth-century barriers of nation and alliance systems, there is still a sense in which we can think of the Afro-Asian steppes as a cultural region. We do not have the word pictures of the old Arabian tent camps, and of the packing and moving process, that we have for the later Mongols. We can look, however, at the contemporary desert-dwelling North African Tuareg and Somali nomads who live on the African Horn and get something of the flavor of this style of nomadic life. The Somalis live spread out over several countries that now abut on the modern state of Somalia and, wherever they live, from 65% to 85% of them are nomads (Silberman 1959: 560). Modern Somalia has substantial trade in forest products and leather and 90% of the world's incense comes from there. There is agriculture in Somalia, of course, but the true nomadic tradition looks down on agriculture. The Somalis do not require vegetables: their main food is milk and, on festive occasions, camel meat. Monteil comments that he has seen sturdy old men—and presumably women!—who have never known any food other than milk (Monteil 1959: 575). Keeping mobile for these people is important to prevent both overgrazing and the human diseases that come with too much interhuman contact in that environment.

> Respiratory complaints are rampant and tuberculosis rates would be higher still if people lived in greater proximity for longer periods. It may be merely an instinct that makes Somali women such keen partisans of nomadism—so tragically at times goading their menfolk to fight, as in the massacre of Italians, in Mogadishu in 1947, as symbols of town and sedentary life, but . . . they know that "the first consequence of the transplantation of a nomad group into an agricultural region [in Africa] is an

enormous increase in the habitual unrequited work of the women." In Arabia it means, of course, veiling and seclusion. (Silberman 1959: 568)

Why would a woman trade relative health and freedom for agricultural or urban "slavery"? Everything she owns can easily be piled on a couple of camels, and she is the one who decides where the tents shall be erected when camp is moved. She is interested in a politics that will preserve her freedom of movement and that of her children. A Somali child of 5 is

alert, and is not afraid to go thirty miles alone; it knows the genealogy of its clan over 17 generations; and it can milk. All through [her] life the Somali invests in brain rather than brawn. The satisfactions of nomadism are such that senior members of the education department at Hargesia, "as a good Somali should," return periodically to their herds in the interior. (Silberman 1959: 568)

The desert-dwelling Tuareg are of special interest to us because the status of women is still high among them after centuries of Moslem rule. The Tuareg are a Berber people, and the Berbers have many of the characteristics of the Arab Bedouins. No one is sure what the ethnic origin of the Berbers is. Like the Arab Bedouins, they live in the bleakest part of their country by preference, and they have the same traits of fierce independence and contempt for city dwellers.

The Tuareg women, to whom the proverb about walking with the head high refers, apparently even today take part in tribal councils and have a tradition as warriors. They are also known as preservers of tradition and learning, and, "where the ancient script, which has a similarity to the old Minoan script of Crete, is still used, women are more versed in it than men" (Drinker 1948: 71-72). Singing at evening tribal gatherings is done by women, not by men; men are the audience. Tuareg women of rank organize and judge sings.

The division of labor among the Tuaregs, with regard to maintenance activities, is determined by the needs of the herds and the scarcity of water. The men must sometimes lead the herds far afield in search of water, and the women remain at the camp doing the typical food preparation, craft work, and child tending of the nomad society. The path they travel in their moves over any one year is a familiar one, determined by grazing and water resources. Nomadic women must be the best packers in the world, because they do so much of it.

The important role of Tuareg women in ceremonial life is probably a reflection of the amount of time they spend together in camp, able to plan and organize tribal activities. The men, dispersed much of the time, have less opportunity for such planning. As among the Arab Bedouins, the society is ranked, rather than stratified, and few permanent advantages accrue to anyone.

The fact that even today the Tuaregs have traditions (not exercised for some time) of women warriors is an interesting bit of evidence of the persistence of this aspect of cultural history. It should at least be noted that the earliest of the Amazon traditions come from Bedouin country; the European Amazons mentioned in the last chapter were a later tradition. Diner ([1932] 1965), who draws largely on the writers of antiquity, tells us how the Amazon women, herders and warriors, flourished at the foot of the Atlas Mountains, presumably in the early days of Egyptian glory, "clad in red leather armor, snakeskin shoes, and with python-leather shields" (Diner [1932] 1965: 133). They are supposed to have encountered the mainland survivors of the Atlantis civilization, made an alliance with them, and, in general, according to the sources Diner draws on, swarmed over North Africa. She quotes Strabo: "There have been several generations of belligerent women in Libya. The Gorgons (Amazons) against whom Perseus waged war, were described as a people of great courage" (Diner [1932] 1965: 134). (It should be noted that Libya in Roman times was what is now Morocco, Algeria, and Tunis.) Further, in Diner's own text:

> These tribes were in rebellion against the Atlantean colony. The Amazons, under the stipulations of the new alliance, were asked for help. Thus there came a battle of Amazons against Amazons. Thirty thousand Libyan horsewomen under Myrine delivered a pitched battle to the Gorgons, won the day, and took . . . many prisoners. ([1932] 1965: 134-35)

Later the Amazons under Myrine are supposed to have fought their way through Egypt, Arabia, Syria, and Phrygia. The mention of their being unlucky at sea and of most of the army drowning in the Mediterranean is perhaps the most realistic note in this tale. Nomads do hate the sea. We do not have to subscribe to a major conquest by Amazon women of North Africa and Syria, however, to accept the possibility that there were women's armies among the Berbers.

Given the wide distribution of Amazon legends in different types of steppe countries, it may be that nomadism under certain conditions encourages all-women armies. (To my knowledge, however, similar legends have not arisen among the Turko-Mongolian nomads.) All Amazon legends refer to the women as being herders and as living on cattle blood, meat, and milk. That they would have remained long without men seems unlikely. Even the legends allow for that:

> The Libyan Amazons, who removed their right breasts, had compulsory military service for all girls for a number of years, during which they had to refrain from marriage. After that, they became a part of the reserves and were allowed to reproduce their kind. The women monopolized

government and other influential positions . . . lived in a permanent
relationship with their sex partners, even though the men led a retiring
life, could not hold public office, and had no right to interfere in the
government of state or society. Children, who were brought up on mare's
milk, were given to the men to rear. (Diner [1932] 1965: 136)

While such stories of total role reversals have a certain ideological
attraction—for women at least—they fade away under close scrutiny. The
partial role reversal of the women warriors, however, does not. We will
find that phenomenon in every century up to and including our own.
Because nomads must train their women to fight, for survival's sake, it may
be that all-women armies first originated in nomadic societies.

To return to our Bedouin warriors of ancient times, one could say that
Queen Zenobia of Palmyra, the northernmost Arab city-state, on the edge of
Syria, was the last of the queens in the Bedouin warrior tradition. She herself
was probably a Macedonian, and Palmyra was by 250 C.E. well integrated into
the settled life of Asia Minor. Nevertheless, it is worth noting that Zenobia
defeated the Roman armies and extended her conquests to the Roman provinces of Asia Minor and part of Egypt. This gives some indication of the
potentials still alive in the Bedouin tradition at that period. By the time
Emperor Aurelian of Rome finally defeated her, she had organized allies from
the Persians, the Saracens, the Armenians, and the Syrians. She led her own
armies wearing a glittering helmet, but in defeat she bargained for her own
safety and is somewhat criticized by historians for ending her days in luxury
outside Rome. Had the nomad blood run thin?

Another late example of female Bedouin leadership is the case of La
Kahina (the Prophetess), the queen of a tribe in the Aures Mountains who led
a confederation of Berber tribes to drive the Moslems back into Tripolitania in
the 670s C.E. She was apparently a good military strategist and had some
success on the battlefield, but the tribal alliances proved too temporary
and fragile. La Kahina did not have the diplomatic skills to deal either with
the Moslems or with the groups outside her own immediate tribe. She
finished by destroying cities and surrounding plains in an attempt to make
the region unattractive to the Moslems and succeeded only in making
herself extremely unattractive to both Moslems and nomads.

Perhaps more typical of the military roles of Bedouin women are the
activities of the Lady of Victory cult. The cult's function was to incite
patriotism and to lash patriots into ferocious fighting. The Lady of Victory
was a woman of high social standing about whom the feminine cult
members, likewise of high rank, gathered in the pavilion sacred to the local
or tribal deity. There, with war songs accompanied by their lute playing,
they stirred their warriors to martial fervor. Around the Lady of Victory and
her retinue the battle raged until it was lost or won. Hind al-Hunud, an

enemy of Mohammed, was described as "holding to the heathen practices of Arabia, and as a follower of this cult." Hind herself played the Lady of Victory in a battle with Mohammed's followers, brandishing a sword with great gusto (Beard 1946: 293-94).

The Bedouin and Berber women certainly played a noteworthy role in Afro-Asian history. They and their men mapped and organized the resources of Arabia and North Africa, providing also a steady stream of leadership into Mesopotamian and Egyptian kingdoms. Their role was, however, not as prominent as that which their counterparts of the Eurasian steppes were to play. In the end, the harshness of the African steppes led to more of a niche adaptation than an organizing adaptation. Within the limits set by that environment, however, women seem to have shared leadership with men to an extent that we will not find in settled societies. Even though they did not tend the herds as directly as men did, the public spaces of the deserts were their spaces as well as the men's. Everywhere was home.

In 661 C.E., a Bedouin woman named Maysun, probably from one of the fringe tribes bordering on Syria, married the first Umayyad caliph, who had previously been the governor of Syria. Maysun was a poet and gave voice to the sorrow of every nomad who must leave the open spaces for the closed ones:

> Breeze-flowing tents I prefer
> to ponderous halls
> And desert dress
> to diaphanous veils.
> A crust I'd eat in the awning's shade,
> not rolls,
> And watched by a dog that barks
> not a cat that smiles,
> I'd sleep to the wind's time,
> not to the tambourine.
> A youth's impetuous sword,
> not a husband's wiles,
> Uncouth slim tribesmen I love,
> not corpulent men.
>> (in Stewart 1967: 108;
>> used by permission)

Nomads of the Eurasian Steppes

Moving from the Afro-Asian desert steppes to the grassy steppes of Eurasia puts us in a totally different ecosystem and a different style of nomadic culture. Grasslands exist in Arabia too, but they are sparser.

There are also deserts in Eurasia but, with grasslands plentiful, the steppe dwellers had more horses than did their Afro-Asian counterparts and more land in which to move around. Two great chains of folded mountains created the Eurasian steppes over eons of time: first the T'ien Shan and Altai ranges, and later the Himalaya, shaped an arc within which lies Turkestan and Mongolia. The moister Russian steppes to the west and the drier Iranian steppes to the south complete the total area of steppe terrain, which includes as much as 5% of the land surface of the planet. This land is easy to travel, and roads are not needed. While the mountainous regions create obstacles for movement, over the centuries, numerous tribes have beaten tracks over the rougher parts of the terrain. The steppes are the archetypal "trackless wastes."

The desert Arabs of the south threatened only the Egyptian-Syriac-Mesopotamian plain. The nomads of the north, however, ranged over China, India, Asia Minor, and Europe during the last two millennia B.C.E. and halfway into the second millennium C.E. Genghis Khan for the Mongols, Attila for the Huns, and Tamerlane for the Turks have become the three great symbols of nomad penetration into the civilized world. These nomad incursions are usually treated as interruptions of the serious business of history by barbarians who are sooner or later tamed. It is supposed that droughts and internecine war among nomadic tribes bring them tumbling into the plains. The actual history of the movements of steppe populations is much more complex than this theory indicates and cannot be traced in detail here. For our own purposes in tracking women's roles in successive changes of social structure through the centuries, we need only take note of each of the main nomadic thrusts and how they affected the settled populations and then explore in detail one set of steppe tribes. Because the Mongols have the best documented history, they are the ones we will explore.

In the tangle of tribal groups that have emerged in the Eurasian steppe from time to time, we are conscious of two main groups: those of Iranian stock who move into the western steppes (Scythians and Sarmatians) and the Turko-Mongol peoples of the eastern steppes. What has determined their movements? We have already mentioned the dynamics of the push-pull process. Given the fertility of the land and the ease of transport, with both horses and draft animals available to haul wagons, there was less reason to limit population in the steppes than in the Arabian desert. So populations multiplied and took the room they needed. Drought would certainly sometimes move whole sets of tribes from one area to another. But movement must also have come from sheer human love of exploration and adventure. The view of the world from the back of a horse is much more likely to feed a thirst for exploration and adventure than the view of the world from on foot.

The earliest steppe dwellers were hunters and gatherers. By 6000 B.C.E., some herders would be pushing north from the farmlands of the fertile crescent. By 2500 B.C.E., with the horse, herders would be able to spread over the steppes far more rapidly. The first great federation of nomad tribes that appears in historical chronicles is that of the Hsiung-nu, who first pressed over Chinese borders in the ninth century B.C.E. The Hsiung-nu were eventually driven out of the eastern steppes and appear several hundred years later at the gates of Europe as the Huns. The Huns and other Turko-Mongolian tribes appear very bloodthirsty when they ram the walls of civilization, but not less so than the Indo-European Scythians and Sarmatians. All had a certain delight in the flowing of blood, including gashing their faces with knives at funerals "so that blood flows with their tears." It was also the general custom to make the skulls of their enemies into drinking cups.

Which of the steppe peoples, the eastern Hunnic Turko-Mongols or the western Scythian-Sarmatians, were the famous Aryan invaders of India? No one knows exactly, but it is now generally considered that the Aryan invasion was a relatively minor incursion resulting in a few steppe bands settling in India. Like so many of these nomadic incursions, the effects on the settled peoples are all out of proportion to the number of nomads involved.

It is interesting to let the historical imagination speculate a bit about those nomadic incursions. From everything we know about the nomad women, they would come in with their men boldly and move about freely. It is usually said that Indian women lost their high status after the Aryan invasions, in the course of measures adopted to protect Hindu women and to keep "common" women from polluting ritual observances. Could it be that the Aryan women, with their free ways, frightened the Hindus, so that they put constraints on all women in an effort to control the women of the new elites?

There are no records documenting the earlier invasion of India, however, so we must begin with the Hsiung-nu. Their initial thrust resulted in a series of tribal movements in the 200s B.C.E. that fatally weakened Persia and undid Alexander and Olympia's eastern conquests. The Hellenic world shrank back toward the Mediterranean.

The first Chinese princess, whom we know to have been part of the arduous, centuries-long process of negotiating with the Mongols through the device of the marriage contract, is nameless—she is referred to only as a "Chinese princess or lady-in-waiting." She joined the tent camp of the chief of the Hsiung-nu in 202 B.C.E. under an agreement entered into by the first emperor of the Han dynasty. As records are sporadic, we do not read of a second such alliance until 33 B.C.E.; after that, they are frequently mentioned, and both the kings of China and the Mongolian chiefs looked upon the marriage contract between the sons and daughters of the aristocracy of the empire and the aristocracy of the surrounding tribes as a way of ensuring communication between them and predictability in political relationships. When either side felt very strong, it might refuse such a contract.[12] War usually ensued, and the peace treaty might well be sealed with a marriage contract, after all. Such contracts were the major diplomatic device of that part of the world.

Genghis Khan and his khatun, Borte, were past masters at diplomacy by marriage alliance. We shall focus here on the time of Genghis's ascension to the position of "khan of khans," or khakan, in 1206 C.E. and follow the nomadic empire until it wanes, in the 1400s after Tamerlane. At its greatest extent under Genghis, the khanate reached well into China and Russia, touched the gates of Constantinople, and covered Anatolia and parts of Mesopotamia and northern India. The Persian and Alexandrian empires were postage stamps by comparison.

The evolution of steppe tribes—from loose ad hoc federations and alliances driving out other tribes that were felt to be crowding their space to well-organized alliance systems under one central administration in the great khanates, having representatives at the royal tent court from all the states of Europe and Asia and receiving tribute from a vast empire—is one of the most fascinating sequences in human history. The Mongols' genius in surveying all the areas they moved through—in terms of both physical and social resources, and in "mining" the centers of civilization for their best craft workers and scholars; of alternating threats and raids with alliances and agreements with settled peoples, including matrimonial alliances; and in developing a courier system over an information network that covered all of Europe as well as Asia—is definitely a nomadic-type genius. City dwellers do not make good map makers. When one European army could hardly find its way to the neighboring city-state with which it was at war, Genghis Khan's couriers knew Europe like the backs of their hands.[13]

What would have happened if the women and men who surrounded Genghis's successor, Kublai, had not gotten absorbed by China and essentially abandoned their nomadic commitments? What would a nomad organization of Eurasia have looked like if the nomads had kept their social organization and communication networks, without settling down in cities? Nomads always lost their unique characteristics when they settled in cities, so all their contributions had to be made within the first two generations of settlement. After that, they were totally assimilated and as unable to scan their environment, nomad style, as any of their city neighbors.

There is real tragedy in the dynamics of the accommodation process. The horseback warrior nomad of the steppes always begins by hating cities. Cities are excrescences on the beautiful plain, occupying space that could be yielding fodder for the nomad's stock. The people who live in them are not "human." That is why the warrior wreaks such wanton destruction on the cities; they have no use in the nomad's scheme of things. Thus nomadic women and men fight together to defend common values and to destroy that which stands in the way of those values. There is a touching passage in Grousset's (1970) *The Empire of the Steppes*, in which a Chinese mandarin who had become an adviser to Genghis Khan is described as unable to control his weeping when the khan destroyed Chinese cities, as he often did. In the setting of Genghis's last campaign in Kansu, the beginning of new social learnings for the Mongols is delineated:

> A Mongol general pointed out to [the khan] that his Chinese subjects would be useless to him, since they were unsuited to warfare, and that therefore he would do better to exterminate them—there were nearly 10 million—so that he might at least make use of the soil as grazing land for the cavalry. Jenghiz Khan appreciated the cogency of this advice, but Ye-lu Ch'u-ts'ai protested. "He explained to the Mongols, to whom any such idea was unknown, the advantages to be gained from fertile soil and hardworking subjects. He made clear that by imposing taxes on land and exacting tribute on merchandise, they might collect 500,000 ounces of silver yearly, 80,000 pieces of silk, and 400,000 sacks of grain." He won his point, and Jenghiz Khan ordered Ye-lu to draw up a system of taxation on these lines. (1970: 251)

From that moment on, carnage stopped and infrastructure began; Genghis was known as a just and wise man and would not kill if he saw alternatives. But the process that began with that teaching on the battlefield ended with Genghis's successor Kublai Khan becoming "soft" in the city and losing those unique nomadic perspectives and energies.

Steppe Social Structure and the Role of Women

Steppe society is more pronouncedly patriarchal than is Bedouin society, probably because it is a more warlike society and a richer one. The steppe aristocracy consists of

> the aristocracy of the brave (ba'atur) and of chief (noyan) which . . . officer [sic] and manage the various social classes: warriors or faithful men who were preeminently free, commoners or plebians, and lastly serfs, who theoretically were of non-Mongol stock. Bonds of personal loyalty, feudal style, link individuals at different hierarchical levels. The

army is tightly organized in a hierarchy with units of tens at the bottom and the Khan at the top, with his own elite bodyguard. (Grousset 1970: 222)

What could the place of women be in a society organized for battle? To visualize the situation adequately, one must remember that this was a society on the move. Everything the tribe owned was piled on horses and in wagons. As the khanate grew wealthier, large felt tents were sometimes permanently mounted on wagons, so there did not have to be so much breaking and setting up of camp. Anyone who has traveled with household possessions, whether by wagon or in a motor trailer, knows that the skills of "battening down the hatches" so articles do not get battered and destroyed while on the move are crucial. Whether preparing to move, on the move, or setting up a new camp, everyone had to be involved, everyone was busy, everyone was needed. Furthermore, in this society, the distinction was not always clear between the "army" and the total tribe. One of the first things Genghis did was organize the wagons as part of the tribal battle formation, with women and children trained to shoot and defend the wagons and the babies. We must infer that women were also trained to fight from horseback, because khatuns sometimes fought by their husbands' sides on the battlefield. Probably only women of the warrior aristocracy received such training.

Nomadic society must generate much more of a sense of shared fate between women and men than either agricultural or urban society does, given that both sexes must operate in the same space, under pressure, so much of the time. We will see this later among the Gypsies.

This is not to suggest that there was not also a separation of men's and women's spaces. Raiding, and some of the more substantial battles, may have been conducted at some distance from the tent camp, and herding would take men and boys away from the camp. The major positions of power within army and tribal councils were held by the men. But, within the warrior aristocracy, the role of women in the court, their place in determining succession, and their part as both regents and full rulers were so clear-cut that one can infer a strong matrilineal tradition with the possibility that at some time in the past there were tribal "queens" comparable to the Arabian "queens." During the khanate, however, women usually only ruled as "in-betweens."

When a khan died, his widow acted as regent until a *kuriltai*, a great council of all the tribes, had been called to elect the successor. In some cases, she ruled for several years and could initiate and supervise military activity during that time. She was also active in the council of elders that was responsible for finding candidates and conducting the election (and, usually, determining its outcome in advance). This, plus the fact that women of the warrior class and the aristocracy owned their own herds and tents, suggests the possibility of an earlier "visiting husband" custom in at least some of the tribes. There are matrilineal tribes today in both China and Tibet, confirming the long-standing presence of this cultural tradition on the steppes.

Because all accounts of the Mongols focus almost exclusively on the battlefields, it is difficult, but not impossible, to sort out information on the role of women. It is clear that the khatun, wife of the khan, was in some sense a coregent who had duties of state. She had a large court of her own. While the khan had other wives, each with her own tents, herds, and attendants, only the khatun could co-preside at court with the khan. The company of wives of the khan had some of the characteristics of the Egyptian women's court in that there were women there from the royal families of most of the kingdoms of Europe and Asia. Because each one had her own tents and retinues, the physical space occupied by these women in the royal camp was substantial. Each woman apparently came with her own diplomatic adviser as well as priests, scholars, and the usual array of musicians, servants, and crafts people. Most of these women from abroad were literate, whereas, at the time of Genghis Khan, few of the Mongols were literate. This meant that the women would be maintaining a substantial international correspondence to supplement the khan's courier service.

I have mentioned that negotiation by marriage between the Chinese and the Mongols began to show up in Chinese court records in 202 B.C.E. Genghis Khan developed this practice to a fine art, not only in his personal marriages but also in supervising the marriages of the women of his family and of his main chiefs. It used to be that alliances with Chinese princesses were the great goal of international diplomacy. But in Genghis's time, and for several centuries afterward, princesses of the khanate line were a major diplomatic goal for both nomadic and settled societies. This was more true in the Asian than the Mediterranean world, but the alliance structure straddled both.

The life of the princess-diplomats was by no means an austere one. In 626 C.E., during the Uigur khanate, one of the first great Mongolian khanates, the Mongols surrounded themselves with the luxury of beautiful brocades, fine food, and both Eastern and Western music. A Chinese pilgrim of that year wrote:

> The Khan wore a coat of green satin and allowed all his hair to be seen, his brow alone being bound by several turns of a silken fillet ten feet long, of which the ends hung down at the back. He was attended by some two hundred officers wearing brocade coats, all with their hair braided. The rest of the troops consisted of riders mounted on camels or horses; they

were clad in furs and fine woolen cloth, and carried long lances, banners, and straight bows. . . . [T]he Khan dwelt in a large tent ornamented with golden flowers that dazzled the eyes. The women, also dressed in brocades, sit on couches near the Khan. The Khatun sits beside the Khan. (Grousset 1970: 94)

Two hundred years later, the khans were importing Persian artists and art to their tent court. The pictures produced during this period show the women and men of the khanate aristocracy wearing ceremonial dress, carrying flowers, and accompanied by musicians.

Accounts of khanate courts all agree that the size of the felt-tent camps was impressive, with tents, people, and herds stretching off in every direction as far as eye could see. The khan's tent, 40 feet square in 520 C.E., in later days became almost palace sized. As mentioned, some of these tents were mounted on wagons, so they did not have to be dismantled when camp was moved. One can imagine the Mongols living in huge covered wagons. Outward symbols of their wealth were confined to portable items like luxurious clothing and tapestries and to large retinues of scholars, musicians, crafts people, entertainers, and servants.

Court life would appear to have been as cosmopolitan in the felt tents as in the palaces of the Mediterranean and Europe, if not more so. A European visitor was surprised to find fellow Europeans at Mongka Khan's court, including

a woman from Lorraine called Pacquette, who had been brought from Hungary, and was in the service of one of the prince's Nestorian wives; she herself had married a Russian who was employed as an architect [of tents?]. At the Karakorum court Rubruck also found a Parisian goldsmith named Guillaume Boucher, "whose brother dwelt on the Grand Pont, in Paris." This man was first employed by the Dowager Sorghaqtani and then by Mongka's younger brother Ariq-boga, who was also sympathetic toward Christianity. Rubruck found that at the great court festivals the Nestorian priests were admitted first with their regalia, to bless the grand khan's cup, and were followed by the Muslim clergy and "pagan" monks, that is Buddhists and Taoists. Mongka himself sometimes accompanied his Nestorian wife to the services of this church. "He came, and a gilded bed was brought for him, upon which he sat with the queen his wife, opposite the altar." (Grousset 1970: 280)

Because every woman who entered into a marriage alliance with members of the khanate aristocracy brought her own priests, scholars, and craft workers, and the khan himself brought talent from all Europe and Asia, the concentration of talent from a diversity of cultures in the felt-tent courts must have been substantial.

The impression I have of the women of this warrior aristocracy is that they were unusually direct and forthright by the standards of urban civilization. While there was a woman's world and a man's world, the two mingled freely at court. Women spoke up in touchy political situations and sang, danced, and toasted at banquets and ceremonial occasions.

A rare description of a banquet scene on an occasion honoring Genghis in his prime gives a delightful picture of bands of women and men of the court spontaneously arising by turn to sing and dance in front of each person whose name Genghis called out in a toast (Prawdin 1940: 88). Spontaneity, gaiety, and a love of singing and dancing come through in the few descriptions we have of the social life. These were never "men's-only" occasions. Borte, Genghis's wife, seems to have been a wonderfully independent woman who handled her husband's rise to power with courage and wisdom, stepping in when things became too tense. She appears to have been as respected as he was in councils of state. Oelun, Genghis's mother, may have had a lot to do with his rise in the first place, by her astute survival operations when all the tribes abandoned her and her young son at the death of her khan husband. Once, after Genghis was khan, when he started quarreling with one of his younger brothers, Oelun came into his tent with bared breasts and told him that, whereas the other boys had nursed at only one breast, he, Genghis, had nursed at both and must never quarrel with the brothers with whom he had shared his mother's breasts. The quarrel stopped immediately (Grousset 1970: 218).

Genghis's daughter-in-law, Princess Sorghaqtani, was reputed to be one of the great Mongol stateswomen, and Genghis turned to her for advice regularly. She seems to have had a great deal of administrative responsibility in the expanding khanate. It was due to her that Nestorianism was the major religion of the court, but she also established schools and temples of all religions and managed to have her son named khakan in his time.

In the next generation, only one, Toragana Khatun, stands out as a major stateswoman. She kept the regency for four years after the death of her husband and built up an alliance structure that included a new Buddhist component, turning over the khanate to her son thereafter. Organa Khatun, a contemporary of Toragana in an associated khanate, ruled under the khakan for nine years during an especially tricky period of khanate politics and also managed to place her own son on the throne in the end. Koquz Khatun, again of the same fast-moving era, is one of the few khatuns mentioned as leading the army on the battlefield jointly with her husband. As powerful champions of Christianity, Koquz and her husband were mourned at their death as the "two stars of the Christian faith." The khakan relied heavily on her advice in affairs of state, and so skillful was her diplomacy that her son was the first to marry into the family of the Byzantine emperors.

Politically active women did not operate as lone wolves. Not only were they part of the central power structure, they could also operate from time to time as a sisterhood and pounce on an unlucky khan who was pursuing a policy of which they did not approve. Genghis Khan was more than once the object of a coordinated attack by his mother and his wife.

Other khatuns led armies in battle: The young widow Mandughai in 1470 took to the battlefield to protect the khanate for her 5-year-old son and successfully kept it for him through an eventful 21 years. When one of the last khans was killed on the battlefield in 1696, his wife Goldan was by his side and died with him.

Enough has been said to indicate that the women of the aristocracy were active in the political realm, on the battlefield, in connecting the nomads with larger religious networks, and in other ways that helped develop the unique infrastructure of a nomadic society. Prawdin sums up the contribution of women by saying that

> Mongolian history has a good deal to say about notable women; those who, when widowed, were able to save their tribe from decay, by showing superabundant energy and sagacity; those who rode beside their husbands to war and fought boldly; those who were able regents, skilled intriguers and wise counselors. (1940: 287)

While it is true that the patriarchal pattern often seems to require widowhood for women to show the full range of their abilities, there seems to be ample evidence that women were active during their husbands' lives as well as after their deaths.

The economic life of the steppe tribes, as indicated earlier, sent men out herding, training horses, and fighting, and by and large kept women closer to the camp, maintaining the physical and social fabric of camp life. While the women of the aristocracy were busy with affairs of state, the commoners worked on basic maintenance. It takes a lot of work to maintain a moving camp in good working order. Several writers comment on how hard nomadic women worked. They were responsible for having their husbands' (and their own) battle gear in battle-ready condition at all times, and the production of food and clothing under camp conditions would take a continuous exercise of ingenuity. Not all the women's time went to maintenance tasks, however. Every woman was mistress of the possessions of her tent (and of her herds, if she had any), so women did a great deal of trading. Women with their own herds surely also learned to train their own horses, as some European Gypsy women do to this day. The skill of animal training is one of the very special skills of the nomads. Toynbee (1935) suggests that it was the basis of the remarkable educational system developed by the Ottoman branch of the Mongols, which trained the Janissaries, that kept the Ottoman empire powerful for so long.[14]

Turko-Mongolian nomadic society was full of contradictions. To the extent that it was a highly successful, stratified warrior aristocracy, it partook of the inequalities of settled society that enabled some men and women to command many resources and accomplish a great deal, leaving the rest of the society to work hard on small-scale maintenance activities. To the extent that it was nomadic and developed environmental scanning skills not available to sedentary peoples, it was more flexible and adaptable to new situations. Because it was a society on the move, it was spared the heavy accumulation of possessions, valuing instead people and portable goods like cloth. As the khanate empire grew larger, it was a society that depended on individual skill in the mass setting. The only way camps could move smoothly and efficiently would be for everyone to know how to pack and move at a moment's notice. The only way massive herds of cattle and horses could be handled was with consummate skill in animal training. The scanning and the management skills of nomadic empires at their height were impressive accomplishments. The system could never have worked if women had not been as skilled and flexible as the men were. And children would have had to learn to function in this rapidly moving social environment very early in life; otherwise they would get lost, left behind. Early chroniclers of nomadic movements sometimes describe them in terms of the nomads "piling their women, children and possessions on huge wagons" (Grousset 1970: 7). This was not at all the case—the women did the piling. In terms of fluidity of roles to meet daily life demands, of command of own property, and of freedom to move in the social spaces of the larger environment, Mongolian women both inside and outside the aristocracy probably had some advantage over city women.

The advantage was not long retained with urbanization. The whole story of the evolution of Moslem society from the early caliphates to the Ottoman empire, dependent on nomad inputs at each stage in its development, is the story of the progressive elimination of women from participation in the central spaces of society as each new Turkish group became assimilated to the urban scene. In assisting with the spread of Islam, nomads promoted the demise of their own way of life. Islam became a city religion, as all scholars from Ibn Khaldun on agree. The men who rose in the early Abbasid caliphate, every one of them of Arabian origin, practically all married out of their own nomad society. The negotiation-by-marriage system worked to exclude the very people—nomadic women—who might have kept Turkish rule more open to the participation of women[15] (Stewart 1967: 81). Women were very important in preurban Islam and specifically in promoting the leadership of Mohammed himself. Without the help of his wife, Mohammed might never have had his teachings accepted. (Mary Beard 1946, is clear on the importance of women in early Islam.)

Historians are too inclined to blame the dangerous, bloodthirsty nomads for the seclusion of women: Settled folk had to put their fragile females in harems and behind veils to protect them from the barbarians, the theory goes. If my interpretation is correct, however, it was the distortion of city social patterns that squeezed out women. The nomadic women who came to the city representing another pattern of participation were not strong enough to fight the forces of urbanized role structures.

Celts, Goths, and Others

We have noticed how important wagons were to the Mongols, minimizing the packing job of the nomadic society and keeping them mobile. Wagons were important to the Celts too—so important that we find a number of ceremonial Celtic burials of the 600s B.C.E. in which the dead person is laid out on one. One burial in Burgundy is particularly impressive: A young woman of about 30 is laid out on a wagon, and her tomb is filled with rich grave furniture apparently imported from Greece. She could be one of the famous Celtic queens, but we have no way of knowing which one.

No one knows where the Celts came from, or just when they started coming, but it seems reasonable to assume that they started off from the European end of the Eurasian steppes in the late third or early second millennium B.C.E. As herding and hunting nomads with no particular destination, they very slowly drifted westward. By the middle of the second millennium B.C.E., they were gradually becoming visible in the melange of Central European cultures that included the battle-ax, Urnfield, and Bell Beaker peoples, mentioned in Chapter 5. The Celts could work metals and they were on horseback, so they began showing the traits of the warrior aristocracy we have already seen on the eastern steppes. They seem to have become a warrior-craft worker society using the sedentary farmers' services for food and working the Mediterranean-European trade routes through central Europe. By 600 B.C.E., they were spread all over Czechoslovakia, Hungary, Austria, Switzerland, and south Germany, and, by 400 B.C., they formed the Celto-Ligurian League.

They were an easygoing people, preferring to live outdoors and steadfastly refusing to build towns. They did build roads, however, or rather wagon tracks. While steppe lands could be used for wagon transport with a minimum of road preparation, not so the forests of Europe. The famous

Roman roads, Anne Ross (1970: 78-84) suggests, were simply built over the earlier, carefully laid Celtic wagon trails.

In Roman times, the Celts spread out over France and the British Isles, and Ireland today still bears many of the marks of that ancient Celtic culture. Although their free-flowing antiurban ways led to the disappearance of their culture in the face of Roman social organization in Gaul, the Celts' nomadic culture was sufficiently strong to resist urbanization and Romanization in Ireland, Scotland, and Wales. By the time we see them through Caesar's eyes in the memoirs of the Gallic War, they are already partly sedentary, but even then they build *oppida*, essentially hill forts, rather than towns. This enabled them to control surrounding towns and farmlands without settling down. That we are so aware of a Celtic culture today, a culture stemming from a people who did not acquire a system of writing until the fifth century C.E., is a testimony to the extraordinary ethnic and cultural unity of these nomads who once were spread so widely over Europe. Lacking evidence from any but their enemies, the Romans, I can only conclude that their unity depended on the same kind of nomadic communication infrastructure that characterized the nomads of the Eurasian and Afro-Asian steppes. That it did not result in empires is probably due to their live-and-let-live value system—though the Romans thought they were quarrelsome enough. While they did have a warrior caste, they did not focus their social organization around purposeful military activity. They fought the Romans when they felt crowded by them, but when we see them in Britain, relatively secure from further attack, we find a people dedicated to poetry, hunting, feasting, and quarreling, in that order of importance. Graves (1966), who is obviously much attached to the Celts, tells us that it was the function of the poets to determine when it was time to go to war and when it was time to stop fighting.

While Celtic society was probably more ranked than stratified, because the Celts neither accumulated goods nor developed the degree of hierarchical organization the Mongols had, there seems to have been an aristocracy of warriors and poets. Women were an important part of that aristocracy and served not only as warrior queens but also as directors of military academies. The most famous and best historically verified Celtic queen is Boudicca. Queen of the Iceni tribe in eastern Britain, she led her troops in battle against terror-stricken Romans:

> She was huge of frame, terrifying of aspect, and with a harsh voice. A great mass of bright red hair fell to her knees: she wore a great twisted golden torc, and a tunic of many colors, over which was a thick mantle fastened by a broach. Now she grasped a spear, to strike fear into all who watched her. (Chadwick 1970: 50)

She and her daughters fought at the head of the army and, when she was defeated, she committed suicide rather than fall into the hands of the Romans. Suicide in such a situation was common behavior for Celtic women; the Romans had a very bad reputation.

The picture of the fierce Celtic women comes from the Roman writers, of course. As described in Chadwick,

> a whole troop of foreigners would not be able to withstand a single Gaul if he called his wife to his assistance who is usually very strong and with blue eyes; especially when, swelling her neck, gnashing her teeth, and brandishing her sallow arms of enormous size, she begins to strike blows mingled with kicks, as if they were so many missiles sent from the string of a catapult. (1970: 50)

As might be expected, there was little love lost between Roman and Celtic women. Two more different conceptions of women's roles could hardly be imagined. The Celtic women were lovers of the outdoors, as were the men. They would never seek a roof as long as there was sky overhead. Meadows were the only carpets they prized, and their banquets would be laid out on boards supported by tree stumps, with the lowing of cattle as background music. A woman's wealth and status, like a man's, was the country's

> soft rains, its vast pasturages, those wandering herds. About this simple commerce there developed a life-mode that was at once dangerous and secure, unconcerned and anxious, reckless and rapacious, unambitious and adventurous, as peaceful and as bloody as the desert. (O'Faolain 1969: 50)

These rough-and-ready people were quarrelsome. It was the custom for men to fight by the dining table before meals, to determine who was the bravest man at the table. The bravest got the best cut of meat (Ross 1970: 54-55). This fighting happened indoors or out, and the women apparently enjoyed it too. An Ulster tale tells of three women who, well in their cups, sang so exuberantly in praise of their respective husbands that the celebrants pulled the house pillars down in their enthusiasm for the songs (Ross 1970: 92). This was considered a great joke by all, including the women. What could a woman who lived, loved, and raised children in such a setting think of the elegant Roman matron who needed a fine town house as a setting for her social relationships? There is recorded the reply of the Caledonian woman,

> when Julia Augusta, the wife of Serverus, jested with her about the free intercourse of her sex with men in Britain. She replied, "We fulfill the

demands of nature in a much better way than do you Roman women, for we consort openly with the best men, whereas you let yourselves be debauched in secret by the vilest." (Chadwick 1970: 55)

Non-Celts who did not understand the high status of Celtic women could make bad mistakes. There was the native Welsh tribal leader who set out to make an alliance with the leader of the Celtic Brigantes to throw out the Romans. It happened that the Celtic leader was only the field commander, and it was his wife, Cartimandua, who was the ruling queen. Because she had already allied herself with the Romans, the luckless would-be rebel soon found himself in chains and delivered to the Romans by the angry queen (Chadwick 1970: 65). Less serious, but possibly more embarrassing, was the occasion when Celtic warriors were taken prisoner and brought to Rome. When brought before the Emperor Claudius, they "ignored him and the imperial insignia, and headed straight for the throne of the Empress Agrippina, making their obeisances to her" (Diner [1932] 1965: 251).

The free ways in which Celtic women used sex come out in stories of Queen Medb, who offered "thigh friendship" to the owner of a bull for the loan of it. She also offered thigh friendships in return for assistance in raids and battles. Apparently all parties, including Medb's husband, considered these deals reasonable (Kinsella, cited in Brennan 1975: 9).

There are many matrilineal traces among the Celts, and the clearest are among the Picts, a pre-Celtic group with a heavy Celtic overlay: "The law for succession among the Picts was through the female, and there are grounds for thinking that the bridegroom was usually a visiting prince, and that the marriage arrangement was not regarded as permanent" (Chadwick 1970: 93). The Venerable Bede notes this in his study of the Pictish kings, discovering no succession through fathers until the ninth century C.E. The ancient system

involved visiting princes and a system of purely formal marriages, highly organized and intricately provided for. The organization of the royal family seems to have been at times matrilocal as well as matrilineal, but not usually matriarchal. (Chadwick 1970: 118)

I have said that Celtic society was more ranked than stratified, and yet there is among the later Celts, as we shall see among the Vikings, a contempt for the lower classes that does not easily fit into the picture we are apt to hold in our minds of a casual outdoor society. Much later, in the 1500s C.E., we get a picture of an Irish home of the aristocracy that brings together just those improbable traits of casual simplicity and unconscious arrogance that the Irish themselves see as their own characteristics. The great Hugh O'Neill in Ulster is entertaining a visitor, who "was entertained . . . to a meal and conversation beside fern tables, on fern forms, spread under the canopy of heaven. O'Neill's children were in velvet and gold lace; his bodyguard of beardless boys were stripped to the waist" (O'Faolain 1969: 41). Houses are dirty, milk is strained through straw, the poor are in rags, and even the great, under their fine cloaks, are naked. In the old battle sagas, when casualties are recorded, "we know not the number of peasants and rabble" (O'Faolain 1969: 42). Liberty these people loved, equality they never bothered about. The family was the only social unit taken seriously. Even here it was not the tight authoritarian family we meet so often in urban settings but a family within which and outside of which both women and men had great freedom of movement. It was that freedom that made the Roman matrons think Celtic women "loose."

The warrior-queen tradition of Celtic history fits in well with this pattern of freedom for women. Most of these queens, apart from Cartimandua and Boudicca, are semilegendary. Yet the references to them are so frequent, and take so many forms, that I am inclined to think there really was a "Queen Mab" (Maeve, Medb) of Connaught, in western Ireland; a Queen Morrigan, represented as Morgan le Fay in the Arthurian legend; and perhaps a real Queen Badb, turned in legend into the goddess of battle. They were all fighting queens (Kinsella 1970). For Medb, we even have a description of her position in a battle formation (Ross 1970: 63). There may also have been a "military academy" for young men and women run by the woman Scathach. There are many references to her institution, and she was apparently a prophetess as well as a military strategist and teacher (Chadwick 1970: 135-36). The tradition of women warriors survives, in a

Figure 7.1. Celtic Woman With Neck Ring, Gallo-Roman Period. Redrawn by HBR.

style reminiscent of the Amazon traditions, in the story of the nine witches of Gloucester, who apparently lived together in their own military camp. Only after the ninth century C.E.—when the Celts had become settled and acculturated—are there no new references to women warriors in Celtic countries (Chadwick 1970: 136).

There were also druidesses and women's festivals that survive today via St. Brigid's festivals, but we know as little of them as we know of the whole mysterious druid tradition. Graves and others mention a famous druid university in Cornwall, but we have no details about it. E. M. White (1924: 30) tells us that there were druidesses of three classes. One class performed temple offices but lived with their families; one class assisted the druids and visited their husbands occasionally; one class was a sisterhood living in seclusion. Some druidesses were members of the Sisterhood of Brighit (goddess of poverty, medicine, and smithies, according to White) and were responsible for preserving a holy fire.

Anne Ross cites a passage from Tacitus showing the role of the druidesses in war:

> On the shore stood the opposing army with its dense array of armed warriors, while between the ranks dashed women in black attire like the Furies, with hair dishevelled, waving brands. All round the Druids, lifting up their hands to heaven and pouring forth dreadful imprecations, scared our soldiers by the unfamiliar sight so that, as if their limbs were paralyzed, they stood motionless and exposed to sounds. Then, urged by their general's appeal and mutual encouragements not to quail before a troop of frenzied women, the Romans bore the standard onwards, smote down all resistance, and wrapped the foe in the flame of his own brands. (1970: 145)

Beard describes the Cimbrian tribes that swept down from the north into Rome:

> Among the Cimbrians, priestesses took charge of war captives. Standing on ladders which they carried with them to battle, they cut off the heads of prisoners, caught the blood in pots, and gave it to their men to drink, in the belief that it would double their strength. (1946: 288)

Shadows of the earlier tradition of the queen, the priestess, and the warrioress may be found in the prominent role of "women religious"[16] in the formation of the Christian monastic movement in Ireland. St. Brigid, the Christianized version of the Celtic goddess Brigantia (Brighit), was used to good advantage by the Christian sisters in the first centuries C.E.

Oddly, while the women fight, teach, preach, prophesy, and rule, tradition has it that only the men write poetry. All the great Celtic historical poems were preserved by the *ollaves*, who had to memorize 150 secret code languages and 350 long traditional histories and romances in addition to being versed in philosophy, civil law, music, augury, divination, medicine, mathematics, geography, universal history, astronomy, rhetoric, and foreign languages; in addition, ollaves had to be able to extemporize poetry in more than 50 complicated meters (Graves 1966: 457). Ollave families kept the craft hereditary, like the priestly families, and I find it hard to believe that there were not also women ollaves whose names were erased from the records.

This brief excursion into Celtic history is mainly to give the flavor of women's roles in a nomadic tradition that was carried to the heart of Europe. The brave women of Gaul who fought the Romans were partly Celts, but by Roman times they were also Goths, Visigoths, Vandals, Franks, and Huns. These represented fresh nomadic incursions from the same regions from which the Celts came.

All the accounts we have of these peoples in their first centuries of contact with the Romans involve descriptions of war. Therefore our picture of women is battle oriented. Because these scenes give a reasonably realistic picture of nomadic women on the battlefield, we can to some extent extrapolate back to the Turko-Mongols and to the Bedouins and the Berbers, allowing for differences in geographic settings and details of tribal culture. It is worth quoting at some length from the passages available to us on women on the battlefield. These are all taken from Beard's work on women in history.

First, in Tacitus's description of the influence of women of the German tribes, he begins

by saying that squadrons or battalions of soldiers were composed of families and clans. Close by them, too, are those who are dearest to them, so that they hear the shrieks of the women, the cries of infants. [Women] are to every man the most sacred witnesses of his bravery—they are the most generous applauders. The soldier brings his wounds to his mother and wife. . . . Tradition says that armies already wavering or giving way have been rallied by women who, with earnest entreaties and bosoms laid

Figure 7.2. Statue of Epona, Gallo-Roman Period. Redrawn by HBR.

bare, have vividly represented the horrors of captivity. . . . [The Germans] even believe that sex has a certain sanctity and prescience, and they do not despise their counsels or make light of their answers. . . . They venerated Aurinia [as divinity], and many other women, but not with servile flatteries or with sham deifications. (Beard 1946: 289)

Plutarch describes the encounters between the Romans and the barbarous hordes at Aque Sextiae, 102 B.C.E.:

the fight had been no less fierce with the women than with the men themselves. . . . [The women] charged with swords and axes, and fell upon their opponents uttering a hideous outcry. . . . When summoned to surrender they killed their children, slaughtered one another, and hanged themselves to trees. (Beard 1946: 289)

Dio Cassius mentions that the Romans found bodies of women in armor among the corpses of the Marcomanni and Quadi. "Other Roman writers said that several Gothic prisoners proved to be women and among the Varangians, who attacked the Byzantines, women were found wielding arms side by side with their men" (Beard 1946: 289).

It should be noted that, while women are active on the battlefield, and "heard" in tribal councils, there is no trace of a concept of "rule" by women. Diner does not give the source for her assertion that

when Hannibal marched through Gaul . . . an agreement drawn up between him and the inhabitants stated that any difference of opinion regarding the damage done by his troops in passage and compensations to be paid for it were to be decided exclusively by the supreme council of Gallic women, with no right of appeal from this college of matrons for either party. (Diner [1932] 1965: 253)

That the prophetesses in the Germanic tribes had some part in deciding whether or not and when a battle should be attempted is clear. But the role of women in tribal councils, apart from that of being "heard," is far from clear. Matrilineal succession was practiced among all these tribes, almost without exception, and the widely cited Salic law appears to be a late, medieval addition to Germanic practice. What seems in general to have happened as a result of contact between the Romans and the Gallic and Germanic tribes is that the traditional higher status of women in both Gallic and Germanic traditions was gradually whittled away. Inferior-status rules regarding women drive out higher-status rules. The old Wergild laws of compensation for injury, replacing the terrible eye-for-an-eye law with provisions for monetary compensation, originally placed twice as high a value on women as on men, in terms of compensation for injuries wrought.

TABLE 7.1 Women's Roles in Ancient Gaul

I. Occupations open to both women and men:

  A. Military
    1. combatants
    2. noncombatants providing ammunition, nursing
  B. Construction
    1. building houses, shelters
  C. Political
    1. positions on tribal council
    2. judge for tribal council
  D. Cattle raising
    1. ownership and supervision of herds
    2. milking

II. Roles open predominantly to women:

  A. Agriculture
  B. Sewing, preparation of skins

III. Roles open only to women:

  A. Priestess/forecaster
  B. Prospecting
  C. Goldsmith

SOURCE: Data from Sullerot (1968).

This changed gradually through the Middle Ages (O'Faolain and Martines 1973: 96-106). Later rules are sometimes confused with earlier rules (Simons 1968: 84-85).

A tabulation of women's economic roles during the Gallic era puts the matter of women's participation in a more pedestrian perspective (see Table 7.1). Unquestionably, the Gallo-Celtic-Germanic tradition gave fuller participation to women in all the affairs of society than the Greco-Roman tradition did. The Gallo-Celtic-Germanic tradition is the tradition of a society on horseback, as compared with the settled Greco-Roman society. We will see in the next chapter how this nomadic tradition of fuller participation of women affected the development of the new Europe out of the old Roman Empire. For centuries to come, two traditions will be in conflict: the freer Gallic tradition and the more repressive Greco-Roman tradition. The issue is still before us in the twentieth century.

The Vikings

The Vikings were among the more ruthless of the nomads that history has romanticized. After 1,000 years of peaceful settled agricultural existence, from the eighth through the tenth centuries C.E., the Vikings became the scourge not only of Europe but also of the whole Atlantic from the Faroe Islands to North America and of Byzantium and Arabia too: "From the wrath of the Northmen, O Lord, deliver us" was the prayer in every church and monastery in northern France and England in the ninth and tenth centuries.

What shot the Vikings from the Northland's bow? One factor was the overpopulation in the Northland; another was the power vacuum in Europe, caused by doldrums after the Moslem conquests up to the gates of Vienna. Beyond these stimuli, there is always the imponderable of adventurousness and restlessness. The Vikings had a clearly marked aristocracy, bearing some of the marks of the free-and-easy Celtic style and some of the marks of the more elaborate Mongolian style. Society was divided into royalty, landholders (jarls), peasants, and, at the bottom, serfs. Jarl and peasant women had high status and enjoyed much freedom. The old Icelandic *Song of Rig*, thought to show Celtic influence (Brøndsted 1965: 238), reveals in its descriptions of the jarl and his wife sitting at home the upper-class cult of the body shared by Nordics and Celts. The image of the body beautiful becomes a powerful reinforcer of systems of social stratification:

And the big farmer twisted a bowstring, bent an elbow, made arrows; while the mistress looked at her arms, smoothed her clothes, tightened her sleeves. On her breast was a brooch, her shift was blue, her cap straight, her train long. Her breast was fair, her brow fairer, and her neck whiter than new fallen snow. (Brøndsted 1965: 239)

The serf girl—the farm drudge—looks quite different: "Her legs were crooked, her feet dirty, her arms sunburnt, her nose pendulous" (Brøndsted 1965: 238).

That early racism, and the theme of the ugly troll who lives in dark underground caves in Norse literature, are thought by some to have derived from Stone Age memories of struggles between Neanderthal-type hominids and their fully modern successors in isolated enclaves in the far North where the Neanderthals lingered on past their time. Whatever the reason for the cast of characters in Norse legends, they have had a long life. The image of the superior Nordic woman striding along in flowing dress, draped with an even more flowing cape, showing her white arms, and wearing at her waist her symbol of authority—the keys of the household— moves through the corridors of time to our own century, breeding both a continued racism and the cult of the superwoman.

There is no doubt that Nordic priestesses dressed in a kind of splendid simplicity that created awe in their time and resonates awe in ours. We can see this from the remains of priestesses and representations of them found in the famous peat bogs of Scandinavia (Glob 1969: 107, 119, 121-24), and there are many references to the barefoot, gray-haired women in white dresses and fine linen cloaks who accompany warriors, both on land and on sea, in the literature of the first millennium C.E.[17] Women, both the wise women of the pagan tradition and Christian women, play an important part in the Icelandic sagas.

The picture we get from the *Vinland Sagas* (1966) is of a sex-egalitarian society forged out of the pioneering experience, although only a few women participated in the life of adventurous voyaging. Navigator, seeress, farmer, and spinner—wise women journeyed everywhere with their brothers. It was their talents of discernment the men relied on, when in doubt, about where to steer, where to land, where to raid, and where to colonize. In the class-conscious society of the Northlands, the seeress was a person of great standing, but at sea and in helping found new colonies in Iceland and further west, she helped her less prophetically gifted sisters create a new classless society that functioned very differently than that in the motherland.

These priestesses with the gift of prophecy had an increasingly hard time through the latter part of the first millennium of the Common Era. Many of them had conflicts of loyalty between the old priesthood and the new when Christianity came to be more widely accepted.[18] Their ancient stock of wisdom was often laid aside as Christianity branded it witchcraft.

Our special interest in the Vikings is their scanning skills that led to the long ocean journeys to Greenland, Iceland, and Vinland (Newfoundland). These long sea journeys were a special challenge to women's skill, because household equipment, seeds, and cattle had to be packed in the longboats—tiny enough for what they carried. Packing a longboat was a lot harder than packing a wagon. Scanning skills at sea are different than scanning skills on land, and women's knowledge of signs and portents and clues about environmental resources must have been stretched to the limit on these journeys.

The separation from local peoples that enables one to scan larger horizons is a two-edged device. The Vikings were even more distanced from the populations they encountered than land nomads would be. They inflicted a good deal of mindless cruelty during their raids on settled populations. This raises the question of whether larger perspectives and large-scale scanning skills also contribute to dehumanization. Seeing the larger picture is not an unmixed good, if unaccompanied by a humanizing experience of relationship with that which is seen. The fact that women were such able partners of the Vikings suggests that women are as liable to this dehumanization as men are.

* * *

Each of the nomadic societies we have examined thus far has been vulnerable to destruction by assimilation into settled society once the barrier between the nomad and the settler has broken down. The Mongols, the Bedouins, the Celts, and, after their 200-year fling, the Vikings only retained their distinctive culture and comparative perspective as long as the settled folk could be thought of as the enemy. The contact that humanized also softened the critical scanning faculties that made these societies so dynamic and interesting. This issue remains perplexing as we look at the Gypsies in the next section. While the suspicion and mistrust between the *gajes* and the *Rom* is deplorable, there is no doubt that Gypsies are in danger of losing many of their special skills, as well as their joy, if they are persuaded to leave the road.

The Gypsies

The Gypsies are both the best loved and the most maligned of all nomads. Running away to the Gypsies is a lure for little children that has resulted in some fine pieces of literature on life among the Gypsies in the nineteenth and twentieth centuries. The instinct to take to the road has apparently never quite died out among settled folk.

The protoypical nomads, Gypsies presumably originated in India and pursued the occupations assigned to outcastes by the Laws of Manu— metal smithing, music, and divining. They are the oldest craft and trading nomads and, with the rise of the Turko-Mongolian empires, attached themselves to the traveling camps of the khans. Historians of the Mongols do not mention them, but other evidence seems to point in this direction. The Mongols themselves had minimal craft skills and had to get their wagon and weapon makers from somewhere. It would be among the herding nomads that the Gypsies would have developed their skills in animal training (Clébert 1963: 36-39, 129-30, 145).

By the 1100s C.E., we begin to find mention of them in Europe, and by then they were showing all the skills of adaptation to local terrain and customs they have been showing ever since, traveling with "safe-conduct" passes from kings and emperors over lands and across borders that others could not cross (Clébert 1963: 58). By the early twentieth century, they were excellent passport forgers. Persecutions also started soon after their first appearance, and alternations of guaranties of safe conduct and persecution continue to be their lot (Clébert 1963: 88).

Their mapping skills were equaled by few outside the Gypsy world. In 1596, they were described as having

> the best and most reliable maps on which are marked all the towns, villages, and rivers, the homes of gentry and others, and arrange among themselves a meeting place, with ten days in between at twenty leagues from where they set out. The Captain allocates to each of the oldest men three households to escort there, taking their own short cut, and finding the rendezvous: and for those remaining who are well mounted and armed, he sends them with a good almanac in which are all the fairs of the world, changing accoutrements and horses. (Clébert 1963: 65-66)

The year 1596 sounds extraordinarily like 1992. In spite of intervening wars and the development of ever more rigid national barriers, the Gypsies keep on the move from country to country, knowing no destination except the road itself. The specific composition of any one caravan is ever shifting, yet everyone knows to which *kumpania* they belong. In any caravan, everyone also knows who the senior man is, and who the senior woman is, although they have no title. Some Gypsies have been lured into settlements, finally giving in to the pressure of authorities who do not know how to deal with peoples on the move. But a significant number of the estimated 5 million Gypsies in the world today are still on the move. More than 400,000 were exterminated by the Nazis for having "impure blood" during World War II. It is almost unbelievable that, all through the 1930s and 1940s, they kept crossing and recrossing boundaries of Western Europe, ignoring all categories such as the Allies, the Axis powers, communism, capitalism, ignoring everything but their own inner mandate to keep moving (Yoors 1967: 110, 114).

How was this possible? Because the planet really belongs to the Gypsies. They are the people, the *Rom*. All others are barbarians, intruders who clutter up the landscape with settlements. Gypsies have their own private *Rom* space wherever they go, their own language, their own ways. *Gajes*— the non-Gypsies—are used as resources but otherwise ignored.

Some of the traditional traits we have described for other nomadic folk the Gypsies exhibit almost to perfection. In addition to having excellent maps, they have a communication network of taverns around the world for which they carry telephone numbers on tattered scraps of paper. With these they activate the network when they want to reach each other (Yoors 1967: 110-14). Every Rom checks in at the network tavern nearest to where he is camping. Until recently largely illiterate, they often have gajes write letters for them that are marked "Gypsy mail" and are sent in care of General

Delivery to the post offices of the world's major cities, lying in the "Gypsy mailbox" until claimed (Yoors 1967: 85, 211). When on the road, they leave special Gypsy trail signs, so anyone else coming after them can know who has gone before and where they are headed (Yoors 1967: 210). "Specific districts, provinces or countries [are] divided into 'hunting territories' or reserved areas 'belonging' to a specific kumpania" (Clébert 1963: 243). The Gypsies "native" to the area help all comers with the intricacies of local customs and law. Because everyone is on the move, it is not clear how each *kumpania* manages to keep some wagons always on its own hunting territory. Probably they know by Gypsy mail or Gypsy phone when they are needed to help other bands passing through.

By skillful combination of all these resources, Gypsies manage to keep track of each other to an extraordinary degree and periodically have large tribal gatherings including convocations of the *kris*, the Gypsy judicial council. On such occasions, they announce to all the world that they are going to elect a "Gypsy king"—although such an institution does not exist among them—because they have found that this gets them favorable publicity and permission to camp far longer than local police usually allow. Otherwise, Gypsy caravans tend to be hounded across Europe from camp site to camp site. Great pressure in the last few years has led to the establishment of permitted Gypsy camping sites, but even greater pressures exist to make them abandon the road altogether. So far, most of them have resisted.

Women's Roles Among the Gypsies

Like all nomadic tribes, the Gypsies show signs of matriliny, especially in Southern and Eastern Europe (Yoors 1967: 121-22). Kinship was formerly counted through the mother, but this practice, where it exists, is of minor importance because the father is head of the kinship unit. The father is to the family what the tribal chief is to the tribe, and no other authority figure exists, except in the informal authority of the senior man and the woman elder in each caravan. The tribal chief's role is loose, and he is advised by a council of elders, the old men of the tribe. Every tribe also has a woman elder, who does not actually sit with the tribal council yet is always consulted by them and carries a great deal of weight among the men as well as among the women. Some scholars believe she is the remnant of an earlier matriarchal system. Because the mother in the family is the equivalent of the woman elder in the tribe, one can say that the family is the microcosm of the tribe.

Given that women's and men's spaces and roles are very clearly defined, and there are many taboos surrounding the activities of women, it does not appear on the surface that there is much equality between women and men. Women may not speak at tribal councils. They do not even eat with the men but send food to the men's circle from the individual family campfires where women sit with their children. Yet, from descriptions like Jan Yoors's *The Gypsies* (1967), one realizes that there is a great deal of shared public space between women and men. The campground is one large family space, used in various ways by all family members, and everyone lives outdoors in the campground except in inclement weather. Children may be fed by anyone and sleep anywhere. Women and men observe strict monogamy, and young unmarrieds are strictly chaperoned. Oddly, although all Gypsy marriages are arranged by the heads of household in consultation with wives, and the younger generation are scarcely ever consulted, a high value is placed on romantic love. Once a young couple have been joined in matrimony, they proceed to develop a love relationship that has all the emotional commitment of a Western-style love relationship and appears to be more lasting. Divorce is practically unknown. Young people marry early and have many children, which is why there are so many Gypsies in the world today. Religious ceremonies are devout, but scanty, and take on the forms of the religious community in which they occur. The Gypsies seem to consider all religions as appropriate vehicles for their devotions.

The old herding practices of nomads have developed for the Gypsy men into skill in training and trading horses. When horses disappear, as in the United States, this is translated into dealing in cars. Gypsy men are also famous for the miniature smithies they carry with them. Women bring income into the caravan by telling fortunes, singing, and dancing. Both women and men have become famous circus performers in Europe, as tamers and trainers of wild animals. There are also famous women and men Gypsy musicians. This mixing of traditional sex roles reflects an adaptability of role structure that is not always apparent on the surface.

One has a tremendous impression of the vitality of Gypsy life and of the vitality of its women and men. The zest with which they sing and dance and talk all night long around campfires, "sleeping it off" in the morning when townsfolk are up and about their business, is surely part of the attraction they have for the children who run off to join them. Why did Wilhelm Bach, oldest son of Johann Sebastian Bach, spend much of his life among the Gypsies (Yoors 1967: 150)? He was a musician who preferred playing around Gypsy campfires to being choirmaster in Darmstadt. Those who manage to photograph Gypsies in their own setting show happy people, although the *zigeuner* melancholy is as famous as the Jewish melancholy. A photograph in Jean-Paul Clébert's *The Gypsies* (1963) looks startlingly like a photograph of a hippie commune on the move in the 1970s. What the

Gypsies have that the hippies did not have is centuries of tradition, puritan sex morals, and a capacity for self-discipline as well as for letting loose.

The Gypsies represent an interesting case of nomadism, because, in spite of their mapping and environment-exploiting skills, they have not acted as social organizers in the way that the Arab and Turko-Mongol nomads did. Theirs is a niche adaptation, depending on minimum contact with the outside world, and yet their niche is the world itself. The women's lives seem narrow and circumscribed, hemmed in by taboos, lacking the possibility of political participation, yet those who write about Gypsy tribes describe women who apparently feel very free, who have all the "space" they want. The practice of caring for each other's children means that the Gypsy women who are going off to town to dance or tell fortunes never have to worry about child care. The whole camp is a day-care center. One could imagine that they will feel much less free in the future, when they are settled in towns and their children go to local schools, as authorities now desire. Gone will be the communal arrangements of the campground and the possibility of shared work.

* * *

The view from the road seems on the whole to be a liberating one for women, at least from their own point of view. While all nomadic societies have some relatively sharp division between men's and women's spaces, due to the nature of the subsistence activities, nomadic women have shared work spaces among themselves, which settled women do not have, and there are also significant intersections of men's and women's spaces. There is more role fluidity than the formal division of labor leads one to expect. Traces of matriliny are present in all nomadic groups. Women's political roles are important in most nomadic societies, although not among the Gypsies except through their women elders. The skills that keep a nomadic society functioning smoothly on the road and in the making and breaking of camp, and the skills that enable nomads to scan and use their environments in ways that settled peoples often occupying the same general space do not, seem to be the skills that also create the unique social bond that makes nomad society as clearly bounded in social space as settled societies are bounded in physical space.

The skill that neither nomad nor settler has developed is how to relate the two modes of life creatively. If we lose nomadism, we lose a special kind of world-modeling capability that cannot be replaced by the computer.[19]

We also lose working examples of nonhierarchical segmented societies that might throw light on problems of societal reorganization from centralized hierarchical modes to decentralist nonhierarchical modes.

If, through mistaken goodwill, we draw nomads too close to us, we destroy them. As I suggested at the beginning of this chapter, they, not we, may be the laboratory of the future. It is possible that nomadic women, who have special demands made on them to create a balance between scanning skills and nurturance skills as they move their households daily, may have something to teach us about how to move through the world.

Notes

1. The few sagas that emanate from nomadic cultures do not find their way into our compendiums either as literature or as history. *The Secret History of the Mongols* (Waley 1963), compiled in the year 1240 by Yuen-chao-pi-shih, or the Celtic *Red Book of Hergest*, or the *Thamudenes*, inscriptions on desert rock left by nomads of the Arabian desert early in the first millennium of the Common Era, are known only to scholars.

2. The camel has a somewhat similar effect on the desert, but camels move more slowly.

3. Nelson (1973: 54-55) describes polygamous families living on the Turkish-Syrian border and points out how powerful the senior wife is and how important her role is after widowhood. She is the one who maintains the children and the other wives, controls the land, makes political and economic alliances, and arranges work contracts. The widow, in short, acts like and is recognized as a man. Nelson cites Barbara Aswad's data from a study of landowning patrilineages over a period of 10 years, showing that 19 of 68 "heads" of these patrilineages were women.

4. A recent study of nomadic holy women confirms the possibility that women may be perceived as having greater spiritual and/or healing power than do men and that fierce competition may arise between male and female *marabouts* (Gaudry, in Nelson 1973: 51-52).

5. The magnitude of Farb's contribution transcends the limitations of his title and the constraints that the title put on his own thinking. The interpretations of women's activities are my own, however, and should not be ascribed to Farb.

6. Because science is continuously pushing back dates about human movements, it should be said that this migration may have occurred much earlier.

7. My somewhat unorthodox discussion of the Eskimo draws on information in David Damas's "The Copper Eskimo" (1972) as well as in Farb (1968).

8. This description applies to a period several centuries ago. Today the Shoshone continue a somewhat similar way of life, but it is built around relationships with white settlers. As a niche culture, their way of life has remained more intact than that of other Indian groups, according to Farb (1968).

9. In fact, such sisterhood did develop between Indian and pioneer women on the fringes of colonial settlement areas, but it was too little and too late to act as a moderating force in warfare (De Pauw 1974).

10. See the passages on variability in marriage contracts among the Jews of the Cairo Geniza (Goitein, 1967, vol. 1: 10, 47-49, 57-59) for an illustration of heterogeneity where one might expect very strictly specified procedures. Egyptian marriage-contract literature shows very great variability, going back to ancient times (Wenig 1970).

11. Moscati characterized these southern towns as "a commercial, fiscal and labour organization, bound to a definite territory. Its members are distributed among various classes, from the noble ruling caste to that of serfs. . . . [O]ne may be attached to a tribe by royal decree, that is a group of different origin may be incorporated into the tribe and have equal rights with its existing members" (1959: 115).

12. In 90 C.E., the reigning emperor felt strong enough to refuse a princess to the nomad chief of the Indo-Scythians and successfully stood off the resulting attack. In 565, a northern Chinese king was in such difficult straits that he "humbly" asked for a great khan's daughter in marriage.

13. The couriers were called "arrow messengers." "Every one of these 'arrow' messengers was to be regarded as sacred. The highest prince in the land must make room for him to pass when the sound of his horse's bells was heard; and if his mount grew tired, the best available horse had to be supplied. By day and by night these messengers rode across the steppes and the desert, crossing in a few days distances which usually needed weeks to cover. An 'arrow' messenger's head and body were bandaged to help him endure his long ride. He rode his steed nearly to death, and slept in the saddle, with the result that nothing could happen throughout the broad land of Mongolia without tidings being promptly conveyed to the Khakan" (Prawdin 1940: 93). This system was extended in modified form to cover Europe. Riders could make 250 to 300 miles a day.

14. It is tempting to develop this animal-training theory of human education further. It must have been a very early form of behaviorism.

15. In 1899, Qasim Amin published a book saying that Islam's decline was due to the suppression of women after the days of the prophet.

16. The term *women religious* is used to refer to women in religious orders. I am following the usage of the Catholic church here.

17. Strabo's passage in his *Geography* is a good example (Glob 1969: 124).

18. The replacement of pagan ritual by the worship of the "White Christ" in Iceland was carried out by women, true to the nomad women's role in introducing new religions (Mowat 1965: 74).

19. I am thinking here about computer-assisted modeling of the world such as the work of Donella and Dennis Meadows et al. represented in *Limits to Growth* (1972).

References

Ahmed, Abdel Ghaffar M. 1973. "Tribal and Sedentary Elites: A Bridge Between Two Communities." Pp. 75-96 in *The Desert and the Sown: Nomads in the Wider Society*, edited by Cynthia Nelson. Berkeley: University of California Press.

Beard, Mary R. 1946. *Woman as Force in History: A Study in Traditions and Realities*. New York: Macmillan.

Brennan, Peggy. 1975. "Analysis of Women in Irish History." Unpublished student paper, University of Colorado, Boulder, Department of Sociology.

Brøndsted, Johannes. 1965. *The Vikings*, translated by Kalle Skov. Great Britain: Cox and Wyman.

Buccellati, Giorgio. 1967. *Cities and Nations of Ancient Syria: An Essay on Political Institutions with Special Reference to the Israelite Kingdoms*. Rome: Universita di Roma, Instituta di Studi de Vincino Oriente.

Chadwick, Nora. 1970. *The Celts*. London: Cox and Wyman.

Clébert, Jean-Paul. 1963. *The Gypsies*, translated by Charles Duff. London: Vista Books, Longacre Press.

Damas, David. 1972. "The Copper Eskimo." Pp. 3-50 in *Hunters and Gatherers Today*, edited by M. G. Bicchieri. New York: Holt, Rinehart & Winston.

Davidson, Basil. 1966. *The African Kingdoms*. New York: Time-Life.

De Pauw, Linda Grant. 1974. *Four Traditions: Women of New York During the American Revolution*. Albany: New York State American Revolution Bicentennial Commission.

Diner, Helen. [1932] 1965. *Mothers and Amazons*, translated by John Philip Lundin. New York: Julian.

Drinker, Sophie. 1948. *Music and Women: The Story of Women in Their Relation to Music*. New York: Coward-McCann.

Eberhard, Wolfram. 1967. *Settlement and Social Change in Asia*. Hong Kong: Hong Kong University Press.

Farb, Peter. 1968. *Man's Rise to Civilization: As Shown by the Indians of North America from Primeval Times to the Coming of the Industrial State*. New York: E. P. Dutton.

Glob, P. V. 1969. *The Bog People*, translated by Rupert Bruce-Mitford. London: Faber and Faber.

Goitein, Solomon D. 1967-71. *A Mediterranean Society: The Jewish Communities of the Arab World as Portrayed in the Documents of the Cairo Geniza*. 2 vols. Berkeley: University of California Press.

Graves, Robert. 1966. *White Goddess: A Historical Grammar of Poetic Myth*. New York: Farrar, Straus & Giroux.

Grousset, René. 1970. *The Empire of the Steppes: A History of Central Asia*, translated by Naomi Walford. New Brunswick, NJ: Rutgers University Press.

Khaldun, Ibn. 1969. *The Muqaddimah: An Introduction to History*, translated by Franz Rosenthal; edited and abridged by N. J. Dawood. Princeton, NJ: Princeton University Press. (Written in 1377.)

Kinsella, Thomas. 1970. *The Tain*. London: Oxford University Press.

Meadows, Donella, Dennis Meadows, et al. 1972. *Limits to Growth*. New York: Universe.

Mohammed, Abbas. 1973. "The Nomadic and the Sedentary: Polar Complementaries—Not Polar Opposites." Pp. 97-112 in *The Desert and the Sown: Nomads in the Wider Society*, edited by Cynthia Nelson. Berkeley: University of California Press.

Monteil, Vincent. 1959. "The Evolution and Settling of the Nomads of the Sahara." *International Social Science Journal* 11:572-85.

Morgan, Lewis Henry. 1901. *League of the Ho-De-No Sau-Nee or Iroquois*. New Haven, CT: Human Relations Area Files.

Moscati, Sabatino. 1959. *The Semites in Ancient History*. Cardiff: University of Wales Press.

Mowat, Farley. 1965. *West Viking: The Ancient Norse in Greenland and North America*. Toronto: McClelland and Stewart.

Nelson, Cynthia, ed. 1973. *The Desert and the Sown: Nomads in the Wider Society*. Berkeley: University of California Press.

O'Faolain, Julia and Lauro Martines, eds. 1973. *Not in God's Image: A History of Women in Europe from the Greeks to the Nineteenth Century*. New York: Harper & Row.

O'Faolain, Sean. 1969. *The Irish*. London: C. Nicholls.

Oliver, Roland, ed. 1968. *Dawn of African History*. 2nd ed. London: Oxford University Press.

Prawdin, Michael. 1940. *The Mongol Empire: Its Rise and Legacy*, translated by Eden and Cedar Paul. London: Allen & Unwin.

Ross, Anne. 1970. *Everyday Life of the Pagan Celts*. London: B. T. Bottsford.

Silberman, Leo. 1959. "Somali Nomads." *International Social Science Journal* 11:559-71.

Simons, Gerald. 1968. *Barbarian Europe*. New York: Time-Life.

Smith, W. Robertson. 1966. *Kinship and Marriage in Early Arabia*. 2nd ed., edited by Stanley A. Cook. Oosterhout N.B., the Netherlands: Anthropological Publications.

Spencer, Robert F. 1952. "The Arabian Matriarchate: An Old Controversy." *Southwestern Journal of Anthropology* 8:478-502.

Stewart, Desmond. 1967. *Early Islam*. New York: Time-Life.

Sullerot, Evelyne. 1968. *Histoire et Sociologie du Travail Féminin.* Paris: Société Nouvelle des Editions Gonthier.

Toynbee, Arnold J. 1935. *A Study of History.* Vol. 3., 2nd ed. New York: Oxford University Press.

The Vinland Sagas: The Norse Discovery of America [Groenlendunga Saga and Eirik's Saga]. 1966. Translated by Magnus Magnuson and Herman Polson. New York: New York University Press.

Waley, Arthur. 1963. *The Secret History of the Mongols, and Other Pieces.* New York: Barnes & Noble.

Wenig, Steffan. 1970. *Women in Egyptian Art.* New York: McGraw-Hill.

White, E. M. 1924. *Woman in World History: Her Place in the Great Religions.* London: Herbert Jenkins.

Yoors, Jan. 1967. *The Gypsies.* New York: Simon & Schuster.

8

Barbarians, Civilizations, and Women: Rome, Byzantium, and Islam, 200 B.C.E. to 100 C.E.

Times that are supposed to be decisive cutting points in history never, in fact, are, particularly when we are looking at women's roles. These roles rarely show dramatic shifts. In the time period this chapter deals with, it *almost* looked as if there would be a dramatic shift. There were great expectations, and one might associate the birth of "futurism" with the onset of the Christian era. But that is not strictly correct, because the idea of a future that is different than the past comes out of all the prophetic religions. With Christianity, however, expectations for the future reached a fever pitch and embraced much of the known world with missionary fervor.

Expectations are one thing. Imaging the future in such a way that images can affect behavior is another. Somewhere between denied expectations and faulty imaging, the alternative future originally set forth by Christianity got lost. The loss was for men as well as for women, but for women the tragedy seems the greater, because the expectations were so much higher.

In this chapter, much attention will be given to the developing institutions of Christianity because they are tied up with both the arousing and the crushing of expectancies about alternative ways of life to replace old oppressions. They are also tied up with a special new set of opportunities for women that survived the crushing of expectancies. While this story becomes Eurocentric, events will be examined in the context of happenings in Byzantium and in Islam as well as in Europe.

In the year 200 B.C.E., the Mediterranean world stood on the threshold of a new kind of society. Many problems of communication, of distribution of resources, and of organization of large-scale societal interaction had been solved. During the era of the Roman Republic, a new pattern of women's civic affairs began to develop that held some promise for the future. For several hundred years, the infrastructures of civic peace developed at least as rapidly as the infrastructure of military might.

If we choose the year 200 B.C.E. as our dividing line, we are highlighting the foot-in-two-worlds role of Rome in the great transition from the oppressions of antiquity to the relatively more open societies of the new Europe. In one sense, the Rome of 200 B.C.E., the "modernized" republic entering on its imperial phase, already represented the new world. In another sense, it belonged to the dying world of the first world empires—power reaching into the dark with no understanding of what is to be grasped. We take that period here to be our "running start" on the future. The protest movement on behalf of women's rights in Rome that inaugurated the second century B.C.E. was at least a mild signal of things to come, of reorganized perceptions of social reality (Baldson 1962: 33-37).

A far more definitive signal of those new perceptions came at the end of the millennium with the appearance of a new teacher in the unlikely small town of Nazareth in the Roman province of Syria. While still a young man, he gathered around him a community of people who bypassed the usual sex role definitions. Something very remarkable nearly happened. For the first 100 years of the new era, women were everywhere leaving behind old constraints, stepping into the public sphere, and participating in the creation of a new society. The extent of the persecution of these women by Roman authorities was a measure of the extent to which the old world feared the new roles for women. The rate at which women joined the new Christian movement was a measure of the readiness of women for the new life.

As the movement grew larger, it grew more conservative. There were no models for this new kind of participation of women. Might women squeeze men out of their traditional authority roles? Beginning about 100 C.E., but taking another 300 years to jell completely, a slow process of reviving the earlier domestic role model for women was instituted, and they lost their initial equal status in the new Christian communities.

Yet what had been unleashed could not be stopped. Seeds were sown that took root in even the stoniest soil of stripped-down possibilities for women as social reformers, teachers, scholars, and individuals modeling a new humanness. The new root system also linked with some old root systems—the roles of elite women in the old Mediterranean empires and of the nomad barbarian women now beginning to settle all along the outer fringes of the Roman Empire in Europe and the Near East. Many different traditions of women's participation intersected over the first 1,000 years of the new era. By the year 1000 C.E., women had managed to establish themselves securely enough in the niche positions that had been left to them to be able to participate actively in the postmillennial "second chance" of the late Middle Ages. That is the story in Chapter 1 of Volume 2 of *The Underside of History*.

This current chapter is a tale of the hardiness of women, particularly of how they created an entire system of formation and education for children and adults of differing cultures in the very teeth of increasingly barbarous military action. What armies tore down, they rebuilt again and again. The real infrastructures of the first millennium C.E. were created by women in the face of continuous and destructive use of force by men. Male armies converted "barbarians" to Christianity through techniques of slaughter. Women patiently engaged the survivors in the learning-teaching dialogues necessary for the building of new cultures out of old ones. Of course, not all men were destructive, and not all women were constructive. But never before had the difference between the social-learning model of social change and the military-force model been so clear. On the one hand, we see the dialogue between different cultures; on the other, we see the forced conformity to one culture. Given that history is written largely in terms of the military model, one must search for the evidence of social learnings.

Before launching into a description of women's roles from 200 B.C.E. to the end of the first millennium, it will be useful to review the situation of the Mediterranean world at the beginning of the period with which this chapter is concerned. The threshold of universalism for human societies was already crossed when Rome moved into position as a major actor on the world scene with the final destruction of Carthage in 202 B.C.E. All the basic problems of organizing society on a new scale had already been confronted by Darius and Atossa when they embarked on the first major road-building project of the modern world. The Hellenistic empire took over road building where Persia left off, and we have seen how the Celts had their own wagon tracks in Europe. When Rome began its famous highway network, it was following a well-established communication design. The establishment of local government offices for administration and tax collecting now had a long tradition behind it, and the women and men of the Mediterranean urban elite knew quite a lot about large-scale administration.

By 200 B.C.E., the art of large-scale warfare had also developed considerable sophistication. The Egyptians were the first to move from a simple massing of soldiers to systematic formations; Sun Tzu wrote the first army manual in 500 B.C.E. in China; Cyrus developed the first "modern" standing army; and Alexander developed the "phalanx" system.

The first large-scale minting operation was developed under Darius and Atossa, and the Daric was the basic coin for international trade by 500 B.C.E. The guild system of organization to meet occupational and welfare needs of city dwellers had developed in one form or another in all the major city-states by 200 B.C.E.

There were universities and libraries in Athens, Alexandria, Taxila (now in Pakistan), and Hien-Yang (China). A tradition of published laws went as far back as the Hammurabi of Babylonia and the Athenian Constitution of 308 B.C.E. There were several major systems of teachings of universalistic ethics, developed in China, India, and Persia, and universalism had emerged in the most recent Judaic prophetic teachings to replace an earlier tribal religion. The mystery religions of all the major urban centers were adding a new dimension to the religious-ethical worldview.

By 200 B.C.E., the Mediterranean world had already gone through several cult-of-antiquity periods. Ramses II in Egypt had created a major cultural revival as far back as 1290. Nebuchadnezzar developed a passion for archaeology and tried to re-create the ancient Hammurabian kingdom in the late 500s. Following him, Nabu-naid, the last king of the Chaldees, had uncovered what he thought was a 32,000-year-old set of records of his forebears. Israel under Josiah in the 600s tried to re-create the Israel of ancient prophecy.

With such a rich past, and such an actively inventive current time, the year 200 B.C.E. was like a gift to the human race. Rome appropriated the gift. She could hardly have missed, in terms of civic achievement. Everything had been set up for her. The women and men of Rome provided the energy and entrepreneurship of the newcomer to the further extension and elaboration of an urban-focused way of life that organized vast hinterlands so that resources could be collected, reworked, and redistributed to meet the needs of the rapidly growing populations of the Mediterranean. If Ferdinand Lot's (1961: 221) interpretation is correct, the Romans were not even innovative in the machinery of state but used an unworkable city-state mechanism to rule an empire. Roman law was originally the municipal law of Rome, painfully worked over to apply to the republic of Rome and never adequate for the empire. What Rome did provide, however, were full-time specialists in law who kept records of new precedents and built up a set of written records in every province, which gave a semblance of order to the empire (Mujeeb 1960: 110).

The story of the next 12,000 years is full of ups and downs. The Romans had four "good centuries." By 200 C.E., just at the point when the new small communities of Christians had spread far enough to develop a strong international network of their own, the inadequacies inherent in the Roman village empire plus the pressure of new populations from "barbarian" Europe set in motion a series of interactions that corrupted all the potentials of Romans, tribal barbarians, and Christians alike. Islam's effort, another "new start" on the new society, suffered the same corruption the Roman-Byzantine world suffered, for much the same reasons—though the Moslems were more politically inventive and more tolerant of religious and cultural differences in those they conquered than were the Roman-Byzantine rulers.

Women's Roles: What Went Into the Melting Pot

Given that, in the twentieth century, no society is proud of a history of the seclusion of women, historians writing about the period before and after the start of the Christian era are apt to blame some *other* culture for initiating a practice of seclusion of women from public life. This practice then "contaminates" the historian's own culture. So Sir Steven Runciman, writing of Christian Constantinople, describes the freedom that Byzantium women had, although court ladies did live in specially reserved women's quarters, referred to by the Greek term *gynaeceum:* "But neither she [the empress] nor the ladies of the court led the secluded lives of Muslim women. They emerged as frequently as they liked" (1967: 161).
Ameer Ali writes of women in Islam:

> At the point of the highest blossoming of the Arabian nation, when it held the foremost place in arts and arms, woman was not only on an equality with man but also the object on his part of a chivalrous veneration. Social demoralization, consequent upon political decadence, accentuated the unnerving influence of foreign ideas and foreign customs. "Gradually the noble picture of the free, courageous, independent, self-respecting and therefore respected, Arab matron and maiden disappears from Moslem society and its place taken by that of secluded ladies" who copy in their lives and manners the luxury, the inanity and want of dignity of the inmates of Byzantine or Persian palaces. (1899: 755)

A footnote in the Ali paper informs us that "the seclusion of women was common among the Athenians, the ancient Persians, and apparently the Byzantines. From the latter the Russians are said to have borrowed their terem" (1899: 756). So the Christians blame the Moslems, and the Moslems the Persians. But Persian women, as we saw in

Chapter 6, came into the empire politics of the Mediterranean world with strong tribal traditions of women's participation. When the Persians conquered the Greeks, Persian women had nothing but contempt for gynaeceum-bound Athenian women.

In all the buck passing, nobody blames the Romans for the seclusion of women, because their women were already looked upon as "emancipated." Among the Romans themselves, there were those who blamed the barbarians for the seclusion of women. The Romans, however, saw only "Romanized" barbarians, and the ways of Gallic and Germanic tribes of 500 B.C.E. may have been very different than the laws recorded by 500 C.E.[1] Also, original tribal traditions differed, so those using the barbarians as an excuse for the suppression of women tend to quote Saxon, Thuringian, and Lombard law, while those who would look at tribal life as the source of freedom for women tend to quote Burgundian and Visigothic law[2] (see the section on Germanic tribal law in O'Faolain 1969).

Any simple black-and-white picture that puts in any particular quarter the blame for the growing seclusion of women in the first millennium C.E. is bound to be wrong. We have already noted that the same Athens that produced the gynaeceum gave hospitality to women scholars and produced noted public figures among its hetairae. Women scholars who knew Athenian culture played an important role in the Roman-Byzantine empire for 1,000 years. We have also noted how, after the barbarian Illyrian woman Eurydice became queen of Macedonia, there developed a whole new tradition of women active in international politics, known as the "Macedonian tradition" (Macurdy 1927).

If we are to place blame anywhere, we should look at the cultures of the most active trading peoples, because these were the culture spreaders of this era. Greeks and Hebrews were the most

Figure 8.1. Scene in Women's Quarters, Pompeii; Imperial Villa, First Century C.E., After Third Century B.C.E. Redrawn by HBR.

active traders in the Mediterranean and Europe from 200 B.C.E. forward. Tavard (1973) suggests that an important influence in making fashionable the seclusion of women in the home was the practice of wealthy Jewish merchants who had homes in each of the major cities of the known world. They drew not only on their own traditions but also developed further the institution of the gynaeceum. Greek and Jewish merchants may well have vied with each other in a Veblenian[3] race to have their wives as conspicuously and expensively secluded as possible. On the other hand, as we will see later in this chapter, a study of the Jewish community in Alexandria toward the end of the millennium indicates a high level of activity of women outside the home and considerable freedom of movement for them. Anywhere we look, as soon as details are available, the picture of seclusion becomes more ambiguous.

The constraints on women were real enough but possibly less dramatic than often envisioned. The only way to get an overall view of the multiplicity of cultural patterns is to trace the development of women's roles in each of these traditions over the period under study and then try to arrive at an overall assessment of the situation of women by the year 1000 C.E.

Women in Pagan Rome

The legends of the founding of Rome, including that of the Romans taking the Sabine women in marriage (the 30 matrilineal clans of ancient Rome?), point to matrilineal origins. The patricians, against whom the plebeians revolted to get constitutional rights for women and men in 451 B.C.E., were presumably in origin the patriarchs of the 30 "conquered" matrilinies. Most of the accounts of Roman women previous to 200 B.C.E., however, are accounts of heroic docility. By 195 B.C.E., things were different. The Oppian Law, passed in 215 as a wartime austerity measure—stating that "no woman might own more than half an ounce of gold, or wear clothes of various colors, or ride in a horse-drawn carriage in any town or city or within a mile of its confines, except on the occasion of some public religious ceremony" (Bullough 1973: 38)—was repealed. Roman women had brought their sisters in from the countryside in great masses to demonstrate against the law, and there were lengthy debates in the tribunes. In the now freer political atmosphere, Roman women increasingly moved about in public, crowded the court when important trials were occurring, attended senate meetings, and increasingly participated in their husbands' careers. In addition, they conducted large-scale trading enterprises and had considerable freedom to marry, divorce, remarry, and conduct their own affairs as they chose. As the empire grew in size and wealth and its leading citizens were rewarded with gifts of land, women had increasingly large estates to manage in the countryside (Baldson 1962: 93). Men were getting nervous about the economic and political power of women. It was argued that women should not accompany their husbands to administrative posts outside Rome because they would institute a second, secret government (Bullough 1973: 92). In Asia Minor, according to E. M. White (1924: 287-88), inscriptions have been found giving evidence of women officials in the Roman province there as judges, administrators, priestesses, and founders of hospitals and orphanages.

The household was the real power base for Roman women, however. Most of their activities were carved out under the "wife-and-mother" rubric. The Roman matron of affairs managed her home, her estate, and her business affairs and educated her children, training them in the international politics of the time.

Not all ladies of the upper classes were civic minded; the new wealth of Rome made a festive life possible for those who wanted it. Roman morals, however, continued to be far more straitlaced for women than for men; riotous banqueting was severely frowned upon and punished by stringently enforced adultery laws. Because extramarital sex was legal for prostitutes, some upper-class women registered as prostitutes to protect themselves (O'Faolain and Martines 1973: 56). This is only one of many examples of women's use of laws of prostitution to gain extra freedom of action.

Although I do not know of any specific instances, I can imagine businesswomen registering as prostitutes so as not to have irrelevant laws invoked to hamper their freedom of movement. Is not the following legal opinion suggestive? "It has been decided that adultery cannot be committed [i.e., there is no such thing as adultery] with women who have charge of any business or shop" (O'Faolain and Martines 1973: 65). In a similar vein, for women innkeepers and servant girls,

> chastity is required only of those women who are held by the bonds of the law, but those who, because of their mean status in life, are not deemed worthy of the consideration of the laws shall be immune from judicial severity (O'Faolain and Martines 1973: 65).

I suspect that Rome's women, including in particular its lesbian circles, were extremely ingenious in obtaining freedom of movement within restrictive laws and would cheerfully claim menial status or prostitution on behalf of that freedom.

The elitism of Roman society suggested by this legal separation of the matron from all other women, whether freeborn or slave, is important to remember as we move toward the Christian era. The last 200 years B.C.E. produced a number of women of substantial wealth and privilege. These were the women who lived in the spacious Roman courtyard-centered homes, who enjoyed the public parks, the forum, the temples, the baths, and who had country houses as well. They had no "political rights," but they knew how to do what they wanted to do. The descendants of these women played an important role in the early Christian community in Rome.

The middle-class women lived with their merchant spouses in apartments above the shops that lined the city streets. They could not afford country houses and frequented inns and temples instead. The majority of the population of Rome, the three fourths of the population who were slaves and freed men and women (Goitein 1967-71, vol. 1: 131), did not, however, frequent these places. They lived in airless, noisy, dusty tenements, six to eight stories high (Nash 1944). The women worked in all the little shops that crowded the city streets, and they served the well-to-do as dressmakers, hairdressers, midwives, and wet nurses. They kept Rome's inns and they even served as chariot drivers. There was no shortage of jobs for women. In Pompeii, there were drinking bars on every street corner and 40 bakeries in the town in 200 C.E. Many of the women must have worked in the bathhouses, of which there were 1,000 in Rome by 400 C.E. (Nash 1944).

The selling of sexual services was becoming highly differentiated. At the top of the status scale were the *delicatae* and *famosae*, the Roman equivalent of the hetairae. Then there were the *meretrices*, the officially registered prostitutes; within this group, there were innumerable special labels for women working in different parts of town and specializing in different types of services. Henriques (1962: 124) speaks of the sense of pride and freedom the women in this profession felt in Rome. The *prostibulae*, the unregistered prostitutes, were another matter. The hardships these poverty-pressed women suffered, often with families to support, will be a familiar theme in city life on into the twentieth century.

The situation of slaves was highly varied. On the one hand, we read that 25% to 40% of them were married; that many lived in their own homes, acquired property, and bought their freedom; that they were as well paid as free labor; that they could be initiated into the mystery cults; that there were many different kinds of political, social, and religious associations of slaves; and that they were a political force in the city. We read that educated slaves serving as nurses and teachers were often loved and revered by their young charges and given land and wealth when their pupils grew up. Auge, the ex-slave woman of Pompeii who gained wealth and fame, may have been one of these. We read of slave women co-conspiring with their mistresses in political conspiracies and of their courage in enduring torture when discovered—the slave Epicharis was the heroine of the Pisonian conspiracy. And there was the practice of Delphic manumission, whereby temples could free slaves (Barrow [1928] 1968: 35, 50; Rostovtzeff 1945: 13).

On the other hand, we know there was widespread industrial slavery, with the use of slaves in factories and mines. And, for every story of affection and loyalty between a slave woman and her owners, there are other stories of cruelty, bestiality, and sexual exploitation on the part of masters and mistresses toward their slaves. In general, however, there appears to have been a general decrease in slavery toward the end of the Roman era. Rostovtzeff (1945) says slave labor was becoming economically less profitable. This was less likely to apply to women, who were domestic slaves.

For the most part, slaves, ex-slaves, and working-class women and men lived in the "other Rome" (E. Morris 1974: 44), the crowded, dirty city full of violence, sex, and drunkenness. Yet Rome was an egalitarian city from a topographical point of view. The tenement houses of the workers alternated with the enclosed houses of the well-to-do and the apartment houses of the middle classes. "High and low, patricians and plebeian, everywhere rubbed shoulders without coming into conflict" (E. Morris 1974: 46). To the people who lived there, Rome was probably an exciting place.

By the middle of the second century C.E., with economic decline, Rome had become a "welfare society" and the streets were less fun. There were meal tickets for the plebeians and the poor, child-support payments for families, and festivals and circus games almost every other day. All shops shut at noon so the people could "play." Still, justice was not done, and women and men rioted because they did not get enough bread.

The brutalization displayed at almost daily circus spectacles of an assortment of naked slaves, captives, Christians, and other enemies of the state being torn apart by wild animals or gladiators must have created an odd, anomic state of mind in the average Roman. It certainly affected the women. Wealthy Roman matrons developed passions for gladiators—Eppia, a senator's wife, ran away with one (Auguet 1972: 165). Women were not just observers of combat but participants. While most gladiatrices fought privately, enough fought publicly so that finally combats were "forbidden in which women fought in companies with each other, or women with dwarfs" (de Beaumont 1929: 54).

On the whole, Roman women were well educated. All but the poorest had some kind of schooling. "The poorer ones went to school, the richer stayed at home and had tutors" (O'Faolain and Martines 1973: 70). In the homes of the well-to-do, the role of the mother as tutor to her children, which I mentioned as developing in Greece, was given considerable public attention. In fact, by 200 C.E., several writings on child development had appeared by Soranus, Galena, and others (de Mause 1974: 86), and poets include some tender references to children. Lucretius writes of the slow ripening to maturity of the child and contemplates his own death with sadness:

No longer will you happily come home
To a devoted wife, or children dear
Running for your first kisses, while your heart
Is filled with sweet unspoken gratitude.
(in de Mause 1974: 81)

Affection in family life was hardly invented in Roman times—similar passages can be found in Homer, with the warrior longing for his home and little ones—but the theme becomes more frequent in Roman literature, expressed in the context of a concern for child development. While the writings on the subject come from men,[4] they probably would not have appeared if mothering, as well as fathering, had not taken on new dimensions.

The double maternal and tutorial responsibilities of mothers, particularly in the middle and upper classes, set a standard of education for women that led to the tradition of scholarship among Christian women in the succeeding centuries. Wives performed household cult ceremonies together with their husbands. There were also a variety of mystery cults to belong to outside the home. Many of these were now run by men, however, with women taking subordinate roles. The sibylline sisterhood was turning into a brotherhood.

Figure 8.2. Young Woman From Pompeii With Stylus and Wax Tablet. Redrawn by HBR.

By 200 C.E., Isis temples had spread from Rome to France, Holland, and England. E. M. White tells us that these temples often had husband-wife priest teams, and she suggests that it was the Isis temples in Europe that provided the "black virgin" statues, as Isis worship shifted with the spread of Christianity (1924: 291-93, 315). The nearest equivalent in Rome to the old high priestess roles of the Eastern empires would be the vestal virgins, women of the highest rank, who during the term of their office (averaging 30 years) had a great deal of prestige and power. This power deteriorated as the empire itself deteriorated, especially after 348 C.E.

The institution of the vestal virgins represented the only opportunity for Roman women to hold public office in their own right, and the opportunity appears to have been a dangerous one. The vestals were active in politics but also vulnerable to accusations of unchastity (which led to the death sentence) when the Senate took offense at their activities. A compilation of all the magistrates of the Roman Republic referred to by name between 509 and 31 B.C.E. in contemporary annals includes, from 483 on, 18 vestals (Broughton 1952). Of these, 11 were accused of misconduct, 7 were executed, 1 hanged herself, and 3 were acquitted. Of the other 7, 5 were apparently not politically offensive to the Senate, and 2 were smart enough to remain politically active without getting denounced.[5] While details are scanty, it appears that most of the vestals denounced for misconduct (incest, unchastity) were really political enemies of the senators who denounced them. The intensity of feeling about vestal activities can be inferred from the fact that two of the vestals finally executed were first tried and acquitted, then retried and condemned.

The political power wielded by women from the second century B.C.E. followed the typical pattern of operating within elitist structures. The exercise of political power was to a considerable extent for women an underlife activity that they carried out in their capacity as mistress of a household. It is easy to be misled by this fact, however, into underestimating the amount of power these women had. The politics of the Republic has to be understood in the context of a relatively small group of consular families whose personal and family lives were totally involved in the life of the Republic. This meant, for example, that every marriage was a policy decision, and we know that women took a very active part in designing the marriage-alliance structures. Women are very conspicuous in the pages of *The Roman Revolution* (Syme 1939), a history of the Roman Republic. Because women did not have personal names until toward the end of this era, they are referred to only by family name and appear as the sister of X, the wife, daughter, or mother of Y. But, nameless though they often are, neither their power nor their independence should be underestimated. Servilia, who was Cato's half-sister, Brutus's mother, and Caesar's mistress,

Figure 8.3. Priestess of Isis, Roman. Redrawn by HBR.

was one of the most powerful persons in Rome, though her name appears in no list of magistrates.

The Romans' own "favorite woman" was Cornelia, the mother of the two Gracchi boys, Tiberius and Gaius. She had married a plebeian by choice over her father's disapproval and deliberately educated these two sons (out of a total of twelve offspring) to lead a reform movement of the plebeians against the patricians. Both sons died in the ensuing social unrest, but Cornelia remained a major international figure "visited by men of affairs and men of letters who came from near and far to pay her honor and discuss with her philosophy, letters and the times" (Beard 1946: 98-99). Ptolemy wanted to share the crown of Egypt with her, but she had her own priorities and refused remarriage. The monument erected to her by the Romans after her death indicates the reverence in which she was held. Helvia, the mother of Senecca, practiced a more emancipated version of the Cornelia tradition, and she taught her son to take the equality of the sexes seriously.[6] The woman Seneca married, Marcia, was another promoter of women's emancipation.

Not too long after Helva, a tradition of women's participation in the politics of the succession of emperors began. It continued past the fall of Rome into the politics of the Byzantine empire until 1453, the fall of Byzantium, and even then it continued on in the politics of Europe until the time of the French Revolution.[7] It is a strange, often brutalizing, tradition in which women fall victim to the depths as well as rise to the heights that empire politics permits.

At the turn of the Christian era, Agrippina, wife of Emperor Germanicus (died 19 C.E.), set a new place for women in politics, though still in the old heroic Roman woman's style. "She was," says Tacitus, "a greater power in the army than legates and commanders, and she, a woman, had quelled a mutiny which the emperor's authority could not check" (Mozans 1913: 25). Her daughter Agrippina II, mother of Nero, became Emperor Claudius's wife by persuading him to murder his first wife Messalina. Some writers suggest Agrippina II then had Claudius murdered so she could put Nero on the throne. An astute politician (who used the women's-rights advocate Seneca as her adviser), she was too fond of power for her son's comfort, and in the end he had her murdered. A number of mother-son political partnerships ended in murder. Women who think they are ambitious for their sons often wind up being ambitious for themselves, and disaster usually ensues. The tragedy of this double bind is one of the prices to be paid for underlife politics.

Livia Drusilla, wife of Augustus (Julius Caesar's nephew) and mother of Tiberius, ran into the same trouble that Agrippina II did. She was only exiled and ignored, however, not murdered. Another keen politician, she is sometimes referred to as the "Founder of the Empire" and threaded her way through a complex of intrigue that ended with her success in getting her son Tiberius crowned as emperor.

> At first all public documents were signed by her as well as by Tiberius, and letters on public business were addressed to her as well as to the emperor; and with the exception of her not appearing in person in the senate or the assemblies of the army and the people, she acted as if she were sovereign. (Mozans 1913: 302)

The Senate was about to heap honors on her when Tiberius decided he had had enough and simply moved his court right out of Rome to get away from her. She lived to be more than 80, a political isolate for the rest of her life. Tiberius would not even visit her on her deathbed.

In the next century, Julia Maesa ascended the throne herself and then successively put on the throne a pair consisting of each of her daughters plus a grandson as coregents. Each pair was murdered until the whole grisly sequence was brought to an end with a successful mother-son combination coming to the throne: Mammaea and her son Alexander, the St. Louis of antiquity. Another harmonious mother-son combination was Victoria and her son Victorinus, during a period of great disorganization when the armies controlled the election of emperors. Her own son and grandson were cut down before Victoria's eyes by angry soldiers, but "in contrition" the army asked her to devise a system of political succession for them and called her "The Mother of the Camps."

The whole fascinating story of the involvement of women in the politics of pre-Christian Rome is told in several studies and does not need to be given further detail here (Beard 1946: 301). The transition to the Christian era of Rome comes gradually. The wife and daughter of persecuting Emperor Diocletian (late second century) were both Christians and did what they could to soften the persecutions. Helena, the concubine mother of Emperor Constantine (late fourth

Figure 8.4. Portion of the Frieze of the Ara Pacis Augustae Procession, Gaius Caesar, Julia, and Livia, 13-9 B.C.E. Redrawn by HBR.

century), was the first woman to play a direct role in the support of Christianity. It is not clear whether she was born a Christian or converted, but she was both honored by her son and active in the empire, in spite of her equivocal initial social status. Burckhardt says Constantine was "said to have been accessible to her counsel always. . . . Purposely clothed with official honors, she spent her last years in charitable works, pious pilgrimages, and church foundations" ([1852] 1949: 276). She lived to be more than 80. One of her most memorable contributions to later history was to see the possibility in special sites in the Holy Land as pilgrimage destinations for Christians. She established church foundations at a number of such sites. She also offers one of the rare examples of a happy mother-son relationship in politics.

We have now strayed over the bounds set to this section, which was intended to cover the women of pagan Rome. As we look back over the role of the Roman matron, we can see the source of the role model of the "good wife" rediscovered in the Renaissance. Such a woman served the civic welfare by tending the hearth and educating her children. All her influence was indirectly exercised. In fact, the Renaissance version of the Roman matron downplayed the actual freedom Roman women had—no Roman matron ever went veiled in public, whereas many women in Renaissance Europe did. The concept of public social space becomes very ambiguous in the Roman setting, because, when the home becomes the training ground for the empire, the mother's role as teacher is no longer private. This is the message that the monument to Cornelia, mother of the Gracchis, conveys. This concept of the public role carried out in the private spaces of the home is, however, subject to distortions and manipulations. There are no safeguards for women in this position, and women in the new Christian era rightly rejected it. We will turn now to the aborted revolution in women's roles that Christianity initiated.

Women in the First Millennium of the Common Era

The New Apostolic Communities[8]

One clear message came across to the little communities that banded together to reflect on the teachings of the executed Nazarene, Jesus, and to prepare the way for the new society. Humankind was about to enter a new era that would restore women and men to the condition they were in before the Fall[9]—a situation of perfect love, perfect equality, and perfect justice. For women, this meant most particularly that the Christian woman is therefore no longer under the curse by which she was made servant to her husband and bound to a chain of painful pregnancies triggered by her desire for him. The Christian woman has become free. (Tavard 1973: 45)

The new era was to come very soon, and Jesus would return for its beginning. This meant there was no reason to carry on with old ways; everyone had to be ready for the new way. Some groups lived together in communes in expectation of the Coming, others continued to live in families. When new partnerships were formed, they were based on a new conception of the woman-man relationship. This new conception is described as nonsexual, and therefore celibate, but did not deny intimate companionship between women and men. The church at Corinth, in particular, tried the experiment of nonsexual common life, with the support of the apostle Paul. Human weakness and the delay in the coming of the new era led to problems.

If a man has a partner in celibacy and feels that he is not behaving properly towards her, if, that is, his instincts are too strong for him and something must be done, he may do as he pleases; there is nothing wrong in it; let them marry. But if a man is steadfast in his purpose, being under no compulsion, and has complete control of his own choice; and if he has decided in his own mind to preserve his partner in her virginity, he will do well. Thus, he who marries his partner does well, and he who does not will do better. (1 Cor. 7: 36-38, as quoted in Tavard 1973: 32)[10]

It seems at first that Paul was genuinely caught up in a new vision of sex-transcending relationships as a preparation for the new Kingdom. The letter to the Galatians is apparently one of Paul's early ones:

Before faith came, we were allowed to freedom by the law; we were being looked after till faith was revealed. . . . Now that that time has come we are no longer under that guardian. . . . All baptised in Christ, you have all clothed yourselves in Christ, and there are no more distinctions between Jew and Greek, slave and free, male and female, but all of you are one in Christ Jesus. (Gal. 3: 23-28)

In a way, what is being foreshadowed is the concept of the androgynous society, with minimal sex differentiation between women and men. The theme reappears in Christian writings sporadically through the centuries.

But pressures that arose from experiments such as those at Corinth were too much for Paul and the other elders of the early church. Paul, too, was a product of his times. Even in his advice to the Corinthians, he is clearly implying that the decision about maintaining virginity is the man's, not the woman's. How the women of Corinth viewed the situation we do not know. In any case, Paul appears to have given way under pressure. This is one way to explain all the injunctions about women wearing veils in church, being obedient to husbands, and so on. Probably a lot more in this vein than Paul himself ever put down was added by later emendation.

The basic issue the church has had to deal with ever since Jesus's time is that *the teaching of the new age has been given*, yet the Coming is continually postponed. Can individuals then live, in the historical present time, *as if the new era had come*? On the whole, the church has answered no to this question, but in the first three centuries many people—women most of all—answered yes.

To understand the meaning of that yes, we must place ourselves first of all back in the towns and villages of the Galilee hill country and look at the kind of people Jesus gathered around him: fisherfolk, artisans, women and men. The "authorized" New Testament lists 12 male disciples. The Gnostic version of the Gospels lists eight men and four women as disciples.[11] J. Morris (1973; who points out that the number 12 has special symbolic meanings in Judaism) suggests that there were 12 women disciples paralleling the 12 men.[12] In any case, we can be sure that there were more than 12 who moved around with Jesus and prepared to become teachers. We can also be sure that a number of his followers were women, because there are so many references to women in the Gospels.[13]

To these ordinary working folk, he taught detachment from conventional family roles in preparation for the Kingdom:

> The children of this world marry and are given in marriage, but those who are judged worthy of a place in the other world and in the resurrection of the dead do not marry, because they can no longer die. (Matt. 22: 30)

As it stands in the Gospels it sounds harsh:

> If someone comes to me, and does not hate his father and his mother and his wife and his children and his brothers and his sisters and even also his wife, he cannot be my disciple. (Matt. 10: 37)

The wording has probably been modified by succeeding generations of male scribes. To his followers, the teachings were not a rejection of society but an affirmation of a new way of living.

Visualize a growing nucleus of women and men living in community and traveling around with Jesus, holding meetings, visiting synagogues, talking with people on the streets. These are working-class people who do not have to observe elaborate social taboos. Jesus himself was very easy going and at home with women from all backgrounds, as with men. He was bringing together a new family for a new society, and sex was not at that historical moment on the agenda.[14] Nobody was antisex, they were "beyond" sex. Given that they expected the new dispensation almost momentarily, that was not an unreasonable frame of mind.

It is not difficult to imagine this cheerful band, full of anticipations about the new time. But what kept them going after Jesus's death? The women were the first who were sure they saw him return, then the men also saw him. This shared conviction would greatly intensify the feelings of togetherness of the group. They all flocked to Jerusalem to "see what would happen." It is explicitly mentioned that there were both women and men among the 120 (the number named in the story in Acts 1:15) who met each day in a second-story apartment in the city. All this built up to a gathering on the 50th day after Jesus's death, when people came together with special expectancy. The account in Acts tells us that tongues of fire appeared over the heads of the gathered women and men, and they spoke "with tongues." Peter said a few words at the end of the gathering:

> And it shall come to pass in the last days, saith God, I will pour out of my Spirit upon all flesh: and your sons and your *daughters* shall prophesy. . . . And on my servants and on my *handmaidens* I will pour out, in those days, of my Spirit; and they shall prophesy. (Acts 2: 17-18; italics added)

Think of what it meant for women who had lived the old Judaic pattern of subservience to men to have been part of this group. For them, the Age of the Holy Spirit had indeed already started.

It is significant that the Pentecostal experience happened in Jerusalem, where there were merchants from all over the Mediterranean and Near Eastern world, those who were

> Parthians, and Medes, and Elamites, and the dwellers in Mesopotamia, and in Judaea, and Cappadocia, in Pontus, and Asia, Phyrgia, and Pamphylia, in Egypt, and in the parts of Libya about Cyrene, and strangers of Rome, Jews and proselytes, Cretes and Arabians. (Acts 2: 9-11)

Merchants who had witnessed the event helped spread the news of this unusual occurrence. A number of these were certainly women. We know that there were a number of wealthy widows engaging in trade in the Mediterranean at this time; the presence of some of them at Jerusalem would not be unrelated to the fact that wealthy widows financed so many of the early churches.

The merchant women would have noticed the unusual number of women among the "120" and would have spoken to them afterward. For all their wealth and freedom, these merchant women must have faced many restrictions because of their sex in a male-dominated world. The new teachings would fall on receptive ears.[15]

Women Apostles

Jesus did not start a movement for women but a movement for humans. It is not surprising, however, that women were especially responsive to his ideas. Trapped in the isolation of a sometimes hostile family, women knew how insecure, unjust, and lonely the world was. It is not surprising that the Pentecostal story ends with the baptism of 3,000 persons who decided to remain together, holding all things common and selling their possessions (Acts 2: 44-47). At least half of them must have been women.[16]

They could not all stay around Jerusalem. Some had to keep on with business, to support those who went off to teach. In the end, they dispersed to the far corners of the Mediterranean world, individually and in small groups. A look at the map of Paul's journeys shows that he traveled the seacoast all the way from the seaport nearest to Jerusalem over to Rome, founding or visiting churches all the way. He also trekked inland at various points, but he never missed an important seacoast town. Consequently, Paul and his associates converted many merchants. Christianity followed the trade routes, and traders helped spread it. The traders' perspectives on the world would be different than those of laboring folk, so differing interpretations of the teachings began early. What made Christianity so attractive to traders? Perhaps the fact of their own experience of being outsiders, aliens, often discriminated against, in the various countries where they traded.[17]

Traders or laborers, it was the women who had the greatest stake in the new world and the greatest energy for missionary work. Whenever a new community was founded, the women took the vow of virginity as a matter of course. It was part of the whole liberation phenomenon.

Women did not necessarily feel they needed to be liberated from their husbands, however. A notable wife-husband team in the earliest church community consisted of Priscilla and Aquila. They must have been well-to-do because they had a house on Aventine Hill, which became the first Christian church in Rome. They left for Corinth during the persecutions and provided a house in Corinth for the church too. Priscilla's name is always mentioned first in the Bible, so it is assumed that she was the more active of the two in the community.

Wife, widow, or women outside of traditional families, the phenomenon of enthusiastic virginity gave the early church a lot of trouble. It was bad enough when the first groups of women and men apostles were traveling together, like Paul and Thecla, living "beyond sex" and teaching the new social vision. Many of the women cut their hair short and dressed like men to avoid trouble, but, if they were caught, they faced certain martyrdom for violating both law and custom (Eckenstein 1935: 72-120). The real trouble began when women from well-to-do pagan families streamed into the new church communities. Objections on the part of the families of the newly liberated women became increasingly vociferous. Thecla herself, of an upper-middle-class family, abandoned a fiancé and marriage plans to join the new sect. Her family and fiancé protested but did not forbid it. Thousands of young women were thrown in jail, and unknown numbers of them died by fire, sword, and wild beasts because furious fathers, husbands, and fiancés would rather see them dead than free of the proper duties of every woman.[18] The ferocity of the Roman persecution was not nearly so much because of the teachings about a "new god" as it was because of the practice of women vowing virginity and independence as a prelude to the new era. Think of the loss to the gross national product of the cities of the Roman Empire! Women were removed from the home not only as sex partners and breeders but as household producers.

It was easiest for the widows. There was no one to forbid their vows, and so the first association to grow up within the burgeoning Christian community of the Mediterranean was the Order of Widows, which flourished all through the second century. Early in the century, there were 1,500 members of the Order of Widows in Rome and 3,000 in Antioch (J. Morris 1973: 7). The first churches in Rome and in other major cities, the *domus ecclesia*, were the homes donated by wealthy widows to the local church community.[19] The very earliest assembly places, before Rome became a major center, would be in humbler houses. All the Christian communities mentioned in the Acts of the Apostles are mentioned as meeting in women's houses: "The church in the house of Chloe, in the house of Lydia, in the house of the mother of Mark, in the house of Nympha, in the house of Priscilla [and her husband Aquila]" (J. Morris 1973: 1). In Rome, by the beginning of the next century, another Priscilla, of a wealthy senatorial family, was to give a catacomb to her Christian community for the burial of the dead.

Despite the horror they aroused, both the rebellious young women dressed in men's clothes and the stately widows were in fact very productive members of society. The wealthier of them provided housing and resources not only for meeting places but for schools and hospitals. Many of the women became healers, and it is noteworthy that a number of Roman women doctors were converted to Christianity. St. Theodosius, one of the best known, was martyred in the persecutions under Diocletian.

Status was no protection against being thrown to the lions. Those women already trained as doctors before conversion helped train others, so the association of Christianity with the foundation of hospitals and the practice of healing began very early. There were also herbalists and faith healers. The fact that the entire spectrum of the healing profession should find its way into the first Christian circles is an indication of the diversity of backgrounds from which women entered the communities (Mozans 1913: 271-72).

The Christian belief in the Resurrection led to a rejection of the Roman practice of cremation, so women learned embalming. This was exclusively a woman's occupation from the beginning (Eckenstein 1935: 97). They also fed the living. As the Roman welfare system gradually broke down toward the end of the empire, feeding and helping the poor became one of the major occupations of the Christian communities.

Meeting together for meals was an important part of cementing the bonds of community. The earliest communion rituals were freely participated in by everyone, with no distinction as to special authority or status of any individuals. This denial of special priesthood roles was especially scandalous to the fellow Romans—it was bad enough for men but that the women should participate too! "The very women of the heretics, how bold! who teach, argue, perform exorcisms, promise cures, baptize. Their ordinations are inconsiderate, trivial, changeable. . . . Thus today one is a bishop, tomorrow another" (Dietrick 1897: 42).

In the beginning, Christianity was a challenge to the concept of priesthood as well as to the subjection of women. When specific religious assignments were necessary, they were a dangerous burden rather than a privilege, given the level of persecution in the second and third centuries. There was also a wide variety of beliefs within "the fold," because there was as yet no canon of Christian books. "The majority of Christians worked in scores of perfectly independent cliques, each one of which was fully as 'authoritative' as another" (Dietrick 1897: 38).

Growth in numbers and increase in respectability eventually combined to produce a formal organization of corporate life and a hierarchy of authority. As the patterns of the larger society took over, men's authority roles became more evident. Also, after the "peace of the church" in 313, there was a great increase in membership. Many women who joined knew nothing of the earlier Pentecostal experience or the commitment to celibacy. They were more likely to accept the traditional authority roles of men (Nugent 1941). While women retained the role of deacons for some centuries, they were excluded from the priestly role as soon as it developed. The church fathers consciously referred to priestess roles as being pagan and unthinkable in a Christian church.

Figure 8.5. Women Preparing and Shrouding the Body for Burial, Fifteenth Century C.E. Redrawn by HBR.

Heretics and Martyrs

The gradual concentration of power within the church did not go unnoticed by women—or by men. The heresies that developed between 100 C.E. and the Council of Nicea in 325 C.E., when a secular emperor, Constantine, made deviation from church doctrine a political issue, all had to do with reactions to authoritarianism, sexism, and corruption within the church. Before discussing these issues, it should be pointed out that the majority of women did *not* pay attention to such matters (nor did men). They found the deaconess role a busy and fulfilling one, and matters of ecclesiastical hierarchy seemed remote and uninteresting.

Those who continued to take literally the doctrine of the new era found themselves at odds with the rest of the community. Marcion, a rich ship builder born in 85 C.E., whose father had been the head of the Christian community at Antiope, decided early that Christians in Rome were falling from the faith. He attracted a group of women and men who wished to be ready for the Second Coming and not get led off into marrying and accumulating worldly wealth. In the Marcionian community, there was complete equality of women and men, and women performed baptisms as they had in the earlier days of all the Christian communities. There was also absolute celibacy. Although Marcionians were expelled from the Roman church in 144, so powerful was the appeal of this community that Marcionist churches were still to be found in the Near East until the sixth century (Nigg 1962: 60-72).

Another perfectionist who wanted to "stay ready" was Montanus, who also kept to the original tradition of equal participation of women and men in the church. He began teaching soon after 155 C.E., and many women who saw themselves losing out in the mainstream Christian community joined him. Priscilla and Maximilla were two famous Montanist prophetesses of the late 200s. Again the rebels were expelled, in 177, but the Montanist churches lasted for several more centuries. Nigg (1962: 3-120) recounts the stories of a series of "heretic" leaders who all represented a return to primitive Christianity (this was already necessary only one lifetime after the death of the teacher) and who all attracted women who preferred a rigorously ascetic life and equality in service over soft living in the cities. (Bishops by then were purportedly condoning women having lovers.)

Perhaps the heresy most powerfully associated with equality between women and men is the Gnostic heresy.[20] This never resulted in a sect but was a philosophical thread that linked the pagan mystery religions to Christianity and was an important influence on Paul in the early days of his ministry (Nigg 1962: 26-42). The Gnostic Gospels give a very prominent place to women, especially to Mary Magdalene, thus moderating the exclusive emphasis of the mainstream church on Mary, the mother of Jesus. We have already mentioned the Gnostic tradition in which there were eight men and four women among the disciples (or parallel sets of twelve). Because many Roman women were already adherents of the mystery religions, it was easy for them to become attracted to Gnostic Christianity both in its mystical aspects and in its recognition of the equality of women and men.

During the first and second centuries, when persecution was at its height, martyrs came from the mainstream and heretic sects alike. Famous among the Montanist martyrs are the Carthagenian Perpetua, the prophetess, and her slave girl Felicitas. Vibia Perpetua was a 21-year-old "matron of good family" nursing a new baby, and her slave Felicitas was pregnant, when they were arrested. Perpetua's firm stand first with her family and then with the authorities, as everyone tried to get her to make the required ritual sacrifice to the emperor to save her life, and the striking visions she recounted make this one of the most vivid and convincing stories in *The Acts of the Martyrs* (Musurillo 1972: 106-31).[21] Felicitas, weeping with pain during childbirth in the prison, yet calm the next day when facing the lions, is unforgettable. Fifteen-year-old Blandina of Gaul, who was fearless in the arena though her mistress had feared she could not manage the ordeal because she was so young, is another of the more memorable heroines. Then there are the three young women of Thessalonia—Agape, Irene, and Chione—who escaped to the mountains to establish a women's religious community. They were found and brought to trial for not sacrificing to the emperor. The record of their answers is testimony to the keen intellectual capacities of the women who were being attracted to Christianity (Musurillo 1972: 281-93).

One of the most interesting characters among women of the early church, and one who was not martyred (though she had several narrow escapes), was Thecla, Paul's traveling companion in the ministry. She lived a long, active life for the church, and the site of her final years of retirement in Seleucia became the first monastery for women. The Acts of Thecla is another of the vivid apostolic stories; Thecla's warmth and liveliness as a person come through clearly (Tavard 1973: 55-56).

These vibrant women were something new under the sun. The men who accepted them as fellow workers were a special breed too. Here was the nucleus of the new society.

The shell of the old world was crumbling. Rome was in decline, but the Second Coming was continually being postponed. Gradually, some important changes took place in the rapidly growing church. Now that it was clear that earthly life would be continuing for a while under the old dispensation, family life had to be reevaluated. From the beginning, there had been many husband-wife converts to the new community. Those who had already borne children continued to care for them. Presumably, the women who traveled in the ministry left their small children to be cared for by others in the community, as Quaker women did in the seventeenth century. Couples who did not yet have children vowed celibacy. Soon the wisdom of celibacy began to be questioned. Family values were strong in Roman, Jewish, and Greek traditions, and Mary, the mother of Jesus, was increasingly put forth as a role model for women. In place of celibacy came the duty to raise children to make a strong Christian community on earth in preparation for the Second Coming. Christians with pagan partners were urged to fulfill their partners' needs but not to let this interfere with their prayer life. It was partly over the issue of celibacy that the heretic sects were being expelled from the church.

The Concept of Celibacy

Gradually the idea of two callings evolved. One was the calling to marriage and procreation, to prepare for the Kingdom through the nurture of children. The other was the calling to celibacy, to service outside family life.

The call, or at least the social pressure, to family life is not hard to explain. But the call to celibacy is. The term *call* implies there is a strong inward prompting that leads an individual to make such a choice. That inward prompting, however, may be fostered by such a strong outward pressure that the autonomous act of choice is no longer clear. This tended to happen with celibacy in the Christian church.

Celibacy and eunuchism historically developed together. An aside on eunuchism is necessary here for us to understand the whole phenomenon of celibacy. Whatever the first origins of the practice of castration, Roman history has it that Queen Sammuramat of Assyria (811-808 B.C.E.) was the first person to castrate men (Penzer 1935: 125). Given that there are frequent references in the Old Testament to eunuchs, the practice must have been well established in Mesopotamia before Queen Sammuramat's time. Its rapid spread through the Near East was due to the fact that it was a useful device for ensuring loyal service to a king or queen. Eunuchs, it was reasoned, would not seek private gain because there could be no offspring to whom they could pass rewards. Cyrus was the first "modernizer" to make use of this device when he captured Babylonia in 538 B.C.E. (Penzer 1935: 137-38). From that time on, we find the castration of civil servants in the Persian, Hellenic, Roman, and Byzantine empires.

The single-mindedness-of-service theme would naturally make the institution of eunuchs attractive to religious organizations, and so we find the tradition of eunuch priests established at the Ephesian temple of Artemis.[22] From there, the eunuch priest tradition spread to Rome. This is the background of the Christian involvement with castration, which is the most drastic form of celibacy. "There are eunuchs who have made themselves eunuchs for the sake of the kingdom of heaven" (Matt. 19: 12) is the saying of Jesus that, taken literally, has produced a series of sects of eunuchs lasting right up to the 1700s, when the Skoptai sect of Christian eunuchs was rediscovered in Russia (Penzer 1935: 136). The castration of boys for the papal choir in the Sistine Chapel in Rome was not really religious castration but part of a general secular practice for ensuring male soprano voices.[23] There have been eunuch patriarchs and possibly eunuch popes. The confusion of castration in the service of a deity with castration as a form of punishment similar to slitting noses, cutting off ears and hands, and putting out eyes, as practiced in Persia and the Byzantine empire and also in Rome itself, makes it particularly difficult to look at this issue objectively. It was widely enough practiced in Rome in the first century C.E. for Emperor Domitian to forbid it entirely. Mohammed also forbade it.

As a form of asceticism, castration is unequivocally condemned today. But the principle of celibacy as a means to single-minded service to the deity remains. As we have seen, it seemed a very natural form of behavior to the first Christians, because the Kingdom was coming soon. When it became a matter of deliberate choice, a way of living in the world, it came to have a different meaning.

For those not already familiar with the best traditions of voluntary celibacy, this may seem like a new form of slavery for women. Because of the number of other expectations attached to a woman's sex-partner role, however, freedom from sex can seem like liberation—not just freedom from heterosexual sex but freedom from all human dependencies as expressed in sexual relations. It follows that a religious call to celibacy can be, and is, experienced by lesbians as well as heterosexually oriented women.

The celibacy choice is somewhat easier for women to live with than it is for men, perhaps mainly because of different social conditionings. One does not read in the writings of holy women about their struggles with tempting visions of beautiful men, although the counterpart struggle is standard fare in the writings of holy men.[24] Today we are very conscious of the pathological elements that may enter into decisions for celibacy, but this should not blind us to the simple fact that in all times there have been "passionate" individuals who chose it freely. They choose it not because they are "undersexed" but because they have "another love," a love that spills over to people around them in a somehow different expression of human sexuality.

A woman may choose celibacy, then, to be free of male domination, or because she loves God, or because it is the only way to get into a desirable career such as those offered by the religious orders for women that began springing up in the third and fourth centuries. Or she might be forced to convent life by a family unwilling to give her a large enough dowry for marriage. Much has been written about all the sex that went on in convents, all the strangled babies, and so on, to point up the fraudulent aspects of celibacy for (some? many? most?) of the women so cloistered. Some of the writing is humorous and delightful, as in Boccacio's *Decameron*; some of it angry (McCabe 1931: 52); and some wavering between salaciousness and social commentary, as in Aretino's *Dialogues*.

No doubt, the full range of human behaviors can be found in convents—as elsewhere. It is a pity that women have not had more choices open to them. But, for a significant number of women, the convent was not a prison but a place to live and work that provided them with a sense of fulfillment and a freedom of action in the world they could never otherwise have had. Now we will turn to the evolution of that specialist religious role for women, the nun.

Evolution of the Nun's Role

The specialist religious role for women took two forms from the beginning. There were the women who served the churches and cathedrals, and there were the women who lived apart in a life of prayer. The Order of Widows and Virgins belonged to the first type. These women increasingly lived together in small groups, as, for example, those who lived with the widow Dorcas (Acts 9: 36). In the early days, when Christianity was still a "movement," one could say that these women were doing the practical work of building the institutional base for the new society. They worked closely with their brothers in this church activity. In time, they were formally recognized and ordained to special service and became known as "canonesses." Some of them continued to live in ordinary apartments near the cathedral, simply making their work at the cathedral the major activity of their lives. Others came to live together in a formal community, developing special vows and a rule for community life to deal with the problems of living together. St. Augustine's sister was the head of one of these houses, and his letter of advice to her about how to handle communal difficulties has often been considered the first "rule" for religious women.[25] But the work of canonesses was always "in the world": teaching religion, running schools, caring for the sick, and providing other needed services. They also performed the liturgical services, including choral singing, for the cathedral. Some of them worked entirely outside the church structure, such as the Lady Fabiola, who founded a hospital at Ostia and, according to the eulogies at her death, revolutionized health care in Rome (Mozans 1913: 272-73). For the most part, however, health care came to be associated with residential centers and, later, convents.

The other group of religious specialists were the anchoresses or hermits, those who lived in solitude, often in the desert. They were as much a part of the Christian movement in the third century as were their sisters and brothers who worked in the city churches. The journey to the desert was one of the most important developments in the early Christian communities. A small trickle became by the fourth century a stream of thousands of women and men who sought out desert life. At first, each one lived in solitude, then small communities were formed, then ever larger ones. In spite of their commitment to physical isolation, they were often in touch with the city; they were trying, in fact, often desperately, to help salvage the vision of the Kingdom that seemed in danger of fading in the midst of the corruption of Rome. They perceived themselves to be undertaking a highly specific task of spiritual reconstruction on behalf of the entire church, through prayer and contemplation. Many of those who chose the desert had been active in the city first, like St. Anthony, who had founded a House of Virgins before deciding in 280 C.E. to go to the desert. (He put the House of Virgins under the leadership of his younger sister before he left.)

A fascinating aspect of the growth of the monastic movement is the number of close brother-sister relationships that emerge in the leadership of the movement. The story of spiritual brother-sister relationships—that is, spiritual friendships—is also an interesting one in the movement, but siblings themselves play an important role in the first few generations. This indicates something about the quality of relationship within the families of those who joined the movement.

The warmth and affection between husbands and wives, brothers and sisters, parents and children, in the families of the early Christian communities was to have a profound effect on the monastic movement itself. The family became the model for the monastery.[26] Among monks, the abbot was to be father and mother to his flock. Among nuns, the abbess had a similar parenting role. Spiritual guidance was to become that compound of parental tenderness and stern authority that reflects the basic conflict between the acceptance of the human and insistence on transformation that characterizes Christianity. The sternness was softened by the special love that not infrequently developed between women in convents. There are many beautiful letters in monastic annals describing such love, letters that have their counterparts among monks in monastic orders as well (Boswell 1980: 220). A spiritual lesbian culture could flourish in convents as well as in the world outside, and indeed there would be times when it found physical expression, although male church authorities discouraged this.

The Monastic Movement

One of the many frustrations in trying to write the underside of history is that the rise of the monastic movement is written almost entirely in terms of men; yet women were equally important in its development. The desert fathers are well recorded; the desert mothers are not. The first women and men to make the journey to the desert were very much a part of the upper classes: wealthy, well educated, experienced in the world, often already in a high position of authority. Later, all sorts of people went, including robbers, outlaws, and thugs. The major movement was into the Egyptian desert, although Syria also housed desert seekers. The problem of sheer numbers as well as of diversity of intention drove the original solitaries to form cenobitic, or communal, living groups.

How does one give a flavor of that life in the desert? It was hot. It was dry. It was uncomfortable. There was little food. People lived in caves, in holes in the ground, in twig shelters. If others came near them, they moved further into the desert to gain more solitude. They gloried in every discomfort. Either discomfort or solitude might seem hard enough by itself. Why both together? To become "new in mind and body" (Lacarrière 1964: 205-15). This drastic stripping process was the only way "to gain insight into heavenly things," said Cassian (Workman [1913] 1962: 33). It is a measure of the despair these women and men felt about the way society was going that they had to struggle so hard to regain the vision and insight that Jesus had left with them.[27]

The real impetus for the monastic movement came *after* the official recognition of Christianity by the Roman Empire through Emperor Constantine's Edict of Milan, 313 C.E. This is the point at which the followers of Christianity go from being a persecuted minority to a triumphant, power-wielding majority. The rapidity with which key clerics in Rome adopted all the Roman administrative patterns and incorporated them into the church, keeping both the political and the legal infrastructure alive after the "barbarians" took over Rome, alienated many of those who felt a strong commitment to the Christian vision of a new social order. Workman ([1913] 1962: 6 ff.) suggests that the entire monastic movement in its origins should be seen as a protest against the development of a powerful ecclesiastical hierarchy in Rome.[28] Women would have even more reason to protest that hierarchy than would men, because it was crowding them out more than it was crowding the men out. Monasteries were alternative societies in a world where alternatives seemed to be disappearing.

When there are choices, there are risks, however. It was in the desert that so many monks developed their terrible phobias about women. Nuns stayed on a more even keel, as is delightfully illustrated by the following story:

> A monk ran into a party of hand-maids of the Lord on a certain journey. Seeing them he left the road and gave them wide berth. But the Abbess said to him: If you were a perfect monk, you would not even have looked close enough to see that we were women. (Merton 1960: 32)

As more people flocked to the desert, the need for those already there to care for the sick and needy and to provide teaching grew to the point at which certain individuals, like Pachomius, felt called to bring together disciples to live in a community and organize, however simply, their prayer life and their

Figure 8.6. Hermitess in Holy Grotto. Redrawn by HBR.

service life. Pachomius had a sister, Mary, who initiated the formation of communities for women at Tabbennisi and Tesminé, not far from his settlement. Thalis, a strong-minded woman ascetic, founded 12 convents in Antinoe. Other women joined monasteries already established by men; Shenute headed a desert community of 2,000 monks and 1,800 nuns. The settlement founded by Thecla near Seleucia, mentioned earlier as possibly the first monastic center, became the center for a group known as Apotactics, which was later declared heretical. "It included cells for men and for women and was ruled over by a woman who is referred to as a woman deacon. It enjoyed a high standing in the fourth century" (Eckenstein 1935: 85).

The development of communities did not replace the solitaries. Among the *inclusi*, who lived shut up in caves or cells, were the famous "harlots," like Thais, "the loveliest courtesan in Alexandria," and Pelagia, the beautiful actress of Antioch. Thais appears to have been forced into a sealed cell by a harsh prelate, and the story is not an edifying one, but Pelagia is one of those who chose the new kind of life freely. Here, too, the sexism of the fourth century becomes clear, given that Pelagia "passed" as a hermit in a cell on the Mount of Olives and was widely venerated as Pelagius. It was not discovered until her death that she was a woman. The monks would have hidden the information, but it got out (Waddell 1957: 173 ff.). In Syria, there were women anchorites like St. Marana and St. Cyriaca, who wore chains for 42 years as heavy as any human being could bear, for the sake of penance (Lacarrière 1964: 153).

While pious writings sometimes describe these inclusi as weepy milk-sops, and some may indeed have been so, for the most part, these were the fiercest and proudest of women, laying their lives on the line to reconcile vision and reality. How many of them felt they had to renounce female-ness and become like a man to do it, like Pelagia, we shall never know. We do know of Eugenia, the daughter of an Alexandrian prefect, a Greek and Latin scholar whose studies led her to Christianity in the third century and who cut her hair and entered a monastery as a man. Many years later, after she had long served as abbot, her sex was discovered by chance. (Note the portrayal of St. Eugenie in Figure 8.7. Accused of rape by the woman to her left, she opens her robe, revealing to the abbot on her right that she could not have committed the crime of which she is accused because she is a woman.) Women also lived as men in the desert caves (Eckenstein 1935: 89-91). More of the desert fathers may have been women than we have dreamed of—discoveries of this kind of "passing" are rare; stories about it rarer still. The early era of fuller participation by women in the religious community was over, it seems, and women were already considered sec-ond-class citizens of the Kingdom of Heaven.

Among those who founded communities of religious women in the 300s were St. Augustine's sister and Pachomius's sister, already mentioned;

Theobisia, the sister of Gregory
of Nyssa; Macrina, the sister of
St. Basil; Marcella, the sister of
St. Ambrose; Florentine, sister
of the two bishops of Seville; and
Marguerite, sister of Honoratius.[29]
In each case, we know of them
because their brothers wrote
about them. How many women
who did not have famous brothers to memorialize them also
founded religious houses? The
case of Macrina is particularly
interesting because, according
to Joan Morris at least, she was
the author of the Rule of St.
Basil, supposed to be the first
formally enunciated monastic
rule; her brother took it over
from her when he founded his
monastery several years after
she founded hers (1973: 13-14).

Figure 8.7. St. Eugenie. Redrawn by HBR.

One of the few "quoted"
desert mothers is Synclectica, a
woman of the Macedonian aristocracy who lived as a recluse near Alexandria
and became known as a great teacher, even in her solitude. The quotations I
have discovered from her are striking, fiery declarations. She lived to be 80.
Quotations from her are found in Waddell (1957: 68, 85, 95, 110). Abbess
Matrona and Abbess Sara are two other mothers quoted in Waddell. Asceticism, solitude, and longevity seem to go together for these early Christians.

Secular and Organizational Leadership of Christian Women

In addition to the women who created their own settings, there were
the wealthy Roman matrons of the famous "Aventine Circle" that formed
around St. Jerome. Marcella of this circle founded a convent on her own
estate. Another group, including the wealthy widow Paula and her daughter Eustochium, removed with St. Jerome to Jerusalem, where they formed
a convent and worked closely with Jerome in one of the earliest recorded
spiritual-intellectual partnerships. Paula and Eustochium not only supplied him with all the books he needed for his work but are said to be
themselves the translators of the Psalter ascribed to him and coauthors

with him of the Vulgate translation of the Bible. Jerome himself freely acknowledged the partnership, and his great indebtedness to them, in numerous letters and writings, and he dedicated many of his works to them.

Such circles did not exist unchallenged: "The friendship of Jerome for these ladies led to scandal in later years. In the dedications of his writings it was common for scribes to scratch out their names and substitute 'venerable brothers'!" (Workman [1913] 1962: 118). We are not often told so explicitly about the erasing of women from history.[30]

Jerusalem was an exciting place in those days. Melanie the Elder (345-410), one of the richest women in Antioch, became a disciple of a contemporary of Jerome's, Rufinus. She disposed of her Antioch estate, freeing 8,000 slaves (Levy 1967: 91), and established a convent on the top of the Mount of Olives. Her granddaughter, Melanie the Younger (383-439), was an international figure in intellectual circles, well known at the courts of Rome and Constantinople, but lived as an ascetic. After extensive travels, she retired to Palestine to establish two monasteries. There is a biography of her by a priest associate, Geronios.

Ladies of the Roman aristocracy played a very important part in the development of the international networks of the Christian community in the fourth century. We hear a lot about "rich lady tourists" who traveled from monastery to monastery, received by abbots as honored guests (de Carreaux 1964). Their status as Roman ladies apparently guaranteed them access everywhere. Lady Etheria of Aquitaine was one of the more notable of these. The book she wrote in 385 about her pilgrimage to the Holy Land is a valuable period document (Tavard 1973: 91; Newton 1968: 44-48).

All of the women just mentioned lived and worked in the 300s. There was an amazing explosion of interest and activity on the part of the women elite of the Roman Empire during that one century. Many of them, like Melanie the Elder, were women of affairs with substantial financial enterprises to oversee, and they therefore brought a know-how to their participation in the church that reinforced their already high status. These women were founding convents in the very century that Christianity became the official religion of the Roman Empire. The political power that accrued to the church as the old political machinery of the secular empire was falling to pieces also to some extent accrued to the convents. Women had a platform from which to work that they might never otherwise have acquired. Instead of individual women operating each from her own family base within the aristocracy, women built up a network of convents across Europe.[31] They thus developed an independent power that enabled them to retain a substantial measure of autonomy long after the greater equality accorded women in the earlier centuries had been withdrawn by the male power structure.

The battle on the part of "women religious" to regain the earlier freedom of action began at the close of the next century, in the late 400s. This was the century in which Benedict of Nursia developed a new monastic model balancing spiritual and physical labor. In itself a tremendous "reform" in modifying the excesses of desert asceticism, its function in regard to women religious was somewhat different. It tended to be used as an instrument to urge all religious women into a pattern of seclusion, whether their calling was in that direction or not.

Women of the upper class who wished neither to be active in the world nor to enter a religious order still had some freedom of choice in the matter, if they were of high enough status. Benedict's sister Scholastica, for example, lived a life of solitary retirement near Benedict's mastery without being either an inclusi or in a convent.[32] Scholastica is particularly well known because of her warm lifelong relationship with her brother. How many other women had this kind of freedom we don't know.

The canonesses described earlier had an active vocation of teaching and social service, and retirement from the world was no part of their intention. The freedom of these women, however, was in direct contradiction to the revived social tradition that valued the woman in the home. If women were to continue to be called to the religious life, at least they should be decently secluded in the familistic environment of the convent and not be intruding on the public space of men. Because many women probably did not have any strong feelings about their religious "life-style," it was not hard for religious advisors to guide them into Benedictine convents. Here the emphasis would usually be on prayer and study, with some handwork. They might also teach children inside the convent.

There was no power struggle until after the 900s, when local church authorities tried to control the activities of the independent-minded canonesses in their institutes and to control the royal convents founded by queens and princesses. When bishops confronted women accustomed to wielding authority, the fur began to fly. That story will be told in the next chapter (Chapter 1 in Volume 2). The pope, it should be noted, supported independent monastic authority for women every time it became an issue. From Rome's perspective, an autonomous constituency answerable only to Rome was valuable. Nuns received just as much support from the papacy as monks did in these jurisdictional disputes. It was not until 1874 in Spain that the final blow was struck against the authority of the woman as abbess.

In the meantime, two separate and distinct things were happening within the "women's movement" in the church during the second half of the first millennium of the Common Era. On the one hand, those women who were already inclined toward the scholarly life turned their convents into centers of learning, with fine libraries and high traditions of scholarship. (Daughters of the poor could enter all but the royal convents, but mostly the nuns came from the upper classes.) On the other hand, women who were inclined to a more active involvement in the political life of the new European kingdoms that flourished after the fall of Rome worked with the royal houses of the Goths and the Franks in Christianizing the pagan populations. The scholarly and the activist tradition were not antithetical but complementary.

The real contrast was not between scholars and activists but between the women, both religious and secular, and the sword-happy men of the new European kingdoms. The women were working toward a conversion of ways of thinking, social values, and life-styles. The men were concerned with consolidating political power and used forcible conversion to Christianity as a means to that end. The church itself was already committed to interlocking structures of church and state and to the use of political power for its ends. This, of course, is an oversimplified picture. Many ecclesiastics were concerned with spiritual and social values, and there were certainly women who enthusiastically and ruthlessly used brute force for purely political goals. On balance, however, more women were engaged in a teaching enterprise among the very heterogeneous tribal populations of Europe, and more men were engaged in military action. The first major opportunity for large-scale innovation by the church came about 500, with a solid administrative organization available to it after the fall of Rome. By then, however, the church had reverted to patriarchal domination models for social change.

The Politicization of Christianity: 500-1000 C.E.

In 400 C.E., Rome still had 2,000 officials in the Prefecture of Gaul (Thrupp 1967: 130). In 476, Rome "fell" and, by the end of the century, that infrastructure had crumbled. The medieval historian Lot puts some very complex history very simply by stating that Justinian (reigned 527-65) recaptured the fallen empire and instituted caesaro-papism, or the joint rule of church and state.[33] It seemed clear that the Second Coming was indefinitely postponed, and the church saw the value of Roman law, "adopted it and fitted itself into the framework of ancient legal institutions" (Lot 1961: 49). The process of adaptation succeeded all too well. Lot describes it thus:

> The church becomes accustomed to employing the secular arm for conversions. It grows impaired and loses its powers of assimilation. Personal propaganda will cease from about the fifth century. Henceforth Christianity

will try and obtain recruits only by angling for the confidence of barbarian kings and their courts. Once the ruler has been won over, he is used
for imposing the faith on his subjects by gentle or violent pressure. . . .
Further the victory was too swift and complete. These herds of Roman
and later of barbarian pagans, thrust by consent or force into the bosom
of the church, debased and changed Christian feelings. (1961: 50)

In 500 C.E., there were the competing kingdoms of the Ostrogoths
(Aryan heretics), under Theodoric, and the Franks (pagans), under Clovis.
Justinian was laying the groundwork from Constantinople of what was to
be the new Holy Roman Empire. By 800, the marriage of church and state
was—for a time—complete, with the pope crowning Charlemagne as
emperor of this new Christian empire. All Europe had been converted to
Christianity except the far north. Yet, just 100 years later, Europe was
gasping from Moslem attacks from the Mediterranean and Viking attacks
from the north. The year 1000, which many of the Christian faithful in
Europe devoutly believed would inaugurate the long-postponed Second
Coming, was instead an exhausted interlude, with 500 years of bloody
fighting behind and the Crusades ahead.

The church was not buying any new models of social change. Even the
old educational system of pagan Rome, which provided training in literacy
for all but the poorest, was nearly gone. All that remained of the vision that
was to make a new world was a chain of monasteries and convents across
Europe. Nuns and monks were the only teachers left.[34]

Now let us examine the activities of the women religious who provided
leadership and continuity during this bleak period. In what was to become
a scholar-abbess tradition, Caesaria was one of the first women scholars to
found a convent in Europe (at Arles, in the early 500s). Her brother, a cleric,
helped write the rule for the new house and seems to have been the more
organizationally inclined of the two. He had great reverence for his sister
and writes to her, "I was a lazy youth, you followed learning from the
cradle" (Duckett 1938: 58).

Hilda of Whitby (early 600s) is one of the most interesting women
monastics of an era with many outstanding women. Of royal blood, she
lived on her own to the age of 34 without getting married or taking vows,
an unusual situation. At 34, she evidently decided to enter monastic life
and was almost immediately given the care of the 1-year-old daughter of
King Oswia, who had promised his daughter to a convent if he should win
in battle. (He did.) The estates that went with the royal infant were very
extensive, and Hilda built the double monastery of Whitby at the center
of these estates. Taking in both nuns and monks, she made it one of the
finest centers of scholarship in England. When the highest religious body

in Britain convened in council at Whitby, she was a member of the presidency of the council. The secretariat of the council was headquartered at her monastery.

England had many double monasteries ruled by abbesses toward the end of the first millennium. These monastic foundations were sometimes the size of whole counties, including a number of villages and churches. The abbess was the civil as well as the religious ruler of the area, collected taxes and administered justice, and was not under the jurisdiction of the bishop but answered directly to king and pope (J. Morris 1973: chap. 5).

Caesaria and Hilda link closely to Roman traditions. In Germany, another tradition is tapped, as a long succession of scholar-activist nuns begin with the work of St. Lioba in the mid-700s. The cultural background for Lioba's work in Germany lies in the priestess-prophetess functions of the Germanic tribes. While there is no direct link between the German abbesses and the older prophetesses, Weinhold (1882) may be correct in pointing out the relevance of the earlier tradition. Letters were considered the women's province in many of the "modernizing" tribes in the early Middle Ages, and women of the tribal aristocracies learned to read and write Latin, Greek, and French along with their tribal tongues. The pre-Christian prophetesses themselves are discussed later in this chapter, in the section on women's political roles in the European kingdoms.

St. Lioba was Anglo-Saxon. Orphaned in infancy, she was brought up in a monastery and received her training in England. Greatly revered for her holiness, she became abbess of Tauberbisch of Sheim and may have headed several other convents also. She is described as very beautiful, an outstanding intellect, and an avid reader. She was a favorite political adviser to the princes of Germany.

On the more activist side is the nun Radegunde (died 587 C.E.), daughter of the tribal chief of the Thuringians and captured by King Clothair of the Franks as a child. Here we see the independence of the barbarian woman. She was kept at a villa to be educated, tried to escape but did not succeed, and was married to the king against her will at the age of 12. She proceeded to create an independent life for herself at court and founded a major religious settlement for women at Poitiers. At court, she paid little attention to the king, presiding over her own table as a woman of learning and entertaining visiting scholars. Busy with her own charitable and educational work, she followed her own timetable and was often late for court events, the chronicler tells us. When the king murdered her brother, she simply left the court. Subsequently, she persuaded a frightened bishop to consecrate her as a deaconess.

Cool-headed in bloody times, Radegunde built a solid fortress-villa to protect her 200 nuns on the estate at Poitiers. She taught and looked after the nuns and the people settled on her extensive lands. She was also in correspondence with all the kings and queens of Europe and was continually playing the peacemaker role, trying to avert wars; this was a period of many family murders among the royalty with whom she was associated, so the peacemaking role was not an academic one. A deeply pious woman, she suffered much over the cruelties of her time. She was also a gifted writer and poet. Radegunde is a poignant figure. She literally straddled three worlds: the Germanic prophetess tradition, the Christian monastic tradition, and the new nationalisms of post-Roman Europe. Her anguished writings profoundly convey the gulf between the religious and the nationalist-military vision of the new order in Europe. (For excerpts of Radegunde's writings, see Eckenstein, *Women Under Monasticism*, 1896.)

At the very close of the millennium, one of the most gifted of women religious writers, Hrotsvitha, continued this Germanic tradition by living close to the heart of the German political arena, at the Convent of Gandersheim. For King Otto, she wrote panegyrics. For her nuns, she wrote teaching poems and dramas. The dramas make good reading but will not be found in the standard compendiums of world literature. (For excerpts of Hrotsvitha's work, see Eckenstein 1896.)

By the 900s, there were convents and double monasteries (neighboring religious houses for monks and nuns under a single administration) all over England, Ireland, France, and Germany. Great religious sensitivity, substantial intellectual work, dedicated teaching, and practical political leadership all emerged from the women living quiet but involved lives in these institutions. These were women with knowledge, authority, some resources at their disposal—and a religious vision of the world.

Convent life was not utopia. Many entered convents for reasons of personal convenience with no interest in religious life. When these secular-minded women were wealthy, as they often were, a convent could turn into a great lady's house with a retinue of servants. The character of a monastery depended a good deal on the quality of its abbess. I have picked out the outstanding ones. There were others who were distinguished by nothing so much as their capacity for self-indulgence. Even at their worst, however, these convents provided a place in the world for single, dowryless women.[35] When all possible criticisms have been made of the convent world, the fact remains that many women led spiritually and socially productive lives there.

The convent also provided a base from which women could develop new perspectives on society. It was not just the religious women who developed these perspectives, however. A series of unsung heroines during this entire half-millennium had been coming out of Christian convent schools, marrying pagan kings, and dealing as best they could with extremely turbulent social conditions. Almost the only bit of nonviolent political action going on in this period was the arranging of marriage alliances by popes, bishops, and kings to shore up precarious military alliances.

To do justice to this historical thread, we will go back to 400 C.E. and the declining days of the Roman Empire. At that time, in addition to the women religious, three other sets of "womanpower" stood at the threshold of the new society. First, there were the women of the Roman nobility, more Christian than pagan at this point but still strongly imbued with the traditions of the Roman matron and retaining the political know-how of the women of the Republic. Second, there was the "new" Byzantine nobility, stemming from the separation of the eastern and western halves of the empire after Constantine. This nobility was partly from the old Roman nobility, partly from the best families of Greece, and partly from ruling families of tribes at the borders of Byzantium.[36] Third, there was the "barbarian" nobility of the Germanic and Gallic tribes now alternately fighting and federating to form kingdoms. The women from each of these three groups played a crucial part in the alliance-formation process out of which the new political entities developed. Additionally, because the story of Islam weaves in and out of the story of Europe and Byzantium, the women of Islam have a part in this story.

Political Roles for Women in the New Empires

The Roman Empire, West and East

From the old Roman nobility, Pulcheria was one of the last and best representatives of empire-building women. Born at the turn of the fifth century, she was the daughter of one emperor (Arcadius), was the sister of another (Theodosius II), and ascended the throne of the eastern half of the Roman Empire when she was only 15. When he died, she took the throne for a second time, taking a Roman general for a husband (in name only because she was a vowed virgin) to help hold the empire together. For 40 years, she was an active stateswoman, playing an important part in resolving east-west and church-state conflicts. She laid the groundwork for the Church Council of Chalcedon, which was called to decide whether Rome or Constantinople held ultimate authority. (It is not a surprise that the council failed to achieve consensus.) She was a scholar, trained in medicine and natural science, but also versatile enough to teach her brother horsemanship and military strategy when she undertook his education. She chose for his wife the Athenian Christian scholar Eudocia, to be empress.

Although she lived all her life in the public service, she was known as a deeply religious person vowed both to virginity and to service in the world. She was canonized after her death by the Greek Orthodox church.

Placidia did for the western empire what Pulcheria did for the eastern, in the very same time period. Also daughter of one emperor (Theodosius) and sister of another (Honorius), in 414 she married Atawulf, the barbarian invader of Rome, "to help out" in that period of extreme social disorganization, and she married his successor when Atawulf died two years later. In addition, she was regent for her son Valentinian III for 25 years. Not as good a stateswoman as Pulcheria was, and with nothing like her character, nevertheless, the politics of empire was her life and she worked at it with zest.

Placidia's niece Honoria also participated in alliance making with the barbarians. There are various versions of the Honoria-Attila story. The generally accepted version is that Honoria sent a ring to Attila, chief of the Huns, offering her hand in marriage. He came to make good his claim, and at that point Pope Leo came into the negotiations—to try to save Italy from Attila.[37] Attila died before negotiations could be concluded. All the women of Placidia's family were involved in the process of establishing marital alliances with barbarians. Placidia's cousin Serena married the Vandal chief Stilicon, who played a key part in the defense of Rome against other barbarian tribes.

Politics, scholarship, and institution building were the areas in which these women of the upper class excelled, and increasingly Constantinople was becoming a center for women scholars. In the late 300s, there was already a well-known circle of Christian women scholars there when Eudocia arrived to marry Theodosius. Eudocia became involved in either founding or reorganizing the University of Constantinople (accounts are not clear). She was active in politics, addressed the Senate from time to time, and wrote religious and secular songs. It is thought that she may have initiated the transcription of the Codex Theodosianus, compiled on Theodosius's orders.

We can imagine the consternation in this circle of women scholars when Hypatia, the brilliant pagan mathematician and philosopher, was murdered by some fanatical Christian monks in Alexandria after one of her lectures in 415 C.E. Hypatia is one of the few women scientists that appears in every history of science and was a major intellectual figure in the transitional world of the 400s. She was only 30 when she was murdered.

The continuing contact between Greece and Constantinople is an interesting one. The Greek women we hear of in Byzantium are not the housebound type; they reflect more the hetairan traditions of Aspasia. One of the best known of these is Olympia. A well-to-do widow at 15, she had a long active life as deaconess in the Christian community in Constantinople. The Greek widow Danielis (Figure 8.8), several centuries later, represents the

Figure 8.8. Greek Widow Danielis on a Litter Borne by 300 Youths. Redrawn by HBR.

continuing nature of the contact between the two societies. She was one of the richest merchants in Greece and also had a sharp eye for alliances. Befriending the to-be emperor Basil in his early youth, she had him take vows of spiritual brotherhood with her own son. She then regularly visited him over the years and continued the friendship with the emperor's successor. History does not tell us what benefits the widow derived from the relationship, but they were probably substantial.

The role of the empress of Byzantium after the fall of Rome was an interesting one. She became, in fact, the first lady of the Holy Roman Empire. Charlemagne, the backwoods country boy of Europe who abortively tried to marry the Byzantine empress Irene in 800, never did succeed in making a Carolingian queen "first lady of the empire" in any comparable way. The Byzantine queens played a more public role in government than had been the practice in the western half of the empire and participated regularly in regencies, full rulerships, and succession determinations, more on the Mongolian than the Roman pattern.[38] In fact, two of the empresses were Mongol princesses: Justinian I's wife was the khan's sister, took the name Theodora, and was coruler with Justinian; Constantine V married a Khazar princess.

The Byzantine ruling tradition is a strange one, full of cruelty as well as producing some outstanding civic contributions. The beautiful courtesan Theodora, Justinian I's wife and coruler, set a grand style for the empress role with her double enjoyment of politics and institution building. It was she who rallied palace forces to defend a wavering Justinian when angry mobs stood ready to invade the palace and overthrow the government. In addition to entering with zest into the theological disputes of the day, she also founded hospitals and convents. The Athenian Irene, Emperor Leo's wife, represents a more aggressive mode. She liked ruling so well that she became coemperor with her son after Leo's death, then had his eyes put out so she could be sole ruler. This is the Irene that Charlemagne tried to marry, but she was deposed and exiled first. By traditional standards, she was a good ruler, though ruthless with her enemies. She dealt with complex internal conflicts related to the iconoclasm issue, at the same time skillfully handling the national defense during a series of border wars and rebellions of subject peoples (Naroll et al. 1974: 114-16).

One unusual rule was a triumvirate of mother, daughter, and son: Theodora, Thecla, and Michael. Theodora ruled in her children's minority and had a surprisingly long reign for very troubled times, from 842 to 856. She quieted down the iconoclasm controversy that was a major source of internal bloodshed in that century and dealt, to the apparent satisfaction of her subjects, with continuing border unrest and military action. In the next century, Emperor Constantine VII chose to turn his rule over to his wife Helena, and it was during Empress Helena's reign that Princess Olga of Russia came to Constantinople to be baptized and to cement Byzantine-Russian relations.

Byzantium is a puzzle. The status of women was high—and not only among the nobility. Byzantine women had better protection of their rights by law in regard to property, divorce rights, and children than did European women of the time. Only the poorest women could not read and write. Women went to the university, and there were women doctors and professionals. Guilds were well organized, and women were active in them. At court, it was customary for male administrators to have wives with corresponding administrative responsibilities, complete with their own staffs. Ladies of the middle class who were not professionals were often active in religious foundations and hospitals. Constantinople was at the crossroads of the trade world, and Byzantine women traders dealt with Russians, Arabs, Italians, Persians, Central Asiatics, Jews, Egyptians, and occasional emissaries from France or Germany.

In other words, this was a cosmopolitan, cultured society and a "Christian" one. Yet, the level of interpersonal ferocity in succession politics equals, if it does not exceed, the ferocity of the European barbarians. Every new person on the throne meant hundreds of dead bodies in the city. The practice of punishment by disfigurement meant that people were regularly blinded, were castrated, or had hands cut off. Deposed emperors were customarily blinded and had their noses slit. These practices resulted in the increasing brutalization of the society, which all the elaborately constructed law codes could not counteract.

While it must be remembered that Byzantium was fighting for its life against Slavic tribes on one side and Islam on the other, and often against Rome, too, so that military action was almost continuous from the eighth century on, I am not sure that this explains the level of internal brutality. Much of the upper-class brutality focused on succession, although the rules for succession seemed to be fairly adequate.

Because succession rules are closely linked to marriage-alliance practices, and therefore involve women in a very intimate way, it may be appropriate to make some observations on succession rules here. The comments will also apply to the European situation, to be examined shortly.

Good succession rules, and intelligent marriage-alliance practices, can only work when universalistic criteria for the best person for the job (whether emperor, empress, or other ruling slot) are applied in making choices from the pool of women and men eligible for the job. Neither in marital-alliance making or in choice of the next ruler would there be only one candidate. There were usually at least two to choose from in selecting an emperor, sometimes up to a dozen—sisters, brothers, sons, daughters, cousins, nephews, even grandchildren. Rules about "the oldest" or "a male" were rarely given priority over the realistic criterion of performance promise. Women could make the critical difference at times of selection crises by supporting the choice of the best person. When they were driven by personal ambition, they could sabotage the selection process. This is one reason that queens and empresses sometimes appear so diabolical. When they performed universalistically, we don't even hear about it, but, when they intervened to further their own ambitions, we hear about "petticoat government." In general, the brutalization process worked against an evolving universalism, through a kind of negative resocialization of individuals. Women royalty therefore rarely got the kind of training that could help them counteract the existing dynamic of violence.[39] The importance of the monastic movement in this period was that within convents there were schools where women could learn a different perspective on the social order and observe different behavioral models. Not all the schools were good schools, and not all the pupils were open to this kind of teaching. But it was a possible source of alternatives in a deteriorating society. The importance of that alternative becomes clear at certain historic moments, such as when the Ukrainian grand princess Olga, of the recently formed Russian state, came to Constantinople for baptism in 957 C.E. She was very consciously building a new society inside her own country and chose the resources of the Christian church to help her do it. The alliance structure that she formed between Russia and Byzantium, including a tradition of marriage alliances, was to provide continuity for Byzantine cultural and religious tradition when Byzantium itself was destroyed.

The relationship of Byzantium to the Slavic world, another interesting story, will not be discussed here except in mentioning that the same alliance-by-marriage system practiced between Rome and the barbarians of Europe was practiced between Constantinople and the Slavs. With the fall of Constantinople, the tie was continued by Ivan the Great's marriage to the last emperor's niece Sophia, who took on the job of "civilizing" the court at Moscow (to the Russians' great disgust).

Slavs had their own traditions of strong women rulers and women warriors, such as the legends about Princess Libussa, who is supposed to have founded the first Bohemian dynasty of Premyslidi (some time before 800 C.E.). There are Russian *bylinas* about bold women who carry men off in bags (Halle 1933: 34). Ukrainian women in particular had a strong tradition of training women as warriors as well as a tradition of strong ruling queens (Babiak 1975, based on translations from Ukrainian history): after Princess Olga came Queen Anna Michailivna (1065), Princess Ivannie Ianka, Queen Polots'ka Predslava (1173), and Queen Yaroslavna (1185). These women were all creative diplomats, and most of them were also scholarly historians who contributed to the recordings of the traditions of their people and to the establishment of schools and monasteries where women could be educated. Ianka started the first Ukrainian school for girls. Russia's century of women rulers in the 1700s comes out of this earlier tradition of women rulers.

Before leaving the East and returning to Europe, we will look at the role of women in the rising new world power, Islam, which confronted both Byzantium and Europe toward the end of the first millennium.

Islam[40]

At the start of the seventh century, continuing warfare between Byzantium and Persia had diverted a lot of lucrative trade toward western Arabia, and a new merchant aristocracy was developing that had nothing but contempt for the ways of the majority population of Bedouin nomads. Mohammed, a member of one of the less successful of the urban-based trading groups in Mecca, found at the age of 40 that he had a mission to change the perspectives of the newly powerful merchants. He taught obedience to God and greater justice toward fellow human beings, with particular emphasis on the responsibility of rich merchants for poor nomads. Christianity had been born in the countryside and then moved to the city 600 years before. The religion of Islam, in contrast, started out in the city. Well-to-do merchant women played an important role in both religions. (In Mohammed's case, the first wealthy merchant woman to support him was his own wife, Khadya, who married him in 580 C.E.) Nevertheless, the influence of the nomadic tradition must never be forgotten in evaluating Islam, any more than the influence of the craft-worker and fisherpeople traditions must be forgotten in the evaluation of Christianity. Mujeeb tells us that

> a Muslim must regard all men as equal before God. No privilege can be claimed or denied on ground of sex, family, social position, race, language or country. No such distinction is allowed as was made among the Buddhists between the monks and the laymen, or in Christianity between the Church and the laity. Asceticism is forbidden. Historically and socially the novel feature of the Muslim faith is the application of all obligations to all members of the community. This is itself an aspect of the doctrine that life cannot be divided into the spiritual and the worldly, that religion is according to nature and nature consists of both spiritual and material elements. (1960: 127)

The extent to which the equality doctrine was applied to women by Mohammed himself and by the men of the Moslem culture that evolved from his teachings is a matter of dispute. As in all religions, there are contradictory references to women. At one time, Mohammed said, "The world and all things in it are valuable, but the most valuable thing in the world is a virtuous woman." At another time, "I have not felt any calamity more hurtful to man than woman" (White 1924: 139). There are some strong references to the equality of women and men in the Koran, but they can be variously interpreted. Because the usual presentations of the status of women in Islam by Westerners is heavily slanted toward almost complete subjugation of women, I have chosen to present the more positive side. In practice, the status of women has varied greatly from one Moslem country to another in various periods of history. Overall assessments of the historical status of Moslem women are just now beginning to become available (Mernissi 1991; Toubia [ed.] 1988)!

The Arabic literary traditions must be borne in mind, as well as the sociopolitical aspects of the religious tradition, in considering women's position. In the pre-Islamic era, all the great poets had sisters and daughters who were also poets, whose elegies were widely sung. The singing of elegies was a specialty of female professional mourners at funerals (Huart 1966: 14-15). The poetess tradition continued in Islamic society under the Ummayads. Laila Al-Akhyaliya was a much-loved poetess. Fadl was also a major intellectual figure at the court in Bagdad. Mahbuba, poetess and singer, was a freed harem slave. All these women belong to the eighth century.

It does appear that the doctrine of equality of all persons, referred to above by Mujeeb, was taken seriously by Mohammed in relation to the situation of women. In the course of the new Arabian urbanism, women were already losing their earlier heritage of free participation. Mohammed detailed women's rights of inheritance, administration of property, and freedom to choose a partner and to determine conditions of divorce, all of which urban Arabs were taking away from women (O'Faolain and Martines 1973). One could interpret the history of women in Islam as one long struggle on their part to maintain the rights enunciated by Mohammed in the face of a series of traditions hostile to women's rights in the various Mediterranean countries conquered by the Moslems. Although it appears on the surface that Islam allowed women few rights because of the unilateral right of men to divorce their wives by pronouncing the *talak*, in fact, most of women's property rights and the conditions under which divorces were permitted came to be written into the marriage contract. The *ta'lik ad talak* provisions could be taken by any woman into a court of law to protect her rights against unfair treatment and also to compel her husband to divorce her if he violated the provisions. Recent studies of women's property and divorce rights in Morocco (Maher 1974) and Indonesia (Lev 1972) indicate that women were able to protect their rights in the traditional rural society. With urbanism, it became harder because women became more dependent on men.

The customs of veiling and the harem, from the Moslem point of view, came into Islam from the outside, from the "degenerate" Greeks and Persians. Plural marriages were not eliminated by Mohammed, but, in limiting the number of wives permitted a Moslem to four, he was setting a higher standard for family relationships than prevailed among the upper classes in Byzantium as well as elsewhere in the Middle East.

The merchant and warrior traditions existed for Arabian women before the rise of Islam, as did the tradition of spiritual leadership. In the lifetime of the prophet, his wife represented the merchant tradition and his daughter Fatima the tradition of spiritual leadership. In village Islam, women continued to feel very free. As Maher points out, they knew they had control of the means of reproduction: "As sisters, women get men wives. As wives, women get men children" (Maher 1974: 222). Though Moslem society is a patriarchal one, rural women have apparently always taken a casual attitude toward marriage and kept strong ties with their families of origin, which can be counted on to protect their interests. The high divorce rates associated with that casual attitude have continued from earliest times into the twentieth century. Because most of our information about Moslem women comes from urban settings, where women may be cut off from their matrikin, we have assumed that all Moslem women were as helpless as some urban women have in fact been.

After Mohammed's death, it is less clear what the extent of women's involvement in community life was. Later, after the original tribal welfare state turned into a conquest state, women became involved in succession politics in the caliphate. The pattern is similar to the one already observed in Byzantium and Rome. From 785 on, after the overthrow of the Ummayad caliphate, we hear of the role of the wife of the caliph in matters of succession. The Abbasid caliphate represented in a way the entry of Islam into world politics, and the tradition of alliance by marriage was fully developed under the Abbasids. Persian and Byzantine models were used as models for politics and court life.

Given that both Christianity and Islam held ideals of a religious world state, they inevitably collided on all fronts. Shortly after Mohammed's death in 632, his successors overthrew the Sassanids in Persia and expelled Byzantium from Syria, Egypt, and North Africa. After these military victories, the Moslems advanced to the Atlantic, to the Caucasus, the Oxus, and the Indus without serious opposition. By the time of the reign of Harun-al-Rashid (786-809), Islam was a great and prosperous empire, and by the end of the millennium its cities were centers of knowledge and culture that far outshone any of the cities of Europe—probably even Constantinople (Hazard 1931). It is hard to know how to characterize this complex civilization, let alone the role of women in it. During the last four centuries of the millennium, there were continuous internal strife, consolidations, and successions within the Moslem world. Successions were often attended by bloodbaths as in Persia, Byzantium, and Rome. There was continuous fighting on the borders between Islam and Europe and between Islam and Byzantium. Yet, Islam practiced religious toleration, which Christian Europe did not. Great scholars of all faiths flourished in the major cities of Islam, a thing impossible in the cities of Europe at that time. Islam also allowed a degree of local self-government, which Christian political organization did not allow. When it came to behavior in war, there was little choice between the Christians and the Moslems. Christians sometimes massacred civilian populations on the taking of a town, and so did Moslems.

In the midst of all this ferocity, an extraordinary society developed that was a continuing blend of Arabian nomads and the various urban populations of the Mediterranean world. The nomads were strongest in Syria and periodically established "reform" governments to do away with urban corruption. Side by side with differing political emphases came differing religious emphases. As Islamic society became increasingly differentiated and institutionalized, it began to provide the same kinds of niches for alternative ways of life that Christianity allowed. One set of niches was the monasteries. The Moslem form of the monastery is the *khanqah*, which potentially gives expression to the same range of socioeconomic and spiritual concerns as the Christian monastery. Sufi convents cared for the sick and the poor in much the same way as the Christian convents in Europe did. The Sufi nun Rabi'a is the best known woman mystic from the Moslem monastic tradition. Stolen into slavery as a child, she was freed as a young woman because of her great purity and love of God and was widely revered in her own lifetime.

A contemporary of St. Rabi'a, Sukaina, was a granddaughter of Mohammed's daughter Fatima. She was one of the first "role models" in Islamic history for a new urban elite of women and is supposed to have "invented" the salon. The reunions in her house of poets, scholars, jurists, and other distinguished people of both sexes became the model for similar social gatherings at the residences of other ladies of fashion. Ali laments that, while St. Rabi'a's tomb is a pilgrimage center, Sukaina, one of the great women of Islam, no longer has visitors to her tomb. She set a standard of education and culture for Arabian women that has been important ever since and was *"la dame des dames de son temps"* (Ali 1899: 758). Women began training in law, theology, and "the traditions" at this time, and leading lady jurists are mentioned up to the fall of Bagdad.

In this same early period, a friend of Sukaina's, Umm ul-Banin, was the wife of Al-Walid I, the Ummayad caliph under whom Spain was taken. She is the first queen mentioned as being active in politics and is said to have "frequently interfered in affairs of State . . . on the side of justice and humanity. Most of the great works of benefaction introduced by Walid were due to her inspiration" (Ali 1899: 759). Walid's colleague, the governor of Iraq, complained of petticoat government and advised Walid not to be influenced by her. According to Ali, Walid's response to the complaint was to command the discontented governor to appear before her and receive a lecture!

One of the first women to be involved in the politics of succession was al-Khayzuran, the mother of Harun al-Rashid. Khayzuran engaged in a power struggle with her son Hadi, who succeeded her husband as caliph. When Hadi tried to have her confined in the harem, she had her slaves kill him, thus making it possible for her favorite son, Harun, to ascend the throne (Naroll et al. 1974: 122-23). The next interference was less violent. One of Harun's wives, the Arabian Zubayda, competed successfully against another wife, a Persian concubine, to have Zubayda's son declared the next caliph in 792.

Zubayda seems to have been an unusual person, representing that vigorous Arabian strain that keeps erupting into Islamic culture. She built an aqueduct at her own expense in Mecca, rebuilt Alexandretta after it was destroyed by the Greeks, and generally seems to have played the role of "development expert" for Arabian cities.

Women's intervention in politics continued. In 1021, caliph al-Hakim of the Fatimids in Egypt met death—purportedly with the connivance of his sister, the Sitt al-Mulk. This lady, according to the *Cambridge History of Islam* (Holt 1970), ruled "competently and vigorously" as regent for her 16-year-old nephew for six years. In 1045, rule passed to the deceased caliph's mother, a Sudanese slave, who ruled for five years with a council of ministers including her former master, a Persian Jewish banker. One would like to know more details of that story! One of the heroines of Moslem history is Shajar al-Durr. She was the concubine of Sultan al-Malik al-Salih, who died during the hostilities that ensued when King Louis IX came from France to "take Egypt." Shajar concealed the news of the sultan's death and issued orders in his name, holding the army and the kingdom together until his son arrived to take over the rule. Plot and counterplot led one faction to murder the son and proclaim Shajar sultan, but opposition to her was substantial. The caliph in Bagdad felt insulted at her enthronement because she was a former inmate of his own harem, whom he had sent to the deceased sultan as a gift! We are told Shajar was a woman of remarkable ability, who nonetheless needed help in waging war; therefore she appointed a commander-in-chief who became sultan. She continued to stay on top of a seething situation, ruling for seven years before she was finally murdered.

Most queens played quieter roles but took an active part in promoting colleges and scholarship and making civic improvements. There was a strong tradition of scholarship and learning for women of the upper classes, contrary to the general image Westerners have of women in Islam. Spain is a particularly good example. The account of Moslem Cordova by A. J. Arberry (1967: 175) reveals a cultured society with highly educated women. Education was "perfectly general," with girls and boys attending local elementary schools (except the upper class, who had their own tutors). "Women shared equally with men in the work of pedagogy; not a few became accomplished scholars." Ibn Hazm, a Moslem scholar, testifies that he was educated by women entirely: "I never sat with men until I was already a youth, and my beard had begun to sprout. Women taught me the Koran, they recited to me much poetry, they trained me in calligraphy" (Arberry 1967: 176).[41] This passage is particularly interesting because it confirms my earlier suggestion that the effect of boys spending time in the women's quarters of the house could have positive and mutually reinforcing benefits for both women and boys. Cordova, Granada, Seville, and the other towns of Spain all were known for their women scholars and poets, one of whom acted as secretary to the scholarly Hakam II. Waladah (died 1087) was considered one of the best poets of her age. Women lectured at the universities of Cordova and Valencia.

In Egypt, women of rank and learning played important public roles under the Tulunides and the Fatimids. Women, equally with men, could be members of the "House of Science" (Dar ul-Hikmat), "which combined the characteristics of a scientific institute with those of a masonic lodge, where the esoteric doctrines of the Ismalias were taught" (Ali 1899: 764). Takia was a famous Egyptian scholar and poet in the reign of Saladin. The tradition of women scholars in Egypt was not destroyed by the advent of Moslem rule.

Yet, individual caliphs did from time to time pass decrees drastically limiting the freedom of women. The fact that Ali Hakem, the "mad caliph," could in the tenth century forbid any woman to appear on the streets on pain of death (White 1924: 150) indicates considerable vulnerability in their position.

The women described here are mostly of the aristocracy. Did middle-class women participate in public life and move about freely? According to Ali, during this period, yes. It would not have been possible for the caliphate to send "both men and women spies into the Byzantine Empire in the guise of merchants, travelers and physicians" if women were not already accustomed to such roles in public in their home society (Naroll et al. 1974: 122). The general practice of purdah came considerably later. The lives of working-class women and slaves would be very much the same in Islam as in Rome, Byzantium, and Europe. Possibly Moslems treated their slaves better than Romans and Europeans did.

Life for Middle-Class Jewish Women in Cairo

Materials on the lives of middle-class women in this millennium have been sparse, no matter what part of the world we examine. Owing to a recent study of the documents of the Cairo Geniza from 969 to 1250, we have an unexpected glimpse of the life of the middle-class Jewish woman in this part of the Mediterranean. The documents are a haphazard deposit in the community storage room of the synagogue, consisting of letters, court records, contracts, accounts, and other writings. Not only do they bring the women's underside life to the light, but they bring hope that a further search for these types of records will enable us to learn a lot more about women as householders than we now know.

These middle-class women had female slaves[42] to do their domestic work, a pattern that was surely common among all urban middle-class women of this millennium. The free servant class did not yet exist. From references to slaves in letters, and from frequent references to the freeing of slaves upon the death of the owner, it appears that slaves were often treated as members of the family or as close friends. Sometimes the slaves were European, but more often they were black.

The Cairo women were involved in many enterprises and handled a good deal of capital, according to the court records. They were money lenders and international traders, and they sometimes had business partners who were gentiles. They were teachers and heads of schools, scholars, and copyists. They were sometimes cantors in the synagogues, in which capacity they would function as singers, marriage counselors, and general social workers for the community. There is also mention of a woman visionary. All girls went to school, sometimes to separate classes, sometimes to classes together with boys. Women spent a good deal of time on community service projects of all kinds. They frequently endowed institutions for relief to the poor in their own names and with their own funds. They headed special financial drives for their synagogues, sometimes to raise money to ransom members of the community who had been captured by pirates. They saw to it that the synagogue warehouse was always stocked with food and clothing for distribution to the poor.

Women were evidently free to make appeals for help and justice to the assembled congregation in the synagogue and did so frequently and successfully. Although traditional Jewish law was followed, it is surprising how egalitarian the society appears to have been. This is another piece of evidence that the same law that limits women also protects the rights they do have, if they use it. Two things set Jews apart from other Mediterranean societies in this millennium. One is that they did not practice infanticide. Earlier customs in this regard were effectively stopped long before they were discontinued in other societies. The other is that all girls were educated in regular classes. This equal care for children of both sexes as they were growing up speaks of a special quality of parent-child relations in the Jewish home. We can see in this highly supportive Mediterranean family setting the source for the phenomenon, to be observed later in Europe, of Jewish women of the middle class being trained to be doctors and scholars at a time when practically no European women of that class (except nuns) were being educated.

As we turn from Mediterranean to European society, which was undergoing similar strains of diverse populations having to be accommodated in a rapidly secularizing polity, we will see that women's roles may not be so different in the two cultural areas as has usually been thought.

European Kingdoms

As Byzantium and Islam were experiencing turbulence in the period we have been discussing, Europe was facing its own storms. The Roman tradition was in some sense broken after 476 and, while the church provided some continuity, a whole new set of political units had to be forged out of the remains of the old Roman provinces and the new tribal groups. While these tribal groups had been in touch with Rome for a long time and were by no means nomadic peoples just tumbled out of forest and steppe, the Gothic and Frankish traditions and life-styles were substantially different than the Roman, particularly in that they were essentially nonurban.

The development of an urban culture and of usable communication and administrative networks on a scale that could deal with both the old Roman world and the new parts of Europe that had to be integrated into it required considerably more than the skills of the warrior. The women of the ruling families did have some of the requisite skills and played an important part, along with their sisters in religious orders, in organizing and "gentling" the society.

The old prophetic tribal tradition was still strong in these societies, as I indicated earlier. The great prophetesses and druidesses were venerated not only by their own people but by the Romans. Emperors and generals turned to them for advice. Veleda was a famous prophetess in the reign of Emperor Vespasian. As described by Tacitus, she was of the tribe of Bructeria and lived in a tower on the River Lippe, a tributary of the Rhine. Foreign ambassadors who came to consult with her were not admitted to her presence but only permitted communication through an intermediary (White 1924: 31). Albruna prophesied in the time of Tiberius. Ganna and Gambara were the leading prophetesses in the reign of Emperor Domitian (Weinhold 1882).

Figure 8.9. Pompeiian Sibyl. Redrawn by HBR.

Because the prophetesses originally wrote and interpreted runes, a tradition of literacy developed among them that we have already noted among the aristocratic women of tribal courts and as a carryover into the convent culture of Germany in the very early Middle Ages. (Druidesses were mentioned in the previous chapter on nomads.) They ranged from women who performed temple offices and lived with their families to a sisterhood dwelling in seclusion (White 1924: 30). Burckhardt refers to these women somewhat unceremoniously as "the gypsies of the declining ancient world." The stories he tells of the priestesses are interesting:

> Aurelian inquired of a number of them—perhaps a corporation of priestesses—concerning the succession in the Empire, and surely not in jest, for in such a matter jesting was dangerous. Sometimes they uttered their prophecies unsolicited. One bold woman, indifferent to consequences, called to Alexander Severus in the Gallic tongue: "Depart, hope for no victory, do not trust your soldiers!" A Druid landlady in the country of the Tungrii (near Leige) with whom the Subaltern Diocles, later Diocletian, was reckoning his daily board, said to him: "You are too greedy, too stingy." "I will be generous if I ever become Emperor," he replied. "Do not mock," the hostess answered, "you will become Emperor when you have slain a boar." (Burckhardt [1852] 1949: 69)

The punch line in that particular story, which Burckhardt omits, comes when the subaltern Diocles stabs Aper (*boar* in Latin), the Praetorian Prefect who had murdered the previous emperor, Numerian. This paved the way to his becoming emperor himself and fulfilled the prophecy of the druidess.

It should not be forgotten that the barbarian queens had this tradition of knowledge and power on which to draw. They were accustomed to the exercise of authority. Amalswinthe, daughter of Theodoric, the first barbarian king of Rome, provides a good example of the performance records of these queens. When her father died, she served capably as regent of the empire for two years. Having received an excellent Latin education, she devoted a good deal of her energy during her regency to reorganizing the crumbling educational system of the Roman schools.

Amalswinthe stood at the center of a very strong alliance-by-marriage system that her father had worked out between the Visigoths, the Burgundians, the Vandals, and the Thuringians (Brentano 1964: 49). It was a masterly piece of international negotiation, but Theodoric's successors were not as skilled as he, so there was much blood shed between the various tribes and kingdoms. Amalswinthe herself was strangled by an ungrateful relative she had brought into the alliance system to help rule the country after her father's death.

Contemporaneous with Amalswinthe was Clothilde, the niece of the first Burgundian king. She was married to Clovis, king of the Franks, more or less with the challenging commission to bring about his conversion to Christianity. The Franks were the only really pagan kingdom in Europe—the other tribes had all been converted to Aryan Christianity, which had been declared heretical by the Catholic church. The pope's hand would be much strengthened in dealing with the Aryans if a strong pagan kingdom could be brought directly into the Catholic fold. The entire political future of the church seemed to depend on the success of this maneuver.

Clovis was not an admirable character, and the task did not seem easy, but Clothilde was tough and persistent. She had been through a lot herself, as she had recently escaped into a convent from an uncle who had stabbed her father and strangled her mother. She laid the groundwork for Clovis's believing that God would help him win an important victory, so he converted as a "thank you" to the deity. A mass conversion of his people followed, as expected. St. Gregory's life of Clothilde shows her as a resourceful and determined person (Brentano 1964: 109-14, 119-20). She knew well the limitations of the mass conversion and did what she could to develop institutions that would help education and Christian service to the Franks. One important step was to found a religious house for royal women, thus providing for a new kind of education and socialization for Frankish women of the upper strata. She became a deaconess and lived the last years of her life as a nun, founding a variety of useful institutions including hospitals.

Shortly after Clothilde's time, we hear that Fredegundis, queen of the Franks, and her son King Chlotar "took possession of Paris and other cities after the barbarian fashion" (Brentano 1964: 46). This was evidently an unsuccessful attempt by a royal mother to get control of a kingdom for her son. She died shortly thereafter. Another ambitious woman of the Frankish royalty of that generation, Brunihild (or Brunechildas), was more successful in the short run, although she was executed in the end by Fredegundis's son Chlotar. For a 50-year period, Brunihild managed to remain a chief actor in the Frankish kingdom, several times serving as regent. It is hard to know what this queen was really like because in one chronicle (Gregory's) she is described as a simple girl. In another (*The Chronicle of Fredegar*, in Brentano 1964: 135-46), she appears as a bloodthirsty, brutal person responsible for many deaths. An Aryan and unfriendly to Catholic monasticism, she undercut many of the church's power bases in trying to build her own. She may have been a major builder of European roads, as there are roads in northern France and the Low Countries that were known as "Brunehilde's Roads" (Leighton 1972: 56). She seems to have had a hand in every major appointment in the kingdom throughout her life, except for a couple of interim periods when she was expelled by irate kings. With a passion for ruling, she played the conventional brutal power politics of her day more effectively than most. In the end, King Chlotar had her executed rather spectacularly.

> Brunechildas was brought before Chlotar, who was boiling with fury against her. He charged her with the deaths of ten Frankish kings— namely, Sigebert, Merovech, his father Chilperic, Theudebert and his son Chlotar, Chlotar's son the other Merovech, Theuderic and Theuderic's three sons who had just perished. She was tormented for three days with a diversity of tortures, and then on his orders was led through the ranks on a camel. Finally she was tied by her hair, one arm and one leg to the tail of an unbroken horse, and she was cut to shreds by its hoofs at the pace it went. (Brentano 1964: 145)

The seventh century brings another activist queen, with a gentler style, to the throne of France. Queen Balthild, daughter of Anglo-Saxon royalty, shared in the typical hair-raising childhood experiences of the times. Captured as a child, she was enslaved but escaped and was befriended by a family of rank. Marrying King Chlodwig II, who turned imbecile, she became governing queen of France for the rest of his lifetime and during the minority of her sons. She worked against slavery, forbidding the sale of Christians in France, managed many political reforms, and generally turned a turbulent kingdom into a peaceful one. She was also a strong supporter of the monastic movement, founding a monastery herself and helping many others as well as helping to link the French and English convent networks. There was a great expansion of convents during her reign, and one could say that a whole new educational system was developing for Europe, aided by her efforts. Retiring to a convent when she left the throne, she had the misfortune to witness the resurgence of the politics of blood after her peaceful reign.

In Italy, we have the same alternation of peacemaking queens and brutal queens as elsewhere. Queen Rosamund of the Lombards (late 500s) had a reputation for killing off husbands, but the story of how she got started on her career of crime helps one understand the socialization for brutality that women experienced: Rosamund's husband, King Ratchis, had killed her father and made a drinking cup out of his skull. One day at a banquet, he gaily handed her the cup and ordered her to "drink merrily" with her father (Brentano 1964: 178).

Given this background of violence, it is more extraordinary that we can point to as many peacemakers as we can. In the same sixth century, we find the devout Catholic queen Theodelinda, also of Lombardy, wife of King Agilulf, devoting her political career to the negotiation of a treaty for the Lombards and the Italian governor of Italy with the Roman Empire (then based in Constantinople). She also moderated the effects of the Lombard invasion of Italy and paved the way for the conversion of the Lombards to Catholicism. She was recognized and thanked by Pope Gregory for her work.

Sixth- and seventh-century England produced a series of devout queens who somewhat gentled the male nobility of a country that was divided into several warring kingdoms. Queen Berhta, wife of Aethelbert of Kent, brought the first Christian ecclesiastic to England after a long period of reversion to paganism. Pope Gregory ordered St. Augustine to go and help her with the work of re-Christianizing England, but Augustine was frightened and turned back before he reached England, begging to be let off (Duckett 1938). The pope sternly ordered him back, and he finally made the trip. The credit for re-Christianizing England usually goes to the frightened Augustine. Rarely is Queen Berhta, the courageous woman who was on the scene all the time and made it possible for Augustine to do his work, even mentioned. (Berhta also converted her own husband.)

Queen Berhta's daughter Aethelburg married King Eadwin of Northumbria and in so doing accepted a commission to avert war between Northumbria and Kent. She brought a Christian cleric with her who baptized her husband; she also founded a double monastery and churches in Northumbria.

Princess Eanswith, also of Kent, refused her commission to marry a heathen king, showing that women were not always helpless pawns in these matters. She devoted her life instead to developing a religious settlement and improving the agricultural practices of the farmers on the estates associated with her monastery. Queen Aethelthrith, or Ethelreda, was the wife of two kings in succession. At the age of 30, she married the second, a 15-year-old boy, for reasons of state. She left him shortly afterward to take the veil, founding a monastery at Ely, one of the major English religious foundations. Like St. Hilda (Duckett 1938: 9), Ethelreda was renowned as a teacher and had many of the leading men of England as her students. She was much loved and there are many legends about her.

The queens of the barbarian kingdoms functioned, as we have seen, as diplomats, peacemakers, founders of educational centers, and Christian missionaries. There is one role that has not been mentioned, which is the role of administrator of economic affairs. A study by David Herlihy uncovers an interesting part of the work of the Carolingian queens of France, which by extension Herlihy suggests may have been true of the queens in other Germanic traditions. From an essay on the organization of the royal household by Hincmar of Rheims, written in 882:

> The royal treasurer, the "camerarius," is directly under the queen. Moreover, the queen is responsible for giving to the knights their yearly gifts,

the equivalent of their salaries. This heavy responsibility falls upon the queen in order to free her husband from "domestic or palace solicitude" and to enable him to give all his attention "to the state of the entire kingdom." So too, Agobard of Lyons mentions the Carolingian queens as being in a peculiar way responsible for the "honestas" of the palace. (Herlihy 1962: 102-3)

Evidently, women of the nobility had similar responsibility for the economic administration of the large estates their families held from the king. This seems to be true in Italy and Spain as well as in France (Herlihy 1962: 103).

When we add economic roles to educational and diplomatic functions, we see that women of the elite carried a heavy share of the administrative responsibility for these kingdoms. The men were left free for military activity. Women generally married between the ages of 12 and 15. This means that these difficult diplomatic missions were taken on at very young ages indeed. The fact that, at the age of 15, Pulcheria could rule the Byzantine empire on behalf of her younger brother says a good deal about the maturity, level of education, and purposefulness of royal teenage girls. Their acceptance of marriage as a diplomatic role and their willingness to undertake unlikely alliances for the sake of public order are worth pondering. On points of principle important to them, they did not compromise. Christian queens did not become pagan to please their husbands. It always went the other way. Furthermore, women could and did refuse marriage alliances they did not wish to undertake, like Eanswith. Their record in founding convents, schools, and hospitals is impressive. On the other hand, their best efforts could be swamped by military action. Like everyone else, female and male, they all lived under the shadow of the sword.

We have been looking at elites. Peasant and working-class women of Europe and the Mediterranean worked much as they had in earlier eras. The pattern did not change very much until the industrial revolution and the advent of factories.

There is some interesting information on the economic roles of middle-class women, thanks to the Herlihy study cited above. In an analysis of European documents between 701 and 1200 dealing with landholdings and transfers of property, Herlihy made the interesting discovery that (a) many men identified themselves in legal documents by their matronymic rather than their patronymic (i.e., as sons of their mothers rather than of their fathers), and (b) women were listed as owners of land more often than expected. Identification through the matronymic for men reached a peak in the eleventh century—8% of all identifications in the legal documents studied referred to the mother. To summarize the findings all too briefly, the mother's name was preferred as identification in the following cases: (a) the woman was a freed woman, her husband a serf, and the child's status was determined by the mother; (b) the child was the illegitimate son of a cleric and therefore took identification through the mother; and (c) the mother was better known in the community than the father was and therefore a better identifier. This is indirect but interesting evidence of women's economic importance and community status.

The reputation of women as persons of affairs in the community were both cause and effect of the increasing properties accumulating in their hands. In Spain, France, and Germany, women held as much as 18% of the land, with 12% as the overall figure for 1200. This is land specifically listed as the woman's and does not include the land held for "heirs," usually under her administration, which would bring the total of land under women's administration to as much as 25% in 1100. Wars were, of course, one of the chief reasons for properties accumulating in the hands of women. General population mobility was another reason; in times of emigration, women (who migrate at lesser rates than men do) always take increased responsibility in the area of out-migration (Herlihy 1962: 111). Warriors die, emigrants do not return, and women hold firm. Did the Crusades "help create a women's world back home"? Poems about women weeping for their lovers in a world emptied of men just might be off the mark (Mancabru, as quoted in Herlihy 1962: 113). Maybe these were tears of joy.

Most of the foregoing applies to women in families that are landholders. For working-class women, a more typical picture might be that of a woman marrying a local priest and supporting him; out of this, she would get living quarters, companionship, children, and a certain amount of social status, and he would get economic support. The status of such women in what is technically referred to as a nicholaite family was evidently a problem: "At Vercelli about 960, married priests ordered to put away their wives answered "that unless they were maintained by the hands of their women they would succumb to hunger and nakedness' " (Herlihy 1962: 104). Herlihy presents similar quotes from Ravenna and Verona and concludes:

> Apparently in these nicholaite families, women had assumed economic functions of critical importance. The presence of fair numbers of available, propertied or at least economically resourceful women may have even aggravated the abuse of nicholaiti with the 10th century church, as needy clerics sought a relief from their own poverty in advantageous liaisons. The sons of priests who use a matronymic were perhaps attempting to cover the ignominy of their fathers. But they also give illustration of the prominence and repute of their mothers within the life of the community. (1962: 104)

It would appear that the women of such households might be very well satisfied with their situation. So might the newly freed woman marrying a serf who was ready to move up in the world. More typical than either of the above would be the peasant woman working side by side with her husband on the farm and the woman artisan working side by side with her husband in town workshops.

Life in the first millennium C.E. in Europe was hard. Neither social class nor sex offered protection against the brutalities and the uncertainties of the age. It has not been possible in this chapter to give a picture of the emerging political units of Europe. Only fragments of the political process have been touched on in describing the activities of women. A good subject for further study, however, would be a careful assessment of the kinds of education and communication infrastructures developed by women as compared with the military-based political structures created by men, in terms of the net contributions of each to the social order. This period is one of attempted consolidation, not of attempted redistribution of social goods, so neither women nor men rate high on efforts for social justice. We find none of the land redistribution legislation that in the previous millennium appeared in Persia, Greece, and Rome. In Chapter 1, Volume 2, we will see to what extent the consolidations achieved in this period provide the basis for future social reconstruction.

A Note on Religion and the Status of Women in India

Although Buddhism predates both Christianity and Islam, it is useful to include a discussion of women in Indian Buddhism here to see the situation of women in these three major religions in comparative perspective. I regret the necessity of omitting a similar discussion on religion and women in China and Japan. Adequate sources are not available to me at this time.

When Gautama Buddha (563-483 B.C.E.) experienced enlightenment and began teaching, India was just beginning to experience the long series of invasions, beginning with Darius of Persia, which were to be intensified between 200 B.C.E. and 300 C.E. with the coming first of the Greeks and then of the Scythians and Parthians. In Indian history, this was the period of "barbarian invasions." It was a dark time, and the ideal of renunciation taught by the Upanishads, by Gautama Buddha, and by Mahavira, the Jainist teacher, was compelling. The struggle between more activist traditions in India and the ideal of renunciation continued until about 500 C.E., when Buddhism ceased to be a significant religion in India and had already put down roots elsewhere in Asia. Jainism remained as a small but important ascetic religion. The difference between Jainism and Buddhism on the one hand and earlier Hindu teachings on the other are significant in that the two newer religions were oriented to a concept of perfectibility rather than simply to escaping from the cosmic cycle of karma. To the extent that Buddhism and Jainism emphasized "becoming" rather than "being," they did not lead to passivity or withdrawal.

The teachings on the possibility of "becoming" attracted Indian women in the 500s B.C.E. They had been pushed out of earlier participation in Hindu religious rites through Brahminic "reforms." The age of marriage was creeping toward puberty and below, and there was a greatly increased pressure for all women to marry. It is not surprising that there was a great positive response of upper-class women to the teachings of Gautama.[43] The detachment from the responsibilities of family life and the possibilities of individual fulfillment that the teachings offered were welcomed in a society where most options for a woman's personal development were coming to an end.

As early as 800 B.C.E., a few women of the aristocracy had adopted a special nunlike mode of existence in following the teachings of Prince Parsha of Varanasi. Regular celibate religious orders of monks and nuns who followed Jainist teachings were organized by Mahavira, shortly before Gautama began his teaching (Shanta 1974). The appeal of Jainism has always been limited because of the extreme degree of asceticism required, but even in the twentieth century, it is estimated that there are 4,000 Jainist nuns. They are *sadhvis*, contemplatives who make no distinction between the active and the contemplative, between eremitic (solitary) and cenobitic (community) life. Dressed in white, they wander in perpetual pilgrimage, begging, meditating, praying, preaching. They are much sought after by laywomen as counselors.

Buddhist teachings also require self-discipline but not the extremes of physical self-denial that characterize Jainism. Buddhism therefore spread more widely. Gautama organized men from the very beginning into lay followers and almsmen (monks). It took five years, however, to persuade him to accept women into comparable groups of laywomen and almswomen. Why did it take this long? From the beginning, his teachings appeared to be for women and men equally, and he never denied the spiritual capabilities of women. Finally, Ananda, his disciple and a women's advocate, obtained from him an admission that, because women could attain *arahanship* (enlightenment) as well as men could, there were no rational grounds for opposing the entry of women into a religious order. Apparently his resistance was simply worn down by repeated deputations of women and of men speaking on women's behalf. What had been the nature of his resistance? It is suggested that, because Gautama was a prince and of the conservative ruling class, he felt it was best not to interfere with the traditional duties of women in the family.[44]

Even after the women's order was established, the rules still required that any woman, no matter of what age and dignity, had to defer to the youngest and rawest monk. Women were not allowed to conduct any important ceremonies on their own but had to have almsmen come in to do it. And there were numerous other restrictions on what women could do in their order. Unlike monks, they could not simply take on the state of homelessness and live under a tree; they must live together in convents. They could meditate and they could beg as well as visit in the homes of lay supporters. During the nonrainy season, they could go from convent to convent on prolonged journeys. But there were no daily liturgies, no work with the hands, either craft or farming, no copying of manuscripts—in short, no balanced regime of *orare et labore* as in the Christian monasteries. Nuns were discouraged from reading, with preference given to oral teaching by the monks. Furthermore, there was no emphasis on healing the sick or feeding the poor. The service of the nun to the community was the attainment of *arahanship* and visiting in the homes of lay supporters. That these services were highly prized by laywomen of the upper classes is amply evidenced by the accounts of the many wealthy lay supporters of the nuns.

There are many beautiful stories of women who gained enlightenment, including courtesans. The most famous courtesans in India at this time were evidently not unlike their sisters in Greece; it appears that many of the "Aspasias" were attracted to Gautama. These were women of wealth and civic standing, sometimes with courts of their own. While they stood outside conventional morality, there is no evidence of social condemnation of the courtesan by Buddha. Gautama welcomed them among his disciples and never said anything about repentance. A courtesan could attain enlightenment while still a courtesan, but, if she wanted to *stay* enlightened, she would be expected to adopt celibacy.

Elite women accustomed to authority, whether they remained lay or joined the order, continued to exercise authority. Most women converts, however, seemed not to have enough to do. They got into mischief, and they sometimes got pregnant (as happened to Christian nuns also). Women leaders had a clear ceiling placed on their aspirations: "A woman will not become a Buddha, absolutely holy and perfectly enlightened . . . not a universal monarch," said Gautama (Horner 1930: 291). Gautama often talked about a person becoming "the man in oneself" (Horner 1930: 358). Evidently he both believed and did not believe that women could have the same spirituality as men. We have seen this ambivalence about women in all the world religions. Indian women might have had more energy for the kind of movements their sisters undertook in Christian monasticism if they had had a greater scope of permitted activity at the beginning. In general, the social impact of Buddhism, and of the women's movement in Buddhism, seems to have been minimal in India. The poorer classes did not participate, although in theory they could have. Buddhism faded away, and the more rigorous Jainism remained, though for a tiny minority.

In comparing Christian and Buddhist religious orders, there are many similarities but some critical differences. Christianity did not start out as an elite religion, while Buddhism did. The tendency in both societies was for elite women to enter the religious orders. A significant difference between the two types of orders is that Christian monasticism was committed to educating nuns, to providing them with a rich liturgical life as an aid to prayer, and to linking them with the community through social service. Buddhism did not have this orientation. Nuns of both religions were placed under the authority of men and suffered the same kind of second-class citizenship, even while being pronounced "spiritual equals."

The practices of *suttee* (immolation of widows) and *purdah* (seclusion) were not current when Buddhism and Jainism entered India. Both practices came into being after the Common Era, and purdah only became widespread after 1000 C.E. The entry of Islam into India at that time was seen by some as a democratizing influence—lower-caste Hindus could raise their status by entering the more egalitarian Moslem community—and by others as a support for the enclosure of women, practiced by the Turkic-Moslem ruling elites then entering India.

While the first millennium of the Common Era tends to be treated as a bleak time in India's history from the point of view of women, it is questionable whether the situation of Indian women was really any different than that of women in the other societies we have examined. In addition to the wealthy and independent class of courtesans, there were more and more middle-class women traders as property laws for women loosened up after 600 (Horner 1930: 221). Women also continued to be doctors and teachers. Lower-class women could be dancing girls and musicians as well as work in the usual range of craft and service occupations.

In the political realm, we have Indian women ascending thrones at least as often as their counterparts farther west. Queen Didda of Kashmir ruled as full sovereign for 22 years. Chandragupta and his spouse Kumaradevi (300 B.C.E.) were corulers. Many women, such as the queen mother of Orissa at the end of the ninth century, assumed regency when their husbands (or sons) died. Queen Nayanika headed the Satavahana empire of the Deccan in the second century B.C.E. The Deccan had a strong tradition of women administrators, with women governors of provinces, queens issuing administrative orders, and so on. There were also queens who ruled in wartime and led armies, such as Kurmadevi of Mevad in 1193. Shortly thereafter, Karnavati, a Rajpur queen, led the defense of Chitor after her widowhood; another queen of the same deceased king, Jawahirbai, fought and died at the head of the army.[45] Whether women also participated in the bloody aspects of succession politics I do not know. They probably did, but details are not available.

* * *

The surprising thing that emerges from this chapter is how similar women's roles have been in each of the societies studied, given the great cultural, political, and religious differences between them. Threshold points at which great changes seem to be possible appear in retrospect as having signaled only modest changes in the situations of women. Nevertheless, neither is the conventional image of the exclusion of women borne out. While limitations have been placed on them everywhere, we also see that in any particular society women were never excluded as completely as they are generally thought to have been. Trying to write the unwritten parts of the history of this first millennium inevitably makes one aware of enormous knowledge gaps; even so, there is evidence enough that every society was teeming with active women for the entire 1,000 years.

Notes

1. Hecker (1914) suggests that there are no indications in the law as later codified as to what the original traditions were.

2. E. L. Hallgren (medieval historian, University of Colorado, Boulder, personal communication, 1975) points out that Burgundian and Visigothic laws as we know them were already heavily influenced by Roman law and Christianity.

3. The reference is to the concept of conspicuous consumption developed by Veblen in his *Theory of the Leisure Class* (1899).

4. The practice of men selling their children into slavery also continued, however. Carla Slatt draws attention to a clause in the *Twelve Tables:* "If a father sells his son three times let the son be free of his father" (1975: 2).

5. The following are names of vestal virgins recorded between 483 and 31 B.C., including date of recording (tabulated from Broughton, 1952). *Accused of misconduct and executed* were Oppia (483), Minucia (337), Sextilla (273), Caparronia (266), Tuccia (230), Licinia (123), Aemilia (114), Marcia (114); *accused and acquitted* were Postumia (420), Fabia

(73), Licinia (69); *politically inoffensive* were Perpennia (69), Arruntia (69), Popilla (69), Occia (38), Aemilia (n.d.); and *politically active, "in the clear"* were Claudia (143), Fonteia (91).

6. There is a famous series of letters between Helvia and Seneca (Beard 1946: 327-28).

7. In Islam, women played a similar role in the politics of the succession of the caliphate.

8. Interpretations in this section will be controversial. The theological frame of reference I am drawing on most heavily is that of George Tavard (1973), but conclusions and interpretations are my own.

9. The technical term is *prelapsarian state*—that is, before Eve ate the apple.

10. Different translations of the Bible are used in different passages in this chapter, as certain translations make the points under discussion more clearly than others do.

11. They are John, Philip, Peter, Thomas, James, Andrew, Matthew, and Simon; Mary, the mother of Jesus, Mary Magdalene, Martha, and Salome (Eckenstein 1935: 35-41).

12. These include Mary, the mother of Jesus; Mary, the wife of Cleophas; Mary Magdalene; Joanna, the wife of Herod's steward Chuza; Susanna, the mother of the sons of Zebedee; Salome; Mary, the mother of James; and Mary, the mother of James the younger and Josef. J. Morris bases the idea of a parallel set of men and women disciples on a mosaic in the Church of Saint Praxidis: "There is a double circle around the doorway of the chapel of Saint Zeno consisting of the busts of the apostles with Jesus in the center and of the busts of eight women together with Our Lady in the center and two deacons on either side of her" (1973: 114). This does not add up to 12, but Morris's idea is an interesting one.

13. Abelard was a strong supporter of the idea that the women followers of Jesus played a more important role than church history has given them. According to Abelard, "because the women of Christ's following showed greater devotion to Him, . . . they were consistently honored and favored more highly than His masculine disciples. Only women had been permitted to minister to Christ, to perform for Him, those services of humanity which He Himself had performed for His disciples. More important, women alone had been allowed to perform the 'sacraments,' the anointing of head and feet, by which Christ was made Priest and King" (McLaughlin 1975: 287-334).

14. There is a great deal of evidence in the Acts of the Apostles and the Epistles as well as in the Gospels for this traveling together of women and men. Paul mentions this specifically in 1 Cor. 9: 5 and is always sending greetings in his Epistles to his sister workers.

15. J. Morris, in speaking of Paul's reliance on women missionaries, mentions Lydia, from the distant town Thyatira, who became a member of the community at Philippi: "She was in the purple dye trade . . . a woman of some wealth. After her conversion to Christianity through the teaching of Paul and Silas, she turned her house into a center for the apostles and the faithful. On one occasion . . . after Paul and Silas had been liberated from a prison at Philippi they went immediately to the house of Lydia and met all the brethren there" (1973: 119).

16. "At Thessalonika among the Greek converts there were many rich women who joined Paul and Silas. At Borea 'Many Jews became believers, and so did many Greek women from the upper classes and a number of men.' " Also, Paul's reference to Phoebe as "our sister in the ministry of the church at Cenchrae" is considered by some to be a reference to full ministerial roles for women (J. Morris 1973: 119).

17. One of the first heretics, the wealthy trader Marcion, taught a doctrine of the Stranger God, which suggests very strongly this alienation process (Nigg 1962: 61-62).

18. St. Agnes, 12 or 13 years of age, refused to marry the man her family provided for her and was either beheaded or burned. Her sister Emerenziana, following her example in vowing virginity, was stoned to death. Mothers who publicly took these vows were killed together with their children—Symphorosa with her seven sons and Felicitas with her seven sons (Eckenstein 1935: 113-20).

19. In Dura-Europos (Mesopotamia), a building has been excavated that was first a private home, then a Christian church. Only its baptismal font makes it recognizable as a church (Lassus 1967: 10-11).

20. The Gnostics emphasized the feminine aspect of the Godhead, which helped strengthen the position of women as teachers. Doctrinally, their chief heresy was to differentiate between the heavenly Christ and the earthly Jesus, treating the Resurrection as symbolic only.

21. These acts have been subjected to careful historical study and have been chosen as being "historically authentic" (Musurillo 1972: xi-xii).

22. There may, of course, have been other sources for this practice in the evolution of the sacrificial rites of the mystery religions.

23. Although condemned from time to time, this practice was continued, if Penzer (1935) is correct, until the accession of Pope Leo XIII in 1878.

24. The question of whether women are more or less highly sexed than men is not relevant to this discussion. We are talking about the consequences of socialization, not biology. For a good discussion of the biological issue, see Sherfey (1972).

25. We do not know the name of Augustine's sister. In fact, there is some question about to whom the letter was actually written—one more evidence of the maddening anonymity of women in history (J. Morris 1973: 160, n. 3).

26. I have mentioned earlier the likelihood that new types of family relationships were developing as a result of increased interaction between family members in urban households. Within Christian communities, conditions would be optimal for developing affectionate family life because of the great emphasis on love and mutual support within the community.

27. Three books on the desert fathers (which include some mention of desert mothers also) make this form of life in the early centuries of Christianity very vivid: Helen Waddell, *The Desert Fathers* (1957), Thomas Merton, *The Wisdom of the Desert* (1960), and Jacques Lacarrière, *Men Possessed by God* (1964).

The desert congregations sometimes tended to re-create the problems of Rome. "Abbot Arsenius lived in a cell 32 miles away from his nearest neighbor, and he seldom went out of it. The things he needed were brought there by disciples. But when the desert of Scete where he lived became peopled with hermits, he went away from there weeping and saying: 'Worldly men have ruined Rome and monks have ruined Scete' " (Merton 1960: 49).

28. The movement into the desert and the movement into heretical sects occurred simultaneously. Each group was trying to solve the problem of corruption. The dissenting groups that were active in the cities were expelled, but the desert dwellers, probably because they were not perceived as a threat to the church, were kept in the fold. This is important to the future history of women in the church, because the tolerance of the church for its desert dwellers laid the foundation for the tolerance of the church for a wide variety of activities within the convents and monasteries, the "deserts" of Europe.

29. There was also at least one husband-wife team, St. Paulinus of Nola and his wife Theresia, who founded a double monastery in Nola after abandoning wealth and position in Rome.

30. Several other examples of "erasing the traces" are given by Joan Morris. A fresco in the Catacomb of Priscilla in Rome shows a group of women conducting a eucharistic banquet, and the head of the chief celebrant, by all other clues a woman, has been sandpapered down so it is not possible to tell the sex of the celebrant. Presumably this is to conceal that women once celebrated the Eucharist (1973: 7, 8). Another example is the substitution of the word *blessed* for *ordained* in documents referring to the ordination of women to conceal the earlier practice of ordaining women as abbesses (1973: 19).

31. For fuller accounts of this network, see Duckett (1938), Eckenstein (1896), J. Morris (1973), and de Carreaux (1964).

32. There are conflicting accounts of Scholastica's way of life. Sometimes she is described as the founder and head of a convent but more often as a person living a life of religious retirement.

33. Another way to put this is that the church entered the vacuum created by the decay of the Roman imperial bureaucracy. The bishops became tax collectors and city defenders, because they were the only ones left to do it (de Carreaux 1964).

34. This applies to the Christian world. Pagan priesthoods also continued as teachers.

35. Convents required dowries also, for operating capital, but it was possible to negotiate more modest amounts for a convent dowry than would be thought proper for a marriage dowry.

36. The word *Byzantium* is used in these chapters to refer to the eastern half of the old Roman empire, or the Byzantine empire, rather than to the ancient city of Byzantium.

37. I owe this sorting out of the Honoria-Attila story to E. L. Hallgren, medieval historian at the University of Colorado.

38. The source for Byzantine history, except when otherwise indicated, is Philip Sherrard, *Byzantium* (1966).

39. When they did get such training, it often disqualified them from becoming empress. Casia, the ninth-century nun and poetess, famed both for piety and for literary talent, missed becoming empress because, when she was put in the usual bridal lineup for the emperor's inspection, she spoke up in an "unladylike" way.

40. Except where otherwise indicated, the material in this section is taken from the *Cambridge History of Islam* (Holt 1970), *Atlas of Islamic History* (Hazard 1931), and "The Influence of Women on Islam" (Ali 1899).

41. Another passage in the same Cordova story gives a glimpse into the lives of slave women of the time. It appears that, in some houses at least, they had a status and degree of privacy and autonomy we do not usually associate with the condition of slavery (Arberry 1967: 172).

42. Women slaves far outnumber men slaves in the records.

43. See Horner's *Women Under Primitive Buddhism* (1930) and Bode's *Women Leaders of the Buddhist Reformation* (1893) for full descriptions of the first generation of women disciples. For a more general overview of women in Buddhism, see Paul (1985).

44. The importance of the working-class origin of Jesus in the acceptance of women as equals among the disciples cannot be overestimated in considering the early development of Christianity 500 years later.

45. Altekar ([1956]: 185-90) gives a list of reigning and recent queens of Indian states.

References

Ali, Ameer. 1899. "The Influences of Women on Islam." *The Nineteenth Century Magazine* 45(May):755-74.

Altekar, A. S. [1956] 1978. *The Position of Women in Hindu Civilization*. Banaras, India: Motilal Banarsidass.

Arberry, A. J. 1967. "Muslim Cordoba." Pp. 166-77 in *Cities of Destiny*, edited by Arnold Toynbee. New York: McGraw-Hill.

Auguet, Roland. 1972. *Cruelty and Civilization: The Roman Games*. London: Allen & Unwin.

Babiak, Wira A. 1975. "The Ukranian Woman." Unpublished student paper, University of Colorado, Boulder, Department of Sociology.

Baldson, John Percy Oyvian Dacre. 1962. *Roman Women: Their History and Habits*. London: Bodley Head.

Barrow, R. H. [1928] 1968. *Slavery in the Roman Empire.* New York: Barnes and Noble.

Beard, Mary R. 1946. *Woman as Force in History: A Study in Traditions and Realities.* New York: Macmillan.

Bode, Mabel. 1893. "Women Leaders of the Buddhist Reformation." *Journal of the Royal Asiatic Society* 25:517-66.

Boswell, John. 1980. *Christianity, Social Tolerance and Homosexuality.* Chicago: University of Chicago Press.

Brentano, Robert, ed. 1964. *The Early Middle Ages, 500-1000.* New York: Free Press.

Broughton, T. Robert S. 1952. *The Magistrates of the Roman Republic. Vol. 2. 44 B.C.-31 B.C.* New York: American Philological Association.

Bullough, Vern L. 1973. *The Subordinate Sex: A History of Attitudes Toward Women.* Urbana: University of Illinois Press.

Burckhardt, Jacob. [1852] 1949. *The Age of Constantine the Great,* translated by Moses Hadas. Garden City, NY: Pantheon.

de Beaumont, Edouard. 1929. *The Sword and Womankind.* New York: Panurge.

de Carreaux, Jean. 1964. *Monks and Civilization,* translated from French. New York: Doubleday.

de Mause, Lloyd. 1974. "The Evolution of Childhood." Pp. 1-74 in *The History of Childhood,* edited by Lloyd de Mause. New York: Psychohistory Press.

Dietrick, Ellen Battelle. 1897. *Women in the Early Christian Ministry: A Reply to Bishop Doane, and Others.* Philadelphia: Alfred J. Ferris.

Duckett, Eleanor Shipley. 1938. *The Gateway to the Middle Ages: Monasticism.* Ann Arbor: University of Michigan Press.

Eckenstein, Lina. 1896. *Women Under Monasticism.* Cambridge: Cambridge University Press.

———. 1935. *The Women of Early Christianity.* London: Faith Press.

Goitein, Solomon D. 1967-71. *A Mediterranean Society: The Jewish Communities of the Arab World as Portrayed in the Documents of the Cairo Geniza.* 2 vols. Berkeley: University of California Press.

Halle, Fannine W. 1933. *Women in Soviet Russia.* London: Routledge.

Hazard, Harry W. 1931. *Atlas of Islamic History.* Princeton, NJ: Princeton University Press.

Hecker, Eugene A. 1914. *History of Women's Rights.* New York: Putnam.

Henriques, Fernando. 1962. *Prostitution and Society.* New York: Grove.

Herlihy, David. 1962. "Land, Family, and Women in Continental Europe, 701-1200." *Traditio* 18:89-120.

Holt, P. M., ed. 1970. *Cambridge History of Islam.* 2 vols. Cambridge: Cambridge University Press.

Horner, Isaline Blew. 1930. *Women Under Primitive Buddhism: Laywomen and Almswomen.* London: Routledge.

Huart, Clement. 1966. *A History of Arabic Literature.* Beirut: Khayts.

Lacarrière, Jacques. 1964. *Men Possessed by God: The Story of the Desert Monks of Ancient Christendom,* translated by Roy Monkcom. New York: Doubleday.

Lassus, Jean. 1967. *Landmarks of the World's Art: The Early Christian and Byzantine World.* London: Paul Hamlyn.

Leighton, Albert C. 1972. *Transport and Communication in Early Medieval Europe, A.D. 500-1100.* Newton Abbot, England: David and Charles.

Lev, Daniel S. 1972. *The Islamic Courts in Indonesia: A Study in the Political Bases of Legal Institutions.* Berkeley: University of California Press.

Levy, Jean Philippe. 1967. *The Economic Life of the Ancient World,* translated by John G. Biram. Chicago: University of Chicago Press.

Lot, Ferdinand. 1961. *The End of the Ancient World and the Beginnings of the Middle Ages.* New York: Harper & Row.

Macurdy, Grace. 1927. "Queen Eurydice and the Evidence for Women Power in Early Macedonia." *American Journal of Philology* 48(July):201-14.

Maher, Vanessa. 1974. *Women and Property in Morocco: Their Changing Relation to the Process of Social Stratification in the Middle Atlas.* Cambridge: Cambridge University Press.

McCabe, Joseph. 1931. "How Christianity Has Treated Women." Pp. 49-58 in *Woman's Coming of Age*, edited by Samuel D. Schmalhauser and V. F. Calverton. New York: Liveright.

McLaughlin, Mary Martin. 1975. "Peter Abelard and the Dignity of Women: Twelfth Century Feminism in Theory and Practice." Pp. 287-334 in *Proceedings of the International Symposium of the Centre National de la Récherche Scientifique* (July 2-9, 1972). Paris: Centre National de la Récherche Scientifique.

Mernissi, Fatima. 1991. *The Veil and the Male Elite: A Feminist Interpretation of Women's Rights in Islam.* Reading, MA: Addison-Wesley.

Merton, Thomas. 1960. *The Wisdom of the Desert: Sayings from the Desert Fathers of the Fourth Century.* New York: New Directions.

Morris, E. J. 1974. *History of Urban Form: Prehistory to the Renaissance.* New York: John Wiley.

Morris, Joan. 1973. *The Lady Was a Bishop.* New York: Macmillan.

Mozans, H. J. 1913. *Woman in Science.* New York: Appleton.

Mujeeb, M. 1960. *World History: Our Heritage.* Bombay: Asia Publishing House.

Musurillo, Herbert. 1972. *The Acts of the Christian Martyrs.* Oxford: Clarendon.

Naroll, Raoul, Vern L. Bullough, and Frada Naroll. 1974. *Military Deterence in History: A Pilot Cross-Historical Survey.* Albany: State University of New York.

Nash, Ernest. 1944. *Roman Towns.* New York: J. J. Augusten.

Newton, Arthur Percival, ed. 1968. *Travel and Travellers of the Middle Ages.* New York: Barnes & Noble.

Nigg, Walter. 1962. *Heretics.* New York: Knopf.

Nugent, Sister M. Rosamond (B.S.F.). 1941. *Portrait of the Consecrated Woman in Greek Christian Literature of the First Four Centuries.* Washington, DC: Catholic University of America Press.

O'Faolain, Julia and Lauro Martines, eds. 1973. *Not in God's Image: A History of Women in Europe from the Greeks to the Nineteenth Century.* New York: Harper & Row.

O'Faolain, Sean. 1969. *The Irish.* London: C. Nicholls.

Paul, Diana Yoshikawa. 1985. *Women in Buddhism.* Berkeley: University of California Press.

Penzer, N. M. 1935. *The Harem: An Account of the Institution.* Philadelphia: J. B. Lippincott.

Rostovtzeff, Mikhail I. 1945. *A History of the Ancient World.* 2 vols., rev. ed. Norwood, PA: Norwood.

Runciman, Sir Steven. 1967. "Christian Constantinople." Pp. 150-65 in *Cities of Destiny*, edited by Arnold Toynbee. New York: McGraw-Hill.

Shanta, N. 1974. "The Doctrine and Life of Junia." *Cisterios Studies* 9:2-3.

Sherfey, Mary Jane. 1972. *The Nature and Evolution of Female Sexuality.* New York: Random House.

Sherrard, Philip. 1966. *Byzantium.* New York: Time-Life.

Slatt, Carla Diane. 1975. "A Study of the Effects of Roman Law on Women." Unpublished student paper, University of Colorado, Boulder, Department of Sociology.

Syme, Ronald. 1939. *The Roman Revolution.* Oxford: Clarendon.

Tavard, George H. 1973. *Woman in Christian Tradition.* Notre Dame, IN: University of Notre Dame Press.

Thrupp, Sylvia L. 1967. *Early Medieval Society.* New York: Appleton-Century-Crofts.

Toubia, Nalud, ed. 1988. *Women and the Arab World, The Coming Challenge.* Papers of the Arab Women's Solidarity Conference. Trans. Nahod El Gamal. London and New Jersey: Zed Books.

Veblen, Thorstein. 1899. *Theory of the Leisure Class.* New York: Viking.

Waddell, Helen. 1957. *The Desert Fathers.* Ann Arbor: University of Michigan Press.

Weinhold, Karl. 1882. *Die Deutschen Frauen in dem Mittelalter.* Wien: Druck und Verlug von Carl Geraed's Sohn.

White, E. M. 1924. *Woman in World History: Her Place in the Great Religions.* London: Herbert Jenkins.

Workman, Herbert B. [1913] 1962. *The Evolution of the Monastic Ideal from the Earliest Times Down to the Coming of the Friars: A Second Chapter in the History of Christian Renunciation.* Boston: Beacon.

The pictures on pages 363 to 367 give fragmentary glimpses of women from different lifeways, and the spaces they occupy. The Chief of the Linen Room and wife, and King Mycerinus and Queen, are represented as being of equal status. The Inspector of Scribes on the other hand is depicted with a miniaturized wife reaching to his knees. The gypsies, the old wise woman and the women construction workers are shown as complete, active human beings in the dignity of their roles.

King Mycerinus and Queen Khamerernebti (Hirmer Fotoarchiv München; used by permission)

Chief of the Linen Room (Editions d'Art, Genève; used by permission)

Spanish Gypsies (Paul Almasy; used by permission)

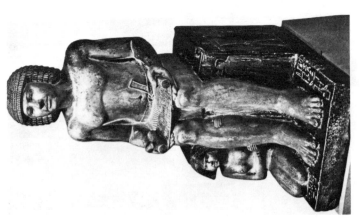

The Inspector of Scribes Sekhema and His Wife (Northamption Museums and Art Gallery; used by permission)

The "Phuri Dai" or Old Wise Woman (Denis Brihat; used by permission)

Woman Kazakh Setting Up a Yurt (Hamburgisches Museum für Völkerkunde; used by permission)

Gypsy Tents and Camps (circa 1960; J. G. Seruzier; used by permission)

Indian Construction Gang (Josef Breitenbach photographer, Thomas Y. Crowell, Inc.; used by permission)

Hypatia (MIT Press; used by permission)

Author Index

Subject Index

About the Author

Elise Boulding is Professor Emerita of Dartmouth College and Senior Fellow in the Dickey Endowment; was Secretary-General of the International Peace Research Association, from 1988 to April 1991; and was Professor and Chair at Dartmouth from 1978 until 1985. From 1967 until 1978, she was in the Department of Sociology and Institute of Behavioral Science at the University of Colorado at Boulder. Born in Oslo, Norway, she received her B.A. degree in English from Douglass College; her M.S. in Sociology from Iowa State University; and her Ph.D. from the University of Michigan. She is the wife of Kenneth Boulding, mother of five children, grandmother of fifteen, and a member of the Society of Friends.

A sociologist with a global view, she has undertaken numerous transnational and comparative cross-national studies on conflict and peace, development, and women in society. Her work in the area of future studies dates from 1961, when she translated, from the Dutch, Fred Polak's classic work, *Image of the Future*. She has worked internationally on problems of peace and world order both as a scholar and as an activist. She served as a member of the governing board of the United Nations University, 1980-85, and was a member of the International Jury of the UNESCO Prize for Peace Education and a former member of the U.S. Commission for UNESCO, 1981-87. She has served as a member of the Commission on Proposals for a National Academy of Peace and Conflict Resolution, which resulted in the establishment by Congress of a U.S. Institute of Peace, and, from 1963-1968 and 1983 to 1987, she served as Editor of the *International Peace Research Newsletter*. Other current international involvements include the World Order Models Project, "Coming Global Civilization," and chairing the International Peace Research Association Commission on Peace Building in the Middle East. From time to time, she has conducted workshops on "imaging a world without weapons."

Her books include *Handbook of International Data on Women* (with Carson, Greenstein, and Nuss; New York: Halsted Press, 1977); *Women in the Twentieth Century World* (Halsted Press, 1977); *From a Monastery Kitchen* (New York: Harper & Row, 1976); *Children's Rights and the Wheel of Life* (Transaction Press, 1979), written especially for the International Year of the Child; *Bibliography on World Conflict and Peace* (with Passmore and Gassler; Westview Press, 1979); *The Social System of the Planet Earth* (with K. Boulding and G. Burgess; Addison-Wesley); *Women and Social Costs of Development: Two Case Studies* (with Moen, Lilleydahl, and Palm); *Building a Global Civic Culture: Education for an Interdependent World* (Syracuse University Press, paperback, 1990); *One Small Plot of Heaven* (Pendle Hill Publications, 1989); *Peace Culture and Society: Transnational Research and Dialogue* (with Clovis Brigagao and Kevin Clements, eds.; Westview Press, 1990); and *New Agendas for Peace Research: Conflict and Security Reexamined* (ed., Lynne Rienner, 1992).

3 5282 00499 8319